CONNECTED VIEWING

As patterns of media use become more integrated with mobile technologies and multiple screens, a new mode of viewer engagement has emerged in the form of *connected viewing*, which allows for an array of new relationships between audiences and media texts in the digital space. This exciting new collection brings together twelve original essays that critically engage with the socially networked, multiplatform, and cloud-based world of today, examining the connected viewing phenomenon across television, film, video games, and social media.

The result is a wide-ranging analysis of shifting business models, policy matters, technological infrastructure, new forms of user engagement, and other key trends affecting screen media in the digital era. *Connected Viewing* contextualizes the dramatic transformations taking place across both media industries and national contexts, and offers students and scholars alike a diverse set of methods and perspectives for studying this critical moment in media culture.

Jennifer Holt is Associate Professor of Film and Media Studies at the University of California, Santa Barbara.

Kevin Sanson is Research Director of the Carsey-Wolf Center's Media Industries Project at the University of California, Santa Barbara.

CONNECTED VIEWING

Selling, Streaming, & Sharing
Media in the Digital Era

Edited by Jennifer Holt and Kevin Sanson

Routledge
Taylor & Francis Group

NEW YORK AND LONDON

First published 2014
by Routledge
711 Third Avenue, New York, NY 10017

and by Routledge
2 Park Square, Milton Park, Abingdon, Oxon OX14 4RN

Routledge is an imprint of the Taylor & Francis Group, an informa business.

© 2014 Taylor & Francis

Library of Congress Cataloging-in-Publication Data

Connected viewing : selling, streaming, & sharing media in the digital era /
    edited by Jennifer Holt and Kevin Sanson.
        p. cm.
    Includes bibliographical references and index.
    1. Multimedia communications.   2. Mass media.   3. Social media.
I. Holt, Jennifer, 1968–   II. Sanson, Kevin.
    TK5105.15.C648 2014
    302.23′1—dc23
    2013028644

ISBN: 978-0-415-81357-0 (hbk)
ISBN: 978-0-415-81360-0 (pbk)
ISBN: 978-0-203-06799-4 (ebk)

Typeset in Bembo
by Apex CoVantage, LLC

Printed and bound in the United States of America by Publishers Graphics,
LLC on sustainably sourced paper.

CONTENTS

PART II
Technology and Platforms   97

PART III
Content and Engagement   181

FIGURES AND TABLES

ACKNOWLEDGMENTS

First and foremost, we would like to thank our contributors for their dedication to this project. It has been a true team effort. These authors have been inspiring to work with over the past year during our collaboration with Warner Bros., and we feel honored to be a part of this creative community of scholars. We would also like to thank all members of the Connected Viewing Initiative research team for their hard work and enthusiasm for the project, and Warner Bros. Digital Distribution for its generosity and partnership in this collaboration. Most especially, we are grateful to Thomas Gewecke, Anuraj Goonetilleke, and Daniel Ornstein for their vision, leadership, and committed support of scholarly research. We are extremely fortunate to have the support of the University of California, Santa Barbara's Carsey-Wolf Center. Constance Penley, Ron Rice, Richard Hutton, LeeAnne French, and Natalie Fawcett made this research endeavor more manageable, and therefore more successful, than we could have done on our own. Michael Curtin was a key source of great ideas, collegial support, and sage advice. Ethan Tussey has assisted the Connected Viewing Initiative from its inception and wore multiple hats very well. John Vanderhoef provided excellent research assistance and copyediting help when we needed it the most. We also wish to acknowledge the support of the University of California Board of Regents.

Conference participants and engaged scholars around the globe have contributed excellent feedback on some of the work in this collection. They include attendees of the Connected Viewing Workshop at Stockholm University, the Society for Cinema and Media Studies Conference in Chicago, and the European Communications Research and Education Association Conference in Istanbul, as well as scholars at the University of Bergen and the American University of

Beirut. We are very thankful for all their thoughtful questions and comments that helped us refine our ideas about connected viewing.

Erica Wetter at Routledge has been an avid supporter of this project from its inception, and we want to thank her for her expertise, leadership, and patience. Matt Caldwell deserves all of the credit for the wonderful cover design.

Other friends, partners, and colleagues have offered helpful commentary and generous support at critical moments throughout the past year. The editors especially wish to thank Hollis Griffin, Lisa Parks, Rico Peña, Alisa Perren, Karen Petruska, Gregory Steirer, Cristina Venegas, and Kristen Warner.

INTRODUCTION

Mapping Connections

Jennifer Holt and Kevin Sanson

An Area of Inquiry

As the media industries adapt to technological change and consumers continuously resist and reshape institutional imperatives, the term *connected viewing* points to an impending revolution in how screen media is created, circulated, and consumed. It refers specifically to a multiplatform entertainment experience, and relates to a larger trend across the media industries to integrate digital technology and socially networked communication with traditional screen media practices. These developments have resulted in the migration of our media and our attention from one screen to many, directed the flow of entertainment content in new patterns, and upended traditional business models. Because of the dramatic ways the phenomenon of connected viewing has affected the contemporary media landscape, it also provides a crucial frame through which we can understand the evolution of film, television, and gaming in the digital era.

Connected viewing is more than digital distribution; it is the broader ecosystem in which digital distribution is rendered possible and new forms of user engagement take shape. It is as much about the aesthetic and social experience of second-screen media as it is about the intermediaries that deliver content to mobile devices, and the gatekeepers regulating our Internet access. Connected viewing spans a wide spectrum of industrial practices, from multiplatform modes of production and distribution to the reconfigured promotional strategies and measurement techniques increasingly necessary to gauge marketing success in the digital space. It also extends to more marginal players, those firms and individuals operating "outside" the mainstream, who are looking to create innovative relationships with the digital, global, and mobile audience. Connected viewing encompasses the new windows, technologies, and platforms that have developed for digital content in film and television; it also incorporates the ways in which that content is bought, sold, "pirated," packaged, policed, redistributed, reimagined, and redefined for a new era in media culture.

Connected Viewing has its origins in the larger intellectual pursuits of the Carsey-Wolf Center's Media Industries Project (MIP) at the University of California, Santa Barbara. As a nexus point for academic and industry dialogue, MIP engages a wide range of industry figures in research endeavors and public programming to develop resources for media industry scholarship. As part of this process, MIP conducted a series of interviews focused on the digital distribution revolution and archived excerpts of those conversations on our website.[1] More than insider opinions, these conversations were shaped by a critical research agenda and prompted industry practitioners to step outside day-to-day pressures, reflect critically on their business practices, and speculate about changes on the horizon. Despite obvious challenges, this type of dialogue holds numerous benefits for scholars and practitioners, not least of which is the opportunity to cultivate greater awareness of the valuable contributions critical media industries research can make to both the private and public spheres.[2]

During an interview with then Warner Bros. digital distribution president (now chief digital officer) Thomas Gewecke, the idea first took shape for a research project focused on connected viewing. In pursuing a conversation with Gewecke about his experiences navigating digital "disruption" (first in the music business and then in film and television), we found an executive intrigued by our line of questioning and excited by the fact that our methods would produce meaningful insights that were very different from those of his own in-house research team. We proposed a collaborative venture that ultimately became the Connected Viewing Initiative: a series of miniconferences and workshops, as well as funding for an international team of scholars to study the multiplatform, socially networked entertainment experience through a variety of analytical frameworks. This is not sponsored research (scholars retained all rights to their work and designed their own projects), nor is it a celebration of Warner Bros. initiatives, or exclusively focused on Warner Bros. properties or questions. Rather, this has been a collaborative venture from the start: We were granted a measure of access to one studio division that is deeply enmeshed with connected viewing, and used these interviews and resources to serve the original agendas of the research team. The findings and analysis were presented to Warner Bros. and then expanded on to form the chapters in this book.

Throughout the course of this research, we consistently heard the studio's desire for innovative approaches to the issue of digital "disruption" in its many forms, outside the purview of market research firms and industry trade journals. This project was designed to respond to that call for creative investigation. The contributors used the longer timelines afforded by academic research, and a diverse array of critical methodologies, to generate fresh insights into the digital media ecosystem. Collectively, they reject the often-inflated speculation of the social and commercial promise of new media technologies heard echoing throughout Los Angeles and Silicon Valley. As a whole, this collection also eschews medium or platform specificity, adopting a more ecumenical perspective on the primary actors currently reshaping the digital entertainment space. *Connected Viewing* looks at the end point of the text and user engagement, and also examines the underlying business models, policies, technologies, and infrastructures that have developed alongside these groundbreaking trends. It provides historical perspective and various methodologies for the study of multiplatform digital media. Ultimately, *Connected Viewing* offers a comprehensive critical framework for the ways in which we might map this moment in media industry transformation.

This initiative has also fostered a community of researchers focused on the connected viewing landscape—a community that will hopefully expand along with this area of interest and its evolving concerns. The value of this community is hard to quantify but remains a testament to the spirit in which this collaborative research endeavor was originally conceived. We envision this collection as a formative articulation of connected viewing's multiple dimensions, and as the beginning of a much longer conversation enriched by the work of researchers worldwide. Each chapter points scholars in slightly different directions for future inquiry, but nevertheless affirms the many developments associated with connected viewing as a growing, vital, and rapidly evolving terrain for further exploration.

Selling, Streaming, Sharing

With patterns of media use customized by search-and-discovery technologies, and with social networking sites beginning to figure more prominently as delivery platforms, connected viewing has become quite important to content providers, distribution networks, policy makers, and viewers. This trend is an outgrowth of convergence culture as explored by Henry Jenkins, and is especially resonant with Jenkins's emphasis on the increasingly blurred boundaries between producers and consumers and distinct delivery systems.[3] Connected viewing also echoes the more egalitarian and participatory phenomenon of what Jenkins, Sam Ford, and Joshua Green have termed *spreadable media,* in which the sharing of digital video across social media platforms betrays an emergent cultural logic of engagement, valuation, and textual meaning in the process of content circulation.[4] While these authors have focused on explaining the complex dynamics of sharing in particular, we are invested in examining an expanded realm of activity related to the circulation of digital media, from business strategies and regulatory mechanisms to user engagement and consumption practices. Chapters in this collection continue to complicate assumptions about the nature of engagement, drawing attention to the impact diverse national media systems and regional and class identities have on the relationships between users and digital media texts. Some take up concerns about the buying and selling of content—and of audiences—across the connected viewing landscape, from video games to mobile devices, while others tackle the ways in which such practices are framed by regulators and the state.

Accordingly, we maintain that connected viewing points to a more fundamental shift in the current media ecosystem, a process in which the various strands of convergence culture have become more fully integrated into the institutional, regulatory, and cultural forces currently shaping media industries worldwide. Michael Curtin has described this juncture as the "matrix era"—a transition from the one-to-many distribution strategies of the broadcast networks to a moment "characterized by interactive exchanges, multiple sites of productivity, and diverse modes of interpretation and use."[5] As such, media companies are currently exploring multiplatform programming strategies, revaluing digital audiences, and experimenting with interactivity and user engagement as they strive to connect viewers with content in this newly emerging media landscape. The "Big Six" global entertainment conglomerates are only one group of players to engage with the array of technological options now before them, and in fact, they have much to learn from the formidable competitors in the connected viewing arena. Stuart Cunningham and Jon Silver explicitly argue this point, drawing attention to market leaders in digital distribution like Apple, Amazon, and Netflix—firms they call "the new King Kongs of the online world."[6] The strategies these companies employ, such as combining connected viewing hardware and software, or user-friendly streaming platforms with library and original content (or in Amazon's case, even cloud services), are widely imitated by large and small firms alike.

There is also a proliferation of third-party second-screen applications, such as Miso, IntoNow, and Viggle, that try to enhance our engagements with media texts in various ways, as discussed by Hye Jin Lee and Mark Andrejevic in their chapter. These apps demonstrate that connected viewing can also inspire innovation and create new space in the marketplace for those operating on the "outskirts" of more mainstream modes of production and distribution, or as independents. Indeed, some of the most central social media apps that have helped to design the connected viewing ecosystem began as the products of small start-ups and entrepreneurial individuals, including GetGlue and Zeebox, not to mention Facebook and Twitter. Ultimately, we find the matrix metaphor particularly useful in this context because it avoids simple top-down, bottom-up binaries in favor of a more expansive, web-like framework. Simply put: it keeps the various intersections within and across the connected viewing landscape at the forefront of our inquiries.

Perhaps no other medium has received as much attention in the connected viewing context as television. Indeed, TV has already been at the center of a number of provocative inquiries related to digital distribution,[7] and its business model has been affected most significantly by the migration of viewers to mobile and multiple screens. Connected viewing, much like the advent of cable, the remote control, or the digital video recorder before it, has already challenged industry and academia alike to grapple with long-held truisms about the medium as a business, techno-cultural form, and cultural object. The extension of television entertainment content across screens and platforms, not to mention a socially networked viewership, has again altered textual practices and expanded the space and time devoted to television consumption.[8] Scholars such as Jennifer Gillan have written about how this opens productive possibilities up for broadcasters as they reimagine the traditional creative and industrial practices that impact audience habits.[9] Yet others such as William Boddy have noted how such dispersal and dislocation cause intense industrial anxiety by threatening to "disconnect" television networks from their financial lifelines: advertisers. As connected viewing further fragments mass audiences, the industry has responded with an array of strategies to reconnect advertisers with viewers, largely by extending advertising across a host of new reception sites and delivery systems.[10] This practice has imbued a rather consumerist ethos to many connected viewing initiatives.

Platform proliferation and audience fragmentation are also upending workplace routines and creative practices. Writers and directors face relentless pressure to produce additional content for social media pages and other websites, as well as to actively participate in multiplatform promotional campaigns, which increases the number of hours in a workday without doing the same for compensation.[11] Even in noncommercial contexts, like the BBC in the UK, connected viewing is altering commissioning priorities and production practices; the public broadcaster now finds itself charged with programming across platforms as part of its remit to "build digital Britain," even though, ironically, the strategy threatens to undo the very national audience it seeks to address.[12]

Contrary to television, the film industry has proven less adaptive to the connected viewing landscape. This is largely because the industry's theatrical revenues are remarkably consistent, and experimenting with premium video-on-demand offerings and other digital windows disturbs critical relationships between distributors and exhibitors. As Elissa Nelson addresses in her chapter, these new windows also threaten to cannibalize highly lucrative global revenue streams and theatrical revenues.[13] Multiple screens and mobile devices also undermine the social protocols and sanctity of the theatrical space, which is a concern that erupted in a much-publicized debate at a 2012 CinemaCon panel. In a discussion about how to lure "today's savvy moviegoers" into the theater, Amy Miles of Regal Entertainment suggested allowing them to text during certain features as a logical concession, to which Alamo Drafthouse's Tim League (whose cinema chain has a strictly enforced no-talking-or-texting policy) responded, "Over my dead body. . . . It's our job to understand that [the theater] is a sacred place."[14]

Most of the innovation has thus emerged in the home entertainment market to compensate for declining revenues in physical media sales, i.e., DVDs. Accordingly, much of the studio's attention is focused on the ownership proposition (an element addressed in Greg Steirer's chapter) and manifests in the form of various video-on-demand, electronic sell-through, and subscription models, or what Chuck Tryon has described elsewhere as "one-click distribution" techniques.[15] Due to the heavily corporate-controlled, restrictive nature of theatrical distribution, some scholars have explored a broader terrain, shifting from an exclusive focus on official distribution networks to less formal processes of circulation that different "connections" (institutional, human, technological) make possible. Ramon Lobato takes up this perspective in his exploration of the informal circuits, or what he calls the "grey zones of semi-legality," across which cinematic content travels, from street corners and church basements to illegal downloads and streaming services.[16] Stuart Cunningham and Jon Silver similarly focus on emergent online venues where they see the greatest potential to disrupt Hollywood's hegemonic grip on global theatrical screens.[17]

We see a similar split in the film industry's production practices. In a panel discussion at the 2012 Produced By Conference, major franchise producers admitted their disinclination toward social media, characterizing it as a necessary evil, even as a promotional tool; one panelist jokingly remarked that he hoped it was all a passing fad.[18] Ultimately, they were reacting to the additional workload and the extra "feedback" loop social media creates for properties already subjected to relentless market testing and focus groups (to producers, angry fans who are upset about a casting decision are just another set of "notes" to address). Once again, the most interest in innovation appears to be coming from the "margins." Independents like Ted Hope, for example, are often more optimistic about the alternative storytelling possibilities, new formats, and business models connecting viewing makes possible, recognizing the potential to expand the opportunities and audiences for stories that might not otherwise be told.[19] Free from the legacy structures and expectations of mainstream media corporations, those working outside such constraints can be more flexible in adapting to the incredible pace of change taking place in digital media distribution right now.

The advent of transmedia storytelling, as explored by the work of Henry Jenkins and others, is a similar expansion of engagement with fans that has influenced many connected viewing strategies.[20] Yet whereas the concept of transmedia is primarily focused on immersive textual experiences, narrative development, and finding ways to tell a story across multiple media platforms, connected viewing addresses the larger industrial landscape in which that text is situated, often speaking to dynamics of delivery, access, and control. Writer-director Scott Frank distances mainstream filmmaking from transmedia storytelling, saying in an interview with MIP that the economics just don't work out to hire a screenwriter to construct a complete story world across platforms and devices: "We cost too much for this." Like Alamo's Tim League, Frank further worries that the transmedia experience distracts from the aura attributed to the filmic text.[21] Unlike the immediacy gained from syncing the second screen to the live broadcast in television, the benefits of an instant connection to the audience via connected viewing strategies have proven to be somewhat more elusive for the film industry.

Dispersion, dislocation, and disconnection are all common tropes used to describe the pitfalls of connected viewing, particularly in the industry trades. It would nevertheless be a mistake to conflate platform proliferation and audience fragmentation with a completely disjointed entertainment experience. There are also countervailing forces at work here, a drawing together of institutions, technologies, and practices that bring multiple screens into alignment and offer audiences a way to enjoy the interactive capabilities of mobile devices and laptops while simultaneously engaging with linear media narratives and texts. Accordingly, connected viewing encompasses both centripetal and centrifugal dynamics, dispersing content across multiple devices and platforms as it creates an expanding array of opportunities for audiences to reconnect with one another, and to engage with media content. Cloud-based "TV Everywhere" services are one example of these competing dynamics, as they simultaneously sell the ability to "disconnect" from your television set, along with the promise of constant connectivity and instantaneous access (to content, to advertisers, to one another), no matter the particular time or place.

As these tensions are increasingly normalized as part of everyday life, more scholars are recognizing this moment as a critical juncture in the evolution of "connectedness." José van Dijck characterizes this shift away from more democratic conceptions of participatory culture toward a rather tenuous form of sociality in her cautionary discussion of our current "culture of connectivity." She argues that social media platforms and interfaces have completely refigured human interactions and reshaped larger societal norms, and that the connectedness we seek out online (to one another and larger communities) has been coopted. In fact, it has become so normalized by corporations interested in managing, manipulating, and monitoring our online behavior that this "connectivity" has fundamentally changed ideological principles, such as privacy, in the process.[22] Similarly, Mark Andrejevic has elsewhere identified connectedness as the comprehensive monitoring of a "super-panopticon" by content companies who turn feedback from transactions and online or viewing activity into the saleable "cybernetic commodity" form of data.[23] At the same time, Clay Shirky has written about the tools and revolutionary potential afforded by the way we use digital technologies, social media, and the Internet, noting that we now have the power to create more connected, powerful communities (and perhaps even a more vibrant democracy) than ever before.[24] As the following chapters attest, connected viewing is both a contributing factor and ongoing consequence of this larger cultural shift in our relationship with technology. While the phenomenon's more egalitarian promises are often compromised by long-standing institutional and regulatory arrangements—another prominent theme of this collection—*Connected Viewing* nevertheless calls for a contingent and complex articulation of the multiple dynamics (and diverse connections) that define this moment of change in the contemporary media industries.

The Connected Viewing Landscape

The industrial strategies and media technologies associated with connected viewing have grown increasingly complex in less than a decade. We have certainly come a long way from one of the first incarnations of connected viewing: the clunky, primitive QUBE system that Warner Cable devised in 1977 to expand television offerings and "connect" viewers to interactive channels via a set-top box and a very large remote.[25] Today, second-screen content, social networking, apps, cloud-based services, and over-the-top (OTT) technologies have all evolved to provide content for a multiscreen ecosystem that is constantly reinventing itself. Netflix was simply a DVD rental service that became a streaming platform accounting for more than one-third of all Internet traffic entering North American homes, and then became an original programming producer creating HBO-type quality programming for its thirty million-plus subscribers . . . all in the span of fifteen years. Netflix users alone streamed over four billion hours of video in the first quarter of 2013.[26] YouTube's parent company, Google, has invested $350 million in "premium channels" and original content to date in order to attract more audiences and higher-end advertisers.[27] At the same time, Internet-enabled, or "smart," TVs have penetrated 25 percent of the US market, and their global sales continue to increase well beyond the US pace; 55 percent of television households in Japan have smart TVs,[28] and it is predicted that there will be 40 percent penetration in the Middle Eastern television market by 2015.[29] The combination of rapid growth in connected and mobile screens, expanding digital delivery options, an unpredictable market for content, and consumer demands for portability and interactivity have created an industrial moment characterized by uncertainty, experimentation, and—depending on whether you are a consumer or provider of connected content—panic, excitement, confusion, or some combination thereof.

The growth of services, platforms, and devices has undoubtedly encouraged "cord cutting" (canceling one's cable subscription), as the home cable connection becomes less necessary with the expanding platforms for digital streaming and video-on-demand available on laptops and mobile devices. Researchers with the Convergence Consulting Group estimate that more than one million customers will "cut the cord" in 2013, representing an uptick in the pace of consumers turning their backs on the cable industry.[30] In some ways, the cord-cutting movement has augmented the phenomenon of connected viewing because all those viewers who are "disconnected" from their cable subscriptions still need a place to get their content, and increasingly, that place is on a mobile screen. According to industry predictions, two-thirds of all mobile data traffic will be video related by 2015.[31]

Digital platforms and OTT services are evolving rapidly as well, particularly as part of gaming consoles; Nintendo's TVii can access cable content, a personal DVR, subscription video-on-demand (SVOD) platforms such as Hulu and Netflix, and social media websites. The Xbox and PS3 currently have access to "TV Everywhere" apps, SVOD services, and social media; and the new Xbox One will also have full integration of pay-TV and live sporting events, specifically NFL content. Set-top boxes such as Roku, Boxee, and Apple TV allow for more connection between the TV screen and the Internet—even without a smart TV, thanks to built-in "TV Everywhere" apps and streaming services like Amazon Instant, Netflix, and HBO Go. It is also becoming easier to live-stream broadcast channels on laptops or mobile devices with the expansion of Aereo, a start-up service launched in New York City that allows computer access to live broadcast TV—although the service's legality is currently being debated in federal court.

Interestingly, it is in the traditional communal viewing space (in addition to the bedroom and the bathroom[32]) where tablets and mobile screens are frequently used for media consumption. A recent study by Motorola indicated that 40 percent of the content viewed in the American living room is on a tablet.[33] Further, according to the recent Pew report on "The Rise of the 'Connected Viewer,'" half of adult cell phone owners now incorporate their mobile devices into their television-watching experiences, making them "connected viewers."[34] Nielsen reports that roughly 40 percent of tablet owners in the United States are using their devices while watching TV, often to engage with social networking services and apps related to the program that is playing on their large-screen television.[35] Multitasking on multiple screens has come to define the act of watching television, even if audiences remain stationary on the couch.

Nielsen launched its first Twitter-based ratings system in the fall of 2013, a recognition of changing (and connected) viewing habits that has been a long time coming, particularly in the realm of audience metrics. This marked the first time that social media's impact on television will be accounted for in any ratings measurement.[36] It also represented an acknowledgement on the part of "old media" institutions that "new media" is indeed an intrinsic part of their business, as well as a pathway for audience engagement with content that is worthy of being counted.

As connected viewing evolves, there will undoubtedly be the continued marriage of hardware and software into one ecosystem (e.g., Apple TV, Xbox), creating proscribed boundaries and parameters delineating our paths into the digital content landscape. Screens will simultaneously become bigger and smaller, viewed by audiences who are both stationary and mobile. And yet, even as we watch on tablets or mobile phones, we are still connected—to social media and other users, to the Internet, to telecommunications networks, to remote storage in "the cloud," and, ultimately, to our content. How those connections are created, and in what form, or to what end, in whose vision . . . those are the questions that inspired the research inquiries in this collection.

Connected Viewing is organized in a manner that we envision as most useful for those teaching this subject in media industry studies courses. The essays are assembled into three admittedly overlapping categories with the goal of providing a productive framework in which to examine this emerging area of study: Industry Structure and Business Models, Technology and Platforms, and Content and Engagement. In the Industry Structure section, Jennifer Holt's chapter focuses on the ways policy issues are having an impact on connected viewing strategies and capabilities, and looks specifically at net neutrality, data caps, and issues related to the jurisdiction of content in the international and largely unregulated space of "the cloud." Hye Jin Lee and Mark Andrejevic address the developing relationship between second-screen apps, audience measurement, and viewer engagement. In their respective chapters, Elissa Nelson and Gregory Steirer investigate the ways the industry might be able to shift business models and their framing of consumer behavior. Nelson's research examines the shifts in and the confusion around digital media windowing strategies, while Steirer's interrogates how different kinds of engagement with content can add value to digital ownership propositions.

Changes in the ways consumers engage with media and shifts in business models could not occur without the attendant explosion in new technologies and platforms. Tackling the range of digital distribution services in Sweden, including industry-sanctioned and unauthorized platforms, Patrick Vonderau examines how connected viewing can be analyzed as a set of strategies that fosters a variety of media uses. Elizabeth Evans and Paul McDonald focus on the UK context, looking at user interactions with online film and television distribution through the themes of behavior, taste, and value, as well as the notion of "free and universal access" that is central to the UK public service media. Joshua Braun highlights an often-forgotten aspect of digital distribution; namely, the role of intermediaries in the online video marketplace, and how the platforms they operate help determine the kind of content consumers can access. Studying the impact individual users have on wider distribution systems, Aynne Kokas looks at the way Chinese netizens recommend content on social media sites, effectively taking a more active role in the curation and distribution of media.

In the Content and Engagement section, chapters address the outgrowth of nontraditional, nonlinear video as a way to rethink the ways that consumers use and access media. Matthew Thomas Payne considers how gamers participate in transmedia play as a way to connect with fellow players, and how these extended forms of immersion add interest in franchises and build users' gaming capital. Building on the centrality of the user experience in connected viewing, Ethan Tussey examines what types of extra content and applications consumers value, and where and when they choose to engage in connected viewing activities, while Chuck Tryon and Max Dawson study viewing habits of students in two different universities, focusing on users' experiences with new distribution models. Sharon Strover and William Moner present a long-term study of how people in different locations, including Texas and Portugal, and of different socioeconomic status, find and access content in media-rich environments.

These chapters attend to a variety of different media and industry relationships, which is integral to the way we are defining this development. Some address film, television, gaming, and social media, either individually, or in relation to one another. Others address the technological infrastructure essential to the existence of connected viewing. Chapters also interrogate the regulatory frameworks and market dynamics that structure what connected viewing does or does not make possible, and they do so without losing sight of what these developments mean for the users who might engage across screens, platforms, and devices. We thus argue connected viewing is an expansive dynamic, a fundamental shift in the digital media ecology, and a cumulative effect of recent technological developments, evolving business strategies, and emergent cultural practices. Connected viewing has opened up new frontiers for development, marketing, and windowing practices, as well as for narrative strategies, media policy, and even research metrics. Rather than isolate one particular dimension from another, the research in this collection affirms the opposite: that the intricate, uneven relationships among these convergent developments are constitutive elements of connected viewing and our ongoing efforts to understand it. In other words, studying connected viewing means making visible the ubiquitous "connections" that increasingly structure, shape, and at times "disrupt" contemporary media industries. By no means are these connections simply innocuous manifestations of selling, streaming, and sharing entertainment content; indeed, they all invoke a broader transformation in the political economy and cultural politics of screen media in the digital era.

Notes

1. Interview excerpts can be found on the Media Industries Project website: http://www.carseywolf.ucsb.edu/mip/critical-conversations.
2. For more on these challenges and opportunities, see Jennifer Holt, "Two Way Mirrors: Looking at the Future of Academic-Industry Engagement," *Cinema Journal,* In Focus: Screen Industry Studies 52, no. 3 (Spring 2013): 183–8.
3. Henry Jenkins, *Convergence Culture: Where Old and New Media Collide* (New York and London: New York University Press, 2006).
4. Henry Jenkins, Sam Ford, and Joshua Green, *Spreadable Media: Creating Value and Meaning in a Networked Culture* (New York and London: New York University Press, 2013).
5. Michael Curtin, "Matrix Media," in *Television Studies after TV: Understanding Television in the Post-Broadcast Era,* eds. Graeme Turner and Jinna Tay (London and New York: Routledge, 2009), 13.
6. Stuart Cunningham and Jon Silver, *Screen Distribution and the New King Kongs of the Online World* (London: Palgrave Macmillan, 2013).
7. For example, see Michael Kackman et al., eds., *Flow TV: Television in the Age of Media Convergence* (London and New York: Routledge, 2010); Jostein Gripsrud, *Relocating Television: Television in the Digital Context* (New York and London: Routledge, 2010); Lynn Spigel and Jan Olsson, eds., *Television after TV: Essays on a Medium in Transition* (Durham and London: Duke University Press, 2004); James Bennett and Niki Strange, eds., *Television as Digital Media* (Durham and London: Duke University Press, 2011); Graeme Turner and Jinna Tay, eds., *Television Studies after TV: Understanding Television in the Post-Broadcast Era* (London and New York: Routledge, 2009); and Darcy Gerbarg, ed., *Television Goes Digital: The Economics of Information, Communication, and Entertainment* (New York: Springer, 2009).
8. P. David Marshall, "Screens: Television's Dispersed 'Broadcast,'" in *Television Studies after TV: Understanding Television in the Post-Broadcast Era,* eds. Graeme Turner and Jinna Tay (London and New York: Routledge, 2009), 41–50.
9. Jennifer Gillan, *Television and New Media: Must-Click TV* (New York and London: Routledge, 2011).
10. For more on this, see William Boddy, "'Is It TV Yet?' The Dislocated Screens of Television in a Mobile Digital Culture," in *Television as Digital Media,* eds. James Bennett and

Niki Strange (Durham and London: Duke University Press, 2011), 76–104; see also William Boddy, "Interactive Television and Advertising Form in Contemporary U.S. Television," in *Television after TV: Essays on a Medium in Transition*, eds. Lynn Spigel and Jan Olsson (Durham and London: Duke University Press, 2004), 113–32.

11. Michael Curtin, Jennifer Holt, and Kevin Sanson, eds., *Distribution Revolution: Conversations about the Digital Future of Film and Television* (Berkeley: University of California Press, 2014). See also John T. Caldwell, "Breaking Ranks: Backdoor Workforces, Messy Workflows, and Craft Disaggregation," *Popular Communication* 8, no. 3 (2010): 221–6.

12. Niki Strange, "Multiplatforming Public Service: The BBC's 'Bundled Project,'" in *Television as Digital Media*, eds. James Bennett and Niki Strange (Durham and London: Duke University Press, 2011), 132–57.

13. For a discussion of the historical importance of theatrical revenues and their critical importance to conglomerate strategies, see Thomas Schatz, "The Studio System and Conglomerate Hollywood," in *The Contemporary Hollywood Film Industry*, eds. Paul McDonald and Janet Wasko (Malden, MA: Blackwell, 2008), 13–42.

14. Richard Verrier, "CinemaCon Panel Lights Up Texting Debate," *Los Angeles Times*, April 25, 2012, http://latimesblogs.latimes.com/entertainmentnewsbuzz/2012/04/cinemacon-panel-lights-up-texting-panel.html.

15. Chuck Tryon, *Reinventing Cinema: Movies in the Age of Media Convergence* (New Brunswick, NJ: Rutgers University Press, 2009). See Chapter 4, "Desktop Productions," in particular.

16. Ramon Lobato, *Shadow Economies of Cinema: Mapping Informal Film Distribution* (London: British Film Institute, 2012).

17. Stuart Cunningham and Jon Silver, "On-line Film Distribution: Its History and Global Complexion," in *Digital Disruption: Cinema Moves On-line*, eds. Dina Iordanova and Stuart Cunningham (St Andrews: St Andrews Film Studies, 2012), 33–66.

18. See Kevin Sanson, "Produced By . . . But for Whom?," *The Buzz* (blog), Media Industries Project, June 29, 2012, http://www.carseywolf.ucsb.edu/mip/buzz-mip-produced-conference.

19. Ted Hope elaborates on his perspective in a videotaped discussion with filmmaker Lance Weiler. For more, see Lance Weiler, "The Evolution of Storytelling," *The Work Book Project* (blog), July 23, 2009, http://workbookproject.com/blog/2009/06/23/culture-hacker-the-evolution-of-storytelling-vid/.

20. See, for example, Henry Jenkins, "Transmedia 202: Further Reflections," *Confessions of an Aca-Fan* (blog), August 1, 2011, http://henryjenkins.org/2011/08/defining_transmedia_further_re.html. Also see the conference archives and videos from the UCLA-USC annual Transmedia, Hollywood event at http://www.transmedia.tft.ucla.edu.

21. Curtin, Holt, and Sanson, eds., *Distribution Revolution: Conversations about the Digital Future of Film and Television*.

22. José van Dijck, *The Culture of Connectivity: A Critical History of Social Media* (Oxford: Oxford University Press, 2013).

23. See Mark Andrejevic, "The Twenty-First-Century Telescreen," in *Television Studies after TV: Understanding Television in the Post-Broadcast Era*, eds. Graeme Turner and Jinna Tay (London and New York: Routledge, 2009), 37; and Andrejevic, *iSpy: Surveillance and Power in the Interactive Era* (Lawrence, KS: University Press of Kansas, 2007).

24. Clay Shirky, *Here Comes Everybody* (New York: Penguin Books, 2008).

25. For an early, somewhat panicked discussion of QUBE's potential, see the special report of the May 1978 *Videocassette and CATV Newsletter* on Warner Cable's Qube, http://www.qube-tv.com/qube-tv/QUBE-REPORT.pdf.

26. Todd Spangler, "Why Netflix Viewing Isn't Comparable to Cablers," *Variety*, April 11, 2013, http://variety.com/2013/digital/news/netflix-now-watched-as-much-as-biggest-cable-nets-analyst-1200349682/.

27. Amir Efrati, "YouTube to Double Down on Its 'Channel' Experiment," *Wall Street Journal*, July 30, 2012, http://online.wsj.com/article/SB10000872396390444840104 577549632241258356.html.
28. Andrew Wallenstein, "The Stupidity of Smart TV," *Variety*, May 16, 2013, http://variety.com/2013/tv/news/the-stupidity-of-smart-tv-1200480143/.
29. *Khaleej Times*, "Smart TVs to Penetrate 40% of Mideast's Market by 2015," September 28, 2012, http://www.khaleejtimes.com/biz/inside.asp?xfile=/data/infotech/2012/September/infotech_September8.xml&section=infotech.
30. The previous four years between 2008 and 2012 had 3.74 million (3.7 percent) of US TV subscribers cancelling their subscriptions. See *Marketing Charts*, "TV Cord Cutters Growing Faster than Expected," April 8, 2013, http://www.marketingcharts.com/wp/television/tv-cord-cutters-growing-faster-than-expected-numbered-1-million -last-year-28437/.
31. *Video Industry News*, "The Growth of Video Streaming Is on the Rise," March 14, 2012, http://www.videoindustrynews.com/2012/03/14/the-growth-of-video-streaming -is-on-the-rise/.
32. One-third of people 18–24 are on social networks in the bathroom. Nielsen Reports, "State of the Media: The Social Media Report," December 4, 2012, 11. Download the report at http://www.nielsen.com/us/en/reports/2012/state-of-the-media-the -social-media-report-2012.html.
33. Motorola Company, "Fourth Annual Motorola Media Engagement Barometer," March 19, 2013. Available for download at http://mediacenter.motorola.com/Content/Detail.aspx?ReleaseID=15389&NewsAreaID=2&ClientID=1.
34. Aaron Smith and Jan Lauren Boyles, "The Rise of the 'Connected Viewer,'" Pew Research Center's Internet & American Life Project, July 17, 2012, http://www .pewinternet.org/Reports/2012/Connected-viewers.aspx.
35. Nielsen Newswire, "40% of Table and Smartphone Owners Use Them While Watching TV," October 13, 2011, http://www.nielsen.com/us/en/newswire/2011/40-of-tablet -and-smartphone-owners-use-them-while-watching-tv.html.
36. Hazel Sheffield, "Nielsen, Twitter Partner for TV Ratings," *Columbia Journalism Review*, December 21, 2012, http://www.cjr.org/behind_the_news/nielsen_and_twitter_ partner_fo.php.

References

Andrejevic, Mark. *iSpy: Surveillance and Power in the Interactive Era*. Lawrence, KS: University Press of Kansas, 2007.

Andrejevic, Mark. "The Twenty-First-Century Telescreen." In *Television Studies after TV: Understanding Television in the Post-Broadcast Era*, edited by Graeme Turner and Jinna Tay, 31–40. London and New York: Routledge, 2009.

Bennett, James, and Niki Strange, eds. *Television as Digital Media*. Durham and London: Duke University Press, 2011.

Boddy, William. "Interactive Television and Advertising Form in Contemporary U.S. Television." In *Television after TV: Essays on a Medium in Transition*, edited by Lynn Spigel and Jan Olsson, 113–32. Durham and London: Duke University Press, 2004.

Boddy, William. "'Is It TV Yet?' The Dislocated Screens of Television in a Mobile Digital Culture." In *Television as Digital Media*, edited by James Bennett and Niki Strange, 76–104. Durham and London: Duke University Press, 2011.

Caldwell, John T. "Breaking Ranks: Backdoor Workforces, Messy Workflows, and Craft Disaggregation." *Popular Communication* 8, no. 3 (2010): 221–6.

Cunningham, Stuart, and Jon Silver. "On-line Film Distribution: Its History and Global Complexion." In *Digital Disruption: Cinema Moves On-line*, edited by Dina Iordanova and Stuart Cunningham, 33–66. St Andrews: St Andrews Film Studies, 2012.

Cunningham, Stuart, and Jon Silver. *Screen Distribution and the New King Kongs of the Online World*. London: Palgrave Macmillan, 2013.

Curtin, Michael. "Matrix Media." In *Television Studies after TV: Understanding Television in the Post-Broadcast Era*, edited by Graeme Turner and Jinna Tay, 9–19. London and New York: Routledge, 2009.

Curtin, Michael, Jennifer Holt, and Kevin Sanson, eds. *Distribution Revolution: Conversations about the Digital Future of Film and Television*. Berkeley: University of California Press, 2014.

Efrati, Amir. "YouTube to Double Down on Its 'Channel' Experiment." *Wall Street Journal*, July 30, 2012. http://online.wsj.com/article/SB10000872396390444840104577549632241258356.html.

Gerbarg, Darcy, ed. *Television Goes Digital: The Economics of Information, Communication, and Entertainment*. New York: Springer, 2009.

Gillan, Jennifer. *Television and New Media: Must-Click TV.* New York and London: Routledge, 2011.

Glasser, Jeff. "Warner's Cable Qube." *Videocassette and CATV Newsletter*, May 1978. http://www.qube-tv.com/qube-tv/QUBE-REPORT.pdf.

Gripsrud, Jostein. *Relocating Television: Television in the Digital Context*. New York and London: Routledge, 2010.

Holt, Jennifer. "Two Way Mirrors: Looking at the Future of Academic-Industry Engagement." *Cinema Journal*, In Focus: Screen Industry Studies 52, no. 3 (Spring 2013): 183–8.

Jenkins, Henry. *Convergence Culture: Where Old and New Media Collide*. New York and London: New York University Press, 2006.

Jenkins, Henry. "Transmedia 202: Further Reflections." *Confessions of an Aca-Fan* (blog). August 1, 2011. http://henryjenkins.org/2011/08/defining_transmedia_further_re.html.

Jenkins, Henry, Sam Ford, and Joshua Green. *Spreadable Media: Creating Value and Meaning in a Networked Culture*. New York and London: New York University Press, 2013.

Kackman, Michael, Marnie Binfield, Matthew Thomas Payne, Allison Perlman, and Bryan Sebok, eds. *Flow TV: Television in the Age of Media Convergence*. London and New York: Routledge, 2010.

Khaleej Times. "Smart TVs to Penetrate 40% of Mideast's Market by 2015." September 28, 2012. http://www.khaleejtimes.com/biz/inside.asp?xfile=/data/infotech/2012/September/infotech_September8.xml&section=infotech.

Lobato, Ramon. *Shadow Economies of Cinema: Mapping Informal Film Distribution*. London: British Film Institute, 2012.

Marketing Charts. "TV Cord Cutters Growing Faster than Expected." April 8, 2013. http://www.marketingcharts.com/wp/television/tv-cord-cutters-growing-faster-than-expected-numbered-1-million-last-year-28437/.

Marshall, P. David. "Screens: Television's Dispersed 'Broadcast.'" In *Television Studies After TV: Understanding Television in the Post-Broadcast Era*, edited by Graeme Turner and Jinna Tay, 41–50. London and New York: Routledge, 2009.

Motorola Company. "Fourth Annual Motorola Media Engagement Barometer." March 19, 2013. http://mediacenter.motorola.com/Content/Detail.aspx?ReleaseID=15389&NewsAreaID=2&ClientID=1.

Nielsen Reports. "State of the Media: The Social Media Report." December 4, 2012. http://www.nielsen.com/us/en/reports/2012/state-of-the-media-the-social-media-report-2012.html.

Nielsen Newswire. "40% of Table and Smartphone Owners Use Them While Watching TV." October 13, 2011. http://www.nielsen.com/us/en/newswire/2011/40-of-tablet-and -smartphone-owners-use-them-while-watching-tv.html.

Sanson, Kevin. "Produced By . . . But for Whom?" *The Buzz*, Media Industries Project. June 29, 2012. http://www.carseywolf.ucsb.edu/mip/buzz-mip-produced-conference.

Schatz, Thomas. "The Studio System and Conglomerate Hollywood." In *The Contemporary Hollywood Film Industry*, edited by Paul McDonald and Janet Wasko, 13–42. Malden, MA: Blackwell, 2008.

Sheffield, Hazel. "Nielsen, Twitter Partner for TV Ratings." *Columbia Journalism Review*, December 21, 2012. http://www.cjr.org/behind_the_news/nielsen_and_twitter_partner_ fo.php.

Shirky, Clay. *Here Comes Everybody*. New York: Penguin Books, 2008.

Smith, Aaron, and Jan Lauren Boyles. "The Rise of the 'Connected Viewer.'" Pew Research Center's Internet & American Life Project, July 17, 2012. http://www.pewinternet.org/ Reports/2012/Connected-viewers.aspx.

Spangler, Todd. "Why Netflix Viewing Isn't Comparable to Cablers." *Variety*, April 11, 2013. http://variety.com/2013/digital/news/netflix-now-watched-as-much-as-biggest -cable-nets-analyst-1200349682/.

Spigel, Lynn, and Jan Olsson, eds. *Television after TV: Essays on a Medium in Transition*. Durham and London: Duke University Press, 2004.

Strange, Niki. "Multiplatforming Public Service: The BBC's 'Bundled Project.'" In *Television as Digital Media*, edited by James Bennett and Niki Strange, 132–57. Durham and London: Duke University Press, 2011.

Tryon, Chuck. *Reinventing Cinema: Movies in the Age of Media Convergence*. New Brunswick, NJ: Rutgers University Press, 2009.

Turner, Graeme, and Jinna Tay, eds. *Television Studies After TV: Understanding Television in the Post-Broadcast Era*. London and New York: Routledge, 2009.

van Dijck, José. *The Culture of Connectivity: A Critical History of Social Media*. Oxford: Oxford University Press, 2013.

Verrier, Richard. "CinemaCon Panel Lights Up Texting Debate." *Los Angeles Times*, April 25, 2012. http://latimesblogs.latimes.com/entertainmentnewsbuzz/2012/04/ cinemacon-panel-lights-up-texting-panel.html.

Video Industry News. "The Growth of Video Streaming Is on the Rise." March 14, 2012. http://www.videoindustrynews.com/2012/03/14/the-growth-of-video-streaming -is-on-the-rise/.

Wallenstein, Andrew. "The Stupidity of Smart TV." *Variety*, May 16, 2013. http://variety. com/2013/tv/news/the-stupidity-of-smart-tv-1200480143/.

Weiler, Lance. "The Evolution of Storytelling." *The Work Book Project* (blog). July 23, 2009. http://workbookproject.com/blog/2009/06/23/culture-hacker-the-evolution-of -storytelling-vid/.

PART I

INDUSTRY STRUCTURE AND STRATEGIES

1

REGULATING CONNECTED VIEWING

Media Pipelines and Cloud Policy

Jennifer Holt

Connected viewing activities such as streaming movies on Facebook, virtually attending BD-Live screening events, or chatting via social media apps about a favorite television show require a significant amount of telecommunications and information infrastructure. This includes everything from wires, cables, switches, buildings, and satellites, to computers, air-conditioning equipment, and vast networks that connect users to high-speed broadband service. These infrastructure elements are among the most basic necessities to sustain this new ecosystem of digital interaction and consumption. However, their ability to continually connect audiences to content cannot be taken for granted. Indeed, these connections between content providers and end users are increasingly at risk, threatened by various trends in regulatory policy and their impact on digital media infrastructure.

In fact, the policies governing broadband access, pricing, and data stored remotely, i.e., "in the cloud," pose some of the biggest challenges to the future development and expansion of connected viewing. These challenges are increasingly difficult to navigate or anticipate, largely because policies governing cloud storage and its attendant infrastructure, or what I will refer to collectively as "cloud policy," are currently in flux. Just as many of the strategies for distributing and engaging with connected viewing content are still evolving, so too are the policies that regulate the conduits on which they rely. In the United States, broadband has been so deregulated that customers currently have no protections against Internet service providers (ISPs) that decide to restrict traffic emanating from various websites, or to specific users.[1] As a result, the survival of net neutrality—a critical element of content's digital flow and, in turn, of connected viewing strategies—is in question. Other similarly important policy debates, such as those affecting the "shareability" and accessibility of data and information stored in the cloud, are presently undergoing intense negotiations as the Federal Communications Commission (FCC), the broadband industry and ISPs, the Supreme Court, content providers, and public interest groups engage in protracted debate. Right now, little has been decided, and the current moment of deliberation is a crucial one for the future viability of connected viewing.

At its core, policy is about power, and this chapter is ultimately about who will have the power to control connected viewing in the coming years. In what follows, I detail the current issues in regulatory policy that will have the most significant impact on connected viewing for content providers and consumers, as well as for service providers. Content providers and audiences are two groups that often have opposing viewpoints on monetizing the digital entertainment space, but in the realm of connected viewing policy, many of their interests are surprisingly well aligned . . . usually against the ISPs (Comcast-NBCUniversal of course being a notable exception, as it is an integrated studio/content provider and the country's largest ISP). Content providers in this context include film and television studios (e.g., Warner Bros., Disney), gaming companies (e.g., Zynga, Electronic Arts), and even aggregators such as Netflix and Hulu. Despite their conflicts over the availability and price of digital content, these companies and their audiences are actually united by their common struggle against the largely unregulated control of Internet and mobile service providers that have power over many dimensions of access in the digital spaces of connected viewing.[2]

Decisions about how broadband pipelines and servers are regulated, how much access costs for consumers, and how cloud-based data are governed will each, in part, determine whether connected viewing has a future. Policy makers can choose to promote consumer-friendly measures on issues such as access and Internet affordability, or they can continue to subject the connected viewing infrastructure to a regime that privileges the power of unregulated ISPs and, consequently, limits the free flow of content and information. As more media content, usage, and sites of engagement shift to the digital space, these issues of diversity, access, and media control are the current regulatory stakes for connected viewing initiatives and, by extension, the future democratic qualities of the Internet and the accessibility of "the cloud."

My research focuses on the US context, but clearly these concerns are international ones, with global ramifications. The legal history of cloud computing and broadband policy in the United States, as well as personal interviews with FCC senior staff, former authors of the National Broadband Plan, public interest advocates, legal counsel for various connected viewing interests, and policy advisors for major cloud computing corporations, have all formed the basis for this chapter. It is clear after distilling these various perspectives that the key developments in the regulatory arena for the connected viewing ecosystem are related to 1) the enforcement of net neutrality; 2) the implementation and legality of bandwidth caps; and 3) the jurisdiction over data servers supporting the storage and transmission of cloud-based media across international borders. As the digital era of distribution unfolds, these issues will ultimately determine the dimensions and sustainability of connected viewing initiatives and, in turn, the future of access and engagement with online entertainment, information, and media culture.

Net Neutrality and Managed Services

Net neutrality—its adoption and preservation—is the most important policy matter for the interests of content providers (of all sizes) and consumers of cloud-based media today. Net neutrality is in fact part of the Internet's original design principle, and it is only in recent years that its applicability has been contested. Essentially, it requires ISPs to carry all data (or "packets") over their wires at the same speed, regardless of who is sending them.[3] That means that ISPs could not be discriminatory in their distribution of content, and therefore could not send it faster—or slower—based on proprietary interests, competitive strategies, or financial arrangements benefiting those who own the digital pipelines. With net neutrality laws, the Internet would in many ways be a more "open," competitive environment, and less susceptible to the consolidated power of ISPs.

That consolidation is quite significant at this time, especially in the United States. Comcast Corp., Time Warner Cable Inc., AT&T Inc., and Verizon Communications Inc. currently control 62 percent of the US broadband marketplace,[4] and there are no signs that the government will slow this trend down anytime soon. In fact, one of the former top lobbyists for the telecom and tech industries, Tom Wheeler, has been selected to chair the FCC for President Obama's second term. Public interest advocates are unimpressed and concerned by this choice. Among them is Sasha Meinrath, who heads the Open Technology Institute at the New America Foundation, which advocates for net neutrality, among other issues. Meinrath put some of the dangers for the connected viewing audience in perspective when he said, "I am skeptical that the former chief lobbyist of the wireless and cable industries will be capable of holding his former clients accountable for their ongoing shortcomings."[5] These shortcomings include the lack of adherence to net neutrality principles, without which those who control the broadband pipelines have unchecked power over how they deliver the data that flow through them.

The concept of net neutrality essentially applies the principle of common carriage to broadband service, similar to its application for telephone service. Common carriers are considered essential infrastructure for the national economy and public welfare, and include certain transportation and communications services, such as railroads and telecommunications. Therefore, they are subject to strict regulations, and they are and must be available to the general public without prejudice.[6] In other words, their providers cannot discriminate against those who wish to use the services, or provide preferential treatment to certain customers. This standard of nondiscrimination, if supported properly through law and applied to Internet service, could potentially be used to wrest some measure of control from the highly powerful ISPs, and ensure the public a freer and more open Internet with less risk of interference from those controlling its distribution.

Unfortunately, the present viability and realization of net neutrality as a legal standard for broadband regulation is in crisis. In the United States, Internet provision is currently being regulated without common carrier requirements, theoretically allowing ISPs to charge companies more to have their content delivered to consumers in a privileged digital "express lane" of sorts. Service providers are also able to privilege their own content if they are integrated with content companies (e.g., Comcast). This could have dramatic implications for what counts as "choice" in the digital television landscape outside public service systems. As Robert McChesney explains, if ISPs were allowed to legally discriminate among users, "they could effectively privatize the Internet and make it like cable television."[7] That scenario offers a model of already-deregulated, consolidated, government-sanctioned regional monopolies that could hypothetically begin charging certain users even more for the privilege of using their pipes, and shut out those who could not afford it. Smaller, independent content providers and digital audiences facing a diminished spectrum of online options will stand to lose the most.

Currently, the courts are deciding whether the FCC actually has any authority at all to regulate ISPs. This was debated as Internet providers were reclassified by federal agencies and the courts four times in five years between 2000 and 2005, ultimately coming before the Supreme Court in the *Brand X* case. The court's decision in this case classified cable Internet providers as *information services* (instead of as *telecommunications services,* which are more stringently regulated), thus liberating these ISPs from any common carriage requirements.[8] Shortly thereafter, the FCC reclassified *all* wireline broadband Internet providers as information services, even those provided by DSL technology/telephone companies. The agency used various rationales, including the argument that "[c]onsistent regulatory treatment of competing broadband platforms will enable potential investors in broadband network platforms to make market-based, rather than regulation-driven, investment and deployment decisions."[9] The FCC's neoliberal approach effectively cut the public right out of the equation in the name of market-based efficiencies.

Brand X and the FCC's subsequent reclassification of ISPs in 2005 would have dramatic implications for the connected viewing landscape, in that those decisions rendered the FCC somewhat powerless in the arena of broadband regulation, and put the bulk of power into the hands of service providers as gatekeepers. In fact, as law professor and former presidential advisor Susan Crawford has put it, the result of the FCC's approach has been, incredibly, that "the essential communications network of our time, access to the Internet, has no basic regulatory oversight at all."[10] This bore out in the landmark *Comcast Corp. v. FCC* case, when Comcast—the largest ISP in the United States—filed suit against the FCC for attempting to regulate its network management practices in 2008. This case had its beginnings a year earlier when a software engineer and barbershop quartet enthusiast, Robb Topolski, noticed that Comcast was interfering with/slowing down his peer-to-peer sharing of rare audio material that was in the public domain, a practice known as "throttling." An AP reporter picked the story up after reading Topolski's post about his discovery on a discussion board for broadband enthusiasts. The report set off a firestorm around net neutrality violations and Comcast's discrimination against certain Internet users.[11] Comcast was publicly censured (but not fined) by the FCC, in the agency's first attempt to impose net neutrality restrictions. To say that attempt backfired is an understatement, as Comcast turned right around and sued the FCC, claiming it did not have the authority to even censure Comcast for the way it treated its customers. To the disappointment of many public interest and policy observers, the DC Circuit Court of Appeals ruled in April 2010 in favor of Comcast. The court's ruling effectively affirmed that, under the Telecommunications Act of 1996, the FCC does not have the statutory power to regulate ISPs and therefore cannot control the network management practices of ISPs.[12] As a result, the country's regulatory agency for communications lacks any legal authority to actually enforce its own net neutrality policies.

Nevertheless, the FCC set out new net neutrality rules in December 2010, as articulated in the Open Internet Order.[13] In the Order, the agency stipulates that broadband providers must maintain transparency; must not block lawful content, applications, or services; and may not unreasonably discriminate in their transmission of content. According to the FCC, these rules were adopted "to ensure that the Internet remains a powerful platform for innovation and job creation; to empower consumers and entrepreneurs; to protect free expression; to promote competition; to increase certainty in the marketplace by providing greater predictability for all stakeholders regarding federal policy in this area; and to spur investment both at the 'edge,' and in the core of our broadband networks."[14] In theory, they would protect content providers and consumers from throttling, and declared that the ISPs cannot adjust their connection speeds on wired Internet service. Yet the enforceability of the Open Internet Order remained in question.

Importantly, the net neutrality rules put forth by the FCC's Order (referred to as "fake net neutrality" by Free Press[15] and other open Internet advocates) would not apply to wireless. Despite this significant exemption, as wireless is indisputably the future of Internet access and how the majority of users now connect to the web,[16] the rules are currently being challenged in courts by Verizon. This lawsuit was initiated in 2011 because Verizon, one of the largest Internet providers in America, claimed that the Open Internet rules violate its rights to free speech, are unconstitutional, and go beyond the FCC's authority.[17] This is rather unusual because the FCC rules in question are almost a direct replication of a proposal—a rather indecent one—put forth by Verizon and Google in 2010 as a blueprint for how the agency might regulate them moving forward.[18] After the FCC basically incorporated the legislative framework recommended by Verizon and Google, Verizon filed a lawsuit against the agency for overreaching its authority. Verizon preferred that Congress retain rulemaking power over the Internet, not the FCC, and explained its appeal of the Open Internet Order in part by stating, "We are deeply concerned by the FCC's assertion of broad authority for sweeping new regulation of broadband networks and the Internet itself. We believe this assertion of authority goes well beyond any authority provided by Congress, and creates uncertainty for the communications industry, innovators, investors and consumers."[19] Arguments in the Verizon case are expected to begin in the fall of 2013 in the DC Circuit Court of Appeals, with a verdict to follow in the winter of 2014. It remains to be seen whether rules so weak that they propose only to regulate wired Internet connections on providers' terms can actually stand up to the lawsuits of those same providers. The history of the rules thus far suggests that net neutrality still has a difficult road ahead.

In addition to the legal battles over net neutrality, there are also threats to the competitive market of digital media distribution posed by media corporations themselves. There is a lingering, widespread concern that service providers aligned with/owned by content providers will begin privileging their own content at any moment, or disadvantaging that of their competitors and perpetuating their "ongoing shortcomings." Comcast, for one, owns not only one of the largest cable, Internet, and phone providers in the United States but also NBC, Universal Studios, and properties including E! network, Bravo, MSNBC, Telemundo, and part of Hulu, as well as on-demand platforms—all of which are delivered through Comcast's own pipelines. This ownership combination of distribution networks and content will undoubtedly favor Comcast in the digital arena, allowing it to potentially discriminate against competing content providers and limit options for connected audiences.

Another issue of concern is that of service providers limiting bandwidth available to their competitors in order to drive consumers toward their own platforms. Verizon, which co-owns the streaming platform Redbox Instant, is a prominent example. The telecom and broadband giant has been accused of slowing the streaming traffic of Netflix, one of Redbox's largest competitors, causing poor service for Netflix subscribers who are Verizon customers.[20] This issue promises to persist, given the enormously high stakes of the digital content delivery business and its rate of expansion. It is clear that in order for the Internet to provide a truly open space for discovery and engagement, the survival of actual net neutrality—for both wired and wireless—must be preserved.

There are still ways in which the biggest Internet companies are currently engineering so-called workarounds to any potential net neutrality rules, while maintaining the façade of being controlled by the FCC's Open Internet Order, despite its precarious legal foundation. One such workaround has taken place in the form of direct payments to broadband providers in order to secure smoother and faster access to their networks. Companies with very deep pockets such as Facebook, Google, and Microsoft have been engaging in this practice in order to compete in an era of increased demand for streaming capacity and subsequent Internet congestion, paying carriers such as Comcast, Time Warner Cable, and Verizon for speedier service. The payments are buying content companies and websites more direct access to the broadband providers' networks, closer to where content delivery originates. This is outside the domain of net neutrality rules, which are focused on the "last mile" of broadband pipeline, i.e., the final portion of delivering connectivity from the provider to the customer. This leaves quite a bit of unregulated territory, which is subject to such informal dealings as dictated by ISPs. Comcast has reported it earns about $30 million per year from such payments—less than 0.1 percent of its total revenue, yet not insubstantial.[21] While technically legal, these payments certainly flout the spirit of the 2010 Open Internet Rules, which are intended to preserve a democratic Internet and maintain similar standards of service regardless of the senders' ability to pay for a speedier delivery of their content at any point in the process. They also disadvantage smaller players who can ill afford to pay for this direct access, and consequently limit the range of creative possibilities for connected viewing.

Another important way companies can avoid the dictates of FCC policy is through Content Delivery Networks (CDNs): a key set of players that are also known as "managed services." This is a category of infrastructure that is exempt from any current net neutrality orders or regulations. CDNs include companies such as Akamai, Level 3, Limelight, CloudFront (Amazon), and Open Connect (Netflix). These networks essentially work to deliver content more quickly and efficiently for various websites and platforms, and their operation is essentially invisible to the end user. They facilitate many connected viewing activities, such as video streaming and downloading. However, they are not regulated by or under the purview of the FCC. As Bruce Gottleib, a former senior advisor to FCC Chairman Julius Genachowski, explains, CDNs are not on the FCC's radar for regulating the connected viewing ecosystem because they were devised by companies that were not in the agency's purview; additionally, the FCC is "very narrowly focused on the pipe to the house [aka 'the last mile']," and "[CDNs] are just not where the agency's attention is."[22]

Joshua Braun's essay in this volume discusses some of these players in the connected viewing landscape as critical "intermediaries," and indeed they are. Partnerships and/or involvement with CDNs will be central to the success of connected viewing strategies for content companies, particularly those companies that do not own broadband networks like Comcast does. Companies such as Apple, Amazon, Comcast, Microsoft, Netflix, and Google have all built out their own CDNs. Amazon's CloudFront CDN is not just for Amazon's services; it is also available as a retail offering for third parties. The CDN owned and operated by Netflix, Open Connect, is working with major ISPs around the world, including Frontier, British Telecom, TDC, Clearwire, GVT, Telus, Bell Canada, Virgin, Cablevision, Google Fiber, Telmex, and more.[23]

New strategies and services have emerged to disseminate the ever-expanding well of streaming video content and websites that enliven connected viewing, but their design does not necessarily (if at all) preserve any commitment to the spirit of net neutrality and an open Internet. CDNs are essential infrastructure in the efficient delivery of streaming media, applications, and social networks to digital platforms, but they are also able to exploit loopholes in policies designed to protect the consumer and preserve competition. Billion-dollar companies making direct payments to ISPs for faster service enact precisely what the end-to-end design principle of the Internet (and the FCC's Open Internet Order) intended to avoid: they diminish the freedoms inherent in this architectural feature, i.e., allow what were supposed to be "dumb pipes" to become gatekeepers and arbiters of control over content. Lawrence Lessig, Tim Wu, and Barbara van Schewick have been among those rigorously advocating for maintaining the end-to-end principle to preserve an open Internet. As van Schewick writes, "Leaving the evolution of the network to network providers will significantly reduce the Internet's value to society . . . doing nothing is not enough to preserve the status quo, let alone to restore the full potential of the Internet."[24] Connected viewing is part of that full, creative potential and, in order to continue developing, it will require infrastructure policy devoted to supporting the end user.

Data Caps for Consumers

Data caps, or limits to the amount of Internet traffic one is allowed to utilize on a single device, and the attendant metered distribution of content over broadband and mobile networks are hot-button, evolving policy issues for connected viewing. According to the Open Technology Initiative at the New America Foundation, data caps are hardly a necessity. In fact, its recent report describes data caps as being "motivated by a desire to further increase revenues from existing subscribers and protect legacy services such as cable television from competing Internet services,"[25] as opposed to being a solution to alleviating congestion, as the ISPs claim. This was further supported by former FCC chairman and current president of the National Cable and Telecommunications Association Michael Powell when he confirmed during a 2013 speech that data caps were not about network congestion. Instead, he explained, "[o]ur principal purpose is how to fairly monetize a high fixed cost."[26] There has also been speculation that data caps are a calculated move by cable companies, which provide both linear television channels and high-speed Internet access, to prevent consumers from accessing video content online (from subscription platforms such as Netflix or Hulu Plus, for example) that they might otherwise have to pay for in a cable subscription. The Department of Justice even launched an antitrust investigation into the use of data caps in 2012 because of such suspicions.[27]

Rationales aside, data caps on both wireline and mobile networks are soon going to be an unpleasant reality for the connected viewing audience. While they are a relatively recent development (first instituted widely by Comcast in 2008), ISPs in the United States are currently in various stages of experimentation with consumer thresholds and market impact for both wireline and mobile caps. The average American household now has five or more connected devices, from laptops and tablets to mobile phones and gaming consoles, and as a result, the demand for bandwidth has increased.[28] Since multiple devices operating in a single household are combined to account for user activity, data caps will become an increasingly central concern for connected viewing. Going over one's cap because of high-resolution video streaming, or contending with new pricing structures designed to charge more for heavier usage, will inject a new financial determinant into the mix, i.e., whether connected viewing will be something that is affordable to most Internet users, or whether ISPs will basically price them out. This is another scenario where the interests of content providers are aligned with their audiences; if viewers cannot afford to stream content and have to limit their online activity, content companies lose as well.

The specific concern of data caps is also intricately related to the larger issues of net neutrality and managed services. The relationship was made clear in a 2012 decision by Comcast to exempt its proprietary Xfinity On Demand service on the Xbox 360 from counting against its monthly data caps. This meant that Comcast would not charge the usage of its own services against the data limit, but that the services of such competitors like Netflix or HBO Go would count. Surprisingly enough, this discriminatory capping is technically legal because the data traffic does not travel over the public Internet; instead, it is routed by Comcast and Microsoft through privately managed services like CDNs, which are not subject to any net neutrality rules, as previously discussed. As one analyst has described this agreement, "Microsoft has extended Comcast's network onto its device and created a fast lane over which Comcast bits can travel."[29] In fact, Comcast itself has actually reasoned that Xbox 360's running the Xfinity app "essentially acts as an additional cable box for your existing cable service," and is therefore more like cable TV than the Internet, and thus excused from the data caps that apply to Xfinity's competitors.[30] Similar issues with data caps are starting to crop up internationally. For example, Germany's Deutsche Telekom recently announced that it would impose strict data caps on home users' Internet downloads by 2016—but would exempt its own TV service, called Entertain.[31]

Data allotments will likely become even more central to connected viewing as broadband speeds increase in the United States and pipelines become capable of delivering media more quickly, expanding the options for connected audiences (the United States is currently eighth in the world in average connection speeds).[32] Further, studies indicate that global mobile data traffic grew 70 percent in 2012, and will increase thirteen-fold between 2012 and 2017.[33] It is predicted that cloud applications will account for 84 percent of total global mobile data traffic by 2017.[34] Managing access to these data will be critical to the future, and all signs point to the inevitable turn away from unlimited plans and toward ISPs treating data as a scarce resource in order to charge more for them.[35] Even President Obama's first FCC chairman, Julius Genachowski, publicly supported metered billing, calling this practice devoted to ISP profits a "consumer-friendly move" that would help drive efficiency in networks and encourage competition.[36]

Currently, however, there remains a great deal of uncertainty about the specifics of new pricing models and their implementation. The only consistency in this conversation over caps is found in the discourse of restriction and scarcity that has dominated much of the public debate and commentary from the ISP industry—echoing similar discourses throughout broadcast history that have often served as rationales for government regulation.[37] A more productive framework for this discussion, according to Blair Levin, who formerly oversaw the development of the National Broadband Plan at the FCC, is one rooted in a "psychology of abundance" that does not impose unnecessary limitations on broadband access. This perspective, he explains, along with regaining our long-lost strategic bandwidth advantage, could spur innovative usage of technologies and promote experimentation. Levin notes, "For most Americans, five years from now, the best network available to them will be the same network they have today . . . [i]nstead of witnessing investment for growth, we are witnessing harvesting for dividends [by the ISPs]."[38] Those dividends are paying off for companies like Comcast and Verizon, but not necessarily for audiences in the digital arena or content providers dependent on those networks. Perpetuating a model of artificial scarcity in the broadband market will only serve to limit the possibilities for connected viewing moving forward.

Jurisdiction over Data in the Cloud

While the inspired, public-relations-devised imagery of "the cloud" might conjure up visions of e-mails, documents, and television episodes residing somewhere celestial, floating in space and readily pulled back down to Earth and accessed on demand, the reality of cloud storage is much less ethereal. The cloud is of course quite material, dependent on a vast series of networked computers and servers (often referred to as "server farms" or data centers), along with related software and infrastructure necessary for their operation. The cloud industry is also rapidly expanding as the digital economy grows increasingly dependent on its services and functions; experts predict that by 2020, the global cloud computing industry will be a $241 billion market.[39] To support all our cloud-reliant activity, it is estimated that there are now more than three million data centers of varying sizes worldwide.[40] It is in these spaces where the data on which all connected viewing relies can be found, and where many potential legal problems begin for its providers, consumers, and regulators.

When we talk of information or streaming media stored in the cloud, we are really referring to data that are collected, fragmented, duplicated, stored, processed—often in different remote locations, even in different countries, on different servers—and then ultimately viewed on an Internet-connected screen of some sort. This means that connected viewing involves cloud applications and services that send data across international borders multiple times in the process of reaching their audience or users. As a result, these data pass through just as many national regimes of privacy laws, intellectual property laws, data processing and protection laws, and other regulations affecting the jurisdiction of and control over that data while they are "in the cloud." This widely distributed, totally uncoordinated legal maze of transnational data flows has created quite a challenge for regulators and the courts when determining who has control over data in the cloud, and exactly where/at what point that control begins and ends. The lack of universal legal standards for a global digital ecosystem also represents a risky environment for connected viewing in the future, particularly as multiplatform engagement relies increasingly on streaming media stored in the cloud.[41]

Data centers have found some precedent as the legally defined geographic locations of data in the cloud. Yet whether data are legally determined to exist in one place or multiple locations (wherever the data are separately collected, processed, and stored) still remains unresolved. Moreover, some services are said to actually "own" the data, while others are merely acting as the "custodians" while they are stored. Overall, the jurisdiction and governance of data—particularly data that is stored, processed, and accessed across international borders—is extremely complex, ill defined, and has thus far proven elusive for regulators attempting to address the many "conflict-of-law" issues. Additionally, the basic economics of the cloud are currently in conflict with some fundamentals of data protection law. According to FCC deputy bureau chief and senior advisor for new technology Michael McKenzie, "data protection law is largely based on an understanding that you know where your data is located within particular borders, whereas the economics of the cloud is dependent on data being able to flow across borders in a fairly seamless way."[42]

While some regulations make data exporters accountable for ensuring the continued protection of transferred personal data no matter what their location, many regulations for cloud data are geographically based.[43] As such, location matters when it comes to determining who controls the data—and, in turn, the media—stored in the cloud. However, decisions about where to locate data centers are influenced most by a variety of factors unrelated to regulatory policies, including proximity to affordable electricity and other energy resources, as well as local infrastructure and tax codes. Electricity costs are key, as data centers are one of the fastest-growing consumers of energy (to both power and cool the servers), and they can consume up to 100 times more energy than a standard office building.[44] Worldwide, server farms use about thirty billion watts of electricity, roughly equivalent to the output of thirty nuclear power plants, and their carbon footprint will likely surpass that of air travel by the next decade.[45] To contend with these significant energy requirements, placing data centers in cool climates has become a common strategy. As such, the Nordic countries have become one burgeoning destination for US companies to build data centers. Facebook, for example, recently built an enormous facility in Luleå, Sweden—its first outside the United States—and will rely on the average daily temperature of 2°C (35.6°F) to do most of the work to cool the server halls, with dams on the nearby Lule River generating the renewable electricity to supply the rest of the facility's power needs.[46]

The power requirements of data centers have created an increasingly complicated and interdependent relationship between data regulation and energy politics, as the allure of cheaper energy to supply data centers often creates jurisdiction shopping for global hosting, and with it, serious privacy concerns about the security of data. This is because those places with the most affordable energy do not necessarily also have the appropriate laws to protect data and/or facilitate the secure exchange of information or entertainment. Google's former senior policy strategist Rick Whitt recognizes the international dimensions of cloud storage, jurisdiction, privacy, and access—particularly the restrictions on information and storage across international boundaries—to be one of the biggest hindrances to a more robust, expansive deployment of cloud strategies. As Whitt characterizes the current climate, "If a country decides it wants to seize the data or it wants to close down the data center or take various steps in that regard, the recourse you have as a multinational company may be rather limited."[47]

The Patriot Act has significantly expanded the US government's ability to compel the hand-over of data, regardless of where the data are located; this has raised major concerns for European and Canadian companies focused on the security of data in their own countries. Developed in response to the September 11 attacks, the Patriot Act "is one of the only laws that affects the entire cloud computing industry" and requires American companies to release data stored in the cloud, even if those servers are located outside US jurisdiction.[48] The issue is often not simply who has access, but also who has the ability to prosecute issues that relate to data being stored in one country and retrieved in another. After all, most international companies have servers all over the globe, and their power to protect the data in those servers is limited without the Patriot Act.

Amazon, for example, has servers in the Netherlands, Ireland, Germany, England, Spain, Italy, France, Sweden, Hong Kong, Japan, Korea, Singapore, Australia, and Brazil.[49] The company is widely considered to be the market leader in infrastructure provision. Amazon Web Services (AWS) has quietly become a "massive utility" that includes GovCloud (cloud services for government agencies) and FinQloud (for financial institutions) and, according to *Wired* magazine, now carries 1 percent of the Internet.[50] The CIA recently signed a $600 million cloud contract with Amazon, and the US Navy is also enlisting AWS to take care of some of its cloud-based storage and data needs.[51] As the public sector's dependence on the private cloud increases, and the stakes for data protection continue to expand well beyond the needs of entertainment companies engaging in connected viewing strategies, perhaps there will be more government support for an internationally focused, future-oriented framework that addresses some of the policy gaps engendered by the global data center. Until now, at least, the American approach to regulating new communication technologies and their impact has generally been more reactive than proactive. As legal scholar Carol Celestine has observed, "The U.S. seems to be content to permit the technology to develop and expand, while addressing concerns as they arise and as the contours of the cloud become more defined."[52] In fact, that lag between policy and technology has only expanded as digital capabilities have grown at a pace far surpassing the speed at which government regulators move.

The European Union, on the other hand, is much more aggressive about protecting its data than most other countries or regions, including the United States. The EU has a Data Protection Directive (also known as Directive 95/46/EC) that establishes seven principles aimed at protecting the privacy of EU data, and requires any data exported out of the European Union to be adequately protected by the receiving country. This presents great concerns for international cloud providers, as the approved list is quite small outside the EU.[53] Meanwhile, the twenty-one member economies of the Asia-Pacific Economic Cooperation (APEC) have a voluntary Privacy Framework that has attempted to protect personal data transferred outside the APEC community, to mixed results.[54] Overall, the global inconsistencies and lack of clarity in the arena of cloud policy are a problem with no solution in sight for the connected viewing landscape—and for the rest of the digital ecosystem that relies on remote storage, the open flow of content across broadband pipes, and abundant bandwidth for public access.

Tomorrow's Logic

The economist Peter Drucker has said, "[T]he greatest danger in times of turbulence is not the turbulence; it is to act with yesterday's logic."[55] Today's policy is being made with yesterday's logic; of that there is no doubt or even much debate. Invitations to think about today's turbulence with tomorrow's logic abound, particularly in relation to connected viewing and media policy. That is not to say that lessons of history do not apply; indeed, they can and should be reflected in the future of media policy. The trajectory of broadcasting alone—as it evolved from a community-oriented innovation into a multibillion-dollar industry controlled by a government largely serving the interests of global corporations—provides a stark example to inform this crucial moment of Internet policy negotiation.

To begin, tomorrow's logic would have content companies thinking of themselves as technology companies, and by extension, conceptualizing content as data, and even understanding global media distribution as the international trade of data. This categorical rethinking would help preserve a focus on policy issues and their importance when determining where and how to store that content. It would also make content companies realize that the lobbying agendas of tomorrow should look different than they do today, a realization that would actually align them much more with the interests of the digital audience in another surprising meeting of interests for these two stakeholders. Currently, many media conglomerates face profound internal conflicts when it comes to lobbying and policy because of the various silos or divisions of their company. What a digital division needs to thrive, particularly in the arena of broadband (nondiscriminatory broadband pipelines, the ability to freely share, fewer restrictions on the flow of data), is almost the opposite of what studio groups want as they grapple with piracy and its many implications. This has created a situation where a company's policy goals as a major, varied content provider are not necessarily in sync or unified with its goals as a digital distributor. Moving ahead, the role of digital content for conglomerates should be a more integral component of lobbying strategy; should they enact such a shift, they, too, would recognize that their interests are on the side of net neutrality.

Tomorrow's logic would also have a greater range of interests and voices officially represented in the policy arena—most notably, that of the public. Robert McChesney and John Nichols, Jeff Chester, and Susan Crawford, among others, have all written extensively and persuasively about the crisis of regulatory capture and the lack of public representation/accountability in media policy.[56] Currently, private companies and nongovernmental bodies are taking the lead in setting policies for cloud computing. The Broadband Internet Technical Advisory Group (BITAG) is one entity gaining momentum in this vacuum in the United States. The advisory group is primarily governed by industry interests, but of the fifteen seats on the board, three are set aside for nonprofit groups or groups unaffiliated with any particular industry sector; there are also three seats set aside for content companies, three for application providers, three for equipment manufacturers, and three for ISPs, or "Internet Connectivity Providers," as categorized by the BITAG bylaws.[57] In light of the proliferation of actors in the digital policy realm, Des Freedman has argued for a recognition of "more subtle distinctions between different forms of regulation," including formal versus informal regulations, as well as those that are national versus supranational, or statutory versus voluntary.[58] These nuanced perspectives would raise awareness of the complex forces at work and help to expand frameworks and discourse beyond the characteristic false dichotomies of policy such as "public/private" or "regulated/unregulated," creating more space and dimension for regulatory interventions.

Histories of such interventions and their successes or failures ultimately demonstrate how law and policy shape our lived experience of media and technology. In trying to relate connected viewing and infrastructure policies, these analyses also map how the relationships between various media industries—cable, broadcast, telecommunications—have shifted. These are the relationships and negotiations that will be determining the flow of content from one screen to the other and, in turn, leaving their impact on the future of media and data transmission. It is significant that this current distribution revolution is being dictated according to terms set primarily by the corporate gatekeepers of content, with government regulators taking their lead. It is up to a vigilant public to ensure that its interests are also a part of this equation, and that its members' voices are heard in these critical conversations about the complex politics of Internet policy so as to ensure that the logic of tomorrow ultimately prevails.

Notes

1. See *National Cable & Telecommunications Association et al. v. Brand X Internet Services et al.*, 545 U.S. 967 (2005); Susan Crawford, *Captive Audience: The Telecom Industry and*

Monopoly Power in the New Age (New Haven, CT: Yale University Press, 2013), 51–63; and Jennifer Holt, "Platforms, Pipelines, and Politics: The iPhone and Regulatory Hangover," in *Moving Data: The iPhone and the Future of Media,* eds. Pelle Snickars and Patrick Vonderau (New York: Columbia University Press, 2012), 145–7.

2. Service providers control many dimensions of access—but not all. Of course, content providers and platforms determine how much they will charge users for access, and what business model they will use (e.g., subscription, pay-per-view, advertiser supported, etc.).

3. For more on the legal aspects of net neutrality, see Tim Wu, "Network Neutrality, Broadband Discrimination," *Journal on Telecommunications and High Technology Law* 2 (2003): 141–78.

4. Quoted in Jon Brodkin, "Verizon, Bandwidth Provider Blame Each Other for Slow Netflix Streaming," *Ars Technica,* June 20, 2013, http://arstechnica.com/information-technology/2013/06/verizon-bandwidth-provider-blame-each-other-for-slow-netflix-streaming/.

5. Jon Queally, "Obama Picks One of Telecom's Most Powerful Industry Lobbyists to Head FCC," *Common Dreams,* May 1, 2013, https://www.commondreams.org/headline/2013/05/01-2.

6. See Tim Wu, *The Master Switch: The Rise and Fall of Information Empires* (New York: Alfred A. Knopf, 2010), 58.

7. Robert W. McChesney, *Digital Disconnect: How Capitalism is Turning the Internet Against Democracy* (New York: The New Press, 2013), 119.

8. See National Cable & Telecommunications Association et al. v. Brand X Internet Services et al., 545 U.S. 967 (2005).

9. Federal Communications Commission, "FCC Eliminates Mandated Sharing Requirement on Incumbents' Wireline Broadband Internet Access Services," August 5, 2005, http://transition.fcc.gov/meetings/080505/sharing.pdf.

10. Susan Crawford, *Captive Audience: The Telecom Industry and Monopoly Power in the New Age* (New Haven, CT: Yale University Press, 2013), 54.

11. For an excellent discussion of this series of events, see Daniel Roth, "The Dark Lord of Broadband Tries to Fix Comcast's Image," *Wired,* January 19, 2009, http://www.wired.com/techbiz/people/magazine/17-02/mf_brianroberts?currentPage=all.

12. More specifically—and ironically—the court ruled that the FCC did not have the power to regulate ISPs based on the FCC's own prior interpretation and application of the Telecommunications Act. See Comcast Corporation v. Federal Communications Commission, 600 F.3d 642, 652–9 (DC Cir. 2010).

13. In Federal Communications Commission, "Preserving the Open Internet, Broadband Industry Practices," December 21, 2010, http://www.fcc.gov/document/preserving-open-internet-broadband-industry-practices-1.

14. Federal Communications Commission, "The Open Internet Guide," http://www.fcc.gov/guides/open-internet.

15. Josh Silver, "FCC Chair Announces Fake Net Neutrality Proposal," Free Press, December 1, 2010, http://www.savetheinternet.com/blog/10/12/01/fcc-chairman-announces-fake-net-neutrality-proposal.

16. See Tom Standage, "Live and Unplugged," *Economist,* November 21, 2012, http://www.economist.com/news/21566417-2013-internet-will-become-mostly-mobile-medium-who-will-be-winners-and-losers-live-and.

17. See comments filed in joint brief for Verizon and MetroPCS, July 2, 2012, USCA Case No. 11–1355, Verizon v. Federal Communications Commission, http://gigaom2.files.wordpress.com/2012/07/verizon-metropcs-net-neutrality-brief-as-filed.pdf.

18. See "Verizon-Google Legislative Framework Proposal," August 10, 2010, http://www.google.com/googleblogs/pdfs/verizon_google_legislative_framework_proposal_081010.pdf.

19. Verizon, "Verizon Files Appeal in Federal Court Regarding FCC Net Neutrality Order," news release, January 20, 2011, http://newscenter2.verizon.com/press-releases/verizon/2011/verizon-files-appeal-in.html.
20. Jon Brodkin, "Verizon, Bandwidth Provider Blame Each Other for Slow Netflix Streaming," *Ars Technica,* June 20, 2013, http://arstechnica.com/information-technology/2013/06/verizon-bandwidth-provider-blame-each-other-for-slow-netflix-streaming/.
21. Shalini Ramachandran and Drew Fitzgerald, "For Web Firms, Faster Access Comes at a Price," *Wall Street Journal,* June 19, 2013, http://online.wsj.com/article/SB10001424127887323836504578553170167992666.html.
22. Author interview with Bruce Gottleib, Washington, D.C., May 22, 2012.
23. Netflix website, "Overview: Netflix Open Connect Content Delivery Network," https://signup.netflix.com/openconnect.
24. Barbara van Schewick, *Internet Architecture and Innovation* (Cambridge, MA: MIT Press, 2010), 388. Also see Lawrence Lessig, *The Future of Ideas* (New York: Vintage Books, 2002).
25. Hibah Hussain et al., "Capping the Nation's Broadband Future?," New America Foundation, December 17, 2012, 1, http://www.newamerica.net/publications/policy/capping_the_nation_s_broadband_future.
26. John Eggerton, "NCTA's Powell: Usage-Based Pricing About Fairness, Not Capacity," *Broadcasting and Cable,* January 17, 2013, http://www.broadcastingcable.com/article/491396-NCTA_s_Powell_Usage_Based_Pricing_About_Fairness_Not_Capacity.php.
27. Thomas Catan and Amy Schatz, "U.S. Probes Cable for Limits on Net Video," *Wall Street Journal,* June 13, 2012, http://online.wsj.com/article/SB10001424052702303444204577462951166384624.html.
28. Olga Kharif, "Average Household has 5 Connected Devices, While Some Have 15-Plus," *Bloomberg,* August 29, 2012, http://go.bloomberg.com/tech-blog/2012-08-29-average-household-has-5-connected-devices-while-some-have-15-plus/.
29. Stacey Higginbotham, "The Technical and Legal Realities of Comcast's Xbox Cap Spat," *GigaOm,* March 27, 2012, http://gigaom.com/2012/03/27/the-technical-and-legal-realities-of-comcasts-xbox-cap-spat/.
30. Moreover, Xfinity is only available to those who have a cable subscription, another "perk" to convince would-be "cord cutters" to keep paying their cable bills (and perhaps drop their Netflix accounts).
31. David Talbot, "All Data Packets Are Equal—Some More than Others," *MIT Technology Review,* May 28, 2013, http://www.technologyreview.com/news/515031/all-data-packets-are-equal-some-more-than-others/.
32. The leaders are South Korea, Japan, Hong Kong, Latvia, Switzerland, the Netherlands, and the Czech Republic. See Akamai Technologies, Inc., "The State of the Internet" 5, no. 4 (Fourth Quarter 2012): 15.
33. Author interview with Mike McKenzie, Washington, D.C., May 21, 2012; and Cisco Systems, Inc., "Cisco Visual Networking Index: Global Mobile Data Traffic Forecast Update, 2012–2017," February 5, 2013, http://www.cisco.com/en/US/solutions/collateral/ns341/ns525/ns537/ns705/ns827/white_paper_c11-520862.pdf.
34. Ibid.
35. This increase in mobile traffic also necessarily introduces new problems of spectrum allocation, and freeing up additional resources for mobile broadband, both of which are central to the future of connected viewing, but extended analysis of those issues falls outside the scope of this chapter.
36. Jason Mick, "FCC Chief Genachowski Plugs 'Pay-Per-Play' Metered Internet Pricing," *Daily Tech,* May 23, 2012, http://www.dailytech.com/FCC+Chief+Genachowski+Plugs+PayPerPlay+Metered+Internet+Pricing/article24754.htm.

37. The concept of scarcity has most often been employed in relation to the spectrum and the availability of broadcast channels, justifying content-based and, less frequently, ownership regulations.

38. Author interview with Blair Levin, Washington, D.C., May 22, 2012; and Blair Levin, "Big Bandwidth: Unlocking a New Competitive Advantage," *All Things D,* July 27, 2012, http://allthingsd.com/20120727/big-bandwidth-unlocking-a-new-competitive-advantage/.

39. *Information Week,* "Forrester Forecasts USD 241 Billion Cloud Computing Market by 2020," April 26, 2011, http://www.informationweek.in/cloud_computing/11-04-26/forrester_forecasts_usd_241_billion_cloud_computing_market_by_2020.aspx.

40. James Glanz, "Power, Pollution and the Internet," *New York Times,* September 22, 2012, http://www.nytimes.com/2012/09/23/technology/data-centers-waste-vast-amounts-of-energy-belying-industry-image.html?pagewanted=all&_r=0.

41. For some consideration of the policy issues involved with cloud computing, see Paul T. Jaeger, Jimmy Lin, and Justin M. Grimes, "Cloud Computing and Information Policy: Computing in a Policy Cloud?," *Journal of Information Technology & Politics* 5, no. 3 (2008): 269–83; Sasha Segall, "Jurisdictional Challenges in the United States Government's Move to Cloud Computing Technology," *Fordham Intellectual Property, Media & Entertainment Law Journal* (Spring 2013): 1105–53.

42. Author interview with Michael McKenzie, Washington, D.C., May 21, 2012.

43. Christopher Kuner, "Regulation of Transborder Data Flows under Data Protection and Privacy Law: Past, Present, and Future," *OECD Digital Economy Papers,* no. 187 (2011), http://dx.doi.org/10.1787/5kg0s2fk315f-en.

44. US Department of Energy, "Data Center Energy Consumption Trends," http://www1.eere.energy.gov/femp/program/dc_energy_consumption.html.

45. James Glanz, "Power, Pollution and the Internet," *New York Times,* September 22, 2012, http://www.nytimes.com/2012/09/23/technology/data-centers-waste-vast-amounts-of-energy-belying-industry-image.html?pagewanted=all&_r=0; and Paul T. Jaeger et al., "Where Is the Cloud? Geography, Economics, Environment, and Jurisdiction in Cloud Computing,"?*First Monday* 14, no. 5 (May 2009), http://firstmonday.org/ojs/index.php/fm/article/view/2456/2171.

46. Richard Orange, "Facebook to Build Server Farm on Edge of Arctic Circle," *Telegraph,* October 26, 2011, http://www.telegraph.co.uk/technology/facebook/8850575/Facebook-to-build-server-farm-on-edge-of-Arctic-Circle.html.

47. Author interview with Rick Whitt, June 4, 2012.

48. Sasha Segall, "Jurisdictional Challenges in the United States Government's Move to Cloud Computing Technology," *Fordham Intellectual Property, Media & Entertainment Law Journal* 1105 (Spring 2013): 1135–6.

49. Amazon CloudFront, http://aws.amazon.com/cloudfront/.

50. Robert McMillan, "Amazon's Secretive Cloud Carries 1 Percent of the Internet," *Wired,* April 18, 2012, http://www.wired.com/wiredenterprise/2012/04/amazon-cloud/; Netflix is also becoming quite a significant cloud computing player, as the company is developing a large suite of open-source tools, software, and services to be used with Amazon's cloud platforms.

51. Reuven Cohen, "U.S. Navy Issues New Cloud Computing Policy," *Forbes,* April 8, 2013, http://www.forbes.com/sites/reuvencohen/2013/04/08/u-s-navy-issues-new-cloud-computing-policy/; and Cade Metz, "Amazon's Invasion of the CIA Is a Seismic Shift in Cloud Computing," *Wired,* June 18, 2013, http://www.wired.com/wiredenterprise/2013/06/amazon-cia/.

52. Carol M. Celestine, "'Cloudy' Skies, Bright Futures? In Defense of a Private Regulatory Scheme for Policing Cloud Computing," *Journal of Law, Technology & Policy* 141 (Spring 2013): 157.

53. Outside the 27 EU countries and three European Economic Area member countries (Norway, Liechtenstein, and Iceland), the recognized countries currently include Andorra, Argentina, Australia, Canada, Switzerland, the Faeroe Islands, Guernsey, Israel, Isle of Man, Jersey, New Zealand, and the Eastern Republic of Uruguay. The United States has a safe-harbor agreement with the EU that allows for data transfer back to the United States. See European Commission, "Commission Decisions on the Adequacy of the Protection of Personal Data in Third Countries," http://ec.europa.eu/justice/data-protection/document/international-transfers/adequacy/index_en.htm.
54. See Christopher Kuner, "Regulation of Transborder Data Flows under Data Protection and Privacy Law: Past, Present, and Future," *OECD Digital Economy Papers*, no. 187 (2011): 17–18, http://dx.doi.org/10.1787/5kg0s2fk315f-en; and Graham Greenleaf, "Five Years of the APEC Privacy Framework: Failure or Promise?," *Computer Law & Security Report* 25 (2009): 28–43, http://ssrn.com/abstract=2022907.
55. Peter Drucker, *Managing in Turbulent Times* (New York: Harper Collins, 1980).
56. For example, see Robert W. McChesney and John Nichols, *Our Media, Not Theirs: The Democratic Struggle against Corporate Media* (New York: Seven Stories Press, 2002); Robert W. McChesney, *Digital Disconnect: How Capitalism is Turning the Internet Against Democracy* (New York: The New Press, 2013); Jeff Chester, *Digital Destiny: New Media and the Future of Democracy* (New York: The New Press, 2007); Susan Crawford, *Captive Audience: The Telecom Industry and Monopoly Power in the New Age* (New Haven, CT: Yale University Press, 2013).
57. See "Amended and Restated Bylaws of Broadband Internet Technical Advisory Group, Inc.," Article V, Section 5.2, 12, http://www.bitag.org/documents/BITAG_Bylaws .pdf.
58. James Curran, Natalie Fenton, and Des Freedman, *Misunderstanding the Internet* (New York: Routledge, 2012), 113.

References

Akamai Technologies, Inc. "The State of the Internet" 5, no. 4 (Fourth Quarter 2012).

Broadband Internet Technical Advisory Group, Inc. "Amended and Restated Bylaws of Broadband Internet Technical Advisory Group, Inc." Article V, Section 5.2, 12. http:// www.bitag.org/documents/BITAG_Bylaws.pdf.

Brodkin, Jon. "Verizon, Bandwidth Provider Blame Each Other for Slow Netflix Streaming." *Ars Technica,* June 20, 2013. http://arstechnica.com/information-technology/2013/06/ verizon-bandwidth-provider-blame-each-other-for-slow-netflix-streaming/.

Catan, Thomas, and Amy Schatz. "U.S. Probes Cable for Limits on Net Video." *Wall Street Journal,* June 13, 2012. http://online.wsj.com/article/SB100014240527023034442045 77462951166384624.html.

Celestine, Carol M. "'Cloudy' Skies, Bright Futures? In Defense of a Private Regulatory Scheme for Policing Cloud Computing." *Journal of Law, Technology & Policy* 141 (Spring 2013): 141–64.

Chester, Jeff. *Digital Destiny: New Media and the Future of Democracy.* New York: The New Press, 2007.

Cisco Systems, Inc. "Cisco Visual Networking Index: Global Mobile Data Traffic Forecast Update, 2012–2017." February 5, 2013. http://www.cisco.com/en/US/solutions/ collateral/ns341/ns525/ns537/ns705/ns827/white_paper_c11–520862.pdf.

Cohen, Reuven. "U.S. Navy Issues New Cloud Computing Policy." *Forbes,* April 8, 2013. http://www.forbes.com/sites/reuvencohen/2013/04/08/u-s-navy-issues-new-cloud -computing-policy/.

Comcast Corporation v. Federal Communications Commission, 600 F.3d 642, 652–9 (DC Cir. 2010).

Crawford, Susan. *Captive Audience: The Telecom Industry and Monopoly Power in the New Age.* New Haven, CT: Yale University Press, 2013.

Curran, James, Natalie Fenton, and Des Freedman. *Misunderstanding the Internet.* New York: Routledge, 2012.

Drucker, Peter. *Managing in Turbulent Times.* New York: Harper Collins, 1980.

Eggerton, John. "NCTA's Powell: Usage-Based Pricing About Fairness, Not Capacity." *Broadcasting and Cable,* January 17, 2013. http://www.broadcastingcable.com/article/491396 -NCTA_s_Powell_Usage_Based_Pricing_About_Fairness_Not_Capacity.php.

European Commission. "Commission Decisions on the Adequacy of the Protection of Personal Data in Third Countries." http://ec.europa.eu/justice/data-protection/document/ international-transfers/adequacy/index_en.htm.

Federal Communications Commission. "FCC Eliminates Mandated Sharing Requirement on Incumbents' Wireline Broadband Internet Access Services." August 5, 2005. http:// transition.fcc.gov/meetings/080505/sharing.pdf.

Federal Communications Commission. "Preserving the Open Internet, Broadband Industry Practices." December 21, 2010. http://www.fcc.gov/document/preserving-open -internet-broadband-industry-practices-1.

Federal Communications Commission. "The Open Internet Guide." http://www.fcc.gov/ guides/open-internet.

Glanz, James. "Power, Pollution and the Internet." *New York Times,* September 22, 2012. http://www.nytimes.com/2012/09/23/technology/data-centers-waste-vast-amounts -of-energy-belying-industry-image.html?pagewanted=all&_r=0.

Greenleaf, Graham. "Five Years of the APEC Privacy Framework: Failure or Promise?" *Computer Law & Security Report* 25 (2009): 28–43. http://ssrn.com/abstract=2022907.

Higginbotham, Stacey. "The Technical and Legal Realities of Comcast's Xbox Cap Spat." *GigaOm,* March 27, 2012. http://gigaom.com/2012/03/27/the-technical-and-legal -realities-of-comcasts-xbox-cap-spat/.

Holt, Jennifer. "Platforms, Pipelines, and Politics: The iPhone and Regulatory Hangover." In *Moving Data: The iPhone and the Future of Media,* edited by Pelle Snickars and Patrick Vonderau, 140–54. New York: Columbia University Press, 2012.

Hussain, Hibah, Danielle Kehl, Benjamin Lennett, and Patrick Lucey. "Capping the Nation's Broadband Future?" New America Foundation, December 17, 2012. http:// www.newamerica.net/publications/policy/capping_the_nation_s_broadband_future.

Information Week. "Forrester Forecasts USD 241 Billion Cloud Computing Market by 2020." April 26, 2011. http://www.informationweek.in/cloud_computing/11-04-26/ forrester_forecasts_usd_241_billion_cloud_computing_market_by_2020.aspx.

Jaeger, Paul T., Jimmy Lin, and Justin M. Grimes. "Cloud Computing and Information Policy: Computing in a Policy Cloud?" *Journal of Information Technology & Politics* 5, no. 3 (2008): 269–83.

Jaeger, Paul T., Jimmy Lin, Justin M. Grimes, and Shannon N. Simmons. "Where Is the Cloud? Geography, Economics, Environment, and Jurisdiction in Cloud Computing." *First Monday* 14, no. 5 (May 2009). http://firstmonday.org/ojs/index.php/fm/article/ view/2456/2171.

Kharif, Olga. "Average Household has 5 Connected Devices, While Some Have 15-Plus." *Bloomberg,* August 29, 2012. http://go.bloomberg.com/tech-blog/2012–08–29-average -household-has-5-connected-devices-while-some-have-15-plus/.

Kuner, Christopher. "Regulation of Transborder Data Flows under Data Protection and Privacy Law: Past, Present, and Future." *OECD Digital Economy Papers*, no. 187 (2011). http://dx.doi.org/10.1787/5kg0s2fk315f-en.

Lessig, Lawrence. *The Future of Ideas*. New York: Vintage Books, 2002.

Levin, Blair. "Big Bandwidth: Unlocking a New Competitive Advantage." *AllThings D*, July 27, 2012. http://allthingsd.com/20120727/big-bandwidth-unlocking-a-new-competitive-advantage/.

McChesney, Robert W. *Digital Disconnect: How Capitalism is Turning the Internet Against Democracy*. New York: The New Press, 2013.

McChesney, Robert W., and John Nichols. *Our Media, Not Theirs: The Democratic Struggle against Corporate Media*. New York: Seven Stories Press, 2002.

McMillan, Robert. "Amazon's Secretive Cloud Carries 1 Percent of the Internet." *Wired*, April 18, 2012. http://www.wired.com/wiredenterprise/2012/04/amazon-cloud/.

Metz, Cade. "Amazon's Invasion of the CIA Is a Seismic Shift in Cloud Computing." *Wired*, June 18, 2013. http://www.wired.com/wiredenterprise/2013/06/amazon-cia/.

Mick, Jason. "FCC Chief Genachowski Plugs 'Pay-Per-Play' Metered Internet Pricing." *Daily Tech*, May 23, 2012. http://www.dailytech.com/FCC+Chief+Genachowski+Plugs+PayPerPlay+Metered+Internet+Pricing/article24754.htm.

National Cable & Telecommunications Association et al. v. Brand X Internet Services et al. 545 U.S. 967 (2005).

Orange, Richard. "Facebook to Build Server Farm on Edge of Arctic Circle." *Telegraph*, October 26, 2011. http://www.telegraph.co.uk/technology/facebook/8850575/Facebook-to-build-server-farm-on-edge-of-Arctic-Circle.html.

Queally, Jon. "Obama Picks One of Telecom's Most Powerful Industry Lobbyists to Head FCC." *Common Dreams*, May 1, 2013. https://www.commondreams.org/headline/2013/05/01-2.

Ramachandran, Shalini, and Drew Fitzgerald. "For Web Firms, Faster Access Comes at a Price." *Wall Street Journal*, June 19, 2013. http://online.wsj.com/article/SB10001424127887323238365045785531701679922666.html.

Roth, Daniel. "The Dark Lord of Broadband Tries to Fix Comcast's Image." *Wired*, January 19, 2009. http://www.wired.com/techbiz/people/magazine/17-02/mf_brianroberts?currentPage=all.

Segall, Sasha. "Jurisdictional Challenges in the United States Government's Move to Cloud Computing Technology." *Fordham Intellectual Property, Media & Entertainment Law Journal* 1105 (Spring 2013): 1105–53.

Silver, Josh. "FCC Chair Announces Fake Net Neutrality Proposal." Free Press, December 1, 2010. http://www.savetheinternet.com/blog/10/12/01/fcc-chairman-announces-fake-net-neutrality-proposal.

Standage, Tom. "Live and Unplugged." *Economist*, November 21, 2012. http://www.economist.com/news/21566417-2013-internet-will-become-mostly-mobile-medium-who-will-be-winners-and-losers-live-and.

Talbot, David. "All Data Packets Are Equal—Some More than Others." *MIT Technology Review*, May 28, 2013. http://www.technologyreview.com/news/515031/all-data-packets-are-equal-some-more-than-others/.

US Department of Energy. "Data Center Energy Consumption Trends." http://www1.eere.energy.gov/femp/program/dc_energy_consumption.html.

van Schewick, Barbara. *Internet Architecture and Innovation*. Cambridge, MA: MIT Press, 2010.

"Verizon-Google Legislative Framework Proposal." August 10, 2010. http://www.google
.com/googleblogs/pdfs/verizon_google_legislative_framework_proposal_081010.pdf.

Verizon. "Verizon Files Appeal in Federal Court Regarding FCC Net Neutrality Order."
News release, January 20, 2011. http://newscenter2.verizon.com/press-releases/verizon/
2011/verizon-files-appeal-in.html.

Verizon v. Federal Communications Commission. Comments filed in joint brief for
Verizon and MetroPCS. July 2, 2012. USCA Case No. 11–1355. http://gigaom2.files
.wordpress.com/2012/07/verizon-metropcs-net-neutrality-brief-as-filed.pdf.

Wu, Tim. "Network Neutrality, Broadband Discrimination." *Journal on Telecommunications
and High Technology Law* 2 (2003): 141–78.

Wu, Tim. *The Master Switch: The Rise and Fall of Information Empires.* New York: Alfred
A. Knopf, 2010.

2

SECOND-SCREEN THEORY

From the Democratic Surround to the Digital Enclosure

Hye Jin Lee and Mark Andrejevic

One of the persistent perceived challenges of the digital era for TV broadcasters has been how to make a notoriously "passive" medium interactive. Once upon a time, in the 1990s, the commercial television industry imagined it could steal the Internet's thunder (or defuse its competition for time and attention) by absorbing it—that is, by transforming the family TV set into an interactive interface for shopping, web browsing, game playing, and on-demand entertainment, as exemplified by Time Warner Cable's Full Service Network project, which ran from 1994–7 in Orlando, Florida. The promotional material for this early digital, interactive service, with images of families gathered around the living room TV, ordering food, shopping, and picking movies to watch, looks singularly unprescient against the background of an increasingly customized, targeted, mobile, multidevice, and multiplatform media world. In its public postmortem of the Full Service Network project, Time Warner Cable conceded that the project had been a failure, plagued by logistical difficulties and the high cost of the connection boxes (upwards of $4,000), but maintained that it had succeeded in its monitoring function: "in terms of providing real-time data on what customers did and didn't like about video on demand and interactivity, it was a genuine success."[1] The project had helped demonstrate the productivity of interactivity as a means of generating real-time data about viewers.

The failed business ventures of interactive television services on cable did not deter various parties, including the computer manufacturers, software designers, and web entrepreneurs, from attempting to deliver on the promise of interactive television by combining Internet access and television viewing into one device in the 1990s and early 2000s. However, as William Boddy's[2] thorough research demonstrates, the interactive television services (from customized stock reports to interactive quiz shows) during the period only received lukewarm reception by the general public. After the initial flops, interactive television is making a comeback in the form of Internet Television (ITV), which provides direct delivery of television programs and movies through on-demand Internet streaming services such as Netflix, Hulu Plus, iTunes, Amazon Instant Video, and so on. To access these video services, users no longer need a computer but simply a television with a game console—such as Sony's PlayStation or Microsoft's Xbox 360—or a media-streaming device made available by Internet-based companies—such as Roku, Boxee, Apple, or Google—that directly streams video from the web to the television set in the living room. While ITV provides greater possibilities for viewers to access an abundance of content on the web and fulfills interactive television's promises of flexibility, customization, and personalization, it also collects a great amount of data generated by viewers through their browsing, search, and selection behaviors. This audience monitoring and control feature of interactive interfaces is particularly enticing to online marketers who are willing to pay more if their ads are more targeted. Television producers are, in other words, coming to realize that convergence does not necessarily converge on one device—interactive TV can come in a variety of different packages, including ancillary interactive screens that supplement the home TV set. As Radha Subramanyam, Nielsen's senior vice president for media analytics, put it, "Five years ago, we thought interactive TV was one screen. Turns out, it's the second screen."[3] The multiscreen, multitasking environment created by so-called "second screen" devices and applications adds an interactive layer to television viewing, delivering on the monitoring, sorting, and customizing functions treasured by marketers and advertisers in the digital era.

Indeed, *second screen* is a credible candidate for 2012 buzzword of the year in the television industry. The term commonly refers to the companion device that people use when watching television, whether it be a smartphone, tablet, laptop, or home computer. The idea of second-screen apps is that if the TV itself is not going to be the primary interactive interface, perhaps it can be synchronized with such an interface in ways that enable the forms of real-time monitoring, customization, and targeting envisioned by the developers and promoters of the interactive commercial economy. As we shall see, making this configuration work relies on several interlocking strategies, including the mobilization of the promise of interactivity for convenience and participation, and an attempt to reverse the time-shifting tide and resuscitate real-time viewing.

The Rise of the Second Screen

Rather than relying on costly physical infrastructure and hardware supplied by cable companies, the television industry has come to realize that it can piggyback on other forms of interactivity that have penetrated the viewing environment. When Nielsen reported in 2010 that almost 60 percent of Americans are online when they watch television, the industry paid attention to the "simultaneity" of people's television-viewing behavior.[4] The great penetration of smartphones and tablets in the United States has encouraged the industry to examine potential ways to capitalize on people's propensity to simultaneously watch and browse (or watch and connect/socialize). The second-screen initiative relies on the insight—readily available to anyone who has spent any time on Twitter, for example—that the constant flow of online commentary relies heavily on externally provided content: something to share, reflect on, and react to.

Thus, when Apple released its long-anticipated iPad in 2010, the possible use of second-screen apps was showcased with ABC leading the way.[5] Before the premiere of its new show *My Generation* on September 23, 2010, ABC promoted the show's companion iPad app. Partnered with Nielsen, the *My Generation* app incorporated Nielsen's new media-sync technology, which listens "for audio watermarks within the broadcast in order to synchronize the first screen (the TV) with the content served on the second screen (the iPad)."[6]

Despite the buzz around the app, the show was eventually cancelled after two episodes because of low ratings. But all was not lost, as ABC went ahead and launched a similar companion app for its popular television show *Grey's Anatomy* in February 2011. ABC's experiment with Nielsen's media sync app turned out to be a failure because many viewers complained that the continuous flood of information from the app was distracting them from watching the show. However, ABC's Backstage Pass app for the Oscars, which provided users an "all-access" interface to the show, turned out to be a hit, prompting ABC, content publishers, and industry watchers to continue developing second-screen apps. What the industry learned from ABC's second-screen app experiments is that these apps do work but that their features need to vary depending on "the show's tone, pace, and style."[7]

They should also have learned that mediated live events—those that are shared remotely by large audiences—lend themselves to second-screen treatment, as evidenced, for example, by the 2012 US presidential election, which was reportedly the most tweeted event in US history.[8] From a programming perspective, the "event" character of multitasking while viewing does not mean that second-screen apps are only viable for forms of live coverage like the election or the Oscars. Rather, the implication is that viewing itself needs to be turned into something that shares the logic of the event: a sense that others are participating at the same time and are interested in sharing their thoughts and responses, at a pace that includes the time and space for interacting, sharing, and reflecting—or simply typing, reading, and navigating a second interface.

In the year subsequent to the success of the Backstage Pass app, many second-screen apps were developed, and more are currently in development.[9] In early 2012, Chuck Parker, a digital media industry blogger, reported that there were more than 110 second-screen apps. That number increased to more than 200 by November 2012. The goal of second-screen apps is to encourage viewers to watch television live, to communicate with others in real time while TV programs are being aired and, as Reggie James, the founder of digital marketing agency Digital Clarity, explains, to turn "TV programs into online events."[10]

In this regard, the attempt to turn all viewing into a networked, social event bucks the current trend of on-demand viewing through time-shifting technologies, such as those allowed by TiVo, DVR, DVD, and online subscription services such as Netflix and Hulu Plus, which promise to allow viewers to shrug off the constraints of network schedules. The development of these time-shifting media technologies has not only allowed audiences to avoid watching shows according to programmers' schedules but also to skip television commercials. This time-shifting practice has posed challenges for network control over television viewership, leading advertisers to question the effectiveness of their advertising plans, since commercials that are "viewed 'late' have often lost their relevance to an advertising campaign and are difficult to track against sales results."[11] Since advertisers lose the power to deliver the impact they want when television loses control of its viewership,[12] it appears that advertisers' concerns over time-shifting technologies are warranted. The fact that second-screen apps are bringing viewers back to real-time television viewing is greatly encouraging to both the advertisers and the networks that continue to rely on advertisers' programming sponsorship. The appeal of second-screen apps is compounded by industry research that indicates viewers who use second screens are more likely to refrain from skipping commercials and are also more likely to engage with commercial content (for instance, by looking up the product online).[13]

Second-screen apps have also been embraced by the industry because of their potential to generate and provide real-time raw data to marketers and advertisers. Considering that "television's interactivity is always necessarily live" as "one must be watching at the time of transmission in order to interact with an application,"[14] interactive apps play an important role in reaggregating audiences when programs air in real time, and in generating "big data" alongside live and social entertainment. The second-screen promise is to reassemble audiences around viewing-as-shared-event and to thereby reconfigure a version of television viewing as social ritual—not because viewing cannot be time-shifted, but because doing so would mean losing out on a proliferating array of interactive affordances and the forms of social networking they enable. Commenting on the on-screen action is not quite as fun when no one else is watching.

Active Engagement in a Passive Medium

In keeping with the goal of generating detailed information about audiences, their viewing behavior, and consumption patterns, technologies that enable consumer monitoring such as digital watermarking, audio fingerprinting, QR codes, and barcode detection are incorporated in a range of second-screen apps.[15] Companies that develop these consumer-monitoring technologies showcase the ways in which the technology can be used to provide more timely and relevant information based on the detection and tracking of audience behavior. After detecting what audience members are watching/hearing on their "first" screen, second-screen apps deliver real-time, relevant information to encourage the audience's further engagement with the program, which in turn generates real-time data on the audience's thoughts, opinions, and reactions that can be monitored and collected by the marketers.

Second-screen apps effectively retrieve this real-time information by inviting viewers to participate in various instant polls, quizzes, and performance ratings. By responding, users provide direct feedback to the networks and advertisers. Most second-screen apps such as Yahoo's IntoNow, Yap.tv, Miso, GetGlue, and Viggle require users to sign in through Facebook or Twitter. By logging in to second-screen apps through their social network accounts, viewers can discover what their friends are watching and choose what to watch based on their friends' recommendations and real-time comments. The goal is to draw on social networking's social graph to make second-screen apps a "real-time social guide for television."[16]

By the same token, the interactive features of second-screen apps are designed to engage the audience members in generating valuable information about themselves, which marketers can use to target them further. The kind of audience labor that interactivity induces participates in "the auto-production of audience commodities," as audiences who freely engage in interactive communication and consumption generate detailed information about themselves (their tastes, behaviors, social relations, and so on), which can be bought and sold among marketers and content providers.[17] At the same time, the hope is that social networks will serve as venues for viral advertising—vehicles for promoting viewership by encouraging potential viewers to tune in to what their friends are watching. From a marketing standpoint, the promise of interactivity is about closing the circle of monitored consumption: linking TV content to ad exposure and consumption behavior.

No second-screen app can track the audience from the living room to the checkout counter yet, but the development of such a system seems imminent based on the direction interactive digital media is taking. Marketers were able to get a taste of how second-screen apps can be used to track the audience from viewing to purchasing through a deal between the CW Network and the shopkick app in May 2011.[18] The partnership between CW and shopkick allowed shopkick users to receive special offers, coupons, and various perks by opening the shopkick app when selected television commercials aired on the CW Network.

The CW and shopkick partnership is a foretaste of the direction that many second-screen apps will take. This partnership also explains why networks, advertisers, and marketers are invested in developing second-screen mobile apps. Cyriac Roeding, chief executive of shopkick, described the significance of the CW-shopkick partnership as follows: "The cellphone is the only interactive medium that you carry with you while you're watching TV *and* while you're shopping in the store. The cellphone is therefore the only interactive medium that can function as the bridge between the TV screen and the store shelf."[19] The fact that

45 percent of cell phone owners are smartphone users and 25 percent of Internet users are tablet users as of September 2012 (with these numbers expected to grow) helps bolster the case that apps are likely to overtake browsers for many online mobile functions.[20]

Along these lines, TV producer and pop culture guru Michael Hirschorn[21] has argued that the digital frontier is shifting from browser dominance to apps and data-pricing plans. Rather than attempting to wall off the existing Internet, in other words, apps add a proprietary layer on top that structures access to content in ways that take advantage of the capabilities—and limitations—of portable mobile devices. Harvard law professor Jonathan Zittrain[22] has similarly argued that as computers become more applianced and tethered to marketers' desires, the Internet will become less about user creativity than about structured consumption and marketing opportunities. In essence, the argument is that, in some ways, the Internet is going through a transition from a technology of creative participation to one of consumption, commerce, and entertainment—although the opposition is a tenuous one, since even commercial apps exploit the creative participation of viewers. Although an argument can be made that the Internet has never really been open, free, and uncontrolled, Hirschorn and Zittrain may be correct to point out how the web is becoming more proprietary, especially as many companies are shifting their focus from maintaining websites to creating and utilizing apps. *Wired* magazine boldly but prematurely pronounced the death of the web on the cover of its September 2010 issue, attributing this demise to the ascendance of closed, proprietary apps that provide simpler and sleeker services. Statistics seem to be on the side of the apps as well: comScore reported that during a three-month period ending in November 2011 mobile users said they used apps more often than web browsers.[23]

One of the biggest differences between browsers and apps may be in the way information is provided to the user. Whereas browsers are more pull-oriented platforms (although admittedly with customized filters), apps are more push-oriented: preselecting customized forms of information and service delivery.[24] They are also less open-ended: one does not surf apps; one uses them for dedicated, specialized purposes. The "push" character of apps makes them attractive for various content publishers and marketers. In an era of information overload in which many companies strive to form feedback-generating relationships with consumers, apps provide a more structured form of targeting and customization. Thus, many media companies have begun to utilize their apps rather than their websites to push their best and most timely content.[25] If browsers allow users to open various windows and roam freely from one site to another, apps (as partitioned digital spaces) create walled gardens, making it inconvenient for users to move from one informational space to another. Apps, in this regard, help to tame the less structured character of the Internet—they bring back (in reconfigured form) some of the time/space channeling of broadcasting. This ability to channel audiences' attention and to customize content, services, and ads helps explain the appeal of app-based platforms to marketers, especially if profits can be generated from technologies that capture the scarce "resource" of viewers' attention.[26]

Internet, "Fanification," and Affective Economics

At the 2006 National Association of Television Program Executives Conference, Stacey Koerner of Global Research Integration and Ken Papagan of Rentrak Corporation argued that, from the point of view of targeting, it is important for television executives to pay more attention to *why* people watch specific shows and *how* they engage with them rather than to focus narrowly on the total audience size (and demographics) of a specific show.[27] Referring to fans as "ideal viewers," Koerner emphasized the way in which online fandom functions as an important source of information for audience engagement.[28] Thanks in no small part to the romanticization of the "active audience" in the academic realm and the drive for more detailed audience data in the commercial realm, fans have come a long way, considering that they were frequently mocked and pathologized before the rise of digital interactivity.[29] In the interactive era, fans have earned the new status of "dedicated consumers"/instant focus groups and are being actively wooed by media industries newly recommitted to capturing and exploiting the attention of "influentials."[30] The marketing strategy of placing the "active, emotionally engaged, and socially networked" consumer at the center of campaigns reflects the imperatives of what marketers call "affective economics": to cultivate consumer loyalty and turn emotional investment into an economic one.[31]

As television networks and franchises build their marketing strategies around audiences' interactive participation, they are fomenting the "fanification" of the audience.[32] Media companies' construction of spaces for fans to socialize, bond over their common favorite shows, and enjoy the collective knowledge shared by larger fan communities can be interpreted as their being "more responsive to their most committed consumers" and allowing fans to exert more influence over the shows they love.[33] There certainly is pleasure in collective viewing, the exchange of knowledge and information, and the sharing of opinions. But there are also palpable advantages to marketers.

The treatment of audience interactivity as a form of online focus-group research has only intensified and accelerated in the era of social media. Thanks to Twitter and Facebook, producers no longer have to wait until their shows have aired to get viewer feedback. For example, at the *Wall Street Journal*'s 2010 D8: All Things Digital Conference, *Modern Family* creator Steve Levitan mentioned that he and his writers use the Twitter back channels to monitor viewer reactions *during* the airing of new episodes on the East Coast. Twitter allows his group of writers to see people laughing in real time and to receive instant feedback on what works and what doesn't. Not only is social media providing instant data to the producers, it is also playing a role in bringing more people who hope to avoid social spoilers back to live television.[34]

At the same time, however, thanks to catch-up TV and file sharing, the Internet has made it less necessary for viewers to watch their favorite shows live. According to a Nielsen report in the first quarter of 2012, 145.5 million people in the United States reported to have watched time-shifted TV, which is a 1.2 percent increase from the fourth quarter of 2011 and an 8.9 percent increase on a year-over-year basis. Similarly, those who watched videos on the Internet grew from 142.4 million in the last quarter of 2011 to 162.5 million in the first quarter of 2012.[35] Even as increasing numbers of people watch television online or time-shift their viewing, Nielsen continues to fail in measuring the unconventional viewership, leading many in the industry to complain about the inaccuracy of the television ratings. Nevertheless, television programs continue to live and die by the Nielsen ratings.[36] The news about social media's role in encouraging more people to watch programs during their broadcast times is therefore welcoming to networks and producers.[37]

Audience Measurement and Interactive Live Television

Even in the era of time-shifting, place-shifting, and platform-shifting that encourages delayed viewing, "liveness" continues to be a defining feature of television.[38] Television has been able to maintain its symbolic authority in part because of its ability to reach a spatially and temporally defined audience (as opposed to, say, online content, which has an audience that is far more open-ended in terms of both time and space).[39] The power of liveness, then, lies in its "sense of collective immediacy and participation."[40] Social networking platforms lend themselves to this sense of collective immediacy, even though they dwell in a realm that blurs any clear distinction between synchronous and asynchronous communication—you do not need to be online at the same time to comment on another user's post, or to have your status update or tweet responded to, commented on, or shared. At the same time, popular networking platforms allow for real-time forms of chat and interaction—and there remains a temporality to the communication. Try tweeting when everyone else is sleeping—it's not quite the same as tweeting when many others are online following the same events in real time. Social media platforms do facilitate asynchronous forms of interaction, but they also thrive on the ability to piggyback on live events: occasions that guarantee lots of people will be available for sharing information, responding to one's posts, and providing fresh commentary and links. The hope that social media can help turn television viewing into a remotely shared event animates the promise of second-screen apps. With this in mind, the interactive affordances of second-screen apps typically rely on live viewing: for an individual to interact with the television, he or she must "be watching at the time of transmission."[41] Thus both the interactive features of second-screen apps and their social networking capability reinvigorate "the need to watch television live at the time of broadcast" and help to aggregate audiences.[42]

As a defining product of the television industry, the audience has been subjected to various efforts to effectively monitor, probe, and parse it. Despite the efforts, gaps between "predicted" audiences, "measured" audiences, and "actual" audiences have always existed, making the audience a particularly elusive commodity.[43] Nonetheless, Nielsen's data have been the standard source that networks and advertisers continue to rely on to determine advertising rates. The data Nielsen provides decide television advertising spending, which grew to $70 billion in 2011.[44]

Predicting the actual audience from a Nielsen report is becoming more challenging as an increasing number of viewers watch television in unconventional ways on an ever-proliferating spectrum of channels. The greater the fragmentation, the bigger the sample size needs to be for the audience to be accurately represented. Realistically, though, a larger sample size for standard ratings measurements is not economically feasible, according to Richard Fielding, the vice president of Starcom MediaVest Group, one of the leading media consulting companies.[45] So audience measurement firms have tried to make up for their lack of scale with more "detailed" information about audiences and new, audience-generated forms of passive (or interactive) self-reporting. As a way to obtain more accurate and detailed information about the audience, Nielsen and other audience measurement companies have invested in creating "passive" measurement devices and technologies that do not require audience input (such as pushing a button or writing a diary) and thus minimize audience recall error.[46] Nielsen experimented with developing passive audience measurement devices that have technologies such as sonar, infrared, facial recognition, or retinal-scanning systems integrated so audio/visual signals of what the audience is watching/listening to can be automatically picked up. However, due to privacy concerns, Nielsen's attempt to launch the passive audience measurement system did not go beyond its experimental stage.[47] Currently, the process of audience measurement is moving from monitoring the television set to monitoring the person, as Arbitron's chief engineer, Ron Kolessar, has observed.[48]

Second-screen apps fulfill the various goals of interested parties: television networks that want higher ratings, audience monitoring companies that dream of voluntary ubiquitous audience monitoring (on a large scale), advertisers who dream of more detailed information about their audience, and an audience that allegedly wants more interactive and social television experiences. For advertisers and marketers, second-screen apps provide an additional platform to display ads even as they increase the relevancy and addressability of ads. Many second-screen apps use automatic content recognition technology such as audio watermarking and audio fingerprinting,[49] which allows them to automatically track and record what the viewer is watching in an unobtrusive way. In this sense, second-screen apps serve as "passive," "invisible" measurement devices. The other advantage that second-screen apps have for marketers and audience monitoring companies is that they can accumulate a vast amount of information without making the audience feel as if it is being monitored.

The Social Network Hook: Amplification, Social Guide, and Social Rating

Most second-screen apps require users to log on with their Facebook or Twitter accounts (although there is the third, less popular option of logging on with a generic e-mail account). It has become the norm for second-screen apps to incorporate social networks, which is not a surprising trend considering that many people are already connected to some form of social media when watching television.[50] Social networks are used in various ways to put the audience to work without making the labor apparent. First, they are effective tools for amplifying marketers' messages. Television networks can use online chats to create promotional materials and generate buzz around their programs. It has become common for networks to rely on social media chatter to figure out their hits and misses.[51] One company that provides social ratings of television shows is Trendrr, a social media monitoring company. On April 4, 2011, Trendrr launched the first social TV ratings chart site. Trendrr.TV's data are generated by tracking all the social media activities fueled by Twitter, Facebook, and second-screen platforms such as GetGlue and Viggle during the airtime of all major network and cable programs (within a three-hour window before and after a show airs) in a twenty-four-hour cycle. By collecting and sharing data about the audience through its charts, Trendrr.TV claims to connect content producers and marketers with their audiences. As CEO Mark Ghuneim writes on the company's home page, "real-time social data is the heartbeat of the new TV economy."[52]

One of the other basic functions of second-screen apps is to serve as channel guides. Yap TV provides a channel guide by timeline (a regular, "TV Guide" style) or genres (reality, drama, comedy, and so on). Viggle also provides a channel guide by timeline with some of the key television shows prominently displayed in its feature section (these are the shows that receive bonus points for check-ins). Zeebox, an app that originated in the UK and was subsequently introduced in the United States with the partnership of NBCUniversal and HBO, also provides a channel guide by timeline. All these apps typically allow viewers to search for what to watch by following "trending" categories. Even the apps without a timeline channel guide, such as Miso, IntoNow, and GetGlue, have a "trending" feature to help users discover what show is being talked about the most on Twitter or in the respective second-screen app community. Based on the trending television list, users can decide which television show to tune to, making second-screen apps a form of "social guide." One's social network—situated within the context of what Facebook founder Mark Zuckerberg calls the "social graph"—serves as a form of collaborative filtering to help sort through the available programming.[53]

The importance of so-called social ratings is growing alongside the role played by social media in amplifying content/brand awareness and shaping online conversations and viewing behavior. However, the industry consensus is that despite inaccuracy and unreliability in its measurement, the numbers that Nielsen provides remain the default standard that advertisers and networks will use in making decisions.[54] Networks and marketers are paying more attention to social ratings, but they do so with the understanding that these will complement and not replace Nielsen ratings.[55] However, Nielsen is aware of its need to improve and change the way it measures audience viewership and engagement with televised content due to the rise of social TV. On December 17, 2012, Nielsen announced that it would be partnering with Twitter, which has become the new real-time digital watercooler, for a multiyear project called the Nielsen Twitter TV Rating, scheduled to launch in the fall of 2013. The Nielsen Twitter TV Rating will deliver an industry standard metric for the reach of TV conversation on Twitter and complement Nielsen's existing TV ratings. Steve Hasker, president of global media products and advertiser solutions at Nielsen, explained that the Nielsen Twitter TV Rating will be a "significant step forward for the industry, particularly as programmers develop increasingly captivating live TV and new second-screen experiences, and advertisers create integrated ad campaigns that combine paid and earned media."[56] The Nielsen Twitter TV Rating is anticipated to be a game changer in the current social TV ecosystem, as this rating metric is not only TV specific but also "ordained by the TV measurement gods."[57]

Although the number of people who share TV experiences is greater in the Facebook community, a report from TVGuide.com in May 2011 revealed that a considerably higher percentage of Twitter users comment on and share their TV experiences during broadcast, making the social networking site a valuable amplification tool for networks and advertisers.[58] With the integration of Twitter, second-screen apps are able not only to provide a "trending" list of television shows, which functions as a social guide, but also to offer more streamlined and filtered Twitter chatter about television shows.

Instant Focus Groups

Like all apps, second-screen apps are designed to push information to users rather than have them spend time searching and browsing. However, second-screen developers have discovered that television viewers tend to use their computers or mobile devices to search for information (mostly on Wikipedia and IMDb) related to the television show they are watching.[59] This finding has been instrumental in the development of content-sync second-screen apps that push timely and relevant information to viewers, generating new forms of feedback that can be recorded and mined.[60] Such apps determine what show is being watched in order to, in a sense, anticipate and preempt actual search requests so as to "deliver relevant companion content directly to viewers during pertinent times as they watch TV."[61] Like other targeted applications, they seek to anticipate user demand before it is expressed. For example, Nielsen's content-sync *Grey's Anatomy* app was designed to push information about the soundtrack, behind-the-scenes photos, background information about characters as well as actors, and so on. But as Nielsen's sync app demonstrated, pushing information too hard can distract viewers from watching the show, which is reportedly the reason why the *Grey's Anatomy* app never took off.[62]

The burgeoning popularity of the social web has thus helped to generate a trove of information about the audience, resulting in the rise of analytics companies such as Trendrr and Bluefin that aggregate social media commentary. Viggle, the first loyalty-based second-screen app, reportedly has more than one million registered users whom it rewards with points that can be spent for prizes such as e-gift cards for Best Buy, Starbucks, and so on. Points are generated whenever users check in to television shows (featured shows give out bonus points in addition to check-in points), answer Viggle live quizzes correctly, or watch Viggle sponsors' commercials. During the airing of live events such as the Grammys, Oscars, or the Olympics, Viggle asks its users to answer questions about some of the commercials that air for bonus points. Viggle also features instant polls, voting, and user evaluations/ratings that allow users to compare their responses with those of other users of the app.[63] For example, throughout the 2012 presidential debates in the United States, Viggle provided extra points to users who correctly answered its trivia questions about the candidates, presidential debates, the debate moderators, and US presidential history. In true market research fashion, it also asked its users personal information such as their political affiliations, whether the debates had any effect on changing their voting decisions, and so on. Viggle sought to double as marketer and focus group aggregator by inviting viewers to take instant polls (which candidate wore a better tie, who appeared feistier in the debate, etc.) and to evaluate the candidates' performances by clicking on emoticons ranging from a very unhappy face to a big smiley face.

If the Internet has encouraged users to participate in providing information about themselves in exchange for convenience and self-expression, second-screen apps are encouraging audience members to provide information about themselves through an additional strategy: gamification. Gamification refers to the incorporation of game mechanics into traditionally nongaming products or activities as a means of increasing user engagement. One app that is well known for gamification is Foursquare, which rewards users with points and unique badges whenever they check in to their locations (particularly restaurants) and post reviews. The more points the users earn, the more rewards and discounts they receive for their loyalty. This gamification strategy has been picked up by some second-screen apps, including Miso and GetGlue.[64] When Miso launched in March 2010, it was immediately dubbed the Foursquare of television because of its check-in and social recommendation features, points systems, and badge-earning opportunities.[65] Similarly, GetGlue has become one of the most popular second-screen apps (with more than three million users in 2012), thanks to its incorporation of game mechanics. GetGlue encourages users to participate by rewarding them with branded stickers for checking out preselected entertainment titles that range from television shows to movies. Whenever users earn twenty stickers, they can request that GetGlue mail the actual stickers to them for free (although the request can be made only once a month, regardless of the number of stickers the user has accumulated). In addition to Miso and GetGlue is the aforementioned Viggle, which gamifies users' media consumption by allowing them to collect points that can be used to collect tangible rewards.[66] Users can earn points by watching sponsored companies' commercials or by playing sponsored interactive games. By partnering with various media (like television networks such as USA and Bravo) and advertising companies to sponsor its interactive features, Viggle claims to provide users with highly targeted, contextually relevant experiences.[67]

The Marketing Surround and the Digital Enclosure

Media scholar Fred Turner[68] has coined the term *the democratic surround* to characterize the utopian hope attached to the prehistory of multiscreen environments designed to provide users with greater opportunities for participation in shaping their information environments. His essay on Edward Steichen's famous *Family of Man* photography exhibit at the Museum of Modern Art in 1955 provides one example of the ur-form of the multi-"screen" display in which viewers are surrounded by images from which to choose, providing them with the opportunity to pick their own paths through the information environment.[69] As Turner puts it, Steichen "gave Americans what he and they saw as a democratic degree of freedom in relation to imagery and so to one another."[70] Drawing on Turner's suggestion that these multi-"screen" forms of information display anticipate subsequent developments in digital multimedia, we might describe the development of second-screen apps as another manifestation of the promise of the "democratic surround": that users will be provided with greater degrees of freedom and more meaningful forms of participation in constructing their mediated information environments. There are echoes of this promise in author Michael Lewis's reception of another digital technology that made TV more interactive: TiVo. The fact that TiVo made it easier than ever before to customize one's viewing to fit one's schedule made it, according to Lewis, an empowering and democratic technology. Against the background of new forms of digital convenience, he observed, "[t]he entire history of commercial television suddenly appears to have been a Stalinist plot erected, as it has been, on force from above rather than choice from below."[71]

However, it is worth noting Turner's own caveat about the empowering promise of the "democratic surround" (with reference, once again, to *The Family of Man* exhibit): "Though visitors moved at their own pace through the galleries, though they could enjoy an enormous variety of visual opportunities for pleasure and engagement with others both like and unlike themselves, they also made their choices in terms that had been set for them, long before they entered the room. In other words, even as it freed Americans from the massifying effects of totalitarianism and its media, *The Family of Man* invited them to adjust themselves to a softer but equally pervasive system of management."[72]

This is perhaps a more convincing description of the multiscreen forms of interactivity mobilized by the television industry and its various commercial apps than the revolutionary rhetoric of Michael Lewis's paean to TiVo. After all, second-screen apps promise to counteract the forms of flexible viewing enabled by DVR technology—working to reassemble audiences that have fragmented in time and space thanks to platform-shifting and time-shifting. Moreover, second-screen apps do not break with previous marketing logic but rather attempt to build on and complete it. The CW-shopkick partnership, for example, is not the first attempt to develop a single-measurement system that links media consumption with product consumption. Before the CW-shopkick deal came Project Apollo, a much-hyped and ambitious joint venture between two monitoring mammoths, Arbitron and Nielsen. Project Apollo was developed and launched with the backing of major marketers, most notably Procter & Gamble. Monitoring more than 70,000 people with portable people meters across the United States, it sought to match all the messages that the monitored audience members saw, heard, read, and encountered with the products they purchased.[73] Although Project Apollo eventually shut down in 2008 (because of its astronomical cost in development and lack of participation from big companies), its spirit continues to live on in the development of second-screen apps. Rather than describing these apps as partaking of the promise of the "democratic surround," we might more accurately describe them as technologies designed to fold television viewing into the monitored embrace of a digital enclosure: a "commercial surround" in which one's activities are recorded, stored, and mined for marketing purposes.

The popularity of such apps will depend on their ability to foster forms of entertaining and meaningful communication and to create added value for television viewers; their functionality will depend on their ability to capitalize on the information they collect. When marketers develop new strategies for monitoring and manipulating consumers, they tend to do so under the banner of the claim that "consumers are king." For instance, A.G. Lafley, CEO of Proctor & Gamble, is well known for his mantra, "the consumer is boss," which comes across as somewhat ironic, considering that P&G is one of the companies that pushes for stronger audience monitoring (also one of the major companies that backed Project Apollo).[74] In keeping with this logic, Radha Subramanyam at Nielsen describes today's proliferation of second-screen apps as a consumer-led revolution with marketers and television programmers merely catching up to the audience's engagement with social media.[75] Commercial social media relies on a similar business model: the provision of informational and communication resources in exchange for access to detailed information that can be used to target, sort, and manipulate audiences more effectively. If the consumer is "king" in such contexts, it is in the "mediatized" sense invoked by Slavoj Žižek in his discussion of digital media:

> [O]riginally this notion designated the gesture by means of which a subject was stripped of its direct, immediate right to make decisions; the great master of political mediatization was Napoleon who left to the conquered monarchs the appearance of power, while they were effectively no longer in a position to exercise it. . . . And, mutatis mutandis, does not the same hold also for the progressive digitalization of our everyday lives, in the course of which the subject is also more and more "mediatized," imperceptibly stripped of his power, all the while under the false impression that it is being increased.[76]

Notes

1. Time Warner Cable, "Full Service Network," http://m.history.timewarnercable.com/the-twc-story/era-1990-1995/Story.aspx?story=56.
2. William Boddy, "Interactive Television and Advertising Form in Contemporary U.S. Television," in *Television after TV: Essays on a Medium in Transition*, eds. Lynn Spigel and Jan Olsson (Durham and London: Duke University Press, 2004), 113–32.
3. Quoted in Randall Stross, "The Second Screen, Trying to Complement the First," *New York Times*, March 3, 2012, http://www.nytimes.com/2012/03/04/business/apps-let-you-supplement-the-tv-show-youre-watching.html?_r=0.
4. Amar Toor, "Study Says 60-Percent of Americans Surf the Web While Watching TV," *Switched*, March 23, 2010, http://www.switched.com/2010/03/23/study-says-60-percent-of-americans-surf-the-internet-while-watch/.
5. ABC's foray into the second-screen app market for iPad was not surprising since Steve Jobs was one of the biggest shareholders of ABC-Disney.
6. Mike Proulx and Stacey Shepatin, *Social TV: How Marketers Can Reach and Engage Audiences by Connecting Television to the Web, Social Media, and Mobile* (Hoboken, NJ: John Wiley & Sons, 2012), 91.
7. Proulx and Shepatin, *Social TV*, 101.
8. Chris Taylor, "Election Night Hits Record High: 20 Million Tweets," *Mashable*, November 6, 2012, http://mashable.com/2012/11/06/election-night-twitter-record/.
9. Somrat Niyogi, CEO of Miso, claims that more than 100 second-screen apps have been developed since Miso came out in 2010.
10. Kristen Nicole, "Where's the Data Fit into Social TV Platforms and Ads?," *Silicon Angle*, April 13, 2012, http://siliconangle.com/blog/2012/04/13/wheres-the-data-fit-into-social-tv-platforms-and-ads/.
11. Joseph Turow, *The Daily You: How the New Advertising Industry is Defining Your Identity and Your Worth* (New Haven, CT: Yale University Press, 2011), 162; see also Jennifer Gillan, *Television and New Media: Must-Click TV* (New York: Routledge, 2011), 26.
12. Turow, *The Daily You*.
13. NBCUniversal.com, "Bravo Deconstructs the Multi-Screener with Robust Behavioral Study on Today's TV Viewing Habits," October 22, 2012, http://www.nbcuniversal.presscentre.com/Content/Detail.aspx?ReleaseID=13183&NewsAreaID=2&ClientID=5.
14. James Bennett, "'Your Window-on-the-World': The Emergence of Red-Button Interactive Television in the UK," *Convergence: The International Journal of Research Into New Media Technologies* 14, no. 2 (2008): 172.

15. Mark Andrejevic, "The Twenty-First-Century Telescreen," in *Television Studies After TV: Understanding Television in the Post-Broadcast Era*, eds. Graeme Turner and Jinna Tay (London and New York: Routledge, 2009), 31–40.
16. Proulx and Shepatin, *Social TV*, 45.
17. Andrejevic, "The Twenty-First-Century Telescreen," 34.
18. Launched in 2010, shopkick is the first mobile app that gives users rewards and special offers for simply walking into stores. Users are given more rewards if they actually make purchases. shopkick is able to verify the purchase and give out extra rewards if the user links his or her credit/debit card information to the app and uses that card when making purchases at shopkick's participating retailers, such as Target, Best Buy, and American Eagle.
19. Brian Stelter and Bill Carter, "Networks Try a Social Media Spin at the Upfronts," *New York Times*, May 18, 2011, http://www.nytimes.com/2011/05/19/business/media/19adco.html?_r=0; also in Proulx and Shepatin, *Social TV*.
20. Joanna Brenner, "Pew Internet: Mobile," Pew Research Center's Internet & American Life Project, December 4, 2012, http://pewinternet.org/Commentary/2012/February/Pew-Internet-Mobile.aspx.
21. Michael Hirschorn, "Closing the Digital Frontier," *Atlantic*, June 8, 2010, http://www.theatlantic.com/magazine/archive/2010/07/closing-the-digital-frontier/308131/.
22. Jonathan Zittrain, *The Future of the Internet—And How to Stop It* (New Haven, CT: Yale University Press, 2008), 20.
23. comScore, "comScore Reports November 2011 U.S. Mobile Subscriber Market Share," December 29, 2011, http://www.comscore.com/Insights/Press_Releases/2011/12/comScore_Reports_November_2011_U.S._Mobile_Subscriber_Market_Share; mobile data users' preference for apps over browsers was well reflected in the collective frustrations iPhone/iPad users expressed in various Apple forums when Apple removed its YouTube app (along with its Google Maps app) from its devices with the iOS6 upgrade because of its feud with Google (which owns YouTube). Even though Apple users could still access YouTube through the Safari browser, many iPad/iPhone users claimed it to be a hassle and demanded the YouTube app be made available again. Google eventually launched its own YouTube app for iPhone on the App Store for users to download for free.
24. Ryan Kim, "Mobile Users Lean toward Apps over Browsers," *GigaOm*, December 30, 2011, http://gigaom.com/2011/12/30/mobile-users-lean-toward-apps-over-browsers/.
25. Hirschorn, "Closing the Digital Frontier."
26. Kevin Kelly, "How Money Follows Attention—Eventually," *MIT Technology Review*, October 28, 2010, http://www.technologyreview.com/news/421457/how-money-follows-attention—eventually/.
27. Cited in Sharon Marie Ross, *Beyond the Box: Television and the Internet* (Malden, MA: Wiley-Blackwell, 2008), 76.
28. Ross, *Beyond the Box*, 77.
29. S. Elizabeth Bird, *The Audience in Everyday Life: Living in a Media World* (New York: Routledge, 2003).
30. Jonathan Gray, Cornel Sandvoss, and C. Lee Harrington, *Fandom: Identities and Communities in a Mediated World* (New York: New York University Press, 2007).
31. Henry Jenkins, *Convergence Culture: Where Old and New Media Collide* (New York: New York University Press, 2006), 20.
32. Kaarina Nikunen, "The Intermedial Practices of Fandom," *Nordicom Review* 28, no. 2 (2007): 114.
33. Henry Jenkins, "Afterword: The Future of Fandom," in *Fandom: Identities and Communities in a Mediated World*, eds. Jonathan Gray, Cornel Sandvoss, and C. Lee Harrington (New York: New York University Press, 2007), 362.
34. Peter Kafka, "Why TV Still Won't Embrace the Web Quite Yet," *All Things D*, June 8, 2010, http://allthingsd.com/20100608/why-tv-still-wont-embrace-the-web-quite-yet/.

35. Nielsen Company, "State of the Media: Cross-Platform Report Q1 2012," September 11, 2012, http://www.tvb.org/media/file/Nielsen-Cross-Platform-Report-Q1–2012-final .pdf.

36. Philip Napoli, *Audience Economics: Media Institutions and the Audience Marketplace* (New York: Columbia University Press, 2003).

37. In the 2012 report, 27 percent of respondents in the TVGuide.com study said they watch more live TV to avoid spoilers, a 7 percent increase from the report in 2010. See TVGuide.com, "Social TV Survey: Social Media Is Making You Watch More TV!," February 27, 2012, http://www.tvguide.com/News/Social-TV-Survey-1044086. aspx; and Cory Bergman, "How Social Media Users Multitask While Watching TV," *Lost Remote,* March 22, 2012, http://lostremote.com/how-facebook-and-twitter-impact-the-entertainment-industry_b27074.

38. William Uricchio, "The Future of a Medium Once Known as Television," in *The YouTube Reader,* eds. Pelle Snickars and Patrick Vonderau (London: Wallflower Press, 2009), 31; Graeme Turner, "'Liveness' and 'Sharedness' Outside the Box," FlowTV.org, April 8, 2011, http://flowtv.org/2011/04/liveness-and-sharedness-outside-the-box/.

39. Nick Couldry, *Media Rituals: A Critical Approach* (London: Routledge, 2003). Also, *The Place of Media Power: Pilgrims and Witnesses of the Media Age* (London: Routledge, 2002).

40. Couldry, *The Place of Media Power,* 42; Turner, "'Liveness' and 'Sharedness' Outside the Box."

41. Bennett, "'Your Window-on-the-World,'" 172.

42. Ibid., 180.

43. Napoli, *Audience Economics.*

44. David Goetzl, "TV Ad Spending Appears to Pass $70 Billion for the First Time, Sports Spending Also Growing," *MediaPost,* April 27, 2012, http://www.mediapost .com/publications/article/173472/tv-ad-spending-appears-to-pass-70-billion-for-the.html#axzz2GBXhO4l5; on how Nielsen plays a significant role in determining TV ad spending see Jon Gertner, "Our Ratings, Ourselves," *New York Times,* April 10, 2005, http://www.nytimes.com/2005/04/10/magazine/10NIELSENS.html?_r= 1&pagewanted=all&position=.

45. Cited in Gertner, "Our Ratings, Ourselves." In addition to economic reasons, Napoli (2003) points out that some media organizations that fear any changes to the audience measurement systems may harm their revenue prospects are reluctant to pay for larger sample sizes or improvements in measurement techniques. For example, mass-appeal content providers may be more hesitant to increase sample sizes than niche content providers who can benefit from a bigger audience sample size.

46. Gertner, "Our Ratings, Ourselves"; Napoli, *Audience Economics.*

47. Napoli, *Audience Economics.*

48. Gertner, "Our Ratings, Ourselves"; Pelle Snickars and Patrick Vonderau argue that, by being always connected, devices like Apple's iPhone, iPod touch, and iPad form "part of the ubiquitous computing continuum." See Pelle Snickars and Patrick Vonderau, "Introduction," in *Moving Data: The iPhone and the Future of Media,* eds. Pelle Snickars and Patrick Vonderau (New York: Columbia University Press, 2012), 9. Anne Balsamo similarly argues that the iPhone may be the "first ubiquitous wearable computational device." See Anne Balsamo, "I Phone, I Learn," in *Moving Data: The iPhone and the Future of Media,* eds. Pelle Snickars and Patrick Vonderau (New York: Columbia University Press, 2012), 252.

49. Audio watermarking and fingerprinting are both automatic audio recognition technologies. The difference between the two is the method of audio detection. Whereas audio watermarking recognizes the content by detecting the inaudible program identifier or code, audio fingerprinting recognizes content by analyzing the characteristics of the audio waveforms and comparing them to a vast database of pre-indexed audio content. Shazam is well known for its digital fingerprinting technology, whereas

Nielsen's early Media-Sync and Yahoo's IntoNow second-screen apps use digital watermarking technology. More content recognition technologies are in development, such as automatic video recognition, so content can be recognized even when the sound is on mute. It is also important to point out that not all second-screen apps sync their content with television screens. Apps such as Yap.tv, Miso, and GetGlue do not have content sync features but rather focus on the social networking aspect of the second-screen experience.

50. Proulx and Shepatin, *Social TV.*
51. The shows that are talked about the most in social media do not always garner high Nielsen ratings. For example, according to the network ratings report published in May 2010 by *Networked Insights'* real-time data analytics platform SocialSense, ABC's *Lost,* which ranked No. 10 in the Nielsen ratings, took the No. 1 spot on the social media charts. Shows such as NBC's *Saturday Night Live, Chuck,* or CBS's *How I Met Your Mother,* which had very low Nielsen ratings (below top forty-six), all grabbed top-twenty spots on the social media ranking during SocialSense's research period for its report ("SocialSense TV Rates the Networks").
52. See http://trendrr.tv/.
53. Proulx and Shepatin, *Social TV.*
54. To understand how Nielsen became the standard television ratings measurement company, see Napoli's *Audience Economics.*
55. Mike Mikho, "Why Social Media Needs TV and TV Needs Social," *Ad Age,* October 15, 2012, http://adage.com/article/digitalnext/social-media-tv-tv-social/237759/; Napoli, *Audience Economics.*
56. Nielsen Press Room, "Nielsen and Twitter Establish Social TV Rating," press release, December 17, 2012, http://www.nielsen.com/us/en/insights/press-room/2012/nielsen-and-twitter-establish-social-tv-rating.html.
57. B. Bonin Bough, "Nielsen and Twitter: A Game-Changing Partnership That Will Shape the TV Ecosystem," *Forbes,* December 21, 2012, http://www.forbes.com/sites/boninbough/2012/12/21/nielsen-and-twitter-a-game-changing-partnership-that-will-shape-the-tv-ecosystem/.
58. *Marketing Charts,* "Tweeters More Engaged With TV Shows," July 11, 2011, http://www.marketingcharts.com/direct/tweeters-more-engaged-with-tv-shows-18253/.
59. Kelly Hodgkins, "Nielsen/Yahoo: 86% of Mobile Users Fire Up Their Phone While Watching TV," *IntoMobile,* January 29, 2011, http://www.intomobile.com/2011/01/29/nielsenyahoo-86-of-mobile-users-fire-up-their-phone-while-watching-tv/.
60. One of the leading second-screen app companies, Miso, reported a study it conducted in May 2011 to understand how synchronized content should be delivered to television viewers. The subtitle of Miso's study, "The Miso Sync Experiment," is "Delivering real-time, relevant information on the second screen," which is an indication of second-screen apps' focus on information "relevancy."
61. Proulx and Shepatin, *Social TV,* 89.
62. Breeanna Hare, "Twice as Much TV?: How Networks are Adapting to the Second Screen," *CNN.com,* September 15, 2012, http://www.cnn.com/2012/09/15/showbiz/tv/second-screen-tv-our-mobile-society/index.html?hpt=en_c2.
63. Interestingly, Viggle does not give points for its instant polls or user evaluations/ratings. But with the nonrewarded polls and user evaluations/ratings pushed at the right moment (with relevant content on screen), users might participate if they think doing so brings a content-enriching experience.
64. When Foursquare relaunched its app in July 2012 to reinvigorate its waning influence, it ditched the gamification model (no more points and badges) for a social media application that provides algorithmic and social recommendations based on check-in history and friends' comments. See Francis Bea, "Foursquare Redesign Ditches Gamification, Emphasizes Recommendation," *Digital Trends,* June 7, 2012, http://

www.digitaltrends.com/social-media/foursquare-redesign-ditches-gamification-emphasizes-recommendations/.
65. Proulx and Shepatin, *Social TV.*
66. On November 19, 2012, it was announced that Viggle (the one with deeper pockets) would purchase GetGlue (the one with bigger audience) and that the two companies would merge (Bergman, "How Social Media Users Multitask While Watching TV," 2012).
67. Viggle, "Partner with Us," http://www.viggle.com/partner/.
68. Fred Turner, *The Democratic Surround: How World War Two America Shaped the Politics of Multimedia* (Chicago: University of Chicago Press, forthcoming).
69. Fred Turner, "*The Family of Man* and the Politics of Attention in Cold War America," *Public Culture* 24, no. 1 (2012): 55–84.
70. Turner, "*The Family of Man* and the Politics of Attention in Cold War America," 58.
71. Michael Lewis, "Boom Box," *New York Times,* August 13, 2000, http://www.nytimes.com/library/magazine/home/20000813mag-boombox.html.
72. Turner, "*The Family of Man* and the Politics of Attention in Cold War America," 51.
73. Gertner, "Our Ratings, Ourselves."
74. Ibid.
75. Julianne Pepitone, "Social 'Second Screen' TV Is All About the App," *CNN.com,* April 9, 2012, http://money.cnn.com/2012/04/09/technology/second_screens/index.htm.
76. Slavoj Žižek, *Less Than Nothing: Hegel and the Shadow of Dialectical Materialism* (London: Verso, 2012), 335–6.

References

Andrejevic, Mark. *iSpy: Surveillance and Power in the Interactive Era*. Lawrence, KS: University Press of Kansas, 2007.

Andrejevic, Mark. "The Twenty-First-Century Telescreen." In *Television Studies After TV: Understanding Television in the Post-Broadcast Era,* edited by Graeme Turner and Jinna Tay, 31–40. London and New York: Routledge, 2009.

Balsamo, Anne. "I Phone, I Learn." In *Moving Data: The iPhone and the Future of Media,* edited by Pelle Snickars and Patrick Vonderau, 251–64. New York: Columbia University Press, 2012.

Bea, Francis. "Foursquare Redesign Ditches Gamification, Emphasizes Recommendation." *Digital Trends,* June 7, 2012. http://www.digitaltrends.com/social-media/foursquare-redesign-ditches-gamification-emphasizes-recommendations/.

Bennett, James. "'Your Window-on-the-World': The Emergence of Red-Button Interactive Television in the UK." *Convergence: The International Journal of Research Into New Media Technologies* 14, no. 2 (2008): 161–82.

Bergman, Cory. "How Social Media Users Multitask While Watching TV." *Lost Remote,* March 22, 2012. http://lostremote.com/how-facebook-and-twitter-impact-the-entertainment-industry_b27074.

Bergman, Cory. "What the Viggle-GetGlue Acquisition Means for the Battle over the Second Screen." *Lost Remote,* November 19, 2012. http://lostremote.com/what-the-viggle-getglue-acquisition-means-for-the-battle-over-the-second-screen_b35220.

Bird, S. Elizabeth. *The Audience in Everyday Life: Living in a Media World.* New York: Routledge, 2003.

Boddy, William. "Interactive Television and Advertising Form in Contemporary U.S. Television." In *Television after TV: Essays on a Medium in Transition,* edited by Lynn Spigel and Jan Olsson, 113–32. Durham and London: Duke University Press, 2004.

Bough, B. Bonin. "Nielsen and Twitter: A Game-Changing Partnership That Will Shape the TV Ecosystem." *Forbes,* December 21, 2012. http://www.forbes.com/sites/boninbough/2012/12/21/nielsen-and-twitter-a-game-changing-partnership-that-will-shape-the-tv-ecosystem/.

Brenner, Joanna. "Pew Internet: Mobile." Pew Research Center's Internet & American Life Project, December 4, 2012. http://pewinternet.org/Commentary/2012/February/Pew-Internet-Mobile.aspx.

comScore. "comScore Reports November 2011 U.S. Mobile Subscriber Market Share." December 29, 2011. http://www.comscore.com/Insights/Press_Releases/2011/12/comScore_Reports_November_2011_U.S._Mobile_Subscriber_Market_Share.

Couldry, Nick. *Media Rituals: A Critical Approach.* London: Routledge, 2003.

Couldry, Nick. *The Place of Media Power: Pilgrims and Witnesses of the Media Age.* London: Routledge, 2002.

D2D. "Second Screens and Social TV - Making Waves in the Broadcast World." February 14, 2012. http://digital2disc.com/index.php/news/article/second-screens-and-social-tv-making-waves-in-the-broadcast-world.

Fuchs, Renaud. "Feature: The Rise of Second Screen Applications." *DVD and beyond,* November 12, 2012. http://www.dvd-and-beyond.com/display-article.php?article=1820.

Gertner, Jon. "Our Ratings, Ourselves." *New York Times,* April 10, 2005. http://www.nytimes.com/2005/04/10/magazine/10NIELSENS.html?_r=1&pagewanted= all&position=.

Gillan, Jennifer. *Television and New Media: Must-Click TV.* New York: Routledge, 2011.

Goetzl, David. "TV Ad Spending Appears to Pass $70 Billion for the First Time, Sports Spending Also Growing." *MediaPost,* April 27, 2012. http://www.mediapost.com/publications/article/173472/tv-ad-spending-appears-to-pass-70-billion-for-the.html#axzz2GBXhO4l5.

Gray, Jonathan, Cornel Sandvoss, and C. Lee Harrington. *Fandom: Identities and Communities in a Mediated World.* New York: New York University Press, 2007.

Hare, Breeanna. "Twice as Much TV?: How Networks are Adapting to the Second Screen." *CNN.com,* September 15, 2012. http://www.cnn.com/2012/09/15/showbiz/tv/second-screen-tv-our-mobile-society/index.html?hpt = en_c2.

Hirschorn, Michael. "Closing the Digital Frontier." *Atlantic,* July/August 2010. http://www.theatlantic.com/magazine/archive/2010/07/closing-the-digital-frontier/308131/.

Hodgkins, Kelly. "Nielsen/Yahoo: 86% of Mobile Users Fire Up Their Phone While Watching TV." *IntoMobile,* January 29, 2011. http://www.intomobile.com/2011/01/29/nielsenyahoo-86-of-mobile-users-fire-up-their-phone-while-watching-tv/.

Jenkins, Henry. "Afterword: The Future of Fandom." In *Fandom: Identities and Communities in a Mediated World,* edited by Jonathan Gray, Cornel Sandvoss, and C. Lee Harrington, 357–64. New York: New York University Press, 2007.

Jenkins, Henry. *Convergence Culture: Where Old and New Media Collide.* New York: New York University Press, 2006.

Kafka, Peter. "Why TV Still Won't Embrace the Web Quite Yet." *All Things D,* June 8, 2010. http://allthingsd.com/20100608/why-tv-still-wont-embrace-the-web-quite-yet/.

Kelly, Kevin. "How Money Follows Attention—Eventually." *MIT Technology Review,* October 28, 2010. http://www.technologyreview.com/news/421457/how-money-follows-attention—eventually/.

Kim, Ryan. "Mobile Users Lean toward Apps over Browsers." *GigaOm,* December 30, 2011. http://gigaom.com/2011/12/30/mobile-users-lean-toward-apps-over-browsers/.

Lewis, Michael. "Boom Box." *New York Times,* August 13, 2000. http://www.nytimes.com/library/magazine/home/20000813mag-boombox.html.

Marketing Charts. "Tweeters More Engaged With TV Shows." July 11, 2011. http://www .marketingcharts.com/direct/tweeters-more-engaged-with-tv-shows-18253/.

Mikho, Mike. "Why Social Media Needs TV and TV Needs Social." *Ad Age,* October 15, 2012. http://adage.com/article/digitalnext/social-media-tv-tv-social/237759/.

Miso. "The Miso Sync Experiment: Delivering Real-Time, Relevant Information on the Second Screen." May 12, 2011. http://blog.gomiso.com/2011/05/12/the-miso-sync-experiment-a-special-report-from-miso-labs/.

Napoli, Philip. *Audience Economics: Media Institutions and the Audience Marketplace.* New York: Columbia University Press, 2003.

NBCUniversal.com. "Bravo Deconstructs the Multi-Screener with Robust Behavioral Study on Today's TV Viewing Habits." October 22, 2012. http://www.nbcuniversal .presscentre.com/Content/Detail.aspx?ReleaseID=13183&NewsAreaID=2&Clien tID=5.

Networked Insights Blog. "SocialSenseTV Rates the Networks." May 18, 2010. http:// blogdotnetworkedinsightsdotcom.wordpress.com/2010/05/18/socialsensetv-rates-the-networks/.

Nicole, Kristen. "Where's the Data Fit into Social TV Platforms and Ads?" *Silicon Angle,* April 13, 2012. http://siliconangle.com/blog/2012/04/13/wheres-the-data-fit-into-social-tv-platforms-and-ads/.

Nielsen Company. "State of the Media: Cross-Platform Report Q1 2012." September 11, 2012. http://www.tvb.org/media/file/Nielsen-Cross-Platform-Report-Q1–2012-final.pdf.

Nielsen Press Room. "Nielsen and Twitter Establish Social TV Rating." Press release, December 17, 2012. http://www.nielsen.com/us/en/insights/press-room/2012/nielsen-and-twitter-establish-social-tv-rating.html.

Nikunen, Kaarina. "The Intermedial Practices of Fandom." *Nordicom Review* 28, no. 2 (2007): 111–28.

Niyogi, Somrat. "Please Don't Ruin the Second Screen." *TechCrunch,* May 27, 2012. http:// techcrunch.com/2012/05/27/please-dont-ruin-the-second-screen/.

Parker, Chuck. "The Coming Battle for Second Screen." *The Intersection* (blog). November 27, 2012. http://digitalvideospace.blogspot.com/2012/11/the-coming-battle-for-second-screen.html.

Pepitone, Julianne. "Social 'Second Screen' TV Is All About the App." *CNN.com,* April 9, 2012. http://money.cnn.com/2012/04/09/technology/second_screens/index.htm.

Proulx, Mike, and Stacey Shepatin. *Social TV: How Marketers Can Reach and Engage Audiences by Connecting Television to the Web, Social Media, and Mobile.* Hoboken, NJ: John Wiley & Sons, 2012.

Ross, Sharon Marie. *Beyond the Box: Television and the Internet.* Malden, MA: Wiley-Black-well, 2008.

Snickars, Pelle, and Patrick Vonderau. "Introduction." In *Moving Data: The iPhone and the Future of Media,* edited by Pelle Snickars and Patrick Vonderau, 1–10. New York: Columbia University Press, 2012.

Stelter, Brian, and Bill Carter. "Networks Try a Social Media Spin at the Upfronts." *New York Times,* May 18, 2011. http://www.nytimes.com/2011/05/19/business/media/19adco .html?_r=0.

Stross, Randall. "The Second Screen, Trying to Complement the First." *New York Times,* March 3, 2012. http://www.nytimes.com/2012/03/04/business/apps-let-you-supplement-the-tv-show-youre-watching.html?_r=0.

Taylor, Chris. "Election Night Hits Record High: 20 Million Tweets." *Mashable,* November 6, 2012. http://mashable.com/2012/11/06/election-night-twitter-record/.

Time Warner Cable. "Full Service Network." http://m.history.timewarnercable.com/the-twc-story/era-1990-1995/Story.aspx?story=56.

Toor, Amar. "Study Says 60-Percent of Americans Surf the Web While Watching TV." *Switched,* March 23, 2010. http://www.switched.com/2010/03/23/study-says-60-percent-of-americans-surf-the-internet-while-watch/.

Turner, Fred. *The Democratic Surround: How World War Two America Shaped the Politics of Multimedia.* Chicago: University of Chicago Press, forthcoming.

Turner, Fred. "*The Family of Man* and the Politics of Attention in Cold War America." *Public Culture* 24, no. 1 (2012): 55–84.

Turner, Graeme. "'Liveness' and 'Sharedness' Outside the Box." FlowTV.org, April 8, 2011. http://flowtv.org/2011/04/liveness-and-sharedness-outside-the-box/.

Turow, Joseph. *The Daily You: How the New Advertising Industry is Defining Your Identity and Your Worth.* New Haven, CT: Yale University Press, 2011.

TVGuide.com. "Social TV Survey: Social Media Is Making You Watch More TV!" February 27, 2012. http://www.tvguide.com/News/Social-TV-Survey-1044086.aspx.

Uricchio, William. "The Future of a Medium Once Known as Television." In *The YouTube Reader,* edited by Pelle Snickars and Patrick Vonderau, 24–39. London: Wallflower Press, 2009.

Viggle. "Partner with Us." http://www.viggle.com/partner/.

Zittrain, Jonathan. *The Future of the Internet—And How to Stop It.* New Haven, CT: Yale University Press, 2008.

Žižek, Slavoj. *Less Than Nothing: Hegel and the Shadow of Dialectical Materialism.* London: Verso, 2012.

3

WINDOWS INTO THE DIGITAL WORLD

Distributor Strategies and Consumer Choice in an Era of Connected Viewing

Elissa Nelson

Throughout the mainstream Hollywood film industry, there has been growing attention to windowing, and specifically to increasing experiments with the timing of when films are released in different markets. Digital distribution has allowed for many of the changes in the various ways media content is disseminated and accessed, and with those changes come the attendant challenges faced by studios, consumers, and the entire media industries ecosystem as all parties adjust to new business practices. Connected viewing, which refers to products and services that enhance entertainment experiences and encourage active viewing through the integration of Internet access, multiple screens, and social networking with traditional forms of entertainment, has also resulted in changes in the larger digital distribution landscape. Included among connected viewing strategies are increasing the availability of content via the Internet and enhancing the options by which that content can be accessed. As with the advances in digital distribution, the developments that have resulted from trying to enhance connected viewing experiences have disrupted traditional distribution models, including windowing strategies.

The home entertainment sector (the industry-standard term even though it includes content viewed outside the home on mobile devices) has historically been one of the most profitable revenue streams for the studios but has recently been experiencing dramatic changes. Ever since 1987, the majority of film revenues are earned in ancillary markets, not at the box office.[1] For example, according to the Motion Picture Association of America,[2] domestic box office revenue for 2011 was $10.2 billion; in the same year, the Digital Entertainment Group (DEG), an industry-funded research organization that combines statistics from movies and television, reported that home entertainment, including rentals and sales, DVD and Blu-ray, cable and satellite video-on-demand (VOD), downloads and streaming, totaled $18.4 billion,[3] or approximately 1.8 times as much as domestic box office. With the home entertainment market such a profitable source of revenue, there have been arguments between distributors, exhibitors, and retailers over how to time the release of films in different windows to extract the greatest overall profit without adversely affecting any specific revenue stream.

With the introduction of DVDs in 1997, DVD sales became a cornerstone of the home video market. Although renting had been the dominant trend with VHS tapes, DVDs were priced for purchasing, and ever since, even in the digital market, studios have valued sell-through because of the higher per-transaction profits from owning versus renting.[4] However, after a steady recession and the introduction of competition from low-cost rental services like Netflix and Red-box, DVD sales started to fall: according to the DEG, the peak year for DVD sales was 2004; DVD sales have dropped each year thereafter. The bright spot for growth with all these daunting numbers remains the rapid adoption of digi-tal distribution. The digital market, while still a small percentage of total home entertainment spending, increased by 50 percent in 2011.[5] Indeed, the growth in online movie viewing has been exponential, with IHS Screen Digest estimating increases from 2011–12 at approximately 135 percent.[6]

The studios are still keeping an eye on what remain their most profitable products in home entertainment—DVDs and Blu-ray discs—and are ever aware that sales in one sector can "cannibalize," or eat into, the sales of another. Nevertheless, when dra-matic declines were reported in 2008 to 2009 when DVD sales dropped 13 percent from $10.06 billion to $8.73 billion,[7] the industry went into a tailspin trying to find a means to recoup revenues. Amanda Lotz points out that as far back as 2004, "the rhet-oric of industry leaders shifted from advocating efforts to prevent change to accepting the inevitability of industrial adjustment," where the acceptance of change meant that strategies to increase the availability of content on multiple platforms were becoming more common.[8] Since 2010, studios have noticed the steadily increasing consumption of films in digital formats and have started to see the benefits of making more content available for online distribution; as Marc Graser reported in *Variety*,

> The Hollywood studios, for their part, are finally accepting the notion that digital distribution is the future of the homevideo biz. They've begun to embrace all forms of video-on-demand, given that digital distribution, as a whole, rose 23% during the first half of the year [2010] to generate $1.1 bil-lion for the studios, according to DEG.[9]

The numbers have only increased since then: according to IHS Screen Digest, in 2012, total consumer spending on digital platforms increased to $4.9 billion.[10] With fears of cannibalization always present, the studios continue to seek out the most profitable times and platforms to make films available, and the trend has been to do so by experimenting with release windows in the digital arena.

This chapter is a study of film industry practice that examines how studios are using windowing strategies to provide greater access and added value to media content. Additionally, it looks at the numerous choices consumers face as they navigate the rapidly changing viewing options engendered by digital distribution and enhanced by connected viewing. While television and international distribution are interrelated with and help inform strategies for film, they are markets with diverse operating principles and as such would benefit from their own individual analyses.[11] Instead, the focus here is primarily on what can be gleaned about industry practice by an examination of studio-based film distribution. This analysis of changing windowing strategies addresses the ways that distributors, exhibitors, and retailers ensure their profits are preserved while also calling attention to the ways consumers, even though they are acting within the confines of a controlled system, have the potential to shape market responses via their viewing and purchasing decisions. By concentrating on the multiplicity of distribution options, the business decisions that effect change in the marketplace, and the benefits and problems that develop from those decisions, this research spotlights the growth of new business strategies and the expansion of consumer choice in an era of digital distribution and connected viewing.

Definitions of Windows and Basic Windowing Strategies

The goals of distribution in the film industry are generally to maximize value and revenue streams over the life of a property. One of the primary and most profitable ways this maximization is achieved is through windowing—the strategy of releasing a film in different venues and on different platforms over a period of time, usually with discreet periods of exclusivity and variable pricing. If consumers want to watch a film in its first run, which is usually in theatrical exhibition, they pay a premium price per each consumer, per each viewing. As the film "gets older," after it has been in release for a while, it goes down the chain, and subsequent viewings of the film in different windows, such as second-run and discount theaters, DVD, high-definition Blu-ray DVD, VOD, or television, are frequently lower in cost per individual viewing.

The following is the traditional release pattern for a studio film in the United States since the advent of the home video market in the late 1970s/early 1980s until the late 2000s:

1. Theatrical
2. Airlines/Hotels
3. Home Video (DVD, Blu-ray, VHS, LaserDisc)
4. VOD/PPV (pay-per-view)
5. Premium/Network Cable (pay TV)
6. Broadcast Network (free TV)

Historically, a typical studio film would be released in the theater first and stay exclusively in this window for the first few months. The run would be determined by whether the film had "legs" (had good word-of-mouth and so stayed in the theaters for an extended period), and then there would be a "black" or rest period when the film wouldn't be available except for on airlines and in hotels. The home entertainment window, including DVD and VOD, would be approximately four to seven months later, with pay television at about nine to fifteen months, a subsequent rest period, and free television at twenty-seven to thirty months.[12] The physical copies of the film (VHS, DVD) are generally available on a continuous basis (except for some Disney films that employ a "vault" strategy, restricting their availability, and for films that go out of print). Meanwhile, broadcast and streaming are frequently limited, and viewers usually aren't certain how long a film will be accessible in these formats.

A number of recent changes have complicated traditional release schedules, mostly having to do with studio strategies of shrinking theatrical windows in an attempt to enhance total returns. The National Association of Theatre Owners (NATO), the trade group that represents and advocates for exhibitors, keeps track of studio-specific and industry-wide average release windows. NATO found that the average time between a film's theatrical debut and its appearance in the home market has gone down from 167 days in 2000, to 147 days in 2005, to 132 days in 2010,[13] representing a cumulative change of thirty-five days or 21 percent. The shortening theatrical windows are due to distributors claiming that declining revenues and piracy threats are forcing them to experiment with new release schedules, and because they aren't earning revenues in the rest periods between windows. Distributors also contend that they are merely offering consumers more choice in their viewing options and that the people who want to see a film in a theater won't be dissuaded by the title's availability in the home entertainment market. Meanwhile, distributors also get a greater percentage of the ticket sales the first few weeks a film is in theatrical release (the timespan in which films earn the greatest box office grosses), while exhibitors earn a larger percentage the longer a film stays in the theaters. As a combination of all these factors, movies stay in theaters for a shorter period of time, and windows are shortened throughout the distribution chain.

There have been some experiments, primarily in the independent sector, with day-and-date (simultaneous) theatrical and early VOD releases. In a move that completely collapsed the theatrical window, Steven Soderbergh's *Bubble* (2005) was released in theaters, on cable, and on DVD at the same time. While *Bubble* was only moderately successful,[14] it marked an interest in pursuing a simultaneous release strategy, at least with smaller, independent films. In 2011, both *Melancholia* (d. Lars von Trier), which premiered in an early VOD window before its theatrical debut, earned nearly $16 million at the worldwide box office with a $7.4 million estimated budget, and *Margin Call* (d. J. C. Chandor), which premiered in the day-and-date format, earned about $19.5 million at the worldwide box office on an estimated $3.5 million budget,[15] even though both films had a limited run (only certain theaters will screen films that are showing with early or simultaneous VOD availability). The films that have been released in the day-and-date format since *Bubble*[16] illustrate that a simultaneous release is usually best reserved for smaller, independent films and that there is potential to vary the windows and give consumers more options, but that with resistance from exhibitors, the tactic is still met with limited success. That success is especially limited if the film is a major release; major studios have encountered pushback from exhibitors who refuse to screen films if the theatrical window is encroached. When Universal attempted to shorten the window in 2011 with *Tower Heist*, planning to offer the film on VOD for $60 three weeks after its theatrical debut, theater owners threatened a boycott and Universal ended up abandoning its plans.[17] While consumers do want more choices, they have generally decided that paying extra to stream a film in an earlier window isn't worth the premium price.[18]

Along with shortened theatrical windows, there have also been shifts in traditional home entertainment window patterns. Even though physical sell-through makes up a larger percentage of studio revenues than digital sell-through, digital sales are more profitable on a per-transaction basis (i.e., the distributor's profit margin on an individual digital sale is greater than the margin on a physical sale[19]). Consequently, with dropping DVD sales, and a 60–70 percent VOD margin versus a 20–30 percent margin on DVD rentals,[20] the studios have been eager to experiment with shifting the physical and digital release schedules. In 2008, Time Warner was the first conglomerate to offer all its films simultaneously on DVD and VOD, thereby closing the window between the DVD and VOD releases.[21] Then, in another home market window shift, in 2010 Warner Bros. was the first studio to institute a twenty-eight-day delay between a film's DVD/VOD release and its availability to lower per-transaction profit margin companies like Redbox and Netflix.[22] While this move decreased consumer choice, it aimed to protect studio revenues, and indeed, although some rental companies still stocked their shelves with wholesale DVDs, the delay boosted sales at retailers.[23]

Studios continue searching for the right window/price combination in the digital sphere; in 2012 Warner Bros. negotiated for fifty-six-day rental delays with Netflix, further solidifying the concept of a high-margin sales window.[24] Rental companies, however, are also carving out their own demands in the marketplace, continuing the constant renegotiations that mark the windowing debates. Redbox, a business that depends more on the availability of new DVD releases than Netflix, refused to agree to the Warner Bros. fifty-six-day delay. In fact, after negotiations fell through, instead of waiting for the previously agreed upon twenty-eight days,[25] Redbox started to stock its rental kiosks with wholesale discs as soon as they became available at retail, thus eating into sales that the delay was designed to protect. Later in 2012, Universal, the next distributor to have its contract up with Redbox, decided against extending the rental delay from twenty-eight days to fifty-six days; the studio did not want to risk the loss of profits from retail sales that might result if Redbox stocked its kiosks with the studio's titles before the twenty-eight-day mark.[26]

Expanding Options for Home Entertainment Digital Distribution

Giving consumers various ways to watch digital content through a number of service providers on multiple viewing platforms is part of a connected viewing strategy that strives to offer more options to access digital content. When discerning changes in release windows, and when trying to understand the ways content and service providers maneuver through the new landscape, it's important to differentiate between the many types of digital distribution used in the home entertainment sector. For example, *VOD* is a frequently used, all-encompassing term that refers to ordering a title through a provider that is immediately available for viewing. However, in industry parlance, the term *VOD,* and even the terms *streaming* and *download,* are too broad.

Nuancing the nomenclature of digital distribution allows for more specificity and a greater understanding of how various strategies are affecting windowing and consumer choice. Studios negotiate different licensing rights and get varying revenue splits based on the type of delivery. For example, different types of VOD (see below) correlate to how a title is purchased, how much it costs, whether it is owned or rented, and the time of its availability. There are also different delivery options utilized for VOD, such as downloading (if the title is to be stored on a local drive) or streaming (if the title is stored in a remote location, commonly referred to as "in the cloud" and then transmitted over an Internet connection). If the delivery method is tied to a multichannel video programming distributor (MVPD) like a cable or satellite company, there are limited options for where and on what device the content can be viewed—usually on a television set connected to a service provider box, but sometimes also via mobile devices if users have authenticated their subscriptions and the "TV Everywhere" option is available.[27] On the other hand, if the content is accessible over a stand-alone Internet connection, it is more readily available on computers and video-enabled mobile devices like smartphones, tablets, and laptops, thereby increasing the options for connected viewing. The following is a list of terms, definitions, and examples to describe various types of digital distribution options:

1. Premium Video-on-Demand (PVOD)—films that are available for a high price (between $10 and $60) either before, day-and-date, or soon after the theatrical release; the films are usually streamed from a cable or satellite provider such as Comcast or DirecTV.

2. Transactional Video-on-Demand (TVOD)—films are available for streaming or download around the same time as their release on DVD; they often have to be viewed within a specific timeframe after purchase; examples of Internet

sites include Amazon, Apple/iTunes, and Vudu, and also include one-time purchases via MVPDs; depending on whether films are new or old releases, are standard or high definition, prices can range from $1–$6 for rentals; for both PVOD and TVOD, distributors get a greater split of the revenues than from physical disc rentals.

3. Subscription Video-on-Demand (SVOD)—a subscription service that lets viewers pay a set fee for usually unlimited streaming viewing of available titles (considered "buffet"/"all-you-can-eat" style, as opposed to transactional's "à la carte" model); titles are often available after their run in more profitable windows such as DVD or TVOD; examples are services such as Netflix ($8 per month for streaming) or Amazon Prime ($79 per year), both over-the-top (OTT) services where no cable subscription is required.

4. Free/Advertising Video-on-Demand (FVOD or AVOD)—films are paid for via advertising so they are considered free for the viewer; streaming over websites such as Crackle and YouTube are examples of FVOD or AVOD (as are broadcast network websites, but these primarily have only television shows available), and although consumers have to pay for a subscription to a cable or satellite service, titles available without an extra charge through these providers are often considered to be in this category; titles are released via F/AVOD after more profitable pay windows in line with the traditional pay cable and free network television windows; with SVOD and F/AVOD content owners negotiate licensing fees for the films upfront.

5. Pay-per-View (PPV)—a precursor to VOD and still used for certain live events like sports and concerts, PPV is offered through cable and satellite providers; usually subscribers order titles to stream at a set time; in the 1980s and '90s, PPV was available after the VHS and DVD releases for films, but is usually simultaneous with live events.

6. Electronic Sell-Through or Download-to-Own (EST or DTO)—instead of renting titles for a specified period of time, consumers buy titles (or license the rights to them); new releases often range between $15 and $20; with EST the films can be streamed or downloaded, and if they're streamed, they are usually stored in the cloud and linked to a user's account, such as with industry-backed UltraViolet or Apple's iCloud; titles are available from multiple online retailers and studios' own websites around the same time as the DVD release; EST and DTO are also considered transactional models and have a high profit margin for the content owners.

While the different options above detail ways the studios are traversing various digital distribution strategies, it's also important to note how piracy factors into the equation. Exact figures aren't available for how many films are illegally downloaded, and how many of those viewings would translate to actual revenue-generating transactions (i.e., if the pirated movie weren't "free," it isn't certain consumers would pay to watch it). What's especially troubling for content producers in an era of digital distribution, an open Internet, and peer-to-peer file sharing is that pirated copies offer easy access to pristine versions of the films. In hoping to avoid what happened to the music industry, which suffered at the hands of rampant illegal downloads, the movie business has tried to learn from previous mistakes by giving consumers more attractive options for legal viewing. In addition to the ease of use of services like Netflix and iTunes, the prevalence and continued development of Internet video–capable devices such as smartphones, tablets (especially the massive popularity of the iPad), and smart TVs (TV sets with built-in Internet connections), and the increase in bandwidth speed and quality have also made consuming films via connected devices more appealing. By varying the cost of films, by releasing them earlier in the ancillary markets, and by offering multiple Internet sites where films can be viewed legally, consumers are encouraged to buy instead of steal.

Increasing the Value to Consumers and Decreasing the Threat to Profitability of Digital Viewing

As Chuck Tryon explains in *Reinventing Cinema,* viewing options are becoming more computerized;[28] instead of being stuck with limited options, strict schedules, and immobile viewing ports, viewers can choose what they want to watch, when, and on what device. In a crowded marketplace—in terms of available services, platforms, and content—the options have to demonstrate their added value and utility in order to be viable. If using a product is too difficult to figure out or if enough titles aren't available, with the multiplicity of options, consumers can always look elsewhere. At the same time, the varied options can cause confusion in the marketplace, and there is no one option that suits the needs of every consumer in every viewing situation.[29] Distributors have to find ways to effectively cut through the noise of the teeming digital distribution arena, while balancing the demands of different industry parties with the demands of the consumer.

Different viewing options promise different kinds of "value." DVDs remain popular because of their high image and sound quality, portability and playability on multiple devices, the ability to lend and borrow them with ease, their extra features, and the abundant titles available. On the other hand, digital options offer immediacy of access, ease of acquisition, multiple screen/device capabilities, and increased portability on mobile devices without optical drives; but at the same time sacrifice sound and image quality (even the highest-quality HD doesn't compare to Blu-ray), have a limited availability of titles, and are affected by interoperability problems relating to whether a title purchased from one retailer can be played on any device.

While recognizing that, depending on the situation, viewers have different viewing needs, studios have tried to rectify some of the challenges posed by digital distribution that limit consumer options (and their spending). To encourage consumers to adopt digital formats, studios started to enhance connected viewing options with mobile viewing apps, and started offering digital copies along with the purchase of physical discs. In the hopes of increasing consumer choice and services, studios have become direct-to-consumer retailers via their websites with options for EST and manufacturing-on-demand (MOD—consumers can buy physical or digital copies of otherwise unavailable titles[30]). And while the experiments did not meet with great success, in addition to increasing revenues, another rationale behind offering early-window PVOD and day-and-date releases is to give consumers more ways to view content.

Perhaps the biggest industry-wide and studio-supported connected viewing endeavor used to increase the value of digital ownership is UltraViolet, a digital rights locker that, according to *Home Media Magazine,* "embodies the 'buy once, play anywhere' approach."[31] While UltraViolet strives to add value to digital distribution and the ownership window, it has been met with numerous problems, including its cumbersome sign-up processes, limited title availability/device interoperability, and lack of consumer adoption. Although it doesn't open a new window—UltraViolet is available in the same purchase window as DVDs and high-margin VOD—it does increase the options for how and where content can be viewed. As a connected viewing strategy, it increases the value of digital ownership by offering convenience and accessibility. Importantly, though, as its slow adoption attests,[32] UltraViolet shows the disconnect between what studios want consumers to pay for and what consumers prefer. It's continually extolled and pushed by studios, but has yet to achieve critical mass or even gain mainstream traction. Offering UltraViolet copies as a free add-on to physical copies also illustrates how studios are trying to increase the appeal of profitable digital distribution strategies while trying not to encroach upon sales in other areas.

Indeed, in trying to assess the most profitable ways to maximize windows, studios have to perform a balancing act. Studios need to keep in mind how important high box office grosses are to the success of a film in the long run, and also how ancillary market revenues provide a larger return. They also need to resolve how to capitalize on the marketing push around the initial theatrical release so that it carries over to sustain later releases. In addition, they need to be aware of which ancillary markets, such as physical DVD, television, and digital distribution, are most profitable, which are most popular, which they have to compete with (piracy), and which providers of said revenue-generating windows they need to keep happy (retailers, cable providers, subscription services), and then they have to manage to balance all these options into an efficacious windowing/ pricing strategy so that one doesn't cannibalize the others. They have to achieve this balance of power and profits all while trying to ensure that they are satisfying consumer demand.

The cannibalization fears start at the very beginning of a film's introduction into the marketplace. In describing trends in the theatrical and DVD releases of films in the UK, Hasan Bakhshi describes how the cannibalization and marketing effects play out when determining windows:

In the earliest studies, the window reflects the trade-off that distributors face between so-called "cannibalisation" and "marketing" effects. Distributors prefer longer windows to the extent that they protect box office revenues (cannibalisation effect), but shorter windows in so far as this lets them capitalise on DVD sales while a film remains fresh in the minds of the public (marketing effects).[33]

The sales from each sector help determine the distributors' course of action, and even though home entertainment outpaces theatrical, success in the box office is still important to revenues in all the ancillary markets; box office grosses are a key determining factor in how well a film does in subsequent windows.

Furthermore, and further complicating the balancing act, distributors have to prevent the high profit margin consumers, or those who will pay for the film in its most profitable setting, from defecting into the group of consumers who will pay to watch the film but in lower profit margin windows.[34] These cannibalization effects factor into ancillary window strategies; distributors are concerned about carving into theatrical revenues, as well as whether releasing a film early on VOD or EST will affect its DVD sales and, additionally, how this will affect distributor relationships with other retailers. For example, in 2006, the studios started negotiating to release films and television shows on the iPod, but Walmart, which at that time accounted for approximately 40 percent of DVD sales in the United States, threatened not to carry Disney's *High School Musical* (2006) in its stores if the studios gave Apple a less expensive price for digital copies than the studios were going to charge Walmart for physical copies.[35] The concern was about protecting sales of the higher profit margin product, sales that could be jeopardized if the same title (with comparable quality and convenience of access) was available somewhere else for less.

While quality, convenience, and ease of use are all important elements in making transaction decisions for the consumer, time of availability is also an essential determining factor. From their report investigating the most profitable times to introduce films in dual distribution channels from a marketing science perspective, Ashutosh Prasad et al. postulate that the maximum profits decrease when there are consumer expectations of a short window: "[t]he reasoning is that more customers will wait for the low-margin product."[36] The authors differentiate between people who will go to the theater no matter where the film is available and those who will watch films via other means. However, the availability of films in ancillary windows in quick succession could easily have the effect of making those undecided or not overly enthusiastic about seeing a particular film in a theater decide to wait for a less expensive offering, something of which theater owners and retailers are well aware and about which they frequently voice their concerns.

While studios are assessing release options and gauging consumer demand, frequently the average moviegoer is not aware of the term *windows*—yet there is an understanding, even if not of the exact timeframes, of when and where films will be available. Expectations about windows, even if they're not named as such to the consumer, are important for how audiences decide when and where to watch, but it is debatable whether it would be more or less beneficial to make the general public aware of the ancillary release dates. Additionally, there's no indication that a single timing strategy would work for all films, especially when factoring in the specific box offices and seasonality of particular titles. However, even if standardized windowing were deemed preferable by consumers, the studios can't collaborate to establish a single release schedule and uniform prices. While distributors make release date deals with exhibitors and retailers, if multiple studios were to adopt the same strategies, it would be considered collusion and would break antitrust laws.[37]

In order to determine the optimal windows and prices that will maximize revenues, the studios need to factor in all these considerations in concert with one another. Even though distributors want to improve the value of digital distribution and do so by focusing on connected viewing strategies that increase the availability of content and enhance viewing options, there's an intricate system of power relations between distributors, exhibitors, licensors, and retailers that affects windowing strategies. Studios of course want to enrich their profits, but the self-maximization strategies of one sector of the industry have rippling effects across the whole system. As a result, all the industry players seek to protect their own interests from profit encroachments while at the same time they continue to work together because they all depend on one another for providing content and securing viewing outlets. There's even a complex balance of power within individual studios and conglomerates as the business decisions of one division, such as theatrical or television, have an effect on others, such as home entertainment or cable. And in the midst of all these calculations and negotiations between industry players is the equally important concern of trying to accommodate consumer preference.

Conclusion

During the mid-2000s and into the early 2010s, windowing patterns took dramatically different turns from how they had been traditionally positioned for the nearly three decades prior. One of the most significant departures is that there is no longer a one-size-fits-all mentality about every film following the same release schedule; digital distribution encourages experimentation and allows for the type of film (e.g., blockbuster, independent) to help determine release order. There are still more changes likely to occur, and variable timing between the different windows, but the following is an updated window pattern describing the sequence of possible releases, with notations marking how the windows can be customized and adjusted:

1. Early PVOD and International Theatrical[38]
2. Domestic Theatrical/Day-and-Date PVOD[39]
3. PVOD and Airlines/Hotels

4. DVD/Blu-ray/UltraViolet/EST (purchase window)[40]
5. TVOD/SVOD/Rental DVD and Blu-ray (rental window)[41]
6. Premium Cable/F/AVOD (pay TV)[42]
7. Basic Cable/F/AVOD (pay TV)
8. Broadcast Network (free TV)

It's not surprising that the pattern requires more provisos and is more confusing than it had previously been: the multiplicity of options that have been so notably augmented by connected viewing products and services, while enabling greater choice and more possibilities for experimentation, also leads to complexity. With the current fragmentation of the media landscape, and with each segment of the industry defending its revenue territory if it perceives threats to its profits, no single strategy can fit all titles or all kinds of viewing preferences. Indeed, the proliferation of frequently changing windows illustrated by the schema above indicates an industry trying to navigate through unchartered territory in relation to the sheer ubiquity of options and players.

The continually changing window patterns described above also show that, in addition to balancing the demands of multiple sectors of the Hollywood industry, the relationships between distributors and consumers have to be constantly rene-gotiated as well. Offering more choice as part of connected viewing strategies that emphasize increasing the availability of content and enhancing the methods by which that content can be accessed is not enough to ensure smooth digital tran-sitions; consumer awareness and adoption of those strategies must follow. When Jeffrey Katzenberg, CEO of DreamWorks Animation, spoke about the digital transition in 2006, he mentioned how he hoped it would mirror the transition from VHS to DVD and described that "the consumer decided when VHS was obsolete . . . not the hardware manufacturers, not retail, not us."[43] The statement indicates the power of consumers to shape the market by voicing their preferences via their purchasing decisions.

The reality of consumer influence is of course more complex, and not just because the transition from VHS to DVD saw an increase in profits while mon-etizing digital content at similar rates has proven more difficult for the studios. Consumers make choices within a system controlled by conglomerate structures. However, it's still important to note the interplay of dynamic forces both within dif-ferent sectors of the industry and between industry players and consumers. Digital distribution and the attendant changes to windows illustrate and reinforce the com-plex system of checks and balances that operates within contemporary Hollywood.

Notes

1. Kristin Thompson and David Bordwell, *Film History: An Introduction* (Boston: McGraw-Hill, 2003), 680.
2. Motion Picture Association of America, "Theatrical Market Statistics 2011," http://www.mpaa.org/Resources/5bec4ac9-a95e-443b-987b-bff6fb5455a9.pdf.

3. Daniel Frankel, "NATO Reduces Threat Level," *Variety*, March 14, 2006, http://www.variety.com/article/VR1117939775/.
4. Lisa Richwine, "Ready for Movies in the Cloud? Studios Bet You Are," *Reuters*, October 10, 2011, http://www.reuters.com/article/2011/10/10/us-ultraviolet-idUSTRE7995MX20111010.
5. Ibid.
6. Quoted in Ben Fritz, "Internet to Surpass DVD in Movie Consumption, Not Revenue," *Los Angeles Times*, March 23, 2012, http://latimesblogs.latimes.com/entertainmentnewsbuzz/2012/03/internet-to-surpass-dvd-in-movie-consumption-not-revenue.html.
7. Jacqui Cheng, "DVD Sales Tank in 2009 as Americans Head to the Cinema," *Ars Technica*, January 4, 2010, http://arstechnica.com/business/2010/01/dvd-sales-tank-in-2009-as-americans-head-to-the-cinema/.
8. Amanda D. Lotz, *The Television Will Be Revolutionized* (New York: New York University Press, 2007), 20.
9. Marc Graser, "Is Hollywood on the Road to Recovery?" *Variety*, September 25, 2010, http://www.variety.com/article/VR1118024585/.
10. Tania Loeffler, "Worldwide Consumer Spending on Movies Sees Accelerated Growth in 2012," iSuppli.com, January 21, 2013, http://www.isuppli.com/media-research/news/pages/worldwide-consumer-spending-on-movies-sees-accelerated-growth-in-2012.aspx.
11. For a discussion of differences between film and television digital distribution, see Alisa Perren, "Business as Unusual: Conglomerate-Sized Challenges for Film and Television in the Digital Arena," *Journal of Popular Film and Television* 38, no. 2 (2010): 72–8.
12. Robert Marich, "Studios Fret over Online Crack in Cable Window," *Variety*, October 29, 2011, http://www.variety.com/article/VR1118045204/. For further discussion of digital distribution strategies and release windows, see Dina Iordanova and Stuart Cunningham, eds., *Digital Disruption: Cinema Moves On-line* (St Andrews: St Andrews Film Studies, 2012); and Philip Drake, "Distribution and Marketing in Contemporary Hollywood," in *The Contemporary Hollywood Film Industry*, eds. Paul McDonald and Janet Wasko, 63–82 (Oxford: Blackwell, 2008).
13. National Association of Theatre Owners, "Major Studio Release Windows," http://www.natoonline.org/windows.htm.
14. Diane Garrett, "Windows Rattled: Pix Speed Up Race to DVD," *Variety*, March 21, 2006, http://www.variety.com/article/VR1117940116/.
15. Figures from the Internet Movie Database (www.imdb.com) and Box Office Mojo (www.boxofficemojo.com).
16. Other examples of independent successes with the day-and-date release strategy include *Flawless* (2007) and *All Good Things* (2010). For further discussion, see Ann Hornaday, "The On-Demand Indie Film Revolution," *Washington Post*, August 17, 2012, http://articles.washingtonpost.com/2012-08-17/lifestyle/35490193_1_magnolia-pictures-screens-and-sound-systems-hdnet-movies.
17. Pat Saperstein, "'Margin Call' Changes VOD Picture," *Variety*, December 18, 2011, http://www.variety.com/article/VR1118047677/; Josh L. Dickey and Andrew Stewart, "Universal Aborts 'Tower Heist' VOD Plan," *Variety*, October 12, 2011, http://www.variety.com/article/VR1118044319/.
18. Patrick Goldstein, "Is DirecTV's $30 Movie Rental Test a Flop of 'Ishtar'-like Proportions?" *Los Angeles Times*, July 11, 2011, http://latimesblogs.latimes.com/.m/the_big_picture/2011/07/is-direct-tvs-movie-rental-test-a-flop-of-ishtar-like-proportions-.html.
19. Jeffrey C. Ulin, *The Business of Media Distribution: Monetizing Film, TV and Video Content in an Online World* (Amsterdam: Elsevier, 2010), 218, 311.

20. Georg Szalai, "Time Warner Going Day-and-Date for VOD," *Hollywood Reporter*, April 30, 2008, http://www.hollywoodreporter.com/news/time-warner-going-day-date-110596.
21. Ibid.
22. Marc Graser, "Warner Bros., Redbox Agree on Deal," *Variety*, February 16, 2010, http://www.variety.com/article/VR1118015320/.
23. Marc Graser and Andrew Wallenstein, "WB Extends 56-day Delay on Netflix," *Variety*, January 5, 2012, http://www.variety.com/article/VR1118048183/.
24. Ben Fritz, "Warner Bros. Extends Delay for Rental DVDs," *Los Angeles Times*, January 7, 2012, http://articles.latimes.com/2012/jan/07/business/la-fi-ct-redbox-netflix-20120107.
25. Ben Fritz, "Redbox-Warner Deal Expires, Ending 28-Day Delay," *Los Angeles Times*, January 31, 2012, http://latimesblogs.latimes.com/entertainmentnewsbuzz/2012/01/redbox-warner-deal-expires-ending-28-day-delay.html.
26. Ben Fritz, "Universal Pictures Extends Deal with Redbox," *Los Angeles Times*, March 2, 2012, http://articles.latimes.com/2012/mar/02/business/la-fi-ct-universal-redbox-20120302.
27. "TV Everywhere" allows viewers who have paid for cable subscriptions to stream television content on Internet-connected devices. For additional information, see Brian Stelter, "Campaign Trains Viewers for 'TV Everywhere,'" *New York Times*, September 11, 2011, http://mobile.nytimes.com/2011/09/12/business/media/campaign-trains-viewers-for-tv-everywhere.xml.
28. Chuck Tryon, *Reinventing Cinema: Movies in the Age of Media Convergence* (New Brunswick, NJ: Rutgers University Press, 2009), 6.
29. Ulin, *The Business of Media Distribution*, 310.
30. For more information on MOD, different studio practices, and title availability, see http://dvdnewsflash.wordpress.com/sony%C2%A0dvd-r/.
31. *Home Media Magazine*, "UltraViolet: Consumers' Bridge to the Future," http://www.homemediamagazine.com/digital-evolution/ultraviolet-consumers-bridge-digital-future.
32. Andrew Wallenstein and Marc Graser, "CES: Studio Execs Push UltraViolet," *Variety*, January 8, 2013, http://variety.com/2013/digital/news/ces-studio-execs-push-ultraviolet-1118064347/.
33. Hasan Bakhshi, "The Theatrical Window: Unchartered Waters?," UK Film Council, March 2007, 2, http://www.ukfilmcouncil.org.uk/media/pdf/g/9/Theatrical_window.pdf.
34. Even the prospect of charging more for high-margin, home market windows, such as PVOD, can have a cannibalizing effect. If the returns on high-margin PVOD can offset the potential box office losses of viewers who might otherwise see the film in the theater, the practice might be justified for the distributor, but anything that affects box office numbers can lead to longer-term problems downstream. As Universal discovered when theaters threatened to boycott *Tower Heist*, regardless of whether the audience for PVOD is the same as the audience that would have gone to see the film in the theater in the first place, by presenting more options and encroaching upon the theatrical window, there's more potential for box office erosion.
35. Merissa Marr, "In Hollywood, the Picture Blurs for Studio Profits," *Wall Street Journal*, September 2, 2006, http://online.wsj.com/article/SB115716089734652490.html.
36. Ashutosh Prassad, Bart Bronnenberg, and Vijay Mahajan, "Product Entry Timing in Dual Distribution Channels: The Case of the Movie Industry," *Review of Marketing Science* 2 (2004): 9.
37. Edward Jay Epstein, *The Hollywood Economist: The Hidden Financial Reality Behind the Movies, Release 2.0* (New York: Melville House, 2012), 208.

38. Although certainly not standard for all films, early PVOD for some independent films and an international release prior to the North American release for some blockbusters have been used to drum up word of mouth for the domestic theatrical release (and to combat piracy in international territories). See previous discussions of *Margin Call* and *Melancholia* regarding early PVOD and independent films, and Amy Kaufman, "'Avengers' Conquer World Box Office as U.S. Audiences Wait," *Los Angeles Times*, May 4, 2012, http://articles.latimes.com/2012/may/04/entertainment/la-et-avengers-20120504, regarding experimentation with early international theatrical releases for blockbusters.
39. Domestic theatrical remains the primary initial window for the majority of films that are released theatrically.
40. The order of these releases is in flux, and they are not necessarily simultaneous with one another: for example, DVD can be the same time as or earlier than EST.
41. Frequently, higher-margin TVOD precedes lower-margin SVOD, but the order depends on the specific deals between the distributors and providers. Also, this window can come earlier if retailers buy physical copies wholesale to rent, or if the distributor hasn't negotiated a rental delay with the provider.
42. While industry nomenclature often calls VOD that comes with some cable stations "free VOD," it is noted as pay-TV on this list because a cable subscription is required for access.
43. Marr, "In Hollywood, the Picture Blurs for Studio Profits."

References

Bakhshi, Hasan. "The Theatrical Window: Unchartered Waters?" UK Film Council, March 2007. http://www.ukfilmcouncil.org.uk/media/pdf/g/9/Theatrical_window.pdf.

Cheng, Jacqui. "DVD Sales Tank in 2009 as Americans Head to the Cinema." *Ars Technica*, January 4, 2010. http://arstechnica.com/business/2010/01/dvd-sales-tank-in-2009-as-americans-head-to-the-cinema/.

Dickey, Josh L., and Andrew Stewart. "Universal Aborts 'Tower Heist' VOD Plan." *Variety*, October 12, 2011. http://www.variety.com/article/VR1118044319/.

Drake, Philip. "Distribution and Marketing in Contemporary Hollywood." In *The Contemporary Hollywood Film Industry*, edited by Paul McDonald and Janet Wasko, 63–82. Oxford: Blackwell, 2008.

Epstein, Edward Jay. *The Hollywood Economist: The Hidden Financial Reality Behind the Movies, Release 2.0.* New York: Melville House, 2012.

Frankel, Daniel. "NATO Reduces Threat Level." *Variety*, March 14, 2006. http://www.variety.com/article/VR1117939775/.

Fritz, Ben. "Internet to Surpass DVD in Movie Consumption, Not Revenue." *Los Angeles Times*, March 23, 2012. http://latimesblogs.latimes.com/entertainmentnewsbuzz/2012/03/internet-to-surpass-dvd-in-movie-consumption-not-revenue.html.

Fritz, Ben. "Redbox-Warner Deal Expires, Ending 28-Day Delay." *Los Angeles Times*, January 31, 2012. http://latimesblogs.latimes.com/entertainmentnewsbuzz/2012/01/redbox-warner-deal-expires-ending-28-day-delay.html.

Fritz, Ben. "Universal Pictures Extends Deal with Redbox." *Los Angeles Times*, March 2, 2012. http://articles.latimes.com/2012/mar/02/business/la-fi-ct-universal-redbox-20120302.

Fritz, Ben. "Warner Bros. Extends Delay for Rental DVDs." *Los Angeles Times*, January 7, 2012. http://articles.latimes.com/2012/jan/07/business/la-fi-ct-redbox-netflix-20120107.

Garrett, Diane. "Windows Rattled: Pix Speed Up Race to DVD." *Variety*, March 21, 2006. http://www.variety.com/article/VR1117940116/.

Goldstein, Patrick. "Is DirecTV's $30 Movie Rental Test a Flop of 'Ishtar'-like Proportions?" *Los Angeles Times,* July 11, 2011. http://latimesblogs.latimes.com/the_big_picture/2011/07/is-direct-tvs-movie-rental-test-a-flop-of-ishtar-like-proportions-.html.

Graser, Marc. "Warner Bros., Redbox Agree on Deal." *Variety,* February 16, 2010. http://www.variety.com/article/VR1118015320/.

Graser, Marc. "Is Hollywood on the Road to Recovery?" *Variety,* September 25, 2010. http://www.variety.com/article/VR1118024585/.

Graser, Marc, and Andrew Wallenstein. "WB Extends 56-day Delay on Netflix." *Variety,* January 5, 2012. http://www.variety.com/article/VR1118048183/.

Home Media Magazine. "UltraViolet: Consumers' Bridge to the Digital Future." http://www.homemediamagazine.com/digital-evolution/ultraviolet-consumers-bridge-digital-future.

Hornaday, Ann. "The On-Demand Indie Film Revolution." *Washington Post,* August 17, 2012. http://articles.washingtonpost.com/2012-08-17/lifestyle/35490193_1_magnolia-pictures-screens-and-sound-systems-hdnet-movies.

Iordanova, Dina, and Stuart Cunningham, eds. *Digital Disruption: Cinema Moves On-line.* St Andrews: St Andrews Film Studies, 2012.

Kaufman, Amy. "'Avengers' Conquer World Box Office as U.S. Audiences Wait." *Los Angeles Times,* May 4, 2012. http://articles.latimes.com/2012/may/04/entertainment/la-et-avengers-20120504.

Loeffler, Tania. "Worldwide Consumer Spending on Movies Sees Accelerated Growth in 2012." iSuppli.com, January 21, 2013. http://www.isuppli.com/media-research/news/pages/worldwide-consumer-spending-on-movies-sees-accelerated-growth-in-2012.aspx.

Lotz, Amanda D. *The Television Will Be Revolutionized.* New York: New York University Press, 2007.

Marich, Robert. "Studios Fret over Online Crack in Cable Window." *Variety,* October 29, 2011. http://www.variety.com/article/VR1118045204/.

Marr, Merissa. "In Hollywood, the Picture Blurs for Studio Profits." *Wall Street Journal,* September 2, 2006. http://online.wsj.com/article/SB115716089734652490.html.

Motion Picture Association of America. "Theatrical Market Statistics 2011." http://www.mpaa.org/Resources/5bec4ac9-a95e-443b-987b-bff6fb5455a9.pdf.

National Association of Theatre Owners. "Major Studio Release Windows." http://www.natoonline.org/windows.htm.

Perren, Alisa. "Business as Unusual: Conglomerate-Sized Challenges for Film and Television in the Digital Arena." *Journal of Popular Film and Television* 38, no. 2 (2010): 72–8.

Prassad, Ashutosh, Bart Bronnenberg, and Vijay Mahajan. "Product Entry Timing in Dual Distribution Channels: The Case of the Movie Industry." *Review of Marketing Science* 2 (2004): 1–18.

Richwine, Lisa. "Ready for Movies in the Cloud? Studios Bet You Are." *Reuters,* October 10, 2011. http://www.reuters.com/article/2011/10/10/us-ultraviolet-idUSTRE7995MX20111010.

Saperstein, Pat. "'Margin Call' Changes VOD Picture." *Variety,* December 18, 2011. http://www.variety.com/article/VR1118047677/.

Stelter, Brian. "Campaign Trains Viewers for 'TV Everywhere.'" *New York Times,* September 11, 2011. http://mobile.nytimes.com/2011/09/12/business/media/campaign-trains-viewers-for-tv-everywhere.xml.

Szalai, Georg. "Time Warner Going Day-and-Date for VOD." *Hollywood Reporter,* April 30, 2008. http://www.hollywoodreporter.com/news/time-warner-going-day-date-110596.

Thompson, Kristin, and David Bordwell. *Film History: An Introduction.* Boston: McGraw-Hill, 2003.

Tryon, Chuck. *Reinventing Cinema: Movies in the Age of Media Convergence.* New Brunswick, NJ: Rutgers University Press, 2009.

Ulin, Jeffrey C. *The Business of Media Distribution: Monetizing Film, TV and Video Content in an Online World.* Amsterdam: Elsevier, 2010.

Wallenstein, Andrew, and Marc Graser. "CES: Studio Execs Push UltraViolet," *Variety,* January 8, 2013. http://variety.com/2013/digital/news/ces-studio-execs-push-ultraviolet-1118064347.

4

THE PERSONAL MEDIA COLLECTION IN AN ERA OF CONNECTED VIEWING

Gregory Steirer

Over the last five or six decades, collecting media content has changed from a fringe activity, practiced by fans and self-styled collectors, to an everyday mode of media consumption in which many consumers participate. As it has changed, so too have the economics of media production, as media industries have become increasingly dependent on the sale of media content in collectable forms to consumers. Even in the film and television industries, which among media industries came relatively late to the idea of their products as collectible, the sale of content for personal collections has become an essential part of profit models.[1] The growth of connected viewing in the form of digital distribution and the development of cloud-based services for online consumption, however, have considerably complicated the practice of consumer collecting. Whereas the logic of collecting practices has historically been premised on the physical or objective qualities of material goods, digital goods are (despite their foundation as binary code) functionally immaterial and, for this reason, often treated by consumers and scholars more as information than as objects. Though such a conception may yet prove compatible with traditional collecting practices—or may, indeed, give rise to new ones—media companies have introduced additional complexity by advocating and widely implementing a model for digital goods in which behaviors taken for granted as being natural corollaries of ownership (such as organizing and reselling) are restricted or disabled. Collecting practices thus face an uncertain future in an era of connected viewing.

In this chapter, I offer a new concept of collecting, applicable to both physical and digital media goods, that corrects for deficiencies in previous scholarly approaches to collecting. These previous approaches, hampered by overly conservative understandings of *use,* have tended to preclude the study of media goods as collections and have resulted in a surprisingly barren literature on media goods and collecting practices. The model I introduce is thus intended not only to facilitate this chapter's analysis of connected viewing, but also to lay the groundwork for future work on media collecting of all kinds, both in the physical and digital domains. I employ this model in order to structure analyses of two specific collecting practices in which collectors of physical media goods engage, and to interrogate how well these practices currently translate to the digital realm. These analyses reveal how media companies have constructed connected viewing in such a way as to wrest power back from consumers and retailers and delimit the possible uses of their products after point of sale. I demonstrate that connected viewing as it is currently constructed thus represents a victory of industry interests over those of collectors; this victory, however, has not been without costs, as media companies find themselves facing new problems as a result of consumer disenfranchisement.

Two clarifications are in order at the outset. First, this chapter examines collecting practices as they apply to the five major forms of entertainment-oriented media goods: books, music, film, television, and games. This is not to discount real variations in how consumers collect these different forms of media, but rather to treat such variations as adaptations of a higher-order or more general behavioral logic to the specific material, legal, and social conditions associated with different media forms at different times. That said, collecting practices for the different media forms are not identical, and their differences have arguably grown more extreme within the digital sphere. It is the contention of this chapter, however, that such differences have less to do with the essential natures of the media forms themselves than how different media companies and/or industries have constructed digital versions of these forms for the sell-through marketplace. By examining collecting practices across media forms, we are thus better able to see how specific kinds of consumer behavior both give rise to and are in turn reciprocally produced by industrial imperatives.

Second, brief discussion is necessary on the distinction between the terms *collection* and *collector*. Although English grammar would suggest that a *collector* is merely a person engaged in the process of building a *collection,* use of these terms by scholars has sometimes suggested that the two terms represent fundamentally different ideas. *Collector* is thus frequently employed as a term of psychological characterization; it is used to describe consumers who exhibit obsessive, fetishistic, or passionate behavior toward a specific kind of good.[2] *Collection,* by contrast, typically describes sets of similar or related goods that have been accumulated by individual or institutional agents—irrespective of the psychological natures of the accumulators.[3]

Such a distinction derives from a more substantial (though typically unvoiced) disagreement among scholars over how collecting should be studied. For scholars working in sociology, communications, and consumer research, the objects of study are *collectors:* why people collect, how their passion for a specific set of objects expresses itself in social interactions, and how behaviors associated with collecting represent responses (typically either resistance and/or mediated capitulation) to dominant sociopolitical forces such as economic systems, legal or moral norms, and industry practices.[4] By focusing on individual actors or communities of actors, these scholars hope to illuminate processes of individual and collective meaning-making within specific social and political settings. Because this group of scholars seeks to study collectors (and to do so within a contemporary social science paradigm), its research has typically relied on subjects who self-identify as collectors or who participate in amateur collecting clubs or trading networks. Scholars working in art history, museum studies, or archaeology have, by contrast, traditionally focused on *collections:* how collected objects constitute a set, how these objects' association together alters their individual meanings or introduces new ones, how the set systematizes knowledge and experience, and how the set can serve as a material representation of a specific historical period.[5] Rooting their analyses in material culture, these scholars are interested in what collections can tell us about different social and historical constructions and the kinds of systematizing consciousnesses to which they give rise. In what follows, I try to incorporate both approaches, but my analyses of specific modes of consumer-product interaction hew closer to those of an object-focused approach. In keeping with this perspective, I use the word *collecting* to indicate the practice of accumulating a set of similar or related goods—irrespective of whether the accumulating subject would identify him or herself as a *collector*. I use *collector* in a similar fashion, signifying only a subject engaged in the practice of such accumulation, and not an underlying personality, psychological structure, or mode of self-identification.

Defining Collecting

Despite differences of emphasis within the existing scholarship on collecting, nearly all studies have derived collecting's unique logic from two primary features. The first, and simpler of the two, is that the goods collected bear some kind of logical relationship to one another. As Brenda Danet and Tamar Katriel observe, "they [the goods collected] must be defined as belonging to a superordinate *category*."[6] In an early paper, Susan Pearce distinguishes three forms this superordinate category could take: souvenirs, fetish objects, and systematics.[7] Though she later abandons this terminology, scholars have continued to rely on it to differentiate between associative logics that are personal (souvenirs, fetish objects) or scientific (systematics) in origin.[8] A schema less rooted in personal psychology might instead differentiate between associative logics based on form (for example, paintings), function (weapons), content (Elvis Presley), and provenance (Hermès products). For the purposes of this chapter, personal media collecting will be primarily examined in terms of form and function; I thus restrict my analysis to film/television collecting, music collecting, and the like and ignore cross-media collecting based on content or provenance.

The second feature underlying the logic of collecting pertains to the altera-tion in use-value collected goods undergo when they enter into a collection. In most scholarship, this alteration is described in terms of removal or exclusion, so that collecting is considered the bracketing off of otherwise useful goods from the order of utility. As Russell Belk explains, "Objects of ordinary consumption, even when the objects are part of a set . . . , are primarily intended for use and therefore do not comprise a collection."[9] Though Belk presents this principle as a typologi-cal rule meant primarily to assist in the identification of collections, other scholars have viewed it as the crux of how meaning-making works for collections. For some, the bracketing off from utility reflects socioeconomic processes associated with capitalism and the growing dominance of consumer society. In works such as anthropologist Paul van der Grijp's *Passion and Profit*, Belk's rule thereby becomes a "paradox" in which "they [collectibles] have exchange value without having use value."[10] For other scholars, the loss of utility is not the primary alteration at all, but is rather a necessary corollary to the collected good's shift into pure objectiv-ity. As humanities scholar Susan Stewart proclaims, "[T]he collection represents the total aestheticization of use value."[11] For Stewart, aestheticization describes an order of interaction between subject and object in which sensual experience is paramount; the collected good *qua* object becomes something beheld instead of used. Other scholars following this route have been less careful than Stewart in their delineations of aesthetic experience, so that aestheticization often finds itself associated more with absence of use than with sensory experience. Danet and Katriel thus define "aesthetic attitude" as "(a) non-practical, (b) non-cognitive, and (c) non-personal."[12] Both strands of this research, however, rely on a binary approach that positions use-value as mutually exclusive of valuations based on other principles.

Although this focus on altered use-value has become one of the primary ways in which collecting is defined within the scholarly literature, it presents signifi-cant problems for the study of personal media collecting. If we define use-value roughly as a good's ability to fulfill a particular function or satisfy a particular need extrinsic to the good itself but for which the good was designed, then media goods would seem to lack such value. Whereas hammers, chairs, and teakettles are easily described in terms of their functions or extrinsic uses, novels, films, and music are not. Media goods are thus typically described or assessed in terms of intrinsic value, with use-value serving only as a secondary and nonessential property. Media goods are thus better understood as what Jeremy Rifkin calls "cultural experiences" than they are as commodities in the classical sense; and, as experiences, they are more usefully described in terms of aesthesis and individual identification or participation than in terms of extrinsic utility.[13] Not intended to be used but rather *experienced,* media goods would thus seem to be bracketed off from the order of utility even when they are not part of collections. Similarly, as goods that are also consumed *as* aesthetic experiences, media goods cannot sensi-bly be said to undergo aestheticization when made part of a collection.

A study focused on the collecting of media goods thus requires a revised notion of what use is and how collecting affects it. Dispensing with traditional definitions of use-value rooted in the connection of goods to extrinsic purposes, I propose a model that defines use-value in terms of the various modes of interaction that take place between a consumer and his or her goods so as to produce pleasure and/or personal satisfaction. These modes of interaction include but are not limited to the uses intended by the goods' producers—what I henceforth refer to as *use in the narrow sense,* under which label I include watching a film, listening to a song, reading a book, and playing a game. Value can also be produced for a consumer through numerous other interactions, including those traditionally deemed secondary but proper to the good (organizing, displaying, disposing) and those deemed improper or "misuses" (using a book for a doorstop, using compact discs for target practice). I follow consumer researchers such as Colin Campbell, Morris Holbrook, and Jacob Jacoby in their approach to consumption by also including as modes of interaction actions that *precede* ownership, such as discovering, searching for, and purchasing the good.[14] Table 4.1 represents the most typical interactions, organized according to when they commonly take place in the consumption process.

Not every act of consumption involves all these modes (indeed, some are mutually exclusive), nor will all consumers find in each of these modes a source of value. The point of schematizing them in this fashion is to represent use as a diachronic process consisting of multiple kinds of use from which value may be generated for the consumer.

With the model I am proposing in place, we can reformulate in a less problematic fashion the central observation of the collecting scholarship with respect to use-value: collected goods undergo an alteration in use-value wherein use in the narrow sense ceases to serve as the sole or primary means of value production.

TABLE 4.1 Modes of Consumer-Good Interaction

Preacquisition	Acquisition	Ownership
Discovering/learning of	Searching for	Using in the narrow sense
Sampling	Negotiating for	Displaying
Desiring	Waiting to purchase or receive	Aesthetic contemplation
	Purchasing	Storing
	Stealing	Organizing
	Receiving as a gift	Caring for
	Borrowing	Misusing
		Lending
		Giving
		Selling
		Destroying

In other words, collecting involves both a de-emphasis (but not an exclusion) of use in the narrow sense and an increase in emphasis on other modes of consumer-good interaction, such as organizing and selling. Though this definition is a significant departure from the theoretical model employed by other scholars of collecting, it is consonant with the findings of anthropological studies, which consistently highlight these other forms of use (and not merely "setting apart" or aesthetic contemplation) as significant and regular sources of value to collectors vis-à-vis their own collections.

These other forms of use serve as the primary focuses in my analysis of how connected viewing affects the viability of personal media collecting. Utilizing this model of collecting as consumer-good interactions that produce personal value, I examine how two particular modes of use are impacted by the specific manner in which digital media goods have been constructed: organizing and selling.

Organizing

Collectors of all kinds devote significant time and energy (and sometimes money) to the organization of their collections. Indeed, organizing can sometimes constitute the primary mode of interaction between collectors and specific goods within their collections. For owners of large collections, organizing reflects the need to keep track of what goods are owned and to ensure that these goods remain accessible for future uses. Organizing also functions, however, to provide a framework by which the collected goods become something more than the sum of their parts. As Pearce explains, "[T]he notion of discrimination, of 'this and that' through which a series or a set can be defined and then subcategories with the set distinguished, is central to collecting both intellectually and emotionally."[15] Through discrimination of this kind, organization practices personalize collections to reflect their owners' own priorities and associative linkages.

Integral to all organizing practices is what has, in recent years, come to be called "meta-data." Defined by Tony Gill as "a structured description of the essential attributes of an information object," meta-data provides the information categories and typological gradients on which organization schemes are structured.[16] Such data can encompass both intrinsic or "objective" attributes, such as publication date, genre, and length; and extrinsic or "subjective" attributes, such as personal rating, display value, and monetary worth. All organized collections rely on some form of meta-data, even if the data are limited to only a small number of attributes and expressed solely via spatial arrangement. In many cases, however, organizing practices involve the creation of separate databases, thereby allowing multiple categorizing schemas to be employed simultaneously (as with card catalogues). Collection database software, such as Collectorz's Movie Collector and Deep Prose Software's Booxter, has been developed to facilitate such practices for everyday consumers, and has since become incorporated into the organizing activities of many individual collectors.

In theory, one of the major advantages of digital media goods is that, being essentially immaterial, they need not be arranged in a single, spatial order. As multiple kinds of meta-data attributes are associated with a specific media file, users should thus in principle be able to execute different sorting schemes and filters in order to produce different kinds of organization. A digital music library might thus simultaneously organize tracks by year released, genre, and track length, allowing users to switch between organizing schemes with a simple button press. In addition, because most digital meta-data requires negligible amounts of hardware space, restrictions on the number and kind of attributes associated with a media file should be unnecessary. Just as users of collecting software can add their own personally defined attribute fields to their databases, owners of digital media should be able—given the similar kind of programming principles involved—to do the same with their files' integrated meta-data. For digital media goods, the possibilities inherent in meta-data thus herald new kinds of dynamic, customizable, multilevel organization schemes for collections.[17]

In practice, however, the vast majority of digital media goods currently available in the sell-through market do not offer such schemes. iTunes, which was originally designed to be as much media file organizer as media player, is currently the only major digital media service that utilizes more than a handful of editable meta-data attributes. Other services, such as Amazon Instant Player, the various Kindle platforms, Vudu, UltraViolet, Apple TV, and Xbox Live, utilize only a tiny number of meta-data attributes, none of which are editable (save sometimes a user rating, though this is usually autofilled by aggregated data). No service—including iTunes—enables the creation of user-defined attribute fields. Digital media goods (at least as currently designed) thus paradoxically allow for fewer organizing activities than do physical media goods despite the fact that their immateriality should allow for more. Indeed, most connected viewing services preclude all organizing activity whatsoever by managing the meta-data internally according to programmer-defined rules and auto-filled data. The "shift" from physical to digital goods has resulted in the disappearance of a major mode of consumer-good interaction.

The decision by media publishers and distributors to design connected viewing services in this fashion can be traced to two related developments in personal computing. One is the push, spearheaded by Apple and recently adopted by all other major software and hardware developers, to produce simpler, more "natural" user interfaces. Such interfaces seek to lower barriers to computer use by hiding and predictively automanaging the database functions on which computer software depends. The trend—largely explained by the software industry's desire to expand its market—has therefore been toward ease of use at the expense of breadth of use. Though media companies have been some steps behind software companies in adopting ease of use as a key product paradigm for connected viewing (UltraViolet, the cloud-based electronic sell-through system spearheaded by Warner Bros., has proven to be notoriously complicated to consumers), they too recognize its importance for establishing connected viewing as a mass-market business.[18]

Among media services, Flixster Collections best demonstrates the resulting shift in approach to meta-data. Released for PCs in 2011 after the acquisition of Flixster by Warner Bros. Home Entertainment Group, Flixster Collections is a film/ television file manager, collection database (entries can be made for DVDs), and media player designed to compete with Apple's iTunes. Drawing from a number of online databases, including Rotten Tomatoes (owned by Warner Bros.), IMDb (owned by Amazon), and Facebook, Flixster Collections automatically fills and keeps updated a bevy of meta-data attribute fields associated with goods entered into the database. Users can sort and search according to a limited range of these attributes, but they cannot change the meta-data themselves. Fully automating the practice of organizing a collection, Flixster Collections relieves collectors of the need to categorize or even know much about the media goods they own.

If the desire to create simpler interfaces represents one of the main reasons designers of digital media goods have reduced or disabled organizing activities, the rise of mobile and tablet computing represents the other. Lacking full keyboards and precision-based input devices such as mice and track pads, mobile phones and tablets make data input difficult and error prone. Their small screens also significantly restrict the amount of visual "real estate" available for data display. These limitations, combined with the need for on-screen buttons to be rendered large and discrete enough to facilitate touch-based selection, have encouraged software designers to hide or remove all but the most essential meta-data from media services for these devices. The majority of such services limit information provided to product image, title, genre, and (where applicable) author. Some offer even less: the Vudu player for iPad associates only a single image with each purchased media good (even the goods' titles are excluded). In almost no cases do these services allow users to sort by the attribute fields they display; most rely instead on a single alphabetized list of the goods owned. Some of these services, such as iPhone's iOS 5 movie player, even lack the ability to search by title (one must, instead, scroll down an alphabetized list). The design constraints associated with mobile and tablet computing have thus resulted in digital media goods that both lack the meta-data necessary to render organization meaningful and rule out the sorting and searching options through which organization takes place.

As PC and mobile operating systems continue to converge, consumers will likely find themselves able to perform even fewer organizing practices with their digital media collections than they can today. New, multiplatform services, in order to provide consistent branding and speedier (and simpler) rollouts and updates, will deploy broadly identical interfaces across a variety of devices, with the least "powerful" device (the mobile) determining the organizing activities available on all of them. To some extent, this has already happened with Amazon Instant Player and iTunes Match, both of which offer far simpler interfaces than their PC-based predecessors (the Amazon website and iTunes). As organizing becomes increasingly simplified and managed internally by software, its personalizing function—and the value it generates for individual consumers through such personalization—will thus be severely reduced. Gains for businesses in the form of larger markets and streamlined software management and development will come at the expense of what has previously been a valued form of consumer-good interaction.

Selling

The scholarship on collecting has almost entirely disregarded selling as a practice. Few works mention it at all, while those that do present it as either a minor or "secondary" practice not worthy of sustained analysis.[19] To some extent, this gap in the literature is a reflection of the way Western culture has traditionally constructed consumers and retailers as distinct and separate groups: the former buys and uses goods; the latter sells them. It is also, however, the result of overly narrow definitions of "use" itself, which position selling (and frequently all forms of disposition) as something other than use.[20] The model of collecting presented in this chapter, by contrast, treats selling as a kind of use available to collectors, for whom it may function as a personally valued mode of interacting with the goods collected. Such a model has the added benefit of better accounting for observable behavior on the part of collectors, who sometimes indeed sell parts of their collections.

Selling has the direct effect of reducing or reshaping, and thus further personalizing, an individual's collection, but it also engages the collector in broader, transpersonal systems of valuation. This, more than the need or desire to translate goods into capital, may explain why collectors sometimes engage in small-scale selling or trading and why even those who do not nevertheless frequently pay close attention to how much they might earn if they did (the "monetary value" of a collected good). Secondary markets, defined here as organized networks consisting of multiple unaffiliated "retailers" who sell "used" or previously owned goods, work not only to circulate goods but also to circulate and synthesize dispersed and often divergent valuations of those goods. Through the mechanism of price, which economist Friedrich Hayek observed functions to coordinate and communicate information within free markets, separate personal or "local" valuations of individual goods enter into conversation with one another to produce a single social or "global" valuation.[21] Secondary markets, like all markets, are thus essentially conversations about value; but unlike most primary markets for consumer goods, wherein the most powerful voices belong to profit-driven companies (producers, distributors, and retail stores), most secondary markets for collected or collectible goods lack similar concentrations of power in individual participants and, because the goods have already been produced, exclude producers altogether. Secondary markets thus function for collectors as a kind of public forum about value, and serve, ultimately, to synthesize the different kinds of value individual collectors ascribe to their collected goods into the single, abstract—and thus universally communicable—monetary value of price. In other words, secondary markets turn individual acts of collecting and valuation into social acts. Even the lone collector who never engages in selling participates, through secondary markets, with those collectors who do, and in settling on a price he or she is willing to pay for a good both contributes and responds to that good's socially determined value.

Although the ability to dispose of a good through sale is often viewed as a natural or inalienable right associated with ownership, this ability is in fact the result of a particular legal construction of ownership. In the United States, this construction, previously established by court cases, was codified in the Copyright Act of 1976, which formally granted owners of lawfully made goods the right to sell or dispose of them without authorization from the copyright holder (most other nations have granted owners a similar right).[22] Commonly referred to as the First Sale Doctrine, the right to sell a previously purchased good has become a keystone of modern capitalist economies, which derive significant economic activity from secondary markets of all kinds, including those for media goods, such as books and DVDs, and other products, such as refrigerators and cars.

Despite its broad contribution to economic growth, however, media companies have often viewed (or acted as though they viewed) First Sale as an onerous limitation on their own rights as copyright holders and a danger to their viability as profitable enterprises. The secondary markets that result from First Sale put downward pricing pressure on goods in the primary market; they also render supply difficult to manage by limiting the ability of publishers to control the number of goods in circulation. Worse still, they generate, through sales, revenue that media companies, despite having produced the goods being sold, receive no share of. For these reasons, media companies have thus consistently tried to create business models—typically through licensing or leasing arrangements—that allow them to sidestep First Sale. In the past, these have generally not succeeded. In fact, the first US court case to establish the principle of First Sale, *Bobbs-Merrill Co. v. Straus* in 1908, found that a book publisher could not attach licenses to its books that forbid owners from reselling them at low prices.[23] Since the 1970s, however, media companies have been more successful. During the era of VHS, for example, Hollywood companies used partnerships and leasing agreements to capture revenue from video rental and sales of previously viewed videos.[24] More recently, video game companies have implemented terms of use that disable certain gaming functions when physical copies of their games are purchased on the secondary market; they have also begun providing in-game bonuses (such as extra characters, costumes, or levels) to those who preorder copies from authorized primary market retailers. Despite these actions, secondary markets for physical media goods of all kinds have remained large and easily accessible to consumers.

The development of connected viewing, however, has provided media companies with new and more powerful options for dismantling the rights codified by First Sale. Nearly all the major media companies have relied on some combination of three basic approaches: 1) through digital rights management (DRM) measures, they have rendered digital media files nontransferable; 2) they have contractually excluded the right of resale by appending licensing agreements to sales of digital goods; and 3) they have denied consumers access to the digital media file as a discrete object so that consumers have no object to transfer. Over the last decade, consumers have become familiar with the first approach, which is the oldest and still the most commonly used. Though digital music, which introduced digital-rights-managed media files to the public, is no longer sold in this fashion, many other digital media formats still are—including television shows on iTunes, Kindle e-books, and games purchased through the Sony PlayStation store. The second approach has almost always been paired with the first. For digital music, however, it now constitutes the sole means of preventing resale; DRM no longer inhibits the resale of MP3s or other music file types, but consumers who engage in this practice become liable to litigation. The third approach is the newest and, judging by recent changes to the structures of sell-through services, also the approach most preferred by media companies and service providers. In it, the file or files necessary to use (in the narrow sense) the purchased media good are delivered to devices in such a way that the files themselves are inaccessible to the purchaser. Instead of consumers being able to manage the files, media goods are instead downloaded through auto-mated processes built into apps and programs, which then hide and/or incorporate the files within the programs' own file structures, effectively rendering the files impossible for most consumers to locate and move. This is how nearly all media files are now delivered to tablets, mobile phones, e-readers, and entertainment console boxes; hidden files are also associated with streaming-based sell-through services on PCs (most notably, Amazon Instant Player and iTunes Match).

The result of these practices has been the complete disabling of selling as a mode of consumer-good interaction for digital media goods and the consequent failure of secondary markets for digital media goods to develop. This ostensibly represents a victory for media companies, who now find themselves in almost complete control of how their products are (legally) circulated and the price at which they are sold (or rented). Such control comes at the expense of consum-ers, who find themselves deprived of both a kind of use they have traditionally enjoyed and the communal processes of value ascription to which it gives rise; but such control also comes at the expense of media companies themselves, who, by disabling secondary sales, have introduced new challenges for themselves in deriving the most profit possible from the sale of their products.

First, because this new form of media good cannot be resold or transferred, it involves greater costs to consumers than otherwise identical goods that can be; as a result, the price that has been established for the latter cannot serve companies as a valid guide for establishing the price of the former.[25] Indeed, evidence sug-gests that the price for digital media goods, currently mirroring or exceeding the price for physical media goods, has been set too high.[26] In a competitive market, the correct price would be determined by on-the-ground "experiments" in pric-ing that measure, through sales, the relationship between price and demand. In a physical market for DVDs, for instance, a retailer will respond to disappointing sales numbers for a specific release by lowering the price; in this way, consumers influence prices by buying or refraining from buying preexisting supplies of products. The market for digital media goods, however, does not function as a typical competitive market. Partly due to the delicate and always tenuous nature of publisher-distributor partnerships in the electronic sell-through market, the different retailers/services compete on service but—with very few exceptions—never on price. Unlike in physical retail markets, in which retailers (protected, like secondary sellers, by First Sale) can set prices as high or as low as they like, in digital markets, consumer sale prices for digital media goods are frequently set through negotiation between producers and retailers.[27] The unique inventory model for digital media goods (they exist as bytes that are reproduced upon sale) has also freed retailers from the costs associated with retaining inventory, thus allowing them much greater "bargaining power" when responding to consumer demand than they have with physical media goods. As a result of both of these factors, pricing for such digital goods as films, television shows, and—until recently—music has shown little variability across retailers.[28]

Second, by disabling resale, media companies have deprived themselves of pricing data produced by secondary markets. Without them, collectors have no easy way—other than simply buying or refraining from buying goods at the price set by the media company (a weak instrument, given the lack of costs associated with holding digital inventory)—of participating in the determination of price for digital media goods. The correct price, meaning the price that most closely reflects the monetary value an average consumer would assign to the product, must be wholly determined by media companies themselves.[29] Though this means greater power for publishers and retailers, it also, paradoxically, makes it more difficult for companies to determine what these prices should be.

Whether connected viewing will continue to be constructed in such a way as to foreclose selling on the part of consumers is currently uncertain. Although media companies seem happy with the current construction, some may eventually find that the decreased demand for ownership (or the decreased price needed to sustain demand) resulting from the inhibition of secondary sales is not worth the increased control over pricing and circulation it has provided them. Some gaming companies, such as Wizards of the Coast and Blizzard, have already enabled resale of some digital gaming products in order to increase demand and social participation in markets. With *Diablo III,* Blizzard has even demonstrated how selling can be integrated into the media service itself (in physical markets, selling relies on intermediaries such as eBay and Amazon), thus allowing a service provider to maintain traditional DRM schemes while also deriving revenue through the imposition of a fee from the secondary sales. Both of these companies also employ a sales model that results in limited supply: Blizzard through limited "production runs," Wizards of the Coast through limited windows of sale. Such practices have effectively encouraged collecting by consumers of these goods and have enabled them to participate, through secondary markets for these goods, in social processes of valuation otherwise only available to collectors of physical goods.

Even if media companies remain happy with the current system of restricting resale, however, the law, as it becomes clarified within different nations and trading regions, may ultimately force them to enable selling as a mode of use. Currently, the legal code is unclear on whether the First Sale Doctrine applies to digital goods.[30] The Copyright Act of 1976 includes an exception for software (though not video games) that excludes it from First Sale.[31] Whether digital media goods can in fact legally be defined as software is an open question, but the use of user licenses as conditions of sale would seem to allow media companies and digital distributors to make such a case. So far, however, media companies have not needed to, as court cases regarding sale or transfer have instead revolved around the legality of copying—without which a digital media good cannot be transferred, but which is currently illegal under the Digital Millennium Copyright Act. Most recently, ReDigi, a company and service allowing consumers to "legally" sell their iTunes music purchases, has been sued by EMI for the former's reliance on copying to complete the sale.[32] The recent shift by media companies to temporary and hidden files accessible only through programs may, however, change the terms of the legal debate by shifting the question away from the copying of digital goods to the transferability of licenses.

Conclusion

What is a digital media good, and what can be done with it? Though often described by companies, journalists, and even some scholars as a new format or means of delivery for otherwise familiar media "objects," this chapter suggests that digital media goods (at least in their current form) are better approached as a new kind of consumer good altogether. Whereas previous shifts in format (the record to the cassette tape, the VHS tape to the DVD) preserved broad modes of use associated with collecting—and, in some cases, even introduced new ones—the shift to connected viewing represents a radical reworking of what use is and how it can be performed by consumers. As the above examinations of organizing and selling demonstrate, such reworking restricts or disables broad forms of use, leaving little for consumers to do with purchased digital media goods besides use them in the narrow sense. Such purchased goods are functionally identical to digital media goods accessed through subscription or rental services, such as Netflix, Spotify, and Amazon Prime. Able only to watch their digital films, listen to their digital music, and read their digital books, consumers are thus deprived of the modes of consumer-good interaction that have traditionally constituted collecting. Indeed, because the different forms of value derived by consumers from these practices have served as the very raison d'être for collecting, connected viewing would seem to rule out collecting as a meaningful practice entirely.

There is nothing, however, about the "nature" of connected viewing that guarantees this state of affairs. As I have tried to demonstrate in the analyses above, the digital media good's unique form of objectivity, far from being natural, is a construction, produced and supported (and sometimes challenged) by a variety of actors, including media companies, hardware companies, digital distributors, legislatures, courts of law, and consumers themselves. These different agents possess different levels of power, with the least power currently belonging to consumers.[33] Connected viewing currently precludes traditional forms of collecting only because the most powerful agents—media companies and digital distributors—have constructed it to do so. In some cases, such as the digital media good's lack of transferability, this construction is the result of deliberate efforts on the part of these agents to maintain control of the good and ensure that they are able to profit from its sale. In other cases, such as the disabling of organizing and searching, the construction may be a side effect of other industrial imperatives or even, to some extent, the result of neglect or ignorance. Whatever the case, the current construction of connected viewing is neither static nor binding, but rather a dynamic process, constantly subject to changes in concentrations of power, legal regimes, technology, social norms, and individual values. For the immediate future, however, connected viewing services seem certain to increasingly rule out or disable traditional forms of media collecting.

Notes

1. See Jeffrey Ulin, *The Business of Media Distribution: Monetizing Film, TV and Video Content in an Online World* (New York: Focal Press, 2010), 160–1.
2. See, for example, Frederick Baekeland, "Psychological Aspects of Art Collecting," in *Interpreting Objects and Collections,* ed. Susan M. Pearce (New York: Routledge, 1994), 205–19; and Ruth Formanek, "Why They Collect: Collectors Reveal Their Motivations," in *Interpreting Objects and Collections,* ed. Susan M. Pearce (New York: Routledge, 1994), 327–35.
3. See, for example, Paul McDonald, *Video and DVD Industries* (London: British Film Institute, 2007), 69–70.
4. The paradigmatic example of this approach is Russell Belk, *Collecting in a Consumer Society* (New York: Routledge, 1995).
5. Susan Pearce's work, though sometimes borrowing questions and methods from social science, provides a good example of this approach to collecting. See Pearce, *On Collecting: An Investigation into Collecting in the European Tradition* (New York: Routledge, 1995).
6. Brenda Danet and Tamar Katriel, "No Two Alike: Play and Aesthetics in Collecting," in *Interpreting Objects and Collections,* ed. Susan M. Pearce (New York: Routledge, 1994), 225.
7. Susan M. Pearce, "Collecting Reconsidered," in *Interpreting Objects and Collections,* ed. Susan M. Pearce (New York: Routledge, 1994), 193–204.
8. See, for example, John Windsor, "Identity Parades," in *The Cultures of Collecting,* eds. John Elsner and Roger Cardinal (London: Reaktion Books, 1997), 49–67.
9. Belk, *Collecting in a Consumer Society,* 67.
10. Paul van der Grijp, *Passion and Profit: Towards an Anthropology of Collecting* (Berlin: Lit Verlag, 2006), 8.
11. Susan Stewart, *On Longing: Narratives of the Miniature, the Gigantic, the Souvenir, the Collection* (Durham, NC: Duke University Press, 1993), 151.
12. Danet and Katriel, "No Two Alike," 225.
13. Jeremy Rifkin, *The Age of Access: The New Culture of Hypercapitalism, Where All of Life Is a Paid-For Experience* (New York: Penguin, 2000), 137–67. For a detailed delineation

between material goods and experiences, see B. Joseph Pine II and James H. Gilmore, *The Experience Economy: Work in Theater & Every Business a Stage,* updated edition (Boston: Harvard Business Review Press, 2011), 1–21.

14. See, for example, Colin Campbell, *The Romantic Ethic and the Spirit of Modern Consumerism* (London: Blackwell, 1987); Morris Holbrook, "What Is Consumer Research?" *Journal of Consumer Research* 14 (1987): 128–32; and Jacob Jacoby, "Consumer Research: A State of the Art Review," *Journal of Marketing* 42 (1978): 87–96.

15. Pearce, *On Collecting,* 186.

16. Tony Gill, "Metadata and the Web," in *Introduction to Metadata,* 2nd. edition, ed. Murtha Baca (Los Angeles: Getty Research Institute, 2008), 22.

17. For more on these possibilities, see Melanie Feinberg, "Organization as Expression: Classification as Digital Media," in *Digital Media: Technological and Social Challenges of the Interactive World,* eds. Megan Winget and William Aspray (Toronto: Scarecrow Press, 2011), 115–33.

18. For a detailed description of the UltraViolet service, see Jim Taylor, UltraViolet Demystified, http://uvdemystified.com. For an example of the confusion it has caused consumers, see Andre Yoskowitz, "Studio's 'Ultraviolet' Getting a Bad Rap" [sic], *AfterDawn,* October 21, 2011, http://www.afterdawn.com/news/article.cfm/2011/10/21/ultraviolet_getting_a_bad_rap.

19. See Belk, *Collecting,* 67; Baekeland, "Psychological Aspects," 205; and Roy Shuker, *Wax Trash and Vinyl Treasures: Record Collecting as a Social Practice* (Burlington, VT: Ashgate, 2010), 126–8.

20. For an overview of disposition as a mode of consumption, see Jacob Jacoby, Carol Berning, and Thomas Dietvorst, "What About Disposition?," *Journal of Marketing* 41 (1977): 22–8.

21. Friedrich Hayek, *Individualism and Economic Order* (London: University of Chicago Press, 1948), 86–8.

22. See Frederick Wasser, *Veni, Vidi, Video: The Hollywood Empire and the VCR* (Austin, TX: University of Texas Press, 2001), 102. For this particular section of the act, see 17 U.S.C. §109(a) (1976).

23. See Barbara Simons, "The Copyright Wars—A Computer Scientist's View of Copyright in the U.S.," in *Digital Rights Management: Technological, Economic, Legal and Political Aspects,* eds. Eberhad Becker et al. (Berlin: Springer, 2003), 387.

24. See McDonald, *Video and DVD,* 114–19; Wasser, *Veni,* 101–3, 110–16.

25. See Richard McKenzie, *Digital Economics: How Information Technology Has Transformed Business Thinking* (London: Praeger, 2003), 252–5. Another cost not mentioned by McKenzie is the inability to liquidate the good—that is, translate it into exchangeable capital. Inability to liquidate increases the risks associated with purchase (a consumer is "stuck with it") and prevents the purchased good from functioning as an investment.

26. See both Sharon Strover's and Paul McDonald's chapters in this volume.

27. For an example of one such negotiation, see Eliot Van Buskirk, "Negotiations Leak: Could Variable iTunes Pricing Be on the Table?," *Wired,* May 19, 2008, http://www.wired.com/listening_post/2008/05/apple-squares-o/. Some of these arrangements on price may eventually be seen to constitute price fixing, but for now the Justice Department has shown little interest in digital pricing models outside the e-book market. See Sara Forden, "U.S. Sues Apple for eBook Pricing as Three Firms Settle," *Bloomberg,* April 17, 2012, http://www.bloomberg.com/news/2012-04-17/u-s-sues-apple-for-ebook-pricing-as-three-firms-settle.html.

28. Since 2011, Amazon has been offering lower prices than other retailers for digital music, which the company now treats as a loss leader. The relaxation of uniform pricing for music likely reflects the decreased importance of EST markets in music publishers' business models.

29. More precisely said, the "correct price" for media companies (or any company) is the price at which the number of sales generated results in the highest revenue after the

subtraction of costs. This price need not match the average consumer's own valuation; for goods aimed at mass markets, however, the two usually converge.

30. For more on this question, see Nakimuli Davis, "Reselling Digital Music: Is There a Digital First Sale Doctrine?," *Loyola of Los Angeles Entertainment Law Review* 363 (2009), http://digitalcommons.lmu.edu/elr/vol29/iss3/2; and Joseph Gratz, "Digital Book Distribution: The End of the First-Sale Doctrine?," *Landslide* 3 (2011), http://www.americanbar.org/content/dam/aba/publications/landslide/landslide_june_2011/gratz_landslide_mayjune_2011.authcheckdam.pdf.

31. 17 U.S.C. §109(b) (1976).

32. For more information of the legal issues raised by ReDigi, see Jessica Leber, "A Startup Asks: Why Can't You Resell Old Digital Songs?," *MIT Technology Review*, August 15, 2012, http://www.technologyreview.com/news/428792/a-startup-asks-why-cant-you-resell-old-digital-songs/. It is also worth noting that ReDigi sets by itself the prices of used goods and so does not constitute by itself a secondary market in the full sense.

33. Piracy is usually viewed by scholars as an important demonstration of consumer value, but I remain unconvinced that piracy, as an institution, is in any way a "grass-roots" or bottom-up construction, reflecting the values of individual consumers. Since Napster, the major pirating services have been for-profit enterprises started by entrepreneurs (and often backed by venture capitalists).

References

Baekeland, Frederick. "Psychological Aspects of Art Collecting." In *Interpreting Objects and Collections,* edited by Susan M. Pearce, 205–19. New York: Routledge, 1994.

Belk, Russell. *Collecting in a Consumer Society.* New York: Routledge, 1995.

Campbell, Colin. *The Romantic Ethic and the Spirit of Modern Consumerism.* London: Blackwell, 1987.

"Copyright Law of the United States and Related Laws Contained in Title 17 of the United States Code." Title 17 *U.S. Code.* 2011 ed. http://www.copyright.gov/title17/.

Danet, Brenda, and Tamar Katriel. "No Two Alike: Play and Aesthetics in Collecting." In *Interpreting Objects and Collections,* edited by Susan M. Pearce, 220–39. New York: Routledge, 1994.

Davis, Nakimuli. "Reselling Digital Music: Is There a Digital First Sale Doctrine?" *Loyola of Los Angeles Entertainment Law Review* 363 (2009). http://digitalcommons.lmu.edu/elr/vol29/iss3/2.

Feinberg, Melanie. "Organization as Expression: Classification as Digital Media." In *Digital Media: Technological and Social Challenges of the Interactive World,* edited by Megan Winget and William Aspray, 115–33. Toronto: Scarecrow Press, 2011.

Forden, Sara. "U.S. Sues Apple for eBook Pricing as Three Firms Settle." *Bloomberg,* April 17, 2012. http://www.bloomberg.com/news/2012-04-17/u-s-sues-apple-for-ebook-pricing-as-three-firms-settle.html.

Formanek, Ruth. "Why They Collect: Collectors Reveal Their Motivations." In *Interpreting Objects and Collections,* edited by Susan M. Pearce, 327–35. New York: Routledge, 1994.

Gill, Tony. "Metadata and the Web." In *Introduction to Metadata,* 2nd ed., edited by Murtha Baca, 20–37. Los Angeles: Getty Research Institute, 2008.

Gratz, Joseph. "Digital Book Distribution: The End of the First-Sale Doctrine?" *Landslide* 3 (2011). http://www.americanbar.org/content/dam/aba/publications/landslide/landslide_june_2011/gratz_landslide_mayjune_2011.authcheckdam.pdf.

Hayek, Friederich. *Individualism and Economic Order.* London: University of Chicago Press, 1948.

Holbrook, Morris. "What Is Consumer Research?" *Journal of Consumer Research* 14 (1987): 128–32.

Jacoby, Jacob. "Consumer Research: A State of the Art Review." *Journal of Marketing* 42 (1978): 87–96.

Jacoby, Jacob, Carol Berning, and Thomas Dietvorst. "What About Disposition?" *Journal of Marketing* 41 (1977): 22–8.

Leber, Jessica. "A Startup Asks: Why Can't You Resell Old Digital Songs?" *MIT Technology Review,* August 15, 2012. http://www.technologyreview.com/news/428792/a-startup-asks-why-cant-you-resell-old-digital-songs/.

McDonald, Paul. *Video and DVD Industries.* London: British Film Institute, 2007.

McKenzie, Richard. *Digital Economics: How Information Technology Has Transformed Business Thinking.* London: Praeger, 2003.

Pearce, Susan M. "Collecting Reconsidered." In *Interpreting Objects and Collections,* edited by Susan M. Pearce, 193–204. New York: Routledge, 1994.

Pearce, Susan M. *On Collecting: An Investigation into Collecting in the European Tradition.* New York: Routledge, 1995.

Pine, B. Joseph, II, and James Gilmore. *The Experience Economy.* Updated ed. Boston: Harvard Business Review Press, 2011.

Rifkin, Jeremy. *The Age of Access: The New Culture of Hypercapitalism, Where All of Life Is a Paid-For Experience.* New York: Penguin, 2000.

Shuker, Roy. *Wax Trash and Vinyl Treasures: Record Collecting as a Social Practice.* Burlington, VT: Ashgate, 2010.

Simons, Barbara. "The Copyright Wars—A Computer Scientist's View of Copyright in the U.S." In *Digital Rights Management: Technological, Economic, Legal and Political Aspects,* edited by Eberhad Becker, Willms Buhse, Dick Günnewig, and Niels Rump, 383–404. Berlin: Springer, 2003.

Stewart, Susan. *On Longing: Narratives of the Miniature, the Gigantic, the Souvenir, the Collection.* Durham, NC: Duke University Press, 1993.

Taylor, Jim. *UltraViolet Demystified.* October 2, 2013. http://uvdemystified.com.

Ulin, Jeffrey. *The Business of Media Distribution: Monetizing Film, TV and Video Content in an Online World.* New York: Focal Press, 2010.

van Buskirk, Eliot. "Negotiations Leak: Could Variable iTunes Pricing Be on the Table?" *Listening Post* (blog). *Wired,* May 19, 2008. http://www.wired.com/listening_post/2008/05/apple-squares-o/.

van der Grijp, Paul. *Passion and Profit: Towards an Anthropology of Collecting.* Berlin: LitVerlag, 2006.

Wasser, Frederick. *Veni, Vidi, Video: The Hollywood Empire and the VCR.* Austin, TX: University of Texas Press, 2001.

Windsor, John. "Identity Parades." In *The Cultures of Collecting,* edited by John Elsner and Roger Cardinal, 49–67. London: Reaktion Books, 1997.

Yoskowitz, Andre. "Studios' 'Ultraviolet' Getting a Bad Rap." *AfterDawn* News, October 21, 2011. http://www.afterdawn.com/news/article.cfm/2011/10/21/ultraviolet_getting_a_bad_rap.

PART II
TECHNOLOGY AND PLATFORMS

5

BEYOND PIRACY

Understanding Digital Markets[1]

Patrick Vonderau

> I have some desired futures that I would like to predict so persuasively that
> they will come to pass. I have been doing so for years and can even point to
> some success in this regard.
>
> John Perry Barlow

I.

In October 2009, the 40th Anniversary of the Internet Conference was held at the
University of California, Los Angeles's Henry Samueli School of Engineering and
Applied Science, the "birthplace of the Internet."[2] As one of the featured speak-
ers, Warner Bros. Digital Distribution president Thomas Gewecke presented a talk
about how the Internet was transforming the media industries. In a context that
was celebrating the Internet as a technology connecting anyone from any location
at any time with any device, Gewecke cautiously avoided characterizing change as
merely disrupting established industry routines. After opening his talk with a bow
to the attending John Perry Barlow, cofounder of the Electronic Frontier Foundation, and to The WELL, a pioneering online community for which Barlow had
served as a board member, Gewecke began outlining the contours of what he
saw as a generation-long transition that, in his view, would entail a partial transformation of media companies into "software businesses," and the development
of business models able to put the familiar slogan of 1990s cyberlibertarianism
("Information wants to be free!") into actual working practice.[3] His talk culmi-
nated in a description of connected viewing—"one of the biggest changes" that
he saw as "going to occur; it's occurring right now":

> And that is that the American living room is going to go from being com-
> pletely un-networked to being completely networked. You have a PS3; you

have an Xbox; you have a Wii—and in the future, if you buy a new television, it will be an IP television. If you buy a new Blu-ray player, it will be a
connected Blu-ray player; and you may have an Apple TV or any number
of other devices; they are custom for your video experience, and they all
have either an Ethernet port or Wi-Fi radio in them. And your television-
viewing experience is going to be connected. And that is a fundamental
revolutionary change, and that is going to happen here and around the
world. . . . This is something we did in December with *The Dark Knight*.
We used the Blu-ray technology and the Connected Disc technology to
let thousands of people join a live screening with director Chris Nolan.
They watched the movie with him, they asked him questions, he answered
the questions as the movie went on. . . . One person asked him to convey a
proposal of marriage, which was accepted. We think it is the first ever, Blu-
ray, BD-Live-mediated marriage proposal, our record (*laughter*)—and this is
very much in its infancy, but connected television is a simple idea that will
change what the Internet means for media and for video in particular.[4]

There certainly is an air of paradox surrounding this address—as in the play of
double temporalities, for instance, that constitutes the account of a present future,
a future performed in today's living rooms and yet not fully contained in the
here and now; and in the form of a major Hollywood studio appearing to bow
down to one of the most ardent challengers of the studios' long-held copyright
doctrines. Barlow, apart from being involved with the Electronic Frontier Foundation and The WELL, was widely known as a political activist rallying precisely
against those "aging industries run by aging men," as he then put it in a dispute
with Motion Picture Association of America (MPAA) president Dan Glickman.
Following a raid against nonauthorized Swedish file-sharing website The Pirate
Bay in 2006, Barlow took an explicit stance in favor of those Swedish "17-year-
olds who have turned themselves into electronic Hezbollah because they resent
the content industry for its proprietary practices"—an attitude Gewecke hardly
would have been unaware of.[5]

Even closer to the heart of the paradox, however, appears Gewecke's way of
identifying Barlow's "desired futures" with a living room scenario wrapped entirely
into branded consumer technologies and digital rights management schemes. On
the one hand, Gewecke's "connected viewing" scenario may have evoked Nor-
bert Wiener's cybernetics, the countercultural rhetorics Stewart Brand and the
Whole Earth network have employed since the late 1960s, or even the idea of
a "metaverse," a virtual-reality-based Internet as featured in Neal Stephenson's
science-fiction best seller, *Snow Crash*.[6] At the same time, there hardly could have
been a more explicit counterdraft to the idea of cyberspace than this executive
planning scenario centered around a conventional domestic viewer-consumer
model of television entertainment. Gewecke's talk seemed to turn cyberspace
into a legally safeguarded, walled-garden ecosystem that would exclude deviant

and "unnetworked" forms of use; his talk also signaled a larger, long-coming war on computation and the future of the general purpose computer, a war against which hackers, civil rights activists, and artists have warned for almost a decade.[7]

It thus could be tempting to dismiss this corporate vision of connected viewing as just another instance of industrial self-disclosure that would ultimately aim at disciplining both new technologies and their users. As this chapter will argue, however, such a view would reflect a fundamental misunderstanding of technological visions and of the underlying dynamics marking those emergent digital markets from which they derive. To be sure, Gewecke's argument entailed a form of corporate spin that rendered complex narratives deceptively simple. Based on a mild version of technological determinism, his talk pictured media devices as a force coming from outside of the social, a force capable of transcending history, naturally appealing and irreversibly new. In this Warner Bros. prediction, connected viewing was to enable alternate forms of connectivity while downplaying existing ones—as much as the fact that audiences had divided their attention between television, friends, news feeds, and competing entertainment forms ever since broadcasting technologies became available for private use.

And yet this vision of connected viewing was nothing but *productive*. The history of information technology is ripe with visions set in motion in order to shape the future—just be reminded of "ubicomp" or the "information superhighway"—and connected viewing formed no exception. As other technological visions, it helped to mobilize the future in real time to marshal resources, coordinate activities, and manage uncertainty.[8] Following the 2008 foundation of the Digital Entertainment Content Ecosystem, a consortium developing standards for a digital rights authentication and licensing service, today known as UltraViolet, was created. Just one week after Disney had presented a rival solution, Keychest, Gewecke employed the connected viewing scenario as an organizational instrument to muster allies across the board.[9] Connected viewing thus surfaced as part of a larger attempt to articulate and execute a program designed to cope with the "economy of ideas" John Perry Barlow and others had earlier predicted to emerge.[10]

Entering into a situation where Barlow and a large number of faithful allies had already teamed up not so much as direct adversaries, but rather as competitors in performing expectations about the future, the idea of a "connected viewing experience" was instrumental in organizing a heterogeneous set of associates for building mutually binding agendas—among them, investors, users, lobbyists, even scholars, but also file formats, platforms, apps, protocols, or servicing standards. Rather than being paradoxical, then, the launch of connected viewing related to an industrial strategy and to a dilemma contained, if not in America's living rooms itself, then in the metaphors and technological visions describing their ongoing transformation. As is often the case with innovations, connected viewing served as a screen onto which an existing but denied social conflict could be projected—a conflict hidden in another, even more deeply embedded and ultimately conventional metaphor: that of the "market."

This chapter investigates the "completely networked living room" as a site that is both metaphorical and material, a site for imagining technologies as much as for engaging them. The aim of this investigation is to understand the markets for premium Hollywood content after the so-called turn to the digital. Given that connected viewing already is an old scenario by the Internet's rate of change, we need to shift the analytic angle from looking *into* the future to looking *at* the future, or how the future has been managed and engaged with at a given point of time.[11] As a past future, connected viewing teaches us how metaphors employed in launching a set of digital technologies have contributed to the altering of social practices. Yet technologies also depend on material and social practices to take shape, so that tracing the history of technological visions becomes equally instructive about the ways corporate programs (or consumer ideals, for that matter) are—to borrow from Andrew Pickering—constantly "mangled in practice"; that is, transformed and delineated in a dialectic of resistance and accommodation.[12] Taking my cue from recent writings in economic sociology and infrastructure studies,[13] I am especially interested in the conflict zones and dark borderlands shaping current sites of exchange, and in the tactics of subversion frequently characterizing market practices. The premise of this chapter is that connected viewing is not so much an issue of digital distribution per se, but rather a question of *interoperability*. Engaging with media in a multiplatform, socially networked digital environment, as envisioned by Gewecke, requires both connections between people, organizations, and devices, and an infrastructure on which such connections can be built up and maintained. Connectivity thus presumes that the technical, economical, legal, or social systems being connected indeed are able to interoperate. As I am going to argue, however, understanding digital markets is all about that which inevitably prevents such connectivity. Based on a yearlong research project studying what from the outset would appear as being the ultimate nemeses of any Hollywood executive, "Swedish pirates,"[14] this chapter combines extensive multisited fieldwork with a theoretical reconsideration of what it means to engage in the digital market.[15]

II.

What's in a market? How to define markets remains a key question of any media industries research. Yet there seems to be little consistency in how the notion of the market has been used in that research. Markets are variously described as collections of viewers or media artifacts, devices per household, playdates per territory, geographical regions, social networks, institutions, as techniques for managing demand, or as the sum total of transactions in a given time and space. While this conceptual messiness points to a general trait of markets as objects of knowledge—often identified by their constitutive elusiveness or lack of "object-ivity"[16]—media markets still come attributed with at least a few principle characteristics. To begin with, we may discern a difference—although only a slight one—between industrial and economical views on those markets. Markets may feature as sectors, windows, or cycles, for instance, when media industries need to legitimate or strategize their operations, or when media industry scholars attend to explain them. Economics, on the other hand, is focused on modeling those operations, abstracting the relationship between factors such as individual, preference, or choice into the idea(l) of a working price mechanism. The distinction between the industrial and the economical view is only a slight one, however, because in both views, the "market" is conjured up in terms of a metaphor designating a generic notion of exchange.

In this perspective, media markets form an idealized setting or environment, an "everywhere and nowhere"[17] whose main purpose is to measure the generation of value on a scale from new to old. This certainly is not to downplay the considerable development in economic thought from neoclassic price theory to what recently, in an attempt to brand Mark Granovetter's, Harrison White's, or Rafael Ramírez's earlier work into an economic model as new as the Internet itself, has been termed "social network markets."[18] Still, in economic terms the market remains a model of social order through which the consumer is defined, implying inequalities or "imperfections" in the ways information (such as a film) is strategically distributed in order to keep that information new (and valuable) as long as possible. As an economic metaphor, then, a market is equal to a "visible sphere of regulated and statistically enumerated media enterprise"[19] characterized by a key dynamic between new and old, with value diminishing according to time.[20]

The industrial view on the market described above relates well to such a conventional economic conception, as it helps to explain how value is generated, and lost, while content travels through the "channels" of communication or distribution "pipelines." For instance, when speaking of the Internet, we might refer to the ways online video distribution organizes information through a particular configuration of content, services, service providers, transportation networks, and consumer media ecosystems. Table 5.1 presents a table that, though certainly not exhaustive, may suffice to illustrate the complex ways in which established media businesses engage with players from adjacent and emerging industry sectors in the delivery of online video.

However rudimentary such a table remains, it still gives some first insight into what Gewecke saw as a slow transformation of media industries into "software businesses." Without subscribing to a teleological model of economic history, we may roughly distinguish three dominant paradigms that have been operational in the emergence of the Hollywood system so far: the paradigm of a cinema industry; that of a copyright industry; and, again, the partial turn into a software business.[21] In Hollywood's classic era, ownership of real estate (and talent) formed the economic grounds on which the motion picture business could thrive. Control over markets was based on control over the distribution to studio-owned exhibition venues, with the latter serving as sites to define consumption in terms of exclusionary, temporary access to an ephemeral good. Following the Paramount decree

TABLE 5.1   Charting Online Video Distribution

Item	*Variables*
Content	Is produced and owned, licensed, and aggregated; thus includes variables such as: *types of content* (new movie releases/library titles, promotional videos, user-generated content, etc.), as well as *IP owners, distributors* (iTunes, BSkyB, etc.), and *content aggregators* (Gravity Ventures, Under the Milky Way).
Services	Include a given *type of service* (video-on-demand, catch-up TV, etc.), a *marketing approach* (pay-per-view, subscription service, advertising based, etc.), a *mode of consumption* (streamed viewing, temporary download, purchase to own), and a *release window* or *market reach* (national or supranational availability, geoblocking, etc.).
Service providers	Include *Internet service providers, platform providers* (business-to-business online video management and publishing companies; or delivery providers such as Brightcove, Kaltura, or Ooyala), and *servicing platforms* (online video providers or video-hosting providers such as maxdome, Netflix, MyVideo, etc.).
Transportation networks[1]	Through which online video services are provided, including: (a) *open networks*—the Internet, or what is often called "Internet TV" or "web for video": online video in networks that are either *infrastructure based*, i.e., via a client server and a content delivery network such as Akamai or Limelight; or *noninfrastructure based*, i.e., delivered via peer-to-peer architectures; both relying, in turn, on Internet service providers; (b) and *closed networks* (such as in Internet protocol television, i.e., managed IP traffic).
Consumer media ecosystems	Include *hardware/software manufacturers* (Apple, Sony, Microsoft), *consumer devices/viewing platforms* (television sets, Apple TV, iPad, Xbox, etc.), modes of connections between devices (wireless to cell phone, Ethernet to TV, via set-top box, direct to computer), and analogue/digital consumption environments (interfaces, databases, hyperlinks, protocols).

[1] Due to the ongoing convergence of industries, devices, networks, and services, it does not make much sense to differentiate between cable, satellite, and telecommunication-based infrastructures. See Sanjoy Paul, *Digital Video Distribution in Broadband, Television, Mobile and Converged Networks: Trends, Challenges and Solutions* (Chichester: Wiley, 2011), 3–10. It neither seems advisable to adopt descriptive terms used in nation-specific legislative frameworks, such as the Federal Communications Commission's definition of "multichannel video programming distributors," as European countries do not have a comparable cable history. Cf. Marvin Ammori, "Copyright's Latest Communication Policy: Content-Lock-Out and Compulsory Licensing for Internet Television," *CommLaw Conspectus* 18 (2010), passim.

in 1948, this business model gradually shifted into one based on copyright; control over markets now consisted of the production of copyright-protected content, and in the licensing of such content to players in and outside the traditional motion picture industry—from television networks to toy manufacturers. Although these first two approaches are far from obsolete today, it's hard to overlook the advent of the third paradigm, which, beginning around the mid-1990s, continued to transform, and expand, the entertainment business. With media turning into code, businesses now aimed at control over markets in terms of control in managing IP across platforms, and ultimately, in controlling those platforms, the Internet and the very idea of computing. In short, Hollywood's expansion as an industrial system went along with problem-solving strategies relating to what market control would entail in terms of control over distribution, copyright—and over interoperability (i.e., over the flow of data, the interconnection of devices, and the connection between people and institutions facilitated by both).[22]

Table 5.1 illustrates how this development plays out in the connected viewing scenario. The completely networked living room appears merely as the "front end" to a media infrastructure deeply entangled in making content flow through a pipeline with pipes that differ in terms of ownership, technology, and function. This often leads to conflicts among the various industries involved, thus delaying or complicating access to information and obscuring online video's value proposition.[23] Consider, for instance, how searching for a European film in the iTunes Store activates a library preselected by Under the Milky Way, iTunes's key video-on-demand (VOD) movie aggregator for Europe, an intermediary whose approach to distributive gatekeeping tactics has changed the amount, variety, and accessibility of entertainment program content.[24] In other words, the living room is far from having turned into a place where different technological, social, or legal systems flawlessly interoperate. Rather, it has turned into a site of market struggle over the loss of what once worked as rights-based control over exclusivity, repeat consumption, variable timing, and price points.[25]

Nowhere does this becomes as obvious as when turning to Sweden, the very market invoked in John Perry Barlow's famous public rejection of a "rough industry" in pursuit of "smart kids," or what later became a meme known as the Great Piracy Debate.[26] Despite the country's just over 9.5 million inhabitants, geographically peripheral location, and comparatively small home entertainment market, Sweden is a territory often brought up in debates over the future of monetizing online video. This is because of the country's unique digital infrastructure.[27] To date, Sweden has one of the highest fixed broadband penetrations in Europe (83 percent of all households/enterprises, as of 2011) and is one of the fastest European (if not global) broadband nations, with 49 percent of all households and enterprises having access to a minimum of 100 megabits-per-second (Mbps) downstream broadband connections, a minimum average speed of 22.1 Mbps across the whole country, and an increasing, nationwide adoption of true (fibre) broadband networks. In terms of the networked living room scenario, Sweden appears as an almost-ideal "small world,"[28] with viewing ecology marked by a limited number of ties among infrastructure, platforms, and content. In fact, while key infrastructure remains in Swedish hands—with most fixed broadband subscriptions provided by local suppliers Telia or Com Hem—75.7 percent of all regularly watched online content is from the United States, an amount dominated by recently released American television series (53.2 percent). Following the establishment of SF Anytime in 2002, Sweden even became one of Europe's first countries to introduce transactional online VOD services, backed by a contract signed with Warner Bros. Television International Distribution in 2004, one of the very first deals closed by a US major in Europe in the VOD field. The country thus also stands out in the European context, which remains far from constituting a digital single market, as promoted by the European Commission since 2009, and which otherwise provides a disruptive rather than a sustaining environment for the Hollywood oligopoly's distribution strategies. European access to online video remains characterized by both an overprovision of online services (with 696 legal VOD platforms available already back in 2008)[29] and market fragmentation, the latter the result of complex territorial copyright licensing processes; the low degree of European media companies' integration, cultural, and linguistic differences; and varying forms of government regulation.

Given Sweden's comparatively strong digital infrastructure and its well-organized "geography of innovation,"[30] it is hardly coincidental that the country has emerged as a paradigmatic case against which to judge the future of digital distribution. What comes as more of a surprise, however, is that Sweden has turned into a paradigmatic case precisely by failing to fulfill expectations regarding the monetization of online video. Despite its obvious potential of becoming a cyberlibertarian information economy or, alternatively, a closed and predictable walled-garden ecosystem, Sweden has not contributed much to the realization of any corporate technological vision. Surveys and aggregated market data for 2011 show, for instance, that the adoption of connected devices such as connected TVs, game consoles, hybrid/over-the-top set-top boxes, or Blu-ray players remains low when compared to France, Germany, or the UK.[31] At the same time, Swedish viewers face increasing competition from existing electronic sell-through platforms such as SF Anytime, film2home, Voddler, Viaplay, or Headweb, and more recently introduced services such as Filmnet (C MORE), Netflix, HBO Nordic, or the iTunes Store. However, while packaged home video revenues (i.e., those of DVD and Blu-ray sell-through and rental) continued to fall (by 14 percent in 2011), digital revenues did not compensate for this loss. In fact, as of July 2012, most Swedes report "never" using services such as iTunes (76.3 percent), Viaplay (79 percent), Headweb (85.1 percent), film2home (88 percent), or Netflix (90.1 percent).[32] Although different in terms of its business models, which include monthly subscription streaming (Filmnet, Netflix, HBO Nordic, Viaplay) as much as rental (Voddler, SF Anytime, iTunes) and retail options (iTunes), online viewing is primarily driven by the consumption of catch-up TV shows. Overall, video paid for and watched on the web accounted for *just over 1 percent* in total home video revenues in 2011.[33]

Premised on continuous demand for premium Hollywood content and a sustaining digital infrastructure, the default explanation for this situation in scholarship, trade reporting, and industry consultation usually is, again, "Swedish piracy," or more precisely, peer-to-peer-based file sharing via nonauthorized third-party-servicing platforms such as The Pirate Bay. Famously established by Gottfrid Svartholm Warg, Fredrik Neij, and Peter Sunde in Sweden in 2003, and famously raided by Swedish police on supposed request of the MPAA in May 2006, The Pirate Bay today counts as one of the 100 most visited websites globally and as the world's largest BitTorrent search engine to date.[34] Invoking piracy to explain Swedish market failure points us to an unregulated sphere of exchange outside this market's formally installed boundaries, but also to a major shortcoming in the way the very concept of "market" is employed to chart the digital universe. As one of the key metaphors used to organize and streamline the Internet's transactional spaces, the "market" bears heavily on neoclassical economics, equilibrium models, and the stasis of nineteenth-century physics on which they were founded.[35] And indeed, in the industrial-economic view outlined above, the digital market appears merely as a stage on which a drama of struggle over control takes place, a drama currently staged on the minimal set of a living room.

Challenged by the organic imagery evoked to describe the Internet's economic properties, and facing the idea of pirates surfing a vast ocean of opportunities, media industry scholars have consequently suggested modifying, extending, or altogether abandoning this static model of regulated exchange. Most recently, in building on early anthropological work by Keith Hart, among others, Ramon Lobato has underlined the importance of differentiating between an industrial-economic conception of markets and the multitude of marketplaces around the globe whose economies defy economics as much as industry planning.[36] In turning his attention toward informal media systems, rather than toward Hollywood's well-researched distribution circuits, Lobato has demonstrated the significance of what he calls "shadow economies": the abundant spheres of unmeasured, untaxed, unregulated production and exchange. Given that the Internet currently constitutes a gray zone for trading activities, marked by an "abiding logic of repurposing otherwise legal online infrastructures for informal uses,"[37] it indeed seems useful to abandon the idea of one "Swedish market" for online video, to be mapped in conventional terms as a properly formalized industry sector. That is, instead of following the Hollywood oligopoly's prosecutional efforts of "othering" what appears to be an integral part of Swedish web video consumption, we might rather chart Sweden's manifold media economies on an open "spectrum of formality"[38] that would include regulated as much as unregulated enterprises, gift giving, barter, and theft as much as surveilled access and commerce, carefully following the constant movement of entrepreneurial (or, for that matter, consumptory) activities between the two ends of the spectrum. For instance, instead of simply pointing to the fact that more than 61 percent of all young Swedes between 15 and 25 years old actively engage in nonauthorized file sharing,[39] we may start by pinpointing the differences between commercial piracy as an activity of distributing available videos—that is, the private fair use of video technologies—and as bootlegging, in order to fill in gaps of market failure.[40] We may point to a complex viewing ecology that is not to be defined territorially, but in terms of a set of interdependent intermediaries, equally comprising search engines such as Google and The Pirate Bay, and what they link to: aggregated content behind paywalls (e.g., Netflix, United States), torrent-hosting services (Torrage.com, Sweden), linking sites (sv. film.fm, Israel), cyberlockers (PutLocker.com, the UK), and so on.[41]

In fact, the key reason for the low revenue generated through legal online video transactions in Sweden is not to be found in commercial piracy. It is resulting from the ways Swedish viewers distribute limited time budgets among authorized and nonauthorized services, including IPTV and free public television, free legal video platforms such as SVT Play or YouTube, e-tailers such as CDON, and bootlegging through TankaFetast.com or The Pirate Bay, with a majority of the Swedish online population citing a 50:50 ratio in regard to the authorized/unauthorized services they use.[42] Finally, we also may pinpoint that Hollywood's fear of having its markets deformalized through piracy goes along well with the studios' own strategies, as laid out in the connected viewing scenario, to proactively formalize the informal—to rigorously track, frame, and monetize the ways we share that information once called "television entertainment." Adding Sweden's informal media marketplaces to our view of its markets, then, we may picture Hollywood's "software business" as being currently caught up in a site-specific struggle between "pirate modernity" and "like economy."[43]

Anthropology thus offers productive frameworks for the study of exchange, and highlights the growing number of actors operating outside formally regulated markets. Such frameworks also go well with our contemporary political sensibilities, not least in the humanities, which often (and for good reason) see social relations threatened by the cold inhumanity of neoliberal economics. From this perspective, we might intuitively answer the question of why Sweden's digital market does not account for more than just 1 percent of the country's home entertainment revenue by simply referring to the famous slogan used by the Occupy movement—that is, because "We are the 99 percent!" Accordingly, our analyses would strive to extend the new/old binary of formal market modeling by exploring the dynamics of another binary, mapping digital distribution on a continuous spectrum from formal to informal, "stickiness" to "spreadability," or flow to file.[44] And yet that is only half of the story, because tracing a basic distinction between economics and economies, or markets and marketplaces, does not tell us much about how these markets have come about in the first place!

Indeed, as Bruno Latour reminds us, all dichotomous distinctions are convincing only as long as they are enforced by an asymmetrical bias that treats the two sides of the border differently.[45] As soon as the common prejudice loses hold, Hollywood studio productions become overtly plagiary, Google starts to resemble The Pirate Bay, pirates become capitalists, and creative consumers turn into rational market agents. Coincidental reversals like these demonstrate that the divide between formal and informal culture is, again, just a border—like that between San Diego and Tijuana. It is enforced arbitrarily by police and bureaucrats, but it does not represent any natural boundary. Useful for polemics, teaching, and paradigm wars, Latour instructs that "great divides do not provide any explanation, but on the contrary are things to be explained."[46]

While Lobato himself is very careful in avoiding simplistic explanations, founding an account of Sweden's digital market on any of the binary distinctions, such as "pirate" or "legal services," regularly employed by the market actors themselves would consequently fall short on two grounds. The first reason, obviously, is that binary oppositions are only one derivative form of difference. "Pirate markets" are based on a similar principle of inequality constituting information markets generally. They are as much premised on the industrial stockpiling and delaying of information as formal markets are, although in another way.[47] Rather than constituting a sphere outside economics, even the shadow economy of online video is a world that includes economics as one of its foundational components.[48] It constantly strives to establish a market by drawing an ideological frame around its activities and is as cautious in policing its borders as any conventional market actor. In fact, an enterprise such as The Pirate Bay is hardly *less* regulated, measured, or taxed, but just *differently* so, given that large parts of its infrastructure—such as Internet service providers, web-hosting services, or advertising partners—are perfectly legal. The Pirate Bay even comes complete with its own market research, political lobby groups, policy-making associates, public relations work, and a mainstream market ideology that is not only more consistent than Hollywood's day-to-day strategizing, but also, despite all the neo-Marxist rhetorics, similarly conservative in its adherence to the cyberlibertarian free-market thought advocated by John Perry Barlow and others.[49] The Pirate Bay can actually be seen as a forerunner of what Peter Jakobsson has described as an emerging *openness industry;* that is, one promoting the idea of openness as a business model for the media industry, much in line with the interests of those Internet and technology companies on whose services access to television entertainment today is founded. Exploiting, or building its markets on top of, digital, cultural, and informational commons, the openness industry may operate outside Hollywood's traditional markets created by copyright law—but certainly not outside formal markets in general.[50]

The second reason to refrain from the self-definitions used by market actors themselves finally brings us to the heart of what understanding digital markets ultimately requires. Market actors, as much as trade journalists or scholars, tend to presuppose the existence of a concrete market reality they can act upon or report about. Acting from the "inside" or reasoning from the "outside," they engage in forms of mapping a territory such as that of Swedish online video transactions. But again, these are attempts at charting a *territory*—implying that it is already out there, inscribed in an enduring geography of media use. In doing so, markets are treated ontologically. That is, despite being just a metaphor to evoke and organize market knowledge, the market is seen as *always already given in practice.* This is how companies like Warner Bros. or The Pirate Bay both can account for an objective reality that is actionable. Yet while such an understanding literally does work for someone acting in a given marketplace, media scholarship needs to shift focus away from a substantive notion of market to an analysis of the very *practices* through which markets are constantly made and remade.[51] To overcome the stasis implied in the notion of the market, then, we do not need another notion of market, but to carry further the anthropological project of investigating the processes in which markets are framed and delineated. The question thus is not what lies "inside" or "outside" the frame, or on the formal or informal side of a spectrum, but how this highly moral and economic distinction itself is produced and sustained.[52] As Bruno Latour aptly notes, it is precisely the "divides" or "borders" that need to be explained.

III.

Let's for a moment assume that bootleggers are not essentially different from regular viewers, that the formal or informal "software businesses" serving their needs operate within the very same field, and that in the digital sphere, markets cannot be easily territorialized. Let's also assume that Sweden's "geography of innovation" is neither "disrupting" nor "sustaining" Hollywood. That is, uses of digital technology in this country do not necessarily lead to more direct access to more niches (or to "selling less of more," to invoke Chris Anderson's "long tail" model),[53] nor do such uses imply that the Hollywood studios have the full capacity to shape the speed and direction of commercial development in the networked environment—i.e., the ways their content is used, the kinds of business models and services that can develop there, and so on. How then to account for possible behavioral changes in online viewing as promoted, and arguably also facilitated, by the industry-wide adoption of the connected viewing scenario following its launch in 2009?

Stepping back from the technological determinism underlying many industry accounts, and acknowledging that the Internet means different things in different countries,[54] we may start by asking ourselves why the industry vision of connected viewing *should* relate to the actual viewing of premium Hollywood content in Sweden in the first place. Historically, the introduction of new media technologies has hardly ever led to disruptive changes in viewing patterns, as they are now regularly proclaimed to go along with the digital. As even Thomas Gewecke, evoking Stewart Brand's "clock of the long now" at points in his speech,[55] would acknowledge, changes in the information infrastructure occur in a long-term perspective and a temporal continuum that may span decades, if not even a century. Sweden is a paradigmatic case for any understanding of online viewing also in that it clearly demonstrates the inadequacy of explanations that assume a radical shift in the epistemology and anthropology of exchange. Evidence points not to a fundamental break in the historical anthropology of media markets, but at best to an extension of already-existing networks, or modes of connectivity.[56] If anything has radically changed so far, it is the ideology—not the practice—of economic life, and one should not conflate a description of the former with one of the latter.[57]

Looking, first, at the most obvious level of market activities—that of exchange practices—the Swedish living room presents itself as a *resilient ecology* for online viewing.[58] It appears as a resilient ecology in terms of how Swedish viewers connect, and how they define the value of Hollywood premium content through their actual viewing practices. According to the data generated by our field studies, which investigated online activities among a viewership of 15–25-year-old Swedish residents between November 2011 and August 2012, these practices differ markedly from prevalent visions of home entertainment, as articulated in local consumer journals such as *HemmaBio Tidningen* and industry-supported online forums such as MinHembio.com.

From the perspective of those young Swedish "buyers" whose practices we were investigating, the most salient attribute of the commercial online video market is indeed its failure to match their demand. More than 70 percent reported not finding what they are interested in, and consider most of the content legally available on the Internet "not worth paying for."[59] While it is doubtful the use of nonauthorized services constitutes a social norm per se,[60] the findings certainly demonstrate that actual Swedish exchange practices define the value of online content as being rather low. "Commercial services are defective in their pricing," as one respondent remarked. It "doesn't cost 49 SEK [about $7] to watch a movie; price elasticity for digital films/series/music has not been properly investigated, which is unusual and amateurish."[61] One reason mentioned for this perception of low value is the fact that, in the online world, film and television have turned into "pure information." By that, Swedish viewers did not mean to imply that information "wants to be free" (as Stewart Brand's slogan goes), but that experience and value relate to what they see as an "information problem" associated with the timing, rather than geography, of global media flows. For instance, evoking an analogy to the spoiler phenomenon, a focus group respondent described US cable television series as "fresh produce" in demand of immediate consumption, or devalued otherwise; at the same time, Hollywood mainstream feature films are seen as so generic and/or so always already valueless that they "can wait how[ever] long."[62] In short, the Swedish viewing ecology appears resilient insofar that local practices of viewing Hollywood content online foreground areas of conflict, miscomprehension, or incommensurability—areas that exist between buyers and sellers in any kind of market,[63] but that are better observable in the digital sphere, and also more difficult to smooth out through traditional instruments such as pricing in the particular Swedish case.

Indeed, from the perspective of a "seller," it is these exchange practices, and the resulting turn to bootlegging as a means of compensating for what appears as market failure, that have made Sweden the *most fragmented market for online entertainment in Europe,* according to Warner Bros. European executives.[64] That is, instead of becoming the foundation for a secure, predictable, and well-mannered marketplace, the technological vision of connected viewing is currently seen as having been challenged and transformed through a process of actual market fragmentation. One might argue, however, that it is also the industry's attempt to capitalize on Sweden's unstable conditions for exchange that contributes to this situation. A flurry of recently introduced servicing platforms testifies to this development, with a previously unavailable show like HBO's *Game of Thrones* now offered on public television SVT, and simultaneously as part of competitive programming packages delivered by, for instance, IPTV platform operator Telia, C MORE's Filmnet.se, or HBO Nordic, not to speak of The Pirate Bay—that is, for free; for a monthly flat rate of SEK 79 (approximately $12) via IPTV; through a subscription-based streaming service (for SEK 49 a month, or roughly $7); or again for free via a nonauthorized, advertising-based BitTorrent search engine. With direct legal access to HBO premium cable programming introduced as part of industrial antipiracy countermeasures, all these platforms now compete against one another in offering *the* optimal configuration of service and experience. Meanwhile, the specter of demand continues to escape traditional industry metrics because of the changing information infrastructure on which those and other platforms run—an infrastructure nevertheless looking rather different from what the connected viewing scenario envisioned.

Turning, then, from an observation of current exchange practice to *representational practices* as a second form of market-making activities, we may note even more "resilience" (or at least divergence) than on the first level of observation. Representational practices include activities that contribute to the depiction of markets and/or how they work. Since markets are abstract entities, such activities are as important in shaping markets as actual exchange practices. For in order to evoke "the digital market" for Hollywood content, it is necessary to bridge the temporal and spatial distances between individual exchanges and produce images of this market.[65] While Gewecke's connected viewing scenario did not serve to picture the digital market on the whole, it did map the information infrastructure for market exchanges. The subsequent promotion, and realization, of connected viewing in US consumer culture further developed this scenario along technological lines—in terms of a global "tubes and wires" infrastructure built on top of the Internet, combining the hardware of game consoles, connected televisions, or wirelessly operating tablet computers with the "cultural software"[66] of apps, websites, social networking services, and second-screen content. Arguably made to communicate with, share with, participate with, and engage viewers in an enhanced multitasking, multiscreen experience, this technological infrastructure seemed also, as I have argued already, envisioned to provide a new framework for formalizing hitherto informal market exchanges; for instance, by channeling word-of-mouth via platforms such as Twitter or Facebook.

The actual Swedish infrastructure, however, looks quite different from its American representations. In fact, our findings underlined once more that any conventional "tubes and wires" understanding of information infrastructure, spelled out in terms of a simple laundry list of technical devices or services (such as those itemized in Table 5.1), ultimately falls short in addressing exactly how people connect over entertainment content. Transforming traditional markets into "software businesses" means more than just changing pipes in a pipeline— it means changes in *infrastructural relations.*[67] The question thus is how access to content (or rather, practical solutions to the problem of access to content) is distributed across an infrastructure comprising the global *as much as* the local, the technological *as much as* the social, and technical standards *as much as* servicing standards. Studied from a broader ecological view, Swedish online viewing appears to be resilient because, as a practice of engaging in an emerging market for entertainment, it clearly is embedded in an *already-existing* infrastructure. For instance, despite the high technology uptake, Swedish home theater discourse still essentially builds on a cinematic mode of viewing, with consumer journals such as *HemmaBio Tidningen* and online forums such as MinHembio.com regularly advising on how best to transform domestic space into a movie theater.[68] Identifying home viewing with theatrical viewing means basing viewing practices on a clear distinction between public and private,[69] a distinction abandoned in the connected viewing scenario, as Thomas Gewecke's anecdotal reference to a "Blu-ray, BD-Live-mediated marriage proposal" aptly illustrates.

When it comes to actual Swedish viewing practices, the differences for a digital market built on multitasking, multiscreen experiences become even more apparent. Connectivity is spelled out as being an informal, social, and largely offline phenomenon, marked by small local viewing communities whose members prefer to talk in person after having seen a given film or show. Many Swedes consider online viewing to be less important than listening to music (49.7 percent), going to the cinema (47.1 percent), or reading books (40 percent); while most Swedish viewers (69.4 percent) watch at home or at a friend's place, and in doing so, never engage at all in activities such as tweeting (73.9 percent), blogging (77.4 percent), or chatting (33.1 percent). Although most Swedes use streaming/downloading via a desktop or notebook computer as their new default, with regular free public service television turning into a second-screen or companion-viewing option, a large majority are not even aware of interactive services such as check-in apps (69.4 percent), or never use them. And although 81 percent of all respondents reported to be active on Facebook, 49.9 percent indicated they communicate with fewer than ten people about a show, with most respondents talking to fewer than five people and networks consisting largely of friends and family living close-by in the very same Swedish town (54.4 percent). Finally, it is worthwhile noting that Swedish viewers also engage in representational practices themselves, by constantly mining online services such as IMDb.com and Metacritic.com or the press for supply information. However, viewers who engage in such practices of market monitoring do not necessarily engage or buy more than others. While we did not find evidence that file sharing would reduce sales, we did find proof that viewers who engage in monitoring activities, including the free, mostly nonauthorized "previewing" of content online, make more selective informed choices when it comes to the ownership over physical copies.[70]

Turning our attention to the third and last form of market-making activities, that of *normalizing practices*, we finally come back to where this chapter began. Normalizing refers to the attempt at guiding markets in specific directions by articulating rules of competition or marketing, and—more importantly—by shaping the very standards of exchange.[71] It is here that we finally touch upon what, in the beginning, I identified as a problem of interoperability, a problem pertaining to the infrastructure on which digital markets run. And it is also here that we may eventually grasp the full extent to which technological visions indeed are productive, and necessary, in order for today's software businesses to succeed. The issue of normalization also ultimately sheds light on those dark borderlands or contact zones within which the differences between "formal" and "informal" markets are articulated and enforced. In fact, normalizing practices are at the very heart of the conflict so often evoked in discussions of Sweden's digital market.

If Sweden has become a territory often mapped along a binary opposition between commercial studio distribution and The Pirate Bay, then this is because both parties have successfully mustered large sets of heterogeneous allies across the country. For instance, advocates of the studio model have mobilized local trade organizations (such as Svenska antipiratbyrån, the Swedish Anti-Piracy Bureau), the law (Swedish police, but also the Intellectual Property Rights Enforcement Directive), technological visions (such as connected viewing), and platforms like Spotify, which originated as an antipiracy solution for music consumption and was in talks in 2012 to develop a video version as well. The Pirate Bay, on the other hand, started out by deliberately introducing piracy as a metaphor in 2003, in response to Svenska antipiratbyrån's foundation, and by building on a wave of mainstream sympathy for piracy in the wake of *Pirates of the Caribbean: The Curse of the Black Pearl* released that same summer, a wave that also included the subsequent launch of H&M pirate T-shirts.[72] As a metaphor, then, "piracy" was never defined as countercultural, but rather illustrated the necessity of finding an out-of-the-box solution that would benefit viewers of commercial entertainment. Actively employing the metaphor of piracy in negotiating the value of its branded service, The Pirate Bay engages, as mentioned above, in market research (The Research Bay), political lobby groups (Piratpartiet), policy-making associates (the Cybernorms research group, Lund University), and public relations (at least three documentaries to date), among others. The Pirate Bay's significance thus goes far beyond the exchange practices it facilitates—it greatly contributes to normalizing the idea of copyright infringement being fair use, or indeed, a social norm.[73] Such cultural engagements are often sidestepped when speaking about digital markets and their underlying information infrastructure, but they are vital for understanding them. They form what I call "ontology work," because this is work done to ontologize a market, to endow this market with a reality, spelled out in actionable market metrics and consumer ideals.

Studying digital markets, we thus may benefit from including the actual processes of market making in our analysis, and from taking a long, hard look at infrastructure: the vast set of technologies and organizations enabling market work. An infrastructural turn is beneficial for digital media research, since infrastructure concerns how practices of market exchange may turn into new standards of media use. Subversively engaging in, and arguably mastering, the current fight over servicing standards, The Pirate Bay has cast a light on the clashes between the epistemic cultures engaging in market exchanges. Far from having turned into happy "prosumers," buyers disagree with sellers, and proponents of formal businesses disagree with those of informal enterprises. If anything, then, Sweden's digital market is marked by a lack of *epistemic interoperability*.[74] While we all may longingly await the desired futures of the digital age, we can hardly ignore that when it comes to what we know of one another, Hollywood and our living rooms may stay unconnected for a while.

Notes

1. The research on which this chapter is based was made possible through funding provided by the Carsey-Wolf Center at the University of California, Santa Barbara as part of the Media Industries Project's Connected Viewing Initiative, from 2011–12. The author wishes to thank Jennifer Holt and Michael Curtin for their generous support. My work has greatly benefitted from discussions held with my Connected Viewing Initiative colleagues, especially Sharon Strover, Josh Braun, and Paul McDonald; and I am indebted to my tireless research assistants, Dee Majek and Anders Nilsson. Jens Rydgren, Alexandra Bogren, and Lina Eklund from the Department of Sociology at Stockholm University have provided invaluable insights into the technical part of social science methodology. My understanding of marketing theory has greatly been inspired by a long conversation with Hans Kjellberg, Stockholm School of Economics. Special thanks to Anuraj Goonetilleke (vice president of business strategy, Warner Bros. Digital Distribution) and to Peter Sunde, former spokesman for The Pirate Bay, for sharing their views on each other. The opening Barlow quote is taken from John Perry Barlow, "The Future of Prediction," in *Technological Visions: The Hopes and Fears that Shape New Technologies*, eds. Marita Sturken, Douglas Thomas, and Sandra Ball-Rokeach (Philadelphia: Temple University Press, 2004), 177.
2. Although the University of California, Los Angeles's team sent the first ARPANET message, there are of course several institutions around the world claiming to have laid the grounds for what the Internet is today.
3. Stewart Brand coined this aphorism at the Hackers Conference in Marin County, California, in 1984. For the notion of cyberlibertarianism, see Langdon Winner, "Cyberlibertarian Myths and the Prospects for Community," *ACM SIGCAS Computers and Society* 14, no. 27 (1997): 14–19.
4. The video of Gewecke's talk at the University of California, Los Angeles's 40th Anniversary of the Internet Conference can be found at http://www.youtube.com/watch?v=gKlIlVdw7xs.
5. Adam Livingstone and Richard Taylor, "Hollywood and the Hackers," *BBC Newsnight*, June 9, 2006, http://news.bbc.co.uk/2/hi/programmes/newsnight/5064170.stm.
6. Fred Turner, *From Counterculture to Cyberculture: Stewart Brand, the Whole Earth Network, and the Rise of Digital Utopianism* (Chicago: University of Chicago, 2006), 171.
7. From this point of view, connected viewing appears—in Cory Doctorow's words—"like a boring science fiction adaptation of the Old Testament's book of numbers . . . a kind of enumeration of every permutation of things people do with information

and the ways we could charge them. But none of this would be possible unless we could control how people use their computers and the files we transfer to them." Cory Doctorow, "The Coming War on General Computation," paper presented at the 28th Chaos Communication Congress, Berlin, Germany, December, 2011. http://events .ccc.de/congress/2011/wiki/Documentation. See also Jonathan Zittrain, *The Future of the Internet—and How to Stop It* (New Haven, CT: Yale University Press, 2008); or Jack Goldsmith and Tim Wu, *Who Controls the Internet?: Illusions of a Borderless World* (Oxford and New York: Oxford University Press, 2006).

8. Marita Sturken, Douglas Thomas, and Sandra J. Ball-Rokeach, *Technological Visions: The Hopes and Fears that Shape New Technologies* (Philadelphia: Temple University Press, 2004). See also David E. Nye, "Technology and the Production of Difference," *American Quarterly* 58, no. 3 (September 2006): 597–618.

9. Bruno Latour, "Drawing Things Together," in *Representation in Scientific Practice*, eds. Michael Lynch and Steve Woolgar (Cambridge, MA: MIT Press, 1990), 19–68.

10. John Perry Barlow, "The Economy of Ideas," *Wired*, March 1994.

11. Nik Brown and Mike Michael, "A Sociology of Expectations: Retrospecting Prospects and Prospecting Retrospects," *Technology Analysis & Strategic Management* 15, no. 1 (2003): 4.

12. Andrew Pickering and Keith Guzik, eds., *The Mangle in Practice: Science, Society, and Becoming* (Chicago and London: University of Chicago Press, 1995), 23.

13. For instance, Michael Callon, ed., *The Laws of the Markets* (Oxford: Blackwell, 1998); Martha Lampland and Susan Leigh Star, eds., *Standards and Their Stories: How Quantifying, Classifying, and Formalizing Practices Shape Everyday Life* (Ithaca and London: Cornell University Press, 2009); see also Nicole Starosielski, "'Warning: Do Not Dig': Negotiating the Visibility of Critical Infrastructures," *Journal of Visual Culture* 11, no. 1 (2012): 1–20; and the writings of Lisa Parks; for instance, Lisa Ann Parks, *Cultures in Orbit: Satellites and the Televisual* (Durham: Duke University Press, 2005); or Lisa Parks and James Schwoch, eds., *Down to Earth: Satellite Technologies, Industries, and Cultures* (New Brunswick, NJ: Rutgers University Press, 2012).

14. David Sarno, "The Internet Sure Loves Its Outlaws," *Los Angeles Times*, April 29, 2007, http://www.latimes.com/technology/la-ca-webscout29apr29,0,5609754.story.

15. This research is based on four kinds of sources: 1) new statistical data aggregated by authoritative, nonindustry sources such as the Organisation for Economic Co-operation and Development, Eurostat, the European Audiovisual Observatory, the Swedish Film Institute, Stiftelsen för Internetinfrastruktur (.SE), and Post- och telestyrelsen; 2) statistics, reports, and raw data provided through commercial services such as Screen Digest and Futuresource Consulting, on personal request and partly bound by nondisclosure agreements—data I have only used for comparative, supplementary purposes; 3) publicly available (i.e., online) industry reports and industry statistics, e.g., by Ericsson, Cisco, Nielsen, or the KIA-index, which I have used to a very limited degree and only in order to gain first general insights about digital markets; 4) fieldwork. My fieldwork consisted of numerous qualitative interviews conducted with European and American industry executives, and participant observation. In addition, a first explorative online survey identified relevant consumer practices among Swedish consumers (n = 174 adults and teens 18–25, April 23–24, 2012, sample generated via Facebook). This nonrepresentative convenience sample was supplemented by two focus groups, conducted in Stockholm and using a semistructured questionnaire (n = 5, adults and teens ages 18–25, sixty minutes, May 16–June 18, 2012). To give a more representative picture of Sweden's online population, a second survey was conducted (n = 1.147 teens and adults ages 16–30, July 25–31, 2012, forty-one questions), with national representativeness sampled on region and gender and individual quotas on age (16–18 years: 200; 19–25: 500; 26–30: 300). Findings were largely consistent through all the samples.

16. Karin Knorr-Cetina and Ure Bruegger, "Trader's Engagement with Markets: A Postsocial Relationship," *Theory, Culture & Society* 19, no. 5/6 (2002): 168.

17. Luis Araujo, John Finch, and Hans Kjellberg, eds., *Reconnecting Marketing to Markets* (Oxford and New York: Oxford University Press, 2010), 3.
18. For the legacy, see Mark Granovetter, "Economic Action and Social Structure: The Problem of Embeddedness," *American Journal of Sociology* 91, no. 3 (1985): 481–510; Harrison C. White, "Where Do Markets Come From?," *American Journal of Sociology* 87, no. 3 (1981): 517–47; Rafael Ramírez, "Value Co-production: Intellectual Origins and Implications for Practice and Research," *Strategic Management Journal* 20, no. 1 (1999): 49–65; for the model, see Jason Potts et al., "Social Network Markets: A New Definition of the Creative Industries," *Journal of Cultural Economics* 32 (2008): 167–85; and for this model's praise, see John Hartley, *Digital Futures for Cultural and Media Studies* (Chichester: Wiley-Blackwell, 2012); and Stuart Cunningham, "Emergent Innovation through the Coevolution of Informal and Formal Media Economies," *Television & New Media* 20, no. 10 (2012): 1–16.
19. Ramon Lobato, Julian Thomas, and Dan Hunter, "Histories of User-Generated Content: Between Formal and Informal Media Economies," *International Journal of Communication*, no. 5 (2011): 901. See below for a more extensive discussion of Lobato's arguments.
20. Sean Cubitt, "Distribution and Media Flows," *Cultural Politics* 1, no. 2 (2005): 205. See also Arthur de Vany, *Hollywood Economics: How Extreme Uncertainty Shapes the Film Industry* (New York and London: Routledge, 2004), 11–27; and John Sedgwick and Michael Pokorny, eds., *An Economic History of Film* (London and New York: Routledge, 2004), passim.
21. This rough account of industry change builds primarily on Harold L. Vogel, *Entertainment Industry Economics: A Guide for Financial Analysis* (Cambridge, MA: Cambridge University Press, 2010); see also Sedgwick and Pokorny, eds., *Economic History;* or Tom Schatz, "Film Industry Studies and Hollywood History," in *Media Industries: History, Theory, and Method,* eds. Jennifer Holt and Alisa Perren (Chichester: Wiley-Blackwell, 2009), 45–56.
22. John Palfrey and Urs Gasser, *Interop: The Promise and Perils of Highly Interconnected Systems* (New York: Basic Books, 2012), 5.
23. For a theoretically elaborate account of digital distribution, see Josh Braun, "Electronic Components and Human Interventions: Distribution Television News Online" (PhD diss., Cornell University, 2011).
24. For company information, see www.underthemilkyway.com; for content aggregation more generally, see Ramon Lobato, "The Politics of Digital Distribution: Exclusionary Strategies in Online Cinema," *Studies in Australian Cinema* 3, no. 2 (2009): 167–78. See also Vogel, *Entertainment Industry Economics,* 47, on legacy assets.
25. Vogel, *Entertainment Industry Economics,* 47; and Jeff Ulin, *The Business of Media Distribution: Monetizing Film, TV and Video Content in an Online World* (Amsterdam and Boston: Elsevier, 2010), 299–300.
26. See, for instance, *BBC News,* "Film Piracy: Is It Theft?," August 18, 2006, http://news.bbc.co.uk/2/hi/programmes/click_online/5263208.stm.
27. Following statistical data compiled from, among others, Olle Findahl, *Svenskarna och Internet,* .SE Internetstatistik, 2011; *PTS Uppföljning av regeringens bredbandsstrategi,* May 2012, Rapportnummer PTS-ER-2012:18, May 30, 2012; *PTS Svensk Telemarknad 2011,* Rapportnummer PTS-ER-2012:17, May 29, 2012; OECD Broadband Portal, "OECD Broadband Statistics," www.oecd.org/Internet/broadbandandtelecom/oecdbroadbandportal.htm.
28. Jeffrey Travers and Stanley Milgram, "An Experimental Study of the Small World Problem," *Sociometry* 32, no. 4 (1969): 425–43.
29. This figure was reported for December 2008. See André Lange, *Video On Demand and Catch-Up TV in Europe: A Report Edited by The European Audiovisual Observatory* (Strasbourg: Observatoire Européen de l'Audiovisuel, 2009), 113.
30. Andrew Currah, "Hollywood, the Internet and the World: A Geography of Disruptive Innovation," *Industry and Innovation* 14, no. 4 (2007): 359–84.

31. Data based on Screen Digest market research, January 2012. Many thanks to Richard Broughton, senior analyst, IHS Screen Digest, personal communication.

32. These data result from our own online surveys, conducted via eighty different market research panels through Cint (see above). When the surveys were conducted, Netflix, Filmnet, and HBO Nordic did not yet operate in Sweden.

33. This figure is based on internal market research data, Futuresource Consulting, April 2012.

34. Anders Rydell and Sam Sundberg, *Piraterna: De svenska fildelerna som plundrade Hollywood* (Stockholm: Ordfront, 2009); Jonas Andersson and Pelle Snickars, eds., *Efter The Pirate Bay* (Stockholm: National Library of Sweden, 2010); see also the blogs of Rasmus Fleischer (http://copyriot.se/) and Peter Sunde (http://blog.brokep.com/).

35. Sally Wyatt, "Danger! Metaphors at Work in Economics, Geophysiology, and the Internet," *Science, Technology & Human Values* 29, no. 2 (Spring 2004): 242–61. See also Tarleton Gillespie, *Wired Shut: Copyright and the Shape of Digital Culture* (Cambridge, MA, and London: MIT Press, 2007); and Patricia Loughlin, "Pirates, Parasites, Reapers, Sowers, Fruits, Foxes …The Metaphors of Intellectual Property," *Sydney Law Review* 28, no. 2 (2006): 211–26.

36. See Ramon Lobato, Julian Thomas, and Dan Hunter, "Histories of User-Generated Content: Between Formal and Informal Media Economies," *International Journal of Communication* 5 (2011): 899–914; and Ramon Lobato, *Shadow Economies of Cinema: Mapping Informal Film Distribution* (London: Palgrave Macmillan, 2012).

37. Lobato, *Shadow Economies*, 95.

38. Lobato, Thomas, Hunter, "Histories of User-Generated Content," 900.

39. Even higher numbers are reported in a survey conducted by the Cybernorms research group at Lund University. For instance, see Stefan Larsson and Måns Svensson, *Social Norms and Intellectual Property: Online Norms and the European Legal Development* (Lund: Lund University, 2009).

40. Lucas Hilderbrand, *Inherent Vice: Bootleg Histories of Videotape and Copyright* (Durham and London: Duke University Press, 2009), 22–3.

41. Of our survey respondents (second representative survey, July 2012), 76.6 percent reported to regularly start their search for US premium entertainment content with Google—rather than any nonauthorized (Swedish) platform.

42. Data based on our second representative survey, July 2012. Ranking clearly revealed free streaming via SVT Play and other legal services to be the first, pirate platforms to be the second, and commercial services to be the third choice for accessing content. Only 17.5 percent of our respondents indicated never using unauthorized platforms (while 11.1 percent reported never using commercial). Key reasons for the support of unauthorized services include the lack of very new content on authorized services (74.9 percent) and discomfort with authorized pricing models (70.2 percent).

43. See Ravi Sundaram, *Pirate Modernity: Delhi's Media Urbanism* (London and New York: Routledge, 2010); and Caroline Gerlitz, "Die Like Economy. Digitaler Raum, Daten und Wertschöpfung," in *Generation Facebook: Über das Leben im Social Net,* eds. Oliver Leistert and Theo Röhle (Bielefeld: Transcript, 2011), 101–23.

44. See Henry Jenkins, Sam Ford, and Joshua Green, *Spreadable Media: Creating Value and Meaning in a Networked Culture* (New York: New York University Press, 2013); and Derek Kompare, "Flow to Files: Conceiving 21st Century Media" (paper presented at Media in Transition 2, Cambridge, Massachusetts, May 2005).

45. What follows is a direct paraphrase of Latour's compellingly witty dissection of conventional accounts of scientific progress. Bruno Latour, "Drawing Things Together," 2.

46. Ibid.

47. Sean Cubitt, "Distribution and Media Flows," 206.

48. Such is the main argument of Michel Callon, "Why Virtualism Paves the Way to Political Impotence. Callon Replies to Miller," *Economic Sociology: the European Electronic Newsletter* 6, no. 2 (February 2005): 3–21.

49. More on The Pirate Bay's associates below. For a historically contextualized critique of Barlow and cyberlibertarian ideology, see Turner, *From Counterculture to Cyberculture*, 176. According to Turner, cyberlibertarians "mingled the rhetorical and social practices of systems theory with the New Communalist celebration of disembodied intimacy and geographically distributed communion."

50. Peter Jakobsson, *Öppenhetsindustrin*. Örebro: Örebro Studies in Media and Communication 13, Södertörn Doctoral Dissertations 65, 2012. In fact, one might argue that what we currently observe in the online sphere has nothing to do with formal or informal exchanges in the first place. Rather, what digital markets testify to is the coexistence of, and competition between, firms devoted to creating and taxing scarcity on the one hand, and firms (like Google, or The Pirate Bay) designed to manage the abundance of information via platforms selling advertising on the other. Both Google and The Pirate Bay are search engines facilitating the discovery, access, and unauthorized use of others' copyrighted works. See Siva Vaidhyanathan, *The Googlization of Everything (And Why We Should Worry)* (Berkeley and Los Angeles: University of California Press, 2011), 160.

51. Analytical techniques such as statistics or maps, as much as pricing models or online platform purchase settings, all form part in an ever-ongoing process of market making. They belong to what economic sociologists have called "market devices"—devices that render things, behaviors, and processes economic. The emphasis here is on the process of "rendering," for what is economic is an outcome of a historical, contingent, and disputable process of economization, rather than simply a given. See Luis M. Araujo and Hans Kjellberg, "Shaping Exchanges, Performing Markets: The Study of Marketing Practices," in *The SAGE Handbook of Marketing Theory*, eds. Pauline Maclaran et al. (London: SAGE, 2009), 195–218; and also Fabian Munesia, Yuval Millo, and Michel Callon, "An Introduction to Market Devices," in *Market Devices*, eds. Michel Callon, Yuval Millo, and Fabian Munesia (Chichester: Wiley-Blackwell, 2007), 3.

52. This is obviously one of the key arguments made by Callon, illustrated by his use of the concepts of "framing" and "overflowing," in "Introduction: The Embeddedness of Economic Markets in Economics," in *The Laws of the Markets*, ed. Michel Callon (Malden and Oxford: Blackwell, 1998), 1–57.

53. Chris Anderson, *The Long Tail: Why the Future of Business Is Selling Less of More* (New York: Hyperion, 2006).

54. For instance, see Daniel Miller, *Tales from Facebook* (London: Polity Press, 2011).

55. "Media transitions take a very long time, a generation, for these kinds of shifts to occur," Gewecke underlined several times during his talk; see Thomas Gewecke (speech, 40th Anniversary of the Internet Conference, University of California, Los Angeles, 2009). See also Stewart Brand, *The Clock of the Long Now: Time and Responsibility: The Ideas Behind the World's Slowest Computer* (New York: Basic Books, 1999).

56. Cf. Bruno Latour and Vincent Antonin Lépinay, *The Science of Passionate Interests: An Introduction to Gabriel Tarde's Economic Anthropology* (Chicago: University of Chicago Press, 2009), 87.

57. Daniel Miller, "Turning Callon the Right Way Up," *Economy and Society* 31, no. 2 (2002): 33.

58. In what follows, I build on the model of market practices suggested by Hans Kjellberg and Claes-Fredrik Helgesson, "On the Nature of Markets and their Practices," *Marketing Theory* 7 (2007): 137–62. Kjellberg and Helgesson differentiate between exchange, representational, and normalizing "market-ing" practices.

59. Of our 1,147 respondents in the 15–25-year-old demography (July 2012), 74.5 percent indicated not finding relevant content via authorized services, while 70.2 percent referred to economical considerations as the main reason for using nonauthorized services.

60. Larsson and Svensson, *Social Norms*, passim.

61. Anonymous comment, July 2012 survey. The respondent was referring to the Swedish iTunes Store's pricing policy for movie library titles.

62. Anonymous focus group participant, Stockholm, May 18, 2012.

63. John Finch and Susi Geiger, "Markets Are Trading Zones: On the Material, Cultural, and Interpretative Dimensions of Market Encounters," in *Reconnecting Marketing to Markets*, eds. Luis Araujo, John Finch, and Hans Kjellberg (Oxford: Oxford University Press, 2010), 117.
64. Stefan Lampinen, managing director, Warner Bros. Entertainment Nordic, personal communication, November 30, 2012.
65. Kjellberg and Helgesson, "On the Nature of Markets," 143.
66. Lev Manovich, *Software Takes Command* (London: Bloomsbury Academic, 2008), passim.
67. Geoffrey C. Bowker et al., "Toward Information Infrastructure Studies: Ways of Knowing in a Networked Environment," in *The International Handbook of Internet Research*, eds. Jeremy Hunsinger, Lisbeth Klastrup, and Matthew Allen (Heidelberg and London: Springer, 2010), 99.
68. Both *HemmaBio Tidningen* and MinHembio.com regularly feature photo reports, often provided by home theater owners themselves, showing the design, architecture, and technological equipment of living rooms turned into movie palaces. In an open-response field to a question about potential future purchases of entertainment technology, a majority out of 370 respondents mentioned an interest in buying home cinema equipment (projectors, surround sound systems, etc.), while only one person opted for "a GOOD on demand service with a GOOD offer of films and series" (anonymous comment, July 2012 survey).
69. See Barbara Klinger, *Beyond the Multiplex: Cinema, New Technologies, and the Home* (Berkeley and Los Angeles: University of California Press, 2006), 21.
70. As one survey respondent commented, "Illegal downloading has definitely changed my habits when it comes to how many media I consume, but not my buying habits regarding DVDs. I am buying about as much as earlier, but only favorites which I know beforehand to be good." Another one noted, "The illegal downloading of media allows [me] to sort all the 'junk' out; stuff which is not worth the investment of time or money to search and pay for. Instead, time and money are used for 'experiences' such as e.g. the cinema." Anonymous comments, July 2012 survey. Comments like these abounded.
71. Kjellberg and Helgesson, "On the Nature of Markets," 143.
72. Rasmus Fleischer, "'Piratrörelsen' har aldrig funnits," *Copyriot* (blog), September 28, 2010, http://copyriot.se/. See also Rasmus Fleischer, "Femton gastar på död mans kista—om framtidens nätpolitik," in *Efter The Pirate Bay*, eds. Jonas Andersson and Pelle Snickars (Stockholm: National Library of Sweden, 2010), 259–81.
73. The Cybernorms research group at Lund University teamed up with The Pirate Bay in 2011 to create The Research Bay, and while neither the methodology nor the results of their joint survey seem to have been published, Lund scholars published policy-related articles that claim, again, that file sharing would constitute a social norm. See The Pirate Bay (blog), "TPB Goes Science, Welcome to The Research Bay," April 18, 2011, http://thepiratebay.se/blog/190.
74. Joshua Braun, "Sharing the News: Toward a Construct of Epistemic Interoperability" (paper presented at the International Communication Association Conference, Phoenix, AZ, May, 2012).

References

Anderson, Chris. *The Long Tail: Why the Future of Business Is Selling Less of More*. New York: Hyperion, 2006.

Andersson, Jonas, and Pelle Snickars, eds. *Efter The Pirate Bay*. Stockholm: National Library of Sweden, 2010.

Araujo, Luis M., and Hans Kjellberg. "Shaping Exchanges, Performing Markets: The Study of Marketing Practices." In *The SAGE Handbook of Marketing Theory*, edited by Pauline Maclaran, Michael Saren, Barbara Stern, and Mark Tadajewski, 195–218. London: SAGE, 2009.

Araujo, Luis M., John Finch, and Hans Kjellberg, eds. *Reconnecting Marketing to Markets.* Oxford and New York: Oxford University Press, 2010.

Barlow, John Perry. "The Economy of Ideas." *Wired,* March 1994.

Barlow, John Perry. "The Future of Prediction." In *Technological Visions: The Hopes and Fears that Shape New Technologies,* edited by Marita Sturken, Douglas Thomas, and Sandra Ball-Rokeach, 172–9. Philadelphia: Temple University Press, 2004.

BBC News. "Film Piracy: Is It Theft?" August 18, 2006. http://news.bbc.co.uk/2/hi/programmes/click_online/5263208.stm.

Bowker, Geoffrey C., Karen Baker, Florence Millerand, and David Ribes. "Toward Information Infrastructure Studies: Ways of Knowing in a Networked Environment." In *International Handbook of Internet Research,* edited by Jeremy Hunsinger, Lisbeth Klastrup, and Matthew Allen, 97–117. Heidelberg and London: Springer, 2010.

Brand, Stewart. *The Clock of the Long Now: Time and Responsibility: The Ideas Behind the World's Slowest Computer.* New York: Basic Books, 1999.

Braun, Josh. "Electronic Components and Human Interventions: Distribution Television News Online." PhD diss., Cornell University, 2011.

Braun, Josh. "Sharing the News: Toward a Construct of Epistemic Interoperability." Paper presented at the International Communication Association Conference, Phoenix, AZ, May 2012.

Brown, Nik, and Mike Michael. "A Sociology of Expectations: Retrospecting Prospects and Prospecting Retrospects." *Technology Analysis & Strategic Management* 15, no. 1 (2003): 3–18.

Callon, Michel. "Introduction: The Embeddedness of Economic Markets in Economics." In *The Laws of the Markets,* edited by Michel Callon, 1–57. Malden and Oxford: Blackwell, 1998.

Callon, Michel, ed. *The Laws of the Markets.* Oxford: Blackwell, 1998.

Callon, Michel. "Why Virtualism Paves the Way to Political Impotence. Callon Replies to Miller." *Economic Sociology: the European Electronic Newsletter* 6, no. 2 (February 2005): 3–21.

Cubitt, Sean. "Distribution and Media Flows." *Cultural Politics* 1, no. 2 (2005): 193–214.

Cunningham, Stuart. "Emergent Innovation through the Coevolution of Informal and Formal Media Economies." *Television & New Media* 20, no. 10 (2012): 1–16.

Currah, Andrew. "Hollywood, the Internet and the World: A Geography of Disruptive Innovation." *Industry and Innovation* 14, no. 4 (2007), 359–84.

de Vany, Arthur. *Hollywood Economics: How Extreme Uncertainty Shapes the Film Industry.* New York and London: Routledge, 2004.

Doctorow, Cory. "The Coming War on General Computation." Paper presented at the 28th Chaos Communication Congress, Berlin, Germany, December, 2011. http://events.ccc.de/congress/2011/wiki/Documentation.

Finch, John, and Susi Geiger. "Markets Are Trading Zones: On the Material, Cultural, and Interpretative Dimensions of Market Encounters." In *Reconnecting Marketing to Markets,* edited by Luis Araujo, John Finch, and Hans Kjellberg, 117–37. Oxford: Oxford University Press, 2010.

Fleischer, Rasmus. "Femton gastar på död mans kista—om framtidens nätpolitik." In *Efter The Pirate Bay,* edited by Jonas Andersson and Pelle Snickars, 259–81. Stockholm: National Library of Sweden, 2010.

Gerlitz, Caroline. "Die Like Economy. Digitaler Raum, Daten und Wertschöpfung." In *Generation Facebook: Über das Leben im Social Net,* edited by Oliver Leistert and Theo Röhle, 101–23. Bielefeld: Transcript, 2011.

Gewecke, Thomas. Speech at the 40th Anniversary of the Internet Conference, University of California, Los Angeles, 2009.

Gillespie, Tarleton. *Wired Shut: Copyright and the Shape of Digital Culture.* Cambridge, MA, and London: MIT Press, 2007.

Goldsmith, Jack, and Tim Wu. *Who Controls the Internet?: Illusions of a Borderless World.* Oxford and New York: Oxford University Press, 2006.

Granovetter, Mark. "Economic Action and Social Structure: The Problem of Embeddedness." *American Journal of Sociology* 91, no. 3 (1985): 481–510.

Hartley, John. *Digital Futures for Cultural and Media Studies.* Chichester: Wiley-Blackwell, 2012.

Hilderbrand, Lucas. *Inherent Vice: Bootleg Histories of Videotape and Copyright.* Durham and London: Duke University Press, 2009.

Jakobsson, Peter. *Öppenhetsindustrin.* Örebro: Örebro Studies in Media and Communication 13 Södertörn Doctoral Dissertations 65, 2012.

Jenkins, Henry, Sam Ford, and Joshua Green. *Spreadable Media: Creating Value and Meaning in a Networked Culture.* New York: New York University Press, 2013.

Kjellberg, Hans, and Claes-Fredrik Helgesson. "On the Nature of Markets and their Practices." *Marketing Theory* 7 (2007): 137–62.

Klinger, Barbara. *Beyond the Multiplex: Cinema, New Technologies, and the Home.* Berkeley and Los Angeles: University of California Press, 2006.

Knorr-Cetina, Karin, and Ure Bruegger. "Trader's Engagement with Markets: A Postsocial Relationship." *Theory, Culture & Society* 19, no. 5/6 (2002): 161–85.

Kompare, Derek. "Flow to Files: Conceiving 21st Century Media." Paper presented at Media in Transition 2, Cambridge, Massachusetts, May 2005.

Lampland, Martha, and Susan Leigh Star, eds. *Standards and Their Stories: How Quantifying, Classifying, and Formalizing Practices Shape Everyday Life.* Ithaca and London: Cornell University Press, 2009.

Lange, André. *Video On Demand and Catch-Up TV in Europe: A Report Edited by the European Audiovisual Observatory.* Strasbourg: Observatoire Européen de l'Audiovisuel, 2009.

Larsson, Stefan, and Måns Svensson. *Social Norms and Intellectual Property: Online Norms and the European Legal Development.* Lund: Lund University, 2009.

Latour, Bruno. "Drawing Things Together." In *Representation in Scientific Practice,* edited by Michael Lynch and Steve Woolgar, 19–68. Cambridge, MA: MIT Press, 1990.

Latour, Bruno, and Vincent Antonin Lépinay. *The Science of Passionate Interests: An Introduction to Gabriel Tarde's Economic Anthropology.* Chicago: University of Chicago Press, 2009.

Livingstone, Adam, and Richard Taylor. "Hollywood and the Hackers." *BBC Newsnight,* June 9, 2006. http://news.bbc.co.uk/2/hi/programmes/newsnight/5064170.stm

Lobato, Ramon. *Shadow Economies of Cinema: Mapping Informal Film Distribution.* London: Palgrave Macmillan, 2012.

Lobato, Ramon. "The Politics of Digital Distribution: Exclusionary Strategies in Online Cinema." *Studies in Australian Cinema* 3, no. 2 (2009): 167–78.

Lobato, Ramon, Julian Thomas, and Dan Hunter. "Histories of User-Generated Content: Between Formal and Informal Media Economies." *International Journal of Communication* 5 (2011): 899–914.

Loughlin, Patricia. "Pirates, Parasites, Reapers, Sowers, Fruits, Foxes . . . The Metaphors of Intellectual Property." *Sydney Law Review* 28, no. 2 (2006): 211–26.

Manovich, Lev. *Software Takes Command.* London: Bloomsbury Academic, 2008.

Miller, Daniel. *Tales from Facebook.* London: Polity Press, 2011.

Miller, Daniel. "Turning Callon the Right Way Up." *Economy and Society* 31, no. 2 (2002): 218–33.

Munesia, Fabian, Yuval Millo, and Michel Callon. "An Introduction to Market Devices." In *Market Devices,* edited by Michel Callon, Yuval Millo, and Fabian Muniesa, 1–13. Chichester: Wiley-Blackwell, 2007.

Nye, David E. "Technology and the Production of Difference." *American Quarterly* 58, no. 3 (September 2006): 597–618.

Palfrey, John, and Urs Gasser. *Interop: The Promise and Perils of Highly Interconnected Systems.* New York: Basic Books, 2012.

Parks, Lisa. *Cultures in Orbit: Satellites and the Televisual.* Durham: Duke University Press, 2005.

Parks, Lisa, and James Schwoch, eds. *Down to Earth: Satellite Technologies, Industries, and Cultures.* New Brunswick, NJ: Rutgers University Press, 2012.

Pickering, Andrew, and Keith Guzik, eds. *The Mangle in Practice: Science, Society, and Becoming.* Chicago and London: University of Chicago Press, 1995.

The Pirate Bay (blog). "TPB Goes Science, Welcome to The Research Bay," April 18, 2011. http://thepiratebay.se/blog/190.

Potts, Jason, Stuart Cunningham, John Hartley, and Paul Ormerod. "Social Network Markets: A New Definition of the Creative Industries." *Journal of Cultural Economics* 32 (2008): 167–85.

Ramírez, Rafael. "Value Co-production: Intellectual Origins and Implications for Practice and Research." *Strategic Management Journal* 20, no. 1 (1999): 49–65.

Rydell, Anders, and Sam Sundberg. *Piraterna: De svenska fildelerna som plundrade Hollywood.* Stockholm: Ordfront, 2009.

Sarno, David. "The Internet Sure Loves Its Outlaws." *Los Angeles Times,* April 29, 2007. http://www.latimes.com/technology/la-ca-webscout29apr29,0,5609754.story.

Schatz, Tom. "Film Industry Studies and Hollywood History." In *Media Industries: History, Theory, and Method,* edited by Jennifer Holt and Alisa Perren, 45–56. Chichester: Wiley-Blackwell, 2009.

Sedgwick, John, and Michael Pokorny, eds. *An Economic History of Film.* London and New York: Routledge, 2004.

Starosielski, Nicole. "'Warning: Do Not Dig': Negotiating the Visibility of Critical Infrastructures." *Journal of Visual Culture* 11, no. 1 (2012): 1–20.

Sturken, Marita, Douglas Thomas, and Sandra J. Ball-Rokeach, eds. *Technological Visions: The Hopes and Fears that Shape New Technologies.* Philadelphia: Temple University Press, 2004.

Sundaram, Ravi. *Pirate Modernity: Delhi's Media Urbanism.* London and New York: Routledge, 2010.

Travers, Jeffrey, and Stanley Milgram. "An Experimental Study of the Small World Problem." *Sociometry* 32, no. 4 (1969): 425–43.

Turner, Fred. *From Counterculture to Cyberculture: Stewart Brand, the Whole Earth Network, and the Rise of Digital Utopianism.* Chicago: University of Chicago Press, 2006.

Ulin, Jeff. *The Business of Media Distribution: Monetizing Film, TV and Video Content in an Online World.* Amsterdam and Boston: Elsevier, 2010.

Vaidhyanathan, Siva. *The Googlization of Everything (And Why We Should Worry).* Berkeley and Los Angeles: University of California Press, 2011.

Vogel, Harold L. *Entertainment Industry Economics: A Guide for Financial Analysis.* Cambridge, MA: Cambridge University Press, 2010.

White, Harrison C. "Where Do Markets Come From?" *American Journal of Sociology* 87, no. 3 (1981): 517–47.

Winner, Langdon. "Cyberlibertarian Myths and the Prospects for Community." *ACM SIGCAS Computers and Society* 14, no. 27 (1997): 14–19.

Wyatt, Sally. "Danger! Metaphors at Work in Economics, Geophysiology, and the Internet." *Science, Technology & Human Values* 29, no. 2 (Spring 2004): 242–61.

Zittrain, Jonathan. *The Future of the Internet—and How to Stop It.* New Haven, CT: Yale University Press, 2008.

6

TRANSPARENT INTERMEDIARIES

Building the Infrastructures of Connected Viewing

Joshua Braun

This chapter is an analysis of the firms that provide not the products, but the processes of online video distribution. While others in this volume look at the experience of connected viewing itself, I want to examine some of the infrastructures that underlie it, and the emerging players in our media ecosystem who have come to support the "enterprise"—in all senses of the term—of connected viewing, while thus far remaining relatively unknown to audiences. A major purpose of this chapter is to sketch out this category of distribution players, which I describe as "transparent intermediaries," and to underscore their significance to media studies, communication research, and industry.

As media researcher Joseph Turow[1] and many scholars of technology argue, infrastructure, while it often remains unnoticed and invisible, is uniquely important in that it facilitates the exercise of structural power—a method of regulation that enables or impinges on our autonomy not so much by directly influencing our lived experience as by setting the terms of it. Such observations have led to a sustained scholarly interest in the study of communication infrastructures, from the postal service,[2] railways, and telegraph[3] to satellites,[4] networking protocols,[5] Internet service providers,[6] transatlantic cable landings,[7] and online publishing platforms.[8] I am interested in those infrastructures that impact connected viewing, which determine what content we are able to access, where, and on what terms—in other words, infrastructures for online distribution of media entertainment and information.

Infrastructure on a general level has been defined by Susan Leigh Star as "ecological," part of "the balance of action, tools, and the built environment" underpinning organized social practice.[9] As with Turow, Star highlights the exercise of structural power here, emphasizing that the very definition of infrastructure is inseparable from one's relationship to it—to many people traversing a building, a flight of stairs is infrastructure, while to the person in a wheelchair it is an impediment.[10] As with other scholars of socio-technological systems, Star defines infrastructure very broadly—a tendency that, as we shall see, has proven highly generative in allowing researchers to draw useful connections between diverse artifacts and layers of social activity.

Others, too, have come up with useful definitions of infrastructure more specific to the distribution of media and cultural goods. In *Signal and Noise*, for example, Brian Larkin defines infrastructures as "the material forms that allow for exchange over space" and the institutions "that facilitate the flow of goods in a wider cultural as well as physical sense."[11] Yet as Larkin and others point out, the notion of "material forms" is partly figurative, both (a) in the sense that technical artifacts are deeply imbricated in and inseparable from the less tangible nuances of commerce, law, and other social phenomena;[12] and (b) in that our everyday world is now so densely mediated by digital technologies that many important infrastructural components, such as the software we use, offer up affordances and constraints that are not fully predicated on or dictated by their material forms.[13]

That is to say, the architecture of software and digital spaces has become widely understood to be as important, in many contexts, as the design of material infrastructure. Like Star and other scholars of technology, I take a broad view of what elements constitute infrastructure—a category I take to include not just physical and digital artifacts, but also the heterogeneous social, commercial, and legal strata with which these artifacts intertwine to enable and constrain the actions of content providers and connected viewers. And like Larkin, I wish to focus on infrastructures specific to distribution and the exchange of cultural goods.

More specifically, I am interested here in the growing importance of software infrastructures and software providers of a very particular sort: those whose technologies and activities increasingly enable, but also structure, the distribution of video online and, by extension, our experiences of connected viewing. These firms produce many of the products and services relied on by content providers to place their videos in front of connected viewing audiences. Their products range from ready-made software infrastructures for mass distribution to particular algorithms that promise to increase the visibility of videos in search results. A common feature across these vendors and services is that, unlike branded services and platforms (e.g., YouTube, Netflix) whose role as distribution intermediaries is readily apparent to users, the companies I am discussing are most successful when they are invisible to audiences, serving up white-label products—video players, search functionality, etc.—the selling point of which is that they bear the brand not of the manufacturer, but of the content provider.

There is now a growing number of transparent intermediaries with monikers like Ooyala, YuMe, Tremor Video, and Brightcove that are just as integral to connected viewing as branded services like Hulu or Amazon, but that unlike these household names, remain largely invisible to end consumers. If you're watching online clips branded with Miramax, ESPN, CBS, or The History Channel (among many others), chances are very good that while the video player you see may bear the familiar logo of a television channel or film distributor, it is coming to you via the resources provided by one or more of these invisible firms.

My term for these infrastructure providers—*transparent intermediaries*—is intended to evoke the manner in which we as users effectively "see through" them, our eyes focused on familiar brands and the desired content, often as unaware of the interventions they provide as a fish of the water in which it swims.[14] The term is also a provocation and an invitation for further scholarship—*transparency*, as a descriptive term, also means "open to scrutiny."

The notion of infrastructures as heterogeneous in nature and inseparable from a larger ecology of technologies and interests is essential to making sense of our emerging media landscape. As Lisa Parks[15] has pointed out, we (perhaps increasingly) live in a world in which entertainment shares resources with a broad variety of corporate interests—where oil conglomerates share satellite bandwidth with regional television networks, and where the array of stakeholders whose interests shape our media infrastructures is often dizzying. And so it is with the technologies offered up by transparent intermediaries. To give one example, transparent infrastructure companies called "geolocation firms" provide information to online brands about the physical location from which users are accessing their websites and services. Many and perhaps most of the clients of geolocation companies have little to do with news or entertainment media at all—e-commerce firms, for example, have found that the ability to compare an individual's billing information with the location from which he or she is making a purchase is a highly effective method of detecting credit card fraud.

But online video destinations like Hulu and Netflix use geolocation services, too, as do many television networks and content providers who stream their video direct to online consumers. Specifically, they employ the geographical information provided by these companies to determine whether users are attempting to access content from regions outside the countries in which they operate or beyond their target markets. With the help of this information, content providers and branded video portals and services like Hulu or PlayOn can easily restrict access to their content to audiences in the regions they specify (a practice known as "geofencing"), and even provide different versions of their content catalogues and interfaces to users in different markets ("geotargeting").

This influence exerted via infrastructure over who sees what content is an example of the exercise of structural power. Scholars from Louis Althusser[16] to contemporary communication researchers like Yong-Chan Kim and Sandra Ball-Rokeach[17] have asserted that media infrastructures likely play a major role in defining our sense of which communities we belong to and to whom we have civic responsibilities. These infrastructures provide affordances and constraints that help to determine how we as potential viewers can be segmented into target audiences. They influence which publics we share experiences with.[18]

And just as theater owners and broadcast affiliates before them were not simply inert projectors and rows of seats or providers of towers and cables, these new intermediaries and builders of infrastructure for online distribution are aggressive companies with their own interests, business models, and bottom lines. As we can see, their interests often stretch far beyond media news and entertainment, even as the impact of their choices may be felt by these industries and their audiences of connected viewers.

For these reasons, transparent intermediaries, the infrastructures they build, and the diverse interests "invested and contested"[19] in their design are particularly worthy of scrutiny by media scholars, but this does not necessarily mean they are easy to examine. As Star and Geoffrey C. Bowker[20] point out, a primary feature of infrastructure is that it tends to remain invisible until it is disrupted, making it stubbornly difficult to study. But as new and disruptive means of circulating content have gained ground in recent years, questions about the infrastructures involved in media distribution have begun to hold renewed and increasing interest for media scholars. Perhaps even more directly than questions of production or content, the study of distribution cuts straight to the heart of who has access to culture and on what terms.

In the remainder of this chapter, I use a series of cases to examine the rise of these intermediaries. I do this through the lens of science and technology studies, wherein technical infrastructure and its potential to influence human activity have long been a subject of analysis. This exploration of the manner in which transparent intermediaries fit into the emerging landscape of connected viewing leads to a better understanding of the sorts of influence these firms exert and why they are important to media studies. Ultimately, their provision of sophisticated analytics on distribution and connected viewing activity to media providers is becoming a driver in their rapid growth. As these companies take on the role of providing a new generation of audience ratings metrics, their potential to impact not just who sees video content online, but what sort of content is delivered, is also one of the primary ways in which the activity of these companies may help to shape the media landscape going forward.

Considering the Path of Content

To understand how we might think critically about the players who develop infrastructure for online video distribution, let us think for a moment about the route content takes to the consumer. Scholars of science and technology studies, and particularly those among them who study "socio-technological systems," have spent a great deal of time thinking about routes and distribution, if not so much about media. In short, they've developed a unique and sophisticated lens on how products are made to move, examining, among other things, the construction of power distribution networks,[21] shipping routes,[22] railway systems,[23] public transit lines,[24] freeway systems, and digital packet routing.[25]

To give a useful example, in 1987, John Law[26] published a seminal article, titled "Technology and Heterogeneous Engineering," that examined the creation of a

Portuguese shipping route to India known as "the volta"—a distribution route, as it were, albeit largely for trade goods, not media content. The challenge the Portuguese faced in acquiring the goods they sought involved circumnavigating Africa and returning in one piece (hence the name *volta,* Portuguese for "revolution" or "return"). At first, they tried a brute-force approach, launching boats full of burly oarsmen who attempted to row their way from Europe toward the horn of Africa. The vessels, full of hungry rowers, were forced to hug the shore so they could frequently pull in and take on supplies—a serviceable strategy until the boats reached the desert coast of Africa and the availability of rations dried up, forcing a halt to the journey.

After 200 years, however, the Portuguese were able to develop sailing ships that could ride the winds south while enjoying a more manageable ratio of hungry sailors to larder space. At this point, the problem became turning around. The winds and currents that so conveniently carried Portuguese ships down the coast of Africa greatly complicated their return. Catching favorable winds to return the vessels to their origin meant swinging far out into the ocean—unfortunately, once sailors did this, they lost sight of land and found they had no way to navigate. Solving this problem meant developing new tools and methods of celestial navigation, which meant employing royal astronomers. Deploying these methods meant educating legions of semiliterate sailors, and the complications got yet more sticky and diverse from there.

Attending to these cascading problems meant enrolling the services of numerous parties, from shipwrights to astronomers, sailors to royalty. Like the winds and waves, each of these agents proved recalcitrant[27]—limited in their malleability like ill-fitting springs, each tool developed or human resource enrolled in the service of the distribution route simultaneously added new difficulties to be solved.

When all was said and done, the Portuguese trade route—the volta—quite literally "traced out on the map"[28] the influence of the various recalcitrant actors. The working distribution route bore the impression not just of winds or waves, but also of interests and stresses on the system that were social, political, and economic—it was truly a *socio*-technological system. The manner in which system builders simultaneously marshaled and contended with this broad array of different actors is a process Law[29] refers to as "heterogeneous engineering" in reference to the diverse nature of the components and challenges involved.

What Law suggests about the volta is also true of the socio-technological systems—the infrastructures—underlying media distribution. Like the volta and innumerable distribution systems that came before and after it, online video distribution involves the coordination of many complex layers of human activity—commercial, regulatory, and social, as well as technical—all of which may have consequences for the way we watch, consume, and participate in our audiovisual culture.[30] In other words, for connected viewing.

With all the methods that now exist for sharing and viewing online video, the route that content takes to the consumer can appear particularly complex.

Through the auspices of transparent intermediaries, legacy media sites are now rife with sophisticated embeddable video players—dutifully whitelisted[31] for viewing on Twitter and Facebook—as well as RSS feeds and social media-sharing tools to help make online video available in more places than ever before. More places, but not just any place. As we began to see with the geofencing example, companies can restrict many aspects of online distribution, deploying code that limits the web domains on which content can be embedded, the devices on which it will play, whether it is available to noncable subscribers, etc. In the absence of a fixed route to the consumer, video providers place a "Share" button here, a domain restriction there, and so forth, hoping that, like bumpers on a bowling lane, a diverse combination of affordances and constraints will guide their content in a generally desirable direction. All these techniques are enmeshed in, and made possible by, networks of commercial and legal arrangements, from deals with Facebook to transnational lobbying efforts aimed at reshaping intellectual property laws.

The video volta may be fluid, but like the Portuguese volta before it, it is a creative and evolving combination of resources inextricably bounded at the edges by limitations and constraints, like a river changing course within the walls of a canyon. And these creative solutions are the business of the transparent intermediaries. They are effectively selling voltas—ready-made distribution infrastructures, tailored to and around the possibilities and constraints of contemporary connected viewing. In what follows, I offer several specific examples of various sorts of transparent intermediaries—or as they call themselves, "business-to-business distribution companies"—and how they, along with the heterogeneous actors they enroll and contend with, influence the flow of online content and the terms of its availability.

Nexidia

Not unlike the geolocation firms mentioned previously, Nexidia is a company that specializes in providing a rather specific type of service to a broad variety of clientele stretching far beyond the realm of commercial online video. More specifically, Nexidia—previously Fast-Talk Communications—builds software to make audio and video recordings searchable by key word. Since the early 2000s, its main clients have been covert intelligence agencies looking to data mine audio and video recordings potentially containing sensitive information. While specifics are not always provided in news clippings and press releases pertaining to Nexidia, they suggest that the company's products have been marketed to, and are likely in use by, the CIA, FBI, and armed forces.[32] The software's ability to "retrieve any word, name or phrase from voice data, regardless of speaker or dialect, with up to 98% accuracy and up to 72,000 times faster than in real time"[33] has also made the company a darling of the National Security Agency (NSA), and Nexidia technologies are considered likely to have been among the tools used by the NSA for

combing through recorded phone conversations during the wiretapping contro-
versy of the past decade, wherein the phone calls of thousands of Americans were
recorded and analyzed without judicial warrants.[34]

Nexidia has also heavily marketed its software solutions to companies that
operate call centers, which may wish to run key word searches on incoming calls
to look for patterns in customer feedback, as well as to monitor employees for
compliance to approved scripts. The company has carved out a niche in the legal
world, too, by providing its audio search technology as a tool to aid law firms
combing through audiovisual materials during legal discovery processes.

The array of stakeholders relying on Nexidia's software is thus extremely diverse.
Recently, Nexidia has begun expanding its interest in commercial video, and its
products have now become part of the plumbing of online video distribution
in places. For example, between 2008 and 2009 MSNBC began incorporating
Nexidia's technology into its online video offerings, using it to make web video
searchable by key word. Video has traditionally been considered an "opaque" sort
of media, meaning that it was not the sort of content that could be easily surfaced
or recommended by the text-based search engines and algorithms that make up
users' primary tools for navigating the web.[35] Nexidia's technology made the spo-
ken content of clips legible to text-based search engines, which not only helped to
search-optimize MSNBC.com's offerings, but resulted in a fascinating shift in the
patterns of video consumption on the site. Where previously audiences' navigation
of MSNBC.com videos had been based largely on what was recent or heavily promoted on the website, as users gained the ability to more easily and accurately search
through the actual content of video, they began to locate, access, and share more
clips based on their personal interests. Former CEO Charles Tillinghast recounted,

> [W]hat we're finding is that demand has shifted significantly from the most
> popular videos, the top videos, to the tail, and that we're seeing much more
> take-up on tail viewing of video in a way that we have not seen before. . . .
> the niche stuff. And so it used to be that, in round numbers, that 80 percent
> of the videos watched were the top 100 most popular videos, or 80 percent
> of the streams were amongst the top 100 videos. Now we're seeing that it's
> almost shifting so that the majority of the . . . videos viewed . . . are outside
> of that top 100. So interest is being spread across a large set of topics and
> news stories, and it's not as concentrated on just a few stories that we hap-
> pen to put on the cover.[36]

Tillinghast illustrates the manner in which the incorporation of Nexidia's
technology shifted the path of the video volta, placing different content in front
of audiences and transforming what content was visible on MSNBC and NBC
News sites. Significantly, as all this video was paired with paid advertising, it also
changed the worth of niche content to the company, which may have impacts on
its programming over the longer term.

Moreover, while MSNBC.com did much of the work of integrating Nexidia technology into its own video content management system, Nexidia itself has subsequently begun to expand more aggressively into the commercial video market, developing similar technologies to license to other content companies. Already a heterogeneous product, drawing on demand across industries as diverse as defense, legal discovery, and telemarketing, as Nexidia expands its commercial video offerings the company is engaging in further feats of heterogeneous engineering. A prime example is the manner in which Nexidia is capitalizing on changes to the legal framework surrounding online media.

With the recent passage by Congress of the Twenty-First Century Communications and Video Accessibility Act,[37] content providers whose video is closed captioned on air are responsible for providing similar closed captioning information when the video is placed online. However, that captioning information has heretofore often been omitted when video is encoded for the web and mobile devices, leaving major content providers with massive libraries of caption-less web video that need to be paired and synced with equally large libraries of closed captioning information—a job that would take an immense amount of time to perform manually.

Nexidia's software, meanwhile, can pair the audio tracks hours' worth of video with existing captioning information in seconds. Not surprisingly, Nexidia is busy turning this technical ability into a marketing pitch[38] that will, if the company succeeds, not just solve a one-time problem, but make Nexidia an obligatory point of passage[39] going forward for video providers who want to make their content available online. Additionally, as more video providers buy into Nexidia's tools, the experience of MSNBC.com may well be repeated. Patterns of content consumption and connected viewing may well change as online video becomes findable in new ways and new places, and if so, this is likely to impact the market strategies of video providers as online distribution becomes an ever-larger part of their business models.

YuMe

If Nexidia provides a very specific tool across a broad variety of contexts, other business-to-business firms are much more tightly focused on the online video space. YuMe, for example, is an advertising network that offers rather extensive software platforms and services to advertisers, video publishers, and device manufacturers to undergird ad-supported content distribution. Both advertisers and content providers can use its software to manage the ads they're buying and selling and place them alongside desirable content. The ad network software is integrated with a variety of different web, mobile, and connected TV publishing platforms, and all its functionality can be managed from within a simple point-and-click desktop program.

But there's more going on with YuMe than simple ad sales. As one manager at the company explained, "[T]he development of our infrastructure is really important because without the technology component that we bring to the table, we're just another video ad network."[40] While YuMe's infrastructure is extensive, the following examples demonstrate how the technological infrastructure it provides affects the flow of content and the experience of connected viewing.

First, connected television makers and other device manufacturers can ship their hardware with YuMe's software development tools preinstalled, allowing these manufacturers to potentially take in ad revenue themselves by including ads in their own connected television interfaces, as well as to promote the tools to developers as a way to easily monetize new apps (using the developer kit, YuMe's interstitial and display advertising can effectively be layered on top of any application). This software infrastructure thus allows television set builders to take on novel roles within the media distribution ecosystem such as selling ad space and retailing content.[41]

Another example of how YuMe impacts distribution and the experience of connected viewing concerns embeddable video. The best thing for users about embeddable video is simultaneously the worst thing about it for advertisers: that it can be displayed nearly anywhere. This is appropriately celebrated as being good for consumers and great for free speech. But the lack of control over the context in which videos appear tends to thoroughly frighten advertisers who want their commercials to appear next to brand-friendly content and nothing else. This has made embeddable players, as popular as they are, extremely difficult for video publishers to monetize through advertising.

YuMe made its name, in part, by brokering a technological solution to this problem. Advertisers buy ads through YuMe and, wherever an embedded video player appears, YuMe's service algorithmically surveils the sites on which videos are served to make a determination as to whether they are "brand-safe environments."[42] Pages and sites deemed unacceptable are added to the company's "constantly growing blacklist of more than 1.6 million Web domains." YuMe's software is then able "to confirm that the player is not embedded on a blacklisted domain before serving an ad."[43] YuMe's solution is another example of a video volta—like a ship charting a course between two obstacles, YuMe threads a needle between the demands of publishers on the one hand and advertisers on the other, creating a compromise in which video players can be embedded anywhere, but advertising is only packaged with them in "brand-safe" environments. In this way, video providers are able to generate ad revenue while still delivering content to places it would not have gone otherwise.

Many will rightfully regard this set of tools and strategies as a rather ingenious solution, and it's also worth noting that it's a layering of infrastructure—a heterogeneous solution that takes advantage of, rather than circumnavigates, a traditional ad-supported business model for video content. This is, perhaps, an unsurprising, even laudable, business strategy, as it allows YuMe to capitalize on numerous resources that are ready to hand, including the tremendous inertia of legacy advertising and content industries, as well as the learned behavior of consumers who—at least in the United States—are still accustomed to an ad-supported model for television and who (at least as far as YuMe's market studies show) tend to prefer free, ad-supported online video to pay-for-service fare. And as we've come to understand, in taking advantage of existing social, commercial, and technical infrastructures, strategies like YuMe's also serve to perpetuate those socio-technical systems.

For connected viewing, this all means that, to the extent such ad-supported strategies prevail, we may watch in more ways and more places, yet still have an experience that in many ways resembles traditional ad-supported television. There are, however, some caveats. As technologies like YuMe's ad network software and developer kit—along with similar infrastructures provided by competitors—lower barriers to entry for new publishers who wish to monetize their content, we may see the continued emergence of more diverse sources of video content. Meanwhile, the affordances offered by YuMe for targeting advertising may well mean the emergence of more niche and low-budget video advertisers, for whom traditional mass media video advertising has previously not been cost effective.[44]

Ooyala

Ooyala is a company founded in 2007 by defectors from Google's YouTube product line who saw a lucrative market for providing some of the same tools, along with more than a few new ones, to professional content providers who wished to distribute videos branded with their own imprimatur, rather than YouTube's one-size-fits-all interface and (at the time) amateur-targeted brand.

Like YuMe, Ooyala provides an extensive amount of technical infrastructure to its clients. But if YuMe's services and infrastructure are specialized around a particular (ad-supported) business model for content distribution, Ooyala is comparatively something of a jack-of-all-trades when it comes to online video distribution. The company's online service and software application, Backlot, for instance, includes an interface for managing online video distribution that allows publishers to make a broad array of distribution choices with regard to their videos, including the sorts of devices they will play on, the length of time they're available, the sites on which they can or cannot be embedded—and, of course, which countries they should be available in. To return briefly to the example of geofencing, for companies using Backlot, restricting content to the United States, or any other country, is as easy as ticking a box.

This sort of geographic direction is one of an enormous number of things that Backlot can do to simultaneously facilitate and control the flow of content online. The application provides a litany of options to clients, including an iTunes-like interface for managing and publishing massive libraries of video content that allows publishers to quickly create custom, branded skins for Ooyala's video player, as well as to instantly syndicate videos to specified websites, feeds, social networks, online video portals, and Internet-connected devices. Users can manage myriad brands, as well as both live and recorded content streams, point and click to create paywalls around their content, manage portfolios of advertisements, and—upon loading up a video within the program—place slots for interstitial and display ads alongside content by clicking the desired points on a QuickTime-like clip timeline. In short, Backlot's interface provides a one-stop shop for clients, with tools for executing nearly every traditional distribution decision—region, venue, release dates and windows, exhibition partnerships, sale price, and so on—in a digital environment.

Ooyala, along with its competitors like Brightcove and thePlatform, solves key problems of device compatibility for content publishers—its distribution platform is constantly updated to ensure that video will work across the confusing tangle of file formats, hardware configurations, and display sizes that come with our ever-growing menagerie of phones, tablets, and connected televisions. Rather than undertake cost-benefit analyses to decide whether there's value in developing for every new video-capable device that's released, content providers who outsource their distribution to transparent intermediaries can comfortably assume that their content will play nearly anywhere, allowing connected viewers to tune in on more devices and in more places.

And it is creeping demands like these that are driving the expansion of transparent intermediaries. While on the one hand we might see feature-specific (e.g., geolocation firms, Nexidia), business model-specific (e.g., YuMe), and generalist (e.g., Ooyala) intermediaries as engaging in different market strategies, in some cases they might also be thought of as respective stages in the evolution of distribution firms. Ooyala executive David Gibbons[45] explained how the needs of clients progress over time and, as they accumulate scale, in turn fuel a great expansion in the number of services offered by individual distribution firms:

> In the early days of online video, the key thing was just being able to upload the video and encode it to play back in a player on your browser. . . . And then as that market has progressed, people have realized, "I need to not just upload a video, I need to upload ten thousand videos, because I have this huge content library, and I want to get it all up," at which point you need a much more heavyweight uploading architecture and encoding-and-processing architecture. . . . So that's right away going to put the company into . . . "We need a cloud computing system that can do that." And the next thing you know, [the intermediary is] a cloud computing company, as well as a video processing-uploading company. . . . [Then] add a bunch of different technologies—support for iOS, support for Android—that weren't present [a few years] before into the mix, and you realize, "Okay, we actually have to become mobile experts, bandwidth connectivity experts." . . . And then . . . the next need that arises is they want to understand where it's being watched, how it's being watched, and all of that information about who their audience is, and what their audience likes and doesn't like. So that

puts you into the analytics world. . . . And I could go on, because obviously once you start putting advertising around things, you suddenly need to be an ad network-aware company. . . . As you start to deal with bigger websites, you need to understand how bigger websites are managed through content management systems. . . . And it basically continues expanding.

Like Portuguese merchants who found both the problems and the complexity of their solutions snowballing before them, Gibbons's description demonstrates how distribution networks can quickly evolve toward far greater complexity and heterogeneity. One aspect in particular of these systems—analytics—deserves special attention, and I will turn to it shortly. However, it's also worth noting that there is a teleological aspect to Gibbons's description that isn't just about how distribution firms expand to meet the needs of video providers, but about the way that these clients' own understanding of the market should mature as they grow. As Gibbons himself put it, content providers moving into the online video space are "at different points in understanding the whole value chain that allows video to be delivered directly to consumers."[46] From this perspective, content providers progress through successive, archetypical stages of maturity, beginning with a naive understanding that their video needs to be online, and eventually grokking the necessity of cross-platform playback, advanced analytics, and more.

One way to look at the portrait Gibbons paints of successive client archetypes is that even large generalist intermediaries like Ooyala that aim to support many different sorts of online video providers must by necessity focus their resources by caricaturing and categorizing their customers, perhaps even channeling them into particular and desirable use cases.[47] And as with any tool or infrastructure, these roles and use cases inevitably get inscribed in business-to-business companies' technical offerings and interfaces—in the same way that YuMe's infrastructure, like that of other ad networks before it, reproduces traditional economic roles of advertiser and publisher in new media spaces, Ooyala's Backlot software is replete with tabs and buttons with labels like "Ad Sets" and "Paywalls" that readily reify and reproduce existing business models and industry categories. And while it would be foolish to be needlessly or naively critical of such features—they are, after all, logical and intelligent responses to economic realities—media researchers and critical scholars going forward would do well to plumb and pry at the balance of structure and agency enacted in the technical architectures of online distribution, and the work they do as pieces within heterogeneous systems that reify some cultural and economic categories, while helping to disrupt or reimagine others.

The Importance of Analytics

Within media industries, audiences constitute an essential but complex unknown whose wants, needs, opinions, and interests must be selectively measured and simplified to produce an actionable market. And this is precisely the business in which many of the most prominent business-to-business distribution companies see their future. In enabling millions upon millions of video views, companies like Ooyala, YuMe, and their numerous competitors are simultaneously collecting enormous volumes of information about audiences and their use of content.

Nearly every online firm involved in distribution provides its clients with extensive analytics. Ooyala's Backlot software provides a typical example. It delivers clients regular performance breakdowns for their online content, detailing the number of times a video appeared in users' browsers and devices ("displays"), the number of times it was actually played ("plays"), and the total number of hours of video playback delivered over the requested interval. These performance metrics can be broken down by numerous categories, including the type of device, operating system, and browser on which the video was played; the countries, cities, and client-designated market areas in which it was played; as well as the web domains and specific webpages on which it was viewed. The popularity of videos in different geographic locations can be displayed via tables, graphs, and "heat maps"—actual geographic maps on which target markets, states, or countries are shaded according to their viewing habits.

Clients can also see how many times a video was played by unique users, how many users watched the whole thing, and how many played through 25, 50, or 75 percent of the clip. The immediacy of these viewing metrics can be striking at times—for example, clients can pull up a video and watch the software sketch a graph that plots the number of viewers for each second of the clip. The application also keeps track of more longitudinal measures, such as the average videos watched per viewer per day, the "conversion rate" for each video (i.e., of the number of times it appeared, how often it was viewed), the average amount of time for which it was watched, and the amount of data in gigabytes delivered by the service. Sharing on social networks, via e-mail, and through video embeds is also recorded, and can also be broken down by region, device, and web address.

Turow[48] and other scholars, like Christopher W. Anderson[49] and Josh Heuman,[50] have dutifully underscored the notion that "the manner in which [media producers] imagine their audience has public consequences."[51] Since, no doubt, not everything that we value or find consequential about our cultural identities or public discourse can be easily quantified, measured, binned, graphed, or regressed, and because those things that are measured may be condensed, weighted, and acted upon in different ways by content providers with different commercial interests, an important discussion has arisen among media scholars about the "configuration"[52] and "industrial construction" of audiences.[53]

Turow,[54] in particular, notes how marketers and advertisers use analytics to reduce audiences into categories of "target" and "waste" in ways that have influenced the content publishers put forward. Similar concerns—about the nature of audience measurement and its influence on the type and availability of content produced—have long swirled around the strategic choices and ambiguities surrounding Nielsen's modeling and representation of television audiences, and have only increased as Nielsen itself has sought to take advantage of localized and digital analytics in ways that may or may not accurately represent the habits and interests of minority audiences.[55]

From a civic perspective, the sorts of traditional mass media measured by Nielsen are, at their best, "general-interest intermediaries,"[56] exposing us to views we might not have chosen of our own accord and making the interests of minority and opposition groups visible to the majority. For concerned citizens, what matters about Nielsen statistics is that they succeed in making these groups visible and represent their activity fairly. The politics involved are the politics of representation and the risk of misrepresentation or, worse, omission and invisibility. The worry here is that groups whose viewing activities are not accurately recorded will not be not sought after as audiences. Their interests and views may consequently be less readily represented in the content of media, and thereby omitted from the public agenda. Such concerns have historically invited challenges—warranted or not—to Nielsen's sampling methods, and made changes to them the subject of much political debate.

New media analytics, on the other hand, have the ability to provide "universe data"—a complete record of viewing activity, rather than a random sample. Because of this, they may, at their best, succeed in making visible the existence of interests and publics who were hitherto lost in the noise of previous systems of representation. At the same time, in a world where providers have all the data about their audiences, identifying trends is no longer a matter of what data are statistically significant—everything is—but rather of what data are interesting. And, as social critics point out, this begs the further questions of "interesting to whom?" and "for what reason?"

The obvious answer in a commercially driven media environment is that audiences are interesting when they are profitable. Thus, the worry is that rather than resulting in a better reflection of our myriad organic social interests and concerns, the development of new media analytics has tended, and will continue to tend, toward treating us as consumers rather than citizens, niche markets rather than social groups. Like traditional film and television audiences before, connected viewers will be defined, first and foremost, as consumers. But while this may be a continuation of previous trends, civic-minded critics have long seen the tendency of content providers to treat audiences more as consumers than as citizens as a necessary evil of commercial media. Observers like Turow[57] and Anderson[58] worry that, as audiences are interpellated into ever more convenient, instrumental, and commercially viable social identities, the drawbacks of commercialization may eventually outweigh its benefits.

Conclusion

Even as transparent intermediaries remain invisible to us as audiences and connected viewers, we are increasingly legible to them. Insofar, then, as these firms create the necessary fictions of the market through their algorithmic representations of audiences, we, as producers, consumers, citizens, and connected viewers, must learn to think critically about the systems of media we want in relation to the systems of media that these constructions might favor. And just as importantly, we must learn to think critically about infrastructures that fade into the background. Parks has called this "the politics of infrastructural intelligibility" and issued a call

> for a form of criticism that is organised not upon the spectacle of the monumental or the new, but upon the materiality of the thing—a form of criticism that leads to investigations of the raw materials, resources, labour, affect and energy required to sustain a system.[59]

Understanding the role of transparent intermediaries, along with their interests and their leverage within the media ecosystem, will prove vitally important to understanding how the landscape of connected viewing evolves. As major industry players and small video start-ups alike begin turning to these firms to distribute content and analyze who is using it, transparent intermediaries stand to become just as essential to the media ecosystem as cable providers and broadcast affiliates before them—another layer of infrastructure that enables, but also shapes and constrains in important ways, our connected viewing activity. And at no time will this scholarly and critical attention be more important than it is right now, while these firms are still relatively new, and their own business models and infrastructures are still developing. As their tools and business models acquire more path dependency, they will tend to become invisible once again, while scholars who take note of them will be left to discuss what might have been, rather than what could be.

Notes

1. Joseph Turow, *Media Systems in Society: Understanding Industries, Strategies, and Power* (New York: Longman, 1992).
2. Richard R. John, *Spreading the News: The American Postal System from Franklin to Morse* (Cambridge, MA: Harvard University Press, 1995).
3. James W. Carey, "A Cultural Approach to Communication," in *Communication as Culture* (Boston: Unwin Hyman, 1989), 13–36.
4. Lisa Parks, "Satellites, Oil, and Footprints," in *Down to Earth: Satellite Technologies, Industries, and Cultures,* eds. Lisa Parks and James Schwoch (New Brunswick, NJ: Rutgers University Press, 2012), 122–40; Lisa Parks, "Technostruggles and the Satellite Dish: A Populist Approach to Infrastructure," in *Cultural Technologies: The Shaping of Culture in Media and Society,* ed. Göran Bolin (New York: Routledge, 2012), 64–84.
5. Thomas P. Hughes, *Rescuing Prometheus: Four Monumental Projects that Changed the Modern World* (New York: Pantheon, 1998); Barbara van Schewick, *Internet Architecture and Innovation* (Cambridge, MA: MIT Press, 2010).
6. Andrew Blum, *Tubes: A Journey to the Center of the Internet* (New York: Ecco, 2012).
7. Nicole Starosielski, "'Warning: Do Not Dig': Negotiating the Visibility of Critical Infrastructures," *Journal of Visual Culture* 11 (2012): 38–57.
8. Tarleton Gillespie, "The Politics of 'Platforms,'" *New Media & Society* 12 (2010): 347–64; Tarleton Gillespie, "Can an Algorithm Be Wrong?," *Limn* 1 (2012), http://limn

.it/can-an-algorithm-be-wrong/; Mike Ananny, "Press-Public Collaboration as Infrastructure," *American Behavioral Scientist* 57, no. 5 (2012): 623–42.

9. Susan Leigh Star, "The Ethnography of Infrastructure," *American Behavioral Scientist* 43 (1999): 377.

10. Star, "The Ethnography of Infrastructure," 380.

11. Brian Larkin, *Signal and Noise: Media, Infrastructure, and Urban Culture in Nigeria* (Durham: Duke University Press, 2008), 5.

12. Thomas P. Hughes, "The Evolutions of Large Technological Systems," in *The Social Construction of Technological Systems*, eds. Wiebe E. Bijker, Thomas P. Hughes, and Trevor Pinch (Cambridge, MA: MIT Press, 1987), 51–82; Thomas P. Hughes, *Human-Built World: How to Think about Technology and Culture* (Chicago: University of Chicago Press, 2004); John Law, "Technology and Heterogeneous Engineering: The Case of Portuguese Expansion," in *The Social Construction of Technological Systems: New Directions in the Sociology and History of Technology*, eds. Wiebe E. Bijker, Thomas P. Hughes, and Trevor J. Pinch (Cambridge, MA: MIT Press, 1987), 111–34; Bruno Latour (as Jim Johnson), "Mixing Humans and Nonhumans Together," *Social Problems* 35 (1988): 298–310; Trevor J. Pinch, "The Invisible Technologies of Goffman's Sociology: From the Merry-Go-Round to the Internet," *Technology and Culture* 51 (2010): 409–24.

13. Lawrence Lessig, *Code: Version 2.0* (New York: Basic Books, 2006); Yochai Benkler, *The Wealth of Networks: How Social Production Transforms Markets and Freedom* (New Haven, CT: Yale University Press, 2006); Tarleton Gillespie, *Wired Shut: Copyright and the Shape of Digital Culture* (Cambridge, MA: MIT Press, 2007); Jonathan Zittrain, *The Future of the Internet—and How to Stop It* (New Haven, CT: Yale University Press, 2008); Barbara van Schewick, *Internet Architecture and Innovation* (Cambridge, MA: MIT Press, 2010).

14. One such company, early to the market, even called itself "Transpera," a title intended to evoke this exact notion about the services it provided to content companies.

15. Parks, "Satellites, Oil, and Footprints."

16. Louis Althusser, "Ideology and Ideological State Apparatuses" in *Cultural Theory: An Anthology*, eds. Imre Szeman and Timothy Kaposy (Malden, MA: Wiley-Blackwell, 2011), 204–22.

17. Yong-Chan Kim and Sandra J. Ball-Rokeach, "Civic Engagement From a Communication Infrastructure Perspective," *Communication Theory* 16 (2006): 173–97.

18. It's worth noting here that users' "piracy" of television and film online—and the sophistication of the infrastructures surrounding this activity—can be viewed as an objection to the terms of access set by officially sanctioned systems of distribution. For an excellent overview of this argument, see Michael Z. Newman, "Free TV: File-Sharing and the Value of Television," *Television & New Media* 13 (2012): 463–79, as well as Patrick Vonderau et al. (this volume).

19. Daniel Chamberlain, "Television Interfaces," *Journal of Popular Film and Television* 38 (2010): 84.

20. Susan Leigh Star and Geoffrey C. Bowker, "How to Infrastructure," in *The Handbook of New Media*, eds. Leah A. Lievrouw and Sonia Livingstone (Thousand Oaks, CA: SAGE, 2002), 151–62.

21. Thomas P. Hughes, "The Electrification of America: The System Builders," *Technology and Culture* 20 (1979): 124–61; Thomas P. Hughes, *Networks of Power: Electrification in Western Society, 1880-1930* (Baltimore: Johns Hopkins University Press, 1983).

22. Law, "Technology and Heterogeneous Engineering."

23. John Law and Annemarie Mol, "Local Entanglements or Utopian Moves: An Inquiry into Train Accidents," in *Utopia and Organization*, ed. Martin Parker (Oxford: Blackwell, 2002), 82–105.

24. Glenn Bugos, "System Reshapes the Corporation: Joint Ventures in the Bay Area Rapid Transit System," in *Systems, Experts, and Computers*, eds. Agatha C. Hughes and Thomas P. Hughes (Cambridge, MA: MIT Press, 2000), 113–31.

25. Hughes, *Rescuing Prometheus*.

26. Law, "Technology and Heterogeneous Engineering."

27. Kenneth Burke, *Permanence and Change: An Anatomy of Purpose*, 2nd ed. (New York: Bobbs-Merrill, 1965), 247–72.

28. Law, "Technology and Heterogeneous Engineering."

29. Ibid.

30. Joshua Braun, "Going Over the Top: Online Television Distribution as Socio-technical System," *Communication, Culture & Critique* 6 (2013): 432–58.

31. Social networks like Twitter and Facebook keep "whitelists" of embeddable players that are allowed to appear on their pages, and companies wishing to allow users of these sites to embed their videos must apply to have their players added to the whitelists. Significantly, it is often easier to have a player whitelisted when it is provided by a transparent intermediary, as the same player technology will generally have already been whitelisted for use by other content providers.

32. Fast-Talk Communications, "Fast-Talk Invited to Exhibit on Capitol Hill at Exclusive Small Business Homeland Security Expo," press release, 2002, LexisNexis Academic Database.

33. Dan Verton, "Technology Aids Hunt for Terrorists," *ComputerWorld*, September 9, 2002, http://www.computerworld.com/s/article/74052/Technology_aids_hunt_for_terrorists.

34. James Bamford, *The Shadow Factory: The Ultra-Secret NSA from 9/11 to the Eavesdropping on America* (New York: Knopf Doubleday, 2008), 323–4.

35. Author phone interview with Drew Lanham, May 24, 2012.

36. Andy Plesser, "MSNBC.com Chief Says Video Transcripts Make Editing Scalable with 'Minimal Human Intervention,'" *Beet.TV*, August 24, 2009, http://www.beet.tv/2009/08/msnbccom-chief-says-video-transcripts-makes-editing-scalable.html.

37. Twenty-First Century Communications and Video Accessibility Act, 2010, Pub. L. No. 111–260, 111th Cong., 2nd Sess. (May 4, 2010).

38. Author phone interview with Drew Lanham, May 24, 2012.

39. Michel Callon, "Some Elements of a Sociology of Translation: Domestication of the Scallops and the Fishermen of St Brieuc Bay," in *Power, Action and Belief: A New Sociology of Knowledge?*, ed. John Law (Boston: Routledge & Kegan Paul, 1986), 196–233.

40. Author phone interview, May 21, 2012. This individual went back and forth about whether she wanted to have her quotes attributed by name. As she never provided me with a clear decision, I will err on the side of caution and simply attribute the quote to "a YuMe executive."

41. Though, importantly, we might also think of this development as, in some ways, a return to earlier revenue models, lest we forget that the origins of all the "Big Three" broadcast networks involved ownership/investment by device manufacturers like the Radio Corporation of America and the Columbia Phonograph Company.

42. YuMe Corporation, "Safeguards for Your Brand," 2011, http://www.yume.com/content/brand-security.

43. Ibid.

44. John Battelle, *The Search: How Google and Its Rivals Rewrote the Rules of Business and Transformed Our Culture* (New York: Portfolio, 2005), 153–88.

45. Author phone interview with David Gibbons, August 7, 2012.

46. Ibid.

47. Steve Woolgar, "Configuring the User: The Case of Usability Trials," in *A Sociology of Monsters: Essays on Power, Technology and Domination*, ed. John Law (New York: Routledge, 1991), 57–99.

48. Joseph Turow, "Audience Construction and Culture Production: Marketing Surveillance in the Digital Age," *The ANNALS of the American Academy of Political and Social Science* 597 (2004): 103–21; Joseph Turow, *The Daily You: How the New Advertising*

Industry Is Defining Your Identity and Your Worth (New Haven, CT: Yale University Press, 2011).

49. Christopher W. Anderson, "Deliberative, Agonistic, and Algorithmic Audiences," *International Journal of Communication* 5 (2011): 529–47.
50. Josh Heuman, "Configuring the Viewer in Transition: Communication Policy and the Television Viewer between 'Old' and 'New' Media" (PhD diss., University of Wisconsin–Madison, 2006).
51. Anderson, "Deliberative, Agonistic, and Algorithmic Audiences," 530.
52. Woolgar, "Configuring the User"; Nelly Oudshoorn, Els Rommes, and Marcelle Stienstra, "Configuring the User as Everybody: Gender and Design Cultures in Information and Communication Technologies," *Science, Technology & Human Values* 29 (2004): 30–63.
53. Turow, "Audience Construction and Culture Production," *The Daily You.*
54. Ibid.
55. Heuman, "Configuring the Viewer in Transition."
56. Cass R. Sunstein, *Republic.com 2.0* (Princeton, NJ: Princeton University Press, 2007).
57. Turow, "Audience Construction and Culture Production."
58. Anderson, "Deliberative, Agonistic, and Algorithmic Audiences."
59. Parks, "Technostruggles and the Satellite Dish," 81.

References

Althusser, Louis. "Ideology and Ideological State Apparatuses." In *Cultural Theory: An Anthology*, edited by Imre Szeman and Timothy Kaposy, 204–22. Malden, MA: Wiley-Blackwell, 2011.

Ananny, Mike. "Press-Public Collaboration as Infrastructure." *American Behavioral Scientist* 57, no. 5 (2012): 623–42.

Anderson, Christopher W. "Deliberative, Agonistic, and Algorithmic Audiences." *International Journal of Communication* 5 (2011): 529–47.

Bamford, James. *The Shadow Factory: The Ultra-Secret NSA from 9/11 to the Eavesdropping on America*. New York: Knopf Doubleday, 2008.

Battelle, John. *The Search: How Google and Its Rivals Rewrote the Rules of Business and Transformed Our Culture*. New York: Portfolio, 2005.

Benkler, Yochai. *The Wealth of Networks: How Social Production Transforms Markets and Freedom*. New Haven, CT: Yale University Press, 2006.

Blum, Andrew. *Tubes: A Journey to the Center of the Internet*. New York: Ecco, 2012.

Braun, Joshua. "Going Over the Top: Online Television Distribution as Socio-technical System." *Communication, Culture & Critique*, 6 (2013): 432–58.

Bugos, Glenn. "System Reshapes the Corporation: Joint Ventures in the Bay Area Rapid Transit System." In *Systems, Experts, and Computers*, edited by Agatha C. Hughes and Thomas P. Hughes, 113–31. Cambridge, MA: MIT Press, 2000.

Burke, Kenneth. *Permanence and Change: An Anatomy of Purpose*. 2nd ed. New York: Bobbs-Merrill, 1965.

Callon, Michel. "Some Elements of a Sociology of Translation: Domestication of the Scallops and the Fishermen of St Brieuc Bay." In *Power, Action and Belief: A New Sociology of Knowledge?*, edited by John Law, 196–233. Boston: Routledge & Kegan Paul, 1986.

Carey, James. "A Cultural Approach to Communication." In *Communication as Culture*, edited by James Carey, 13–36. Boston: Unwin Hyman, 1989.

Chamberlain, Daniel. "Television Interfaces." *Journal of Popular Film and Television* 38 (2010): 84–8.

Fast-Talk Communications. "Fast-Talk Invited to Exhibit on Capitol Hill at Exclusive Small Business Homeland Security Expo." Press release, 2002. LexisNexis Academic Database.

Gillespie, Tarleton. "Can an Algorithm Be Wrong?" *Limn* 1 (2012). http://limn.it/can-an-algorithm-be-wrong/.

Gillespie, Tarleton. "The Politics of 'Platforms.'" *New Media & Society* 12 (2010): 347–64.

Gillespie, Tarleton. *Wired Shut: Copyright and the Shape of Digital Culture.* Cambridge, MA: MIT Press, 2007.

Heuman, Josh. "Configuring the Viewer in Transition: Communication Policy and the Television Viewer between 'Old' and 'New' Media." PhD diss., University of Wisconsin–Madison, 2006.

Hughes, Thomas P. *Human-Built World: How to Think about Technology and Culture.* Chicago: University of Chicago Press, 2004.

Hughes, Thomas P. *Networks of Power: Electrification in Western Society, 1880-1930.* Baltimore: Johns Hopkins University Press, 1983.

Hughes, Thomas P. *Rescuing Prometheus: Four Monumental Projects that Changed the Modern World.* New York: Pantheon, 1998.

Hughes, Thomas P. "The Electrification of America: The System Builders." *Technology and Culture* 20 (1979): 124–61.

Hughes, Thomas P. "The Evolutions of Large Technological Systems." In *The Social Construction of Technological Systems,* edited by Wiebe E. Bijker, Thomas P. Hughes, and Trevor Pinch, 51–82. Cambridge, MA: MIT Press, 1987.

John, Richard R. *Spreading the News: The American Postal System from Franklin to Morse.* Cambridge, MA: Harvard University Press, 1995.

Kim, Yong-Chan, and Sandra J. Ball-Rokeach. "Civic Engagement From a Communication Infrastructure Perspective." *Communication Theory* 16 (2006): 173–97.

Larkin, Brian. *Signal and Noise: Media, Infrastructure, and Urban Culture in Nigeria.* Durham: Duke University Press, 2008.

Latour, Bruno. "Mixing Humans and Nonhumans Together." *Social Problems* 35 (1988): 298–310.

Law, John. "Technology and Heterogeneous Engineering: The Case of Portuguese Expansion." In *The Social Construction of Technological Systems: New Directions in the Sociology and History of Technology,* edited by Wiebe E. Bijker, Thomas P. Hughes, and Trevor Pinch, 111–34. Cambridge, MA: MIT Press, 1987.

Law, John, and Annemarie Mol. "Local Entanglements or Utopian Moves: An Inquiry into Train Accidents." In *Utopia and Organization,* edited by Martin Parker, 82–105. Oxford: Blackwell, 2002.

Lessig, Lawrence. *Code: Version 2.0.* New York: Basic Books, 2006.

Newman, Michael Z. "Free TV: File-Sharing and the Value of Television." *Television & New Media* 13 (2012): 463–79.

Oudshoorn, Nelly, Els Rommes, and Marcelle Stienstra. "Configuring the User as Everybody: Gender and Design Cultures in Information and Communication Technologies." *Science, Technology & Human Values* 29 (2004): 30–63.

Parks, Lisa. "Satellites, Oil, and Footprints." In *Down to Earth: Satellite Technologies, Industries, and Cultures,* edited by Lisa Parks and James Schwoch, 122–40. New Brunswick, NJ: Rutgers University Press, 2012.

Parks, Lisa. "Technostruggles and the Satellite Dish: A Populist Approach to Infrastructure." In *Cultural Technologies: The Shaping of Culture in Media and Society,* edited by Göran Bolin, 64–84. New York: Routledge, 2012.

Pinch, Trevor J. "The Invisible Technologies of Goffman's Sociology: From the Merry-Go-Round to the Internet." *Technology and Culture* 51 (2010): 409–24.

Plesser, Andy. "MSNBC.com Chief Says Video Transcripts Make Editing Scalable with 'Minimal Human Intervention.'" *Beet.TV,* August 24, 2009. http://www.beet.tv/2009/08/msnbccom-chief-says-video-transcripts-makes-editing-scalable.html.

Star, Susan Leigh. "The Ethnography of Infrastructure." *American Behavioral Scientist* 43 (1999): 377–91.

Star, Susan Leigh, and Geoffrey C. Bowker. "How to Infrastructure." In *The Handbook of New Media,* edited by Leah A. Lievrouw and Sonia Livingstone, 151–62. Thousand Oaks, CA: SAGE, 2002.

Starosielski, Nicole. "'Warning: Do Not Dig: Negotiating the Visibility of Critical Infrastructures." *Journal of Visual Culture* 11 (2012): 38–57.

Sunstein, Cass R. *Republic.com 2.0.* Princeton, NJ: Princeton University Press, 2007.

Turow, Joseph. "Audience Construction and Culture Production: Marketing Surveillance in the Digital Age." *The ANNALS of the American Academy of Political and Social Science* 597 (2004): 103–21.

Turow, Joseph. *Media Systems in Society: Understanding Industries, Strategies, and Power.* New York: Longman, 1992.

Turow, Joseph. *The Daily You: How the New Advertising Industry Is Defining Your Identity and Your Worth.* New Haven, CT: Yale University Press, 2011.

Twenty-First Century Communications and Video Accessibility Act, 2010. Pub. L. No. 111–260, 111th Cong., 2nd Sess. May 4, 2010.

van Schewick, Barbara. *Internet Architecture and Innovation.* Cambridge, MA: MIT Press, 2010.

Verton, Dan. "Technology Aids Hunt for Terrorists." *ComputerWorld,* September 9, 2002. http://www.computerworld.com/s/article/74052/Technology_aids_hunt_for_terrorists.

Woolgar, Steve. "Configuring the User: The Case of Usability Trials." In *A Sociology of Monsters: Essays on Power, Technology and Domination,* edited by John Law, 57–99. New York: Routledge, 1991.

YuMe Corporation. "Safeguards for Your Brand." 2011. http://www.yume.com/content/brand-security.

Zittrain, Jonathan. *The Future of the Internet—and How to Stop It.* New Haven, CT: Yale University Press, 2008.

7

AMERICAN MEDIA AND CHINA'S BLENDED PUBLIC SPHERE

Aynne Kokas

In the People's Republic of China (PRC) media industries, digital media usage is deeply entwined with two central forms of content restriction—corporate intellectual property right enforcement and government censorship. At the same time, with China's rapidly growing media market garnering more and more attention from Hollywood,[1] regulation of distribution channels for Hollywood films is a major area of concern for both PRC regulators and studios. Yet still much contemporary evidence—from the rapid circulation of dissident Ai Weiwei's incendiary take on PSY's "Gangnam Style"[2] video to the ample availability of unauthorized digital versions of *Mad Men* on the Chinese search engine Baidu—highlights how both regulators and media corporations are fighting what appears to be a losing battle with netizens over who controls access to content.[3]

In this chapter, I argue connected viewing squarely occupies the space between access and control in the PRC marketplace. Chinese social media sites provide users with user commentary about foreign films they cannot legally access. They also make visible both authorized and unauthorized means to access the content they discover on social media. As such, connected viewing creates what I call a "blended public sphere," a digital space in which conversations about different modes of access counter the rigorously controlled Chinese media landscape. In the first section of this chapter, I examine the genesis of connected viewing in the Chinese context, from DVD street vendors to robust, online communities. In the second section, I focus on the user forums devoted to entertainment content on the social network Douban. Here, I provide a detailed analysis of how this activity points to the growth of a blended public sphere in which everyday users subtly flout the regulation of content. In the final section, I examine the significance of the blended public sphere as it relates to the future of connected viewing. Thus, this chapter reveals the ways in which connected viewing complicates the roles played by corporations and regulators as (frequently unsuccessful) gatekeepers to media content, and it further underscores the increasingly blurring distinctions between terms like *authorized* and *unauthorized, legal* and *illegal*.

Strongly regulated access to theatrical content in the PRC creates a sizeable gap between new films available in the domestic market and releases elsewhere in the world. I have identified three categories of Hollywood films that are most affected by this gap. The first type of film is one with no legal distribution window in China. In order to watch these films, Chinese audiences must completely circumvent government restrictions to watch pirated versions. The second type of film is released legally in China but in a different release window than the United States, creating a gap between the date when content is legally available in American theaters and the date it is legally available in Chinese theaters. In the case of the second type of film, the window between American and Chinese releases creates an opportunity for pirates to digitize and upload a digital copy of the film that can undercut theatrical box office revenue. The third type of film is a co-production legally released in China and the United States at the same time, but edited for the Chinese market to meet content requirements of the State Administration of Press, Publication, Radio, Film and Television (SAPPRFT), formerly known as the State Administration of Radio, Film and Television (SARFT). Though Chinese audiences may have timely access to the film, they lack authorized access to the unedited version released in other markets.

The latter two types of films present the most interesting case for our examination of connected viewing. In both the cases, the films are distributed legally in China, even if some of the films are slightly modified in their domestic versions. As a result, Chinese government and Hollywood partners have not only financial incentive to drive legal consumption in the theatrical window, but also a disincentive to rigidly control social media buzz about the film that may increase box office revenue. However, users begin to use social media platforms to discuss content at the point of their earliest easiest access, rather than their earliest legal access. When users access and discuss Hollywood films via unauthorized means, such connected viewing activity weakens regulation that affects both digital distribution and social media. Additionally, user-generated forums help normalize unauthorized access, as online discussions assume such behavior is a rather routine or mundane aspect of content consumption. This corresponds to findings from other studies that examine the frequency of piracy activity among different communities: the lack of seriousness with which community members viewed violations of piracy regulations correlated strongly with the overall level of piracy in the group—in short, higher levels of indifference result in higher levels of piracy.[4]

Connected viewing in the Chinese context, then, highlights the tensions between government content control, industry intellectual property rights regulation, and the netizen's resistance to both. In other words, activity on social networking platforms illustrates how users both engage with and flout the overlapping restrictions resulting from foreign intellectual property right protection and Chinese government regulation. Users employ social networks as a way to develop awareness of studio content through peers and interest groups, and thus acquire knowledge of current yet unavailable media. This ultimately has created a system in which users have incentive to circumvent content controls, and has contributed to a nearly 300 million-person market for virtual private networks (VPNs)—proxy servers used to circumvent PRC firewalls.[5] The relative ease with which users can evade the gap between content discussed on social networking platforms in the PRC and the content available through cheap- and unauthorized-distribution digital channels has created a world in which hacking the Internet in China is a common reality.

Drawing on the work of Miriam Hansen, Jinying Li has made valuable interventions in articulating the space of pirated film in the PRC as an alternative public sphere. Li focuses on film buffs who have developed their own organizations and spaces for screening pirated films—particularly those films that are not legally admitted to the market—and identifies this behavior as a form of civil engagement in the PRC.[6] I would argue, however, that the relationship between social networking platforms and commercial films in highly regulated markets demands an additional category to describe discourses that meld conversations about multiple modes of access to authorized and unauthorized content—what I am calling a blended public sphere, a site where government monitors both heavily regulate but also miss transgressive digital behavior.[7]

Characterizing connected viewing in this way helps account for the imperfectness of the censors and the vibrant, ever-changing character of user behavior on online forums. To some extent, discourses on digital social forums are always blended. However, the dramatic contrast between the high level of regulation on Chinese sites and the gigantic community of playfully disobedient Chinese netizens makes the Chinese digital sphere a particularly compelling space in which to observe this phenomenon. For example, social media forums in which users can discuss unauthorized access to commercial films that will eventually become legally available in some form start to blur the lines that distinguish acceptable behavior and content.[8] The mixing also highlights the complexity that connected viewing injects into regulatory structures of SAPPRFT (formerly SARFT)[9] and the Federal Communications Commission, as well as the international lobbying efforts of the Motion Picture Association of America.

Connected viewing points to the existence of a public sphere in which social media activity around Hollywood films stems in part from unauthorized access and content; it is also highly monitored by regulatory agencies[10] and studios. Chinese social media sites, then, are both deeply imbricated with government and industry oversight and a dynamically growing market where users actively seek out any means to meet their entertainment needs. However, under regulation and censorship by the State Internet Information Office,[11] social media spaces in China—regardless of the presence of politically challenging content—cannot entirely constitute an alternative public sphere. Indeed, social media sites blend regulation and transgression of digital content standards. The sites point to unauthorized access but are authorized themselves. This blended public sphere then acts as a digital gateway to unauthorized spaces, like media consumption via pirated videos or VPN servers. The blended public sphere operates as a highly regulated digital space in which surveillance carefully, but imperfectly, monitors user activity, at the same time as the immense dynamism of social media posts allows users to routinely push regulatory boundaries.

As Tao Zhu et al. highlight,[12] Chinese digital surveillance includes a combination of filtering technologies, police surveillance, and policy approaches. However, for innocuous practices that point to illegal activity—like discussing soon-to-be-released films and the different ways to access them, whether authorized or not—regulatory priorities leave space for subverting digital regulation. Moreover, as Zhu et al. highlight in the case of Chinese social network Weibo, censorship focuses on sensitive users and sensitive content first.[13] Illegal, unauthorized digital access to films with release dates in China highlights the behavior of active fans, not of activists. Discussions of unauthorized entertainment content are neither obvious triggers for filtering mechanisms, nor exciting sites for police surveillance. Media piracy facilitates a blended public sphere precisely because of the relative mundaneness of unauthorized access to blockbusters online.

I elected to examine the individual film pages and user forums on Douban because it is one of the largest Chinese-language social media platforms. It is especially well known for its sophisticated user recommendations[14] generated by the platform's taste-based algorithm. Because of Douban's role as a media trendsetter,[15] it offers a particularly fertile place to examine the relationship between film viewing and user commentary on Chinese social media at the vanguard of popular culture. Douban recommends content on three levels.[16] First, the platform selects specific media for individual users based upon the algorithm's response to their activity on the site. Second, users can discuss content on user forums, either providing other users with explicit recommendations to see/avoid films or sharing insights that may pique the interests of other users. Finally, users can create their own carefully selected exhibitions of content to visualize for other users both their current viewing history[17] and anticipated future screenings.[18] While I limit the scope of this chapter to user discussions in individual film forums, all these recommendation practices constitute a bouquet of activities whose multiplicity make them particularly difficult to control.

Indeed, the process through which users learn about content not (yet) legally available in the PRC market points to one of the major policy challenges in the globalization of the PRC media industries—namely, how to support digital innovation[19] and still regulate content.[20] When users access films online, they contribute to the growth of the digital media culture in China and also undermine the regulatory mechanisms put in place by PRC leadership to control content distribution. While the growth of social media and the film industry is a pillar of Chinese government economic policy,[21] Internet regulation is also a major feature of central government policies to promote stability.[22] Together, these competing priorities create a complex policy-making landscape for regulators, a difficult terrain for studios, and the potential for increased Internet access by netizens. The competing priorities for growth and social stability[23] in the PRC digital media industry create the conditions for a blended public sphere in which users may have open discussions about content likely (or even certainly) accessed through unauthorized means, yet are still under the watchful eye of the State Internet Information Office.[24] At the same time, the practice of accessing digital entertainment content via unauthorized means can further normalize unauthorized access to other types of media. Therefore, growing user awareness of and unauthorized access to content have profit implications for industry players, policy implications for government regulation in the PRC, and sociocultural implications for the growth of the digital public sphere in China. This blended public sphere offers a space through which everyday people—not necessarily activists—practice flouting government control of media.[25]

Connected Viewing in China

Unauthorized access to digital entertainment content has been deeply imbricated in the fabric of Chinese viewing at least since the 1990s, when digital reproduction of filmed entertainment became easy and cheap. Video CD (VCD)[26] was one of the first "digital" forms in the contemporary transnational culture of video piracy in the PRC, emerging in the last decade of the twentieth century. As the pirated market for VCDs waned, ubiquitous street vendors emerged, yelling out "DVD, DVD" in the corners of China's "Silicon Valley," Beijing's Zhongguancun neighborhood, to meet the demand for pirated content. At the same time, companies like Warner Bros. saw their home video distribution profits evaporate in the PRC.[27] The heavily regulated theatrical market in the PRC created a scarcity of product, and thus helped cultivate taste among Chinese audiences for unauthorized entertainment content that they could only find on pirated VCDs and DVDs.

By the mid-2000s, Chinese websites were streaming US films and television series for Chinese audiences. Strict government film import quotas and equally stringent content standards constrained legal distribution in the market to the point that unauthorized access became commonplace.[28] Ultimately, government restrictions and foreign copyright controls created a rich social culture surrounding the unauthorized access of content, where a high number of power users uploaded multiple copies of the same piece of content on a variety of online platforms in order to evade any corporate or government crackdown. It is worth noting that these developments facilitated unauthorized access in the United States, too. Online content aggregators, like SideReel.com, gave any US college student with enough broadband capacity access to an online world of Chinese pirated versions of Hollywood titles. Stories abounded on American college campuses about the experience of watching *Gossip Girl* online with Chinese subtitles, demonstrating that very little unites people across the world as well as "free" content.[29]

This is not to say that interventions intended to curtail unauthorized access have been wholly unsuccessful. Court cases have somewhat stemmed US access to Hollywood content on Chinese websites, although anyone who has spent time on a college campus knows that piracy issues remain as common as underage students drinking cheap beer.[30] Nevertheless, intensive government intervention can reduce intellectual property violations in China. In the period leading up to the XXIX Olympiad, for example, the government actively protected the Olympic trademark as a matter of national pride and state revenue.[31] However, while this effort was largely (though not entirely) successful, the crackdown was part of a specific, time-delimited national government priority. Routine policing of American television series and major Hollywood blockbusters is not similarly prioritized. That said, the 2008 Olympic Games remain a perpetual reminder that an actively enforced central government mandate in the PRC to protect intellectual property can bring about a substantial reduction in intellectual property violations.

In the private sector, interventions to control intellectual property in the Chinese market have been less successful. As part of its China film distribution strategy, in 2005, Warner Bros. attempted to enter the Chinese DVD market at a price point slightly higher than local pirated DVDs, but at more legal retail sites.[32] Initially, media analysts hailed the venture as an exciting possibility.[33] But even without competition from robust unauthorized streaming sites—which were, during this period, still in their infancy—the experiment was unprofitable. The PRC's preexisting market culture privileged inexpensive unauthorized access over slightly more costly legal means.[34]

Unauthorized online access to pirated entertainment content, especially streaming video-on-demand sites, currently is one of the most common forms of media consumption in China.[35] The users of these sites represent a large domestic market, and the skillfulness with which their usage habits elide control continues to make the market a challenge for both government and industry regulators. Market leaders in 2012 included Youku, Ku6, and pps.tv; and some reports estimate the total number of streaming video-on-demand users exceeds 325 million, with over 63 percent of Internet users consuming online video.[36] In April 2012, Youku, an ad-supported site, had 107 million unique users with 2,700 film titles, 2,111 television series titles, and more than 400,000 hours of other professional content, much of which was unauthorized.[37] At the same time, a January 2012 report by the China Internet Network Information Center estimated the size of the entire Chinese Internet user base at a rapidly growing 531 million unique users.[38]

Granted, the impact of increased digital access to social media and streaming content only affects part of the Chinese population.[39] There are hundreds of millions of rural Chinese who lack Internet access and primarily access media through television. Yet even the numbers of digital users in rural populations are growing, with estimates of rural usage in the 400 million range and an estimated mobile growth rate of 10 percent per year.[40] As the proliferation of digital streaming technology and online social networking spaces replaces the street vendor with robust online communities, connected viewing is positioned at the point where consumer desires, government control, and industry regulations converge. Ultimately, the social media pages through which users discuss access to controlled commercial content are a latter-day iteration of discussions with the DVD salesman about the newest *daoban*[41] release. However, in this case, the same discussions now are occurring under the watchful eye of government censors, rather than in back-alley DVD stands. It is in the blend of public discourse, government control, and industry oversight that connected viewing describes the major tension of the growth of the contemporary Chinese digital media industries.

Douban User Forums as Blended Public Sphere

On the Chinese social network Douban, social media user forums about Hollywood films operate as a blended public sphere in which netizens talk about transgressing access regulations within a domain that is carefully watched by both government regulators and industry analysts. Ultimately, unauthorized public engagement with commercial films in a tightly regulated digital community grows the blended public sphere. Idle chatter about the latest release (accessed illegally) opens a digital gateway where users can flout regulations of their viewing habits. This comparatively innocuous play with viewing regulations expands digital forums outside the realm of wholly government-controlled entities into a blended site that is both regulated and free. Douban user forums facilitate blended public spheres in three key ways. First, the site offers an important space in which users can aggregate opinions about Hollywood films that are not (or not yet) legally accessible in the PRC market. Second, the site offers users a space through which to exhibit their tastes for content, whether accessible in authorized ways or not, in digital exhibitions on their personal pages. Third, the site offers users a space to discuss the experience of viewing films that complies with existing regulatory frameworks and yet defies them by allowing references to unauthorized access. Like teenagers returning to homeroom smelling of cigarette smoke, the forums leave traces of unauthorized behavior small enough for regulators to ignore, but substantial enough to tacitly expand acceptable community behavior.

The site creates spaces for users to congregate around a specific entertainment property, to rate it, to discuss it, and to generate digital exhibitions of their favorite content for other users to see. Users can peruse one another's digital libraries to identify new properties or find old titles that fit their taste preferences based on the preferences of their peers. Groups form around specific films, musicians, or book titles, allowing users to easily engage with other fans and identify similar works by visiting the digital exhibitions on their personal pages.[42] Fan "collections" are broken down into categories of "already watched"[43] and "would like to watch."[44] Groups are not limited to entertainment properties released legally in the Chinese market but include domestic and foreign titles, legally and illegally available in the PRC. Of most interest here, Douban is overwhelmingly focused on user-generated content, emphasizing user-generated groups, reviews, and recommendations. Douban's structure not only offers user-generated content centered on specific entertainment properties, but also provides its users with a space in which fan communities form around common taste preferences, regardless of legal constraints on accessing individual films.

Groups focused on Hollywood titles contain both Chinese- and English-language discourses, as the site serves a PRC, global Sinophone, and global Anglophone population. This fact further complicates the politics of authorized access by making unclear when or from where users access content and how those factors correspond to global release windows. Comments first appear at the time of the title's earliest international release date, which could indicate either authorized or unauthorized access by the user. The international scope of the site creates a multitiered class system of access in which Chinese users outside the release location become aware of content before they can access it legally, a dynamic in which the only way to remain current on the discussion is through unauthorized access.

User-generated discussion centered on Rian Johnson's *Looper* (2012) offers particularly helpful insight into the ways users flout regulatory structures on social media forums by demonstrating how different international versions of the same film can catalyze discussions that reveal unauthorized viewing. In order to access both Chinese and US theaters, Johnson made two versions. One version was released to the United States and international territories other than China. A different version was released in China because SAPPRFT (formerly SARFT) censored the Chinese version and investors demanded that more scenes of Shanghai be included in the film's mainland release. The two versions were never both released in the same place at the same time. This is important to note because discussions of the discrepancy in release versions reveal the ways social media forums act as a blended public sphere, a space in which users engage in discussions about various forms of access and content simultaneously.

Three weeks following *Looper*'s release, 43,299 people had provided some sort of commentary about the film, and 23,230 had written reviews. User responses to the film ranged from more common discussions about form and style, like continuity errors, to more surprising discourses about how the film, a science-fiction time-travel narrative, constructed its vision of the future, and of China's future in particular. Significantly, user commentary on the film consisted of both close readings of the authorized release and fan one-upmanship that required access to both versions to fully participate. Some netizens explicitly used the site to compare international and Chinese versions of the film as a way to discuss changes SAPPRFT (formerly SARFT) made to the local version.[45] In particular, the name of one discussion thread was "Are Domestic and International Versions Really So Different? They Are Simply Just Two Different Films."[46] The forums examined the relative merits of the Chinese and American versions, discussing which scenes of Shanghai had been added and deleted. Similarly, they critiqued the performance of actress Fan Bingbing in the film's Chinese release in relation to its American release. While these discussions are not significant on their own, when looked at in the context of the international distribution market, the conversations refer back to unauthorized viewing practices. Ultimately, the subtle maneuvers of users in popular forums undermine regulatory control in a way that can be more pervasive than the activities of users who distribute sensitive political content that is rapidly removed after being censored.[47] Censors can easily block unauthorized content through key word searches. However, by referring to unauthorized access to content that will eventually become legal, users are circumventing the most common mechanics of Internet censorship.

On Douban forums, fans can become accustomed to talking, even bragging about, unauthorized viewing. This is a significant act in a Chinese digital space where users are constantly monitored. Yet user activity highlights one of the weaknesses in Chinese censorship practices—a focus on key word analysis[48] that leaves space for illegal online activities, such as accessing films online that are being distributed in theaters, that might not include a sensitive key word. Though netizens know that censorship exists, to see fellow netizens flout these regulations as part of the social media forum experience increases awareness of both the existence and limitations of Chinese censorship for even the most committed couch potato. Threads like the discussion about the difference between the Chinese and American versions of *Looper* highlight the way in which sites like Douban normalize unauthorized access to content. Indeed, at no point in the discussion does someone in the thread question how or why other netizens had access to both versions of the film. Users went a different direction entirely. One commentator took the opportunity to make an aesthetic recommendation for the Chinese version based upon the American version. The user suggested that the longer segment in Shanghai (which was present in the Chinese version, but not the US version) be removed from the film, in addition to other cuts.[49] Another user took the opportunity to share his/her opinions about the difference between the mainland and international versions of the *Transformers* movies.[50] Comments like these, both of which had been logged on the forum for at least five months at the time of writing—when 90 percent of digital censorship occurs within the first twenty-four hours[51]—suggest that Douban can act as a space for users to candidly discuss unauthorized access to media and also tacitly refer to state film censorship.

In the context of connected viewing, Douban offers users a space to perform the digital labor of recommendation and commentary, but also whet other users' appetite for access. Indeed, Douban itself often obfuscates authorized access to Hollywood theatrical content. In many cases, it is not possible to access legal theatrical versions of the films through the website because while Douban's site links to theaters, the links frequently do not work. In some cases, there are only dead links to the names of cities. In others, there are no theaters at all. It is just as easy (or easier) to find a free unauthorized copy of a film online as it is to pay to watch it. For Guy Ritchie's *Sherlock Holmes: Game of Shadows,* a 2012 Hollywood export to the PRC, a search for the film on search engine Baidu produced a free version before an electronic sell-through (EST) copy.[52] Similarly, the free version of another Hollywood-PRC export, George Miller's *Happy Feet Two* (2011 US release/2012 Chinese release), was also available more easily through a Baidu search for the title of the film than in EST. This, in addition to reports about Chinese users' unauthorized access to streaming video for entertainment content,[53] suggests that at least some of the activity on these films' Douban pages is coming from unauthorized access. Moreover, the intersection of authorized and unauthorized access highlights the way in which social media sites act as a blended public sphere where intensive regulation intermingles with citizen engagement in the alternative public sphere of pirated cinema.

The Future of Digital Distribution

Intellectual property regulation, as well as government regulation, has facilitated a digital culture in the PRC wherein access via unauthorized means has become the norm. My analysis of the social networking website Douban suggests it is a sphere in which users increase their awareness of content while playing with the boundaries of a highly regulated Internet experience. From this perspective, social media connects viewers to one another and to content as they navigate and transgress the regulatory mechanisms also structuring their online consumption behaviors. As such, this analysis draws attention to the complementary interests of Chinese regulators and US media entities, even if the imperfect control they exercise over content serves different priorities.

While it is tempting to try to make rigid distinctions between authorized and unauthorized access via social media, this case study points to an instance when activity on a social media forum is positioned squarely between those very distinctions. The Chinese market, and likely others, suggests users are interested in the most convenient mode of access, regardless of legality. Yet at the same time, users are also likely to continue to use social media as a way to express frustrations about the limitations of their legal viewing experiences. The converging discussions of authorized and unauthorized media viewing exhibited in social media forums point to a dynamic of digital access that is expanding the range of discourse available to users, even in highly regulated digital environments.

Regardless of how we frame the restrictions placed on Chinese netizens—are they necessary policy or economic constraints, unfair controls of media, or somewhere in between?—this mode of connected viewing provides extensive space for understanding and commenting on both authorized and unauthorized access to media content. Engaging with social networking sites, like Douban, users disseminate knowledge, accrue information, and receive recommendations, all for content that they can access relatively simply, yet illegally. As long as this process continues, connected viewing in the PRC will further diminish the effectiveness of political and industrial restrictions on entertainment content. Concomitantly, connected viewing will further facilitate the demand for otherwise inaccessible media properties. A logical outcome from this process is cyclical. Government and industrial regulations will strengthen their grip on access and content, and user recommendations will continue to identify content that is worth circumventing regulations for. Thus, it is possible to understand connected viewing as a blended public sphere wherein Chinese netizens are constantly negotiating, reworking, and weakening the forces that otherwise structure their Internet usage patterns.

Notes

1. Clarence Tsui, "China Will Top U.S. as Biggest Film Market in the World by 2020: Study," *Hollywood Reporter,* November 28, 2012, http://www.hollywoodreporter.com/news/china-will-top-us-as-395366.
2. This video is blocked on Baidu searches but accessible in China via virtual private network (VPN) proxies.
3. Search Baidu for *Mad Men* guanggao kuangren 广告狂人 http://video.baidu.com/v?word=guanggao+kuangren&ct=301989888&rn=20&pn=0&db=0&s=0&fbl=800. This content is blocked in the United States, but available to users on mainland China without a VPN proxy.
4. R.B. Kini, H.V. Ramakrishna, and B.S. Vijayaraman, "An Exploratory Study of Moral Intensity Regarding Software Piracy of Students in Thailand," *Behaviour & Information Technology* 22, no. 1 (2003): 63–70; R.B. Kini, H.V. Ramakrishna, and B.S. Vijayaraman, "Shaping of Moral Intensity Regarding Software Piracy: A Comparison between Thailand and U.S. Students," *Journal of Business Ethics* 49 (2004): 91–104.
5. Personal communication, VPNinja internal market data.
6. Jinying Li, "From 'D-Buffs' to the 'D-Generation': Piracy, Cinema, and an Alternative Public Sphere in Urban China," *International Journal of Communication* 6 (2012): 544.
7. Li, "From 'D-Buffs' to the 'D-Generation,'" 544.
8. In 2012, Hollywood imports (and by extension, state film distribution revenues for Hollywood imports) exceeded revenues for local Chinese films. For more information, see Ben Fritz, "Imports Top Local Films as China Box Office Grows 28% in 2012," *Los Angeles Times,* January 2, 2013, http://articles.latimes.com/2013/jan/02/entertainment/la-et-ct-china-box-office-20130102.
9. Indeed, acknowledging the complexity of digital media regulation, in the regulatory restructuring that occurred during China's 2013 National People's Congress proceedings, lawmakers collapsed the General Administration of Press and Publication into the State Administration of Radio, Film and Television to further centralize content regulation. This move highlights a need to further centralize content regulation due to the complexity of digital distribution patterns. See Raymond Li, "Merger of Media Regulator and Censor, But No Culture Super-Ministry," *South China Morning Post,* March 11, 2013, http://www.scmp.com/news/china/article/1187908/merger-media-regulator-and-censor-no-culture-super-ministry.
10. *Economist,* "Monitoring the Monitors," July 10, 2012, http://www.economist.com/blogs/analects/2012/07/online-censorship.
11. *Xinhua,* "China Sets Up Office for Internet Information Management," May 4, 2011, http://news.xinhuanet.com/english2010/china/2011-05/04/c_13857911.htm.
12. Tao Zhu et al., "Tracking and Quantifying Censorship on a Chinese Microblogging Site," November 26, 2012, arXiv:1211.6166 [cs.IR], 1.
13. Zhu et al., "Tracking and Quantifying Censorship on a Chinese Microblogging Site."
14. Major platforms in this market include microblog service Sina Weibo and social networking site QQ, among others.
15. For more information in the trade press about Douban's role in the vanguard of culture and recommendation on Chinese social media, please see Yang Wang, "The Curious Case of Douban," *Tech Node,* September 3, 2013, http://technode.com/2012/09/03/the-curious-case-of-douban/; and Sunny Ye, "Inside Douban, China's Truly Original Social Network," *Tech Rice,* August 11, 2011, http://techrice.com/2011/08/11/inside-douban-chinas-truly-original-social-network/.
16. One aspect of digital curation on social media that I did not address as part of my work on Douban as it relates to user engagement with Hollywood film properties is the practice of spatial curation, in which users create virtual galleries and commentaries about specific locations. For more information about how socio-locative social media curation works, see Ingrid Erickson's excellent piece, "Documentary With Ephemeral Media: Curation Practices in Online Social Spaces," *Bulletin of Science, Technology & Society* 30, no. 6, (2010): 387–97.

17. These titles are listed under the heading "看过 kanguo," or "have already seen," on an individual user's page.

18. These titles are listed under the heading "想看 xiangkan," or "would like to see," on an individual user's page.

19. Yu Hong, "Reading the Twelfth Five-Year Plan: China's Communication-Driven Mode of Economic Restructuring," *International Journal of Communication*, no. 500 (2011): 1049.

20. Hong, "Reading the Twelfth Five-Year Plan," 1049.

21. Hong, "Reading the Twelfth Five-Year Plan," 1045.

22. Miriam D. D'Jaen, "Breaching the Great Firewall of China: Congress Overreaches in Attacking Chinese Internet Censorship," *Seattle University Law Review* 31, no. 327 (2007): 331.

23. The notion of social stability, or *hexie shehui,* is a common trope in discourses about the growth of the Chinese Internet. Former President Hu Jintao first introduced the idea as an objective for Chinese socioeconomic growth during his tenure. The term highlights a focus on resolving the tension between economic growth and inequality—in this case, unequal access to Internet content. For more information about the "harmonious society" concept, see Kinman Chan, "Harmonious Society," in *International Encyclopedia of Civil Society,* eds. Helmut K. Anheier and Stefan Toeper, 821 (New York: Springer, 2010).

24. Zhu et al., "Tracking and Quantifying Censorship on a Chinese Microblogging Site."

25. Hong, "Reading the Twelfth Five-Year Plan," 1045.

26. Video CD is a digital viewing technology introduced in China in the 1990s that acted as an intermediate technology between VHS and DVD.

27. Shujen Wang, "Piracy and the DVD/VCD Market: Contradictions and Paradoxes," in *Art, Politics and Commerce in Chinese Cinema,* eds. Ying Zhu and Stanley Rosen (Hong Kong: Hong Kong University Press, 2010), 72.

28. Shujen Wang, *Framing Piracy: Globalization and Film Distribution in Greater China* (Lanham, MD: Rowman & Littlefield, 2003).

29. Mei-lan Li, "Reorganization of Cultural Image in Audiovisual Translation—Taking Gossip Girl as an Example," *Journal of Sanming University* (April 2011); Xinhua News Agency Online, 新华网 "Meiju Shoudao Zhongguo Qingnian Repeng," 美剧受到青年的热捧, December 19, 2012, http://news.sohu.com/20121219/n360953078.shtml.

30. For further discussion of this issue, please refer to Max Dawson and Chuck Tryon's contribution to this collection.

31. Erin Swike, Sean Thompson, and Christine Vasquez, "Piracy in China," *Business Horizons* 51, no. 6 (November/December 2008): 495.

32. Wang, "Piracy and the DVD/VCD Market," 83.

33. Wang, "Piracy and the DVD/VCD Market," 83.

34. Warner Bros. Connected Viewing Research Team, personal communication, September 6, 2012.

35. Ambassador Ronald Kirk, "2012 Special 301 Report," Office of the United States Trade Representative, April 2012, 29.

36. Zhongguo Hulianwang Xinxi Zhongxin 中国互联网信息中心. Di 29 Ci Hulianwangluo Fazhan Zhuangkuang Tongji Baogao 第29次中国互联网络发展状况统计报告. (Beijing, January 2012), http://www1.cnnic.cn/IDR/ReportDownloads/201209/P020120904421720687608.pdf.

37. J.P. Morgan Asia Pacific Equity Research, "Youku, Inc.: Darkest Hour Is Just Before the Dawn," August 7, 2012, 2.

38. Zhongguo Hulianwang Xinxi Zhongxin 中国互联网信息中心. Di 29 Ci Hulianwangluo Fazhan Zhuangkuang Tongji Baogao 第29次中国互联网络发展状况统计报告.

39. Ying Zhu and Chris Berry, *TV China* (Bloomington: University of Indiana Press, 2009), 174.

40. *BBC News,* "Rural Chinese Get Online as Mobile Overtakes Desktop," July 19, 2012, http://www.bbc.co.uk/news/technology-18900778.

41. 盗版 daoban. This term is most commonly translated as "pirated."

42. For a sample of how the user digital film exhibition works, log into Douban and see http://movie.douban.com/people/wenxiaogua/.

43. kanguo 看过
44. xiangkan 想看
45. Beiyuan de Huli (Hengzhou) 北原的狐狸(衢州) Guonei he Guowai de Banben Zhen You Nenme Butong? Genben Jiushi Liangbu Butong de Dianying "国内和国外的版本真有那么不同？根本就是两不同的电影" September 30, 2012, http://movie.douban.com/subject/3179706/discussion/49135272/.
46. Beiyuan de Huli (Hengzhou) 北原的狐狸（衡洲) Guonei he Guowai de Banben Zhen You Nenme Butong? Genben Jiushi Liangbu Butong de Dianying "国内和国外的版本真有那么不同？根本就是两不同的电影."
47. Tao Zhu et al., "The Velocity of Censorship: High-Fidelity Detection of Microblog Post Deletions," March 4, 2013, http://arxiv.org/pdf/1303.0597v1.pdf, 11.
48. Zhu et al., "Tracking and Quantifying Censorship on a Chinese Microblogging Site."
49. User 春困秋乏夏打盹 wrote, 想法不错, 就是严重怀疑芒果台投资的, 许晴的片段这么狗血, 还TM反反复复的播, 有 完没完, 有种别只裁8分钟啊, 请将中国元素的的画面都裁掉啊 on October 18, 2012.
50. "Guonei he Guowai de Banben Zhen You Nenme Butong? Genben Jiushi Liangbu Butong de Dianying 国内和国外的版本真有那么不同？根本就是两不同的电影."
51. Zhu et al., "The Velocity of Censorship: High-Fidelity Detection of Microblog Post Deletions," 11.
52. Search performed on February 14, 2013, with the search term «大侦探福尔摩斯2,» the Chinese title of *Sherlock Holmes: A Game of Shadows.*
53. Ambassador Ronald Kirk, "2012 Special 301 Report," 29.

References

BBC News. "Rural Chinese Get Online as Mobile Overtakes Desktop." July 19, 2012. http://www.bbc.co.uk/news/technology-18900778.

Beiyuan de Huli (Hengzhou) 北原的狐狸 (衢州) "Guonei he Guowai de Banben Zhen You Nenme Butong? Genben Jiushi Liangbu Butong de Dianying 国内和国外的版本真有那么不 同？根本就是两不同的电影." September 30, 2012. http://movie.douban.com/subject/3179706/discussion/49135272/.

Chan, Kinman. "Harmonious Society." In *International Encyclopedia of Civil Society,* edited by Helmut K. Anheier and Stefan Toepler, 821. New York: Springer, 2010.

D'Jaen, Miriam D. "Breaching the Great Firewall of China: Congress Overreaches in Attacking Chinese Internet Censorship." *Seattle University Law Review* 31, no. 327 (2007): 331.

Economist. "Monitoring the Monitors." July 10, 2012. http://www.economist.com/blogs/analects/2012/07/online-censorship.

Erickson, Ingrid. "Documentary With Ephemeral Media: Curation Practices in Online Social Spaces." *Bulletin of Science, Technology & Society* 30, no. 6 (2010): 387–97.

Fritz, Ben. "Imports Top Local Films as China Box Office Grows 28% in 2012." *Los Angeles Times,* January 2, 2013. http://articles.latimes.com/2013/jan/02/entertainment/la-et-ct-china-box-office-20130102

北原的狐狸（衢州) Guonei he Guowai de Banben Zhen You Nenme Butong? Genben Jiushi Liangbu Butong de Dianying "国内和国外的版本真有那么不同？根本就是两不同的电影" September 30, 2012, http://movie.douban.com/subject/3179706/discussion/49135272/.

Hong, Yu. "Reading the Twelfth Five-Year Plan: China's Communication-Driven Mode of Economic Restructuring." *International Journal of Communication,* no. 500 (2011): 1049.

J.P. Morgan Asia Pacific Equity Research. "Youku, Inc.: Darkest Hour Is Just Before the Dawn." August 7, 2012.

Kini, R.B., H.V. Ramakrishna, and B.S. Vijayaraman. "An Exploratory Study of Moral Intensity Regarding Software Piracy of Students in Thailand." *Behaviour & Information Technology* 22, no. 1 (2003): 63–70.

Kini, R.B., H.V. Ramakrishna, and B.S. Vijayaraman. "Shaping of Moral Intensity Regarding Software Piracy: A Comparison between Thailand and U.S. Students." *Journal of Business Ethics* 49 (2004): 91–104.

Kirk, Ambassador Ronald. "2012 Special 301 Report." Office of the United States Trade Representative, April 2012.

Li, Jinying. "From 'D-Buffs' to the 'D-Generation': Piracy, Cinema, and an Alternative Public Sphere in Urban China." *International Journal of Communication* 6 (2012): 544.

Li, Mei-lan. "Reorganization of Cultural Image in Audiovisual Translation—Taking GossipGirl as an Example." *Journal of Sanming University*, April 2011.

Li, Raymond. "Merger of Media Regulator and Censor, But No Culture Super-Ministry." *South China Morning Post,* March 11, 2013. http://www.scmp.com/news/china/article/1187908/merger-media-regulator-and-censor-no-culture-super-ministry.

Ma Huyan. 马虎眼 Shenme Yang de Yonghu Shihe Douban? 什么样的用户适合豆瓣 ChinaZ, March 19, 2012. http://www.chinaz.com/manage/2012/0319/240509.shtml.

PRC State Administration of Radio, Film and Television. on1/1211/29/7644618.html. izens/.ing http://www.hollywst updated June 6, 2008 http://www.cfcc- film.com.cn/en/production/200806064.html.

Swike, Erin, Sean Thompson, and Christina Vasquez. "Piracy in China." *Business Horizons* 51, no. 6 (November/December 2008).

Tsui, Clarence. "China Will Top U.S. as Biggest Film Market in the World by 2020: Study." *Hollywood Reporter,* November 28, 2012, 494–5. http://www.hollywoodreporter.com/news/china-will-top-us-as-395366.

Wang, Shujen. *Framing Piracy: Globalization and Film Distribution in Greater China.* Lanham, MD: Rowman & Littlefield, 2003.

Wang, Shujen. "Piracy and the DVD/VCD Market: Contradictions and Paradoxes." In *Art, Politics, and Commerce in Chinese Cinema,* edited by Ying Zhu and Stanley Rosen, 71–83. Hong Kong: Hong Kong University Press, 2010.

Wang, Yang. "The Curious Case of Douban." *Tech Node,* September 3, 2013. http://technode.com/2012/09/03/the-curious-case-of-douban/.

Xinhua. "China Sets Up Office for Internet Information Management." May 4, 2011. http://news.xinhuanet.com/english2010/china/2011-05/04/c_13857911.htm.

Xinhua News Agency Online. 新华网 "Meiju Shoudao Zhongguo Qingnian Repeng." 美剧受到青年的热捧, December 19, 2012. http://news.sohu.com/20121219/n360953078.shtml.

Ye, Sunny. "Inside Douban, China's Truly Original Social Network." *Tech Rice,* August 11, 2011. http://techrice.com/2011/08/11/inside-douban-chinas-truly-original-social-network/.

Zhongguo Hulianwang Xinxi Zhongxin 中国互联网信息中心. Di 29 Ci Hulianwangluo Fazhan Zhuangkuang Tongji Baogao. Beijing, January 2012. http://www1.cnnic.cn/IDR/ReportDownloads/201209/P020120904421720687608.pdf.

Zhu, Tao, David Phipps, Adam Pridgen, Jedidiah R. Crandall, and Dan S. Wallach. "The Velocity of Censorship: High-Fidelity Detection of Microblog Post Deletions." March 4, 2013. http://arxiv.org/pdf/1303.0597v1.pdf.

Zhu, Tao, David Phipps, Adam Pridgen, Jedidiah R. Crandall, and Dan S. Wallach. "Tracking and Quantifying Censorship on a Chinese Microblogging Site." November 26, 2012. http://arxiv.org/abs/1211.6166.

Zhu, Ying, and Chris Berry. *TV China.* Bloomington: Indiana University Press, 2009.

8

ONLINE DISTRIBUTION OF FILM AND TELEVISION IN THE UK

Behavior, Taste, and Value

Elizabeth Evans and Paul McDonald

This chapter connects with "connected viewing" in the specific terms of focusing on delivery services for the online distribution of film and television programs. As the following outlines, *digital distribution* is itself a bit of an umbrella term for various types of services, including "catch-up TV," download-to-own or electronic sell-through (EST), pay-per-view (PPV), subscription video-on-demand (SVOD), and video sharing. Furthermore, such services are always divided between what Ramon Lobato describes as "formal" and "informal" economies, where the former represents a corporately ordered and controlled sphere, and the latter is characterized by "economic production and exchange occurring within capitalist economies but outside the purview of the state."[1] While the formal/informal distinction certainly relates to divisions between legal and illegal economies, the informal sphere is not exclusively defined by infringing activity, for blunt distinctions are forever blurred by a complex "grey zone of semi-legality."[2]

Discussing the international experience of digital television, Graeme Turner argues,

> [O]nce the mass media lose their 'massness' . . . they become much more radically conjunctural, much more volatile and contingent in response to the precise configuration of the forces of change in particular social-historical circumstances. We need to be responsive to that volatility in our accounts of what is going on as television becomes digital.[3]

As Turner notes, too frequently the American experience is assumed to define the present and future of digital television, and yet it is abundantly clear that the precise configuration of any nation's or region's experience of television is going to be the product of the complex interplay among a number of specific conjunctural factors—and only one of these will be technological.[4]

Frequently, universalizing visions of digital transformation are the stuff of assertion, for "projections of technological change are often—indeed notoriously—short of substantive evidence."[5] The same challenges of respecting different contextual circumstances and grounding observations in empirical scrutiny equally confront accounts of online distribution. Rather than impose a singular universalizing vision of how digital online delivery transforms the business and consumption of mediated exchanges, it is forever necessary to continually recognize and interrogate profound differences in how digital media is deployed, organized, monetized, used, adopted, understood, and evaluated across local, international, or regional contexts. In the rush to understand the newness of "new" media, it should not be assumed that just because they own the technologies of laptops, smartphones, and tablet computers, modern media consumers in all parts of the developed world are watching moving images in radically new ways, consuming anywhere, anytime, by selecting from the sheer heterogeneity of a rich "long tail" of unfettered choice. Any tendency toward such utopian visions of connected viewing requires a reality check, demanding empirical scrutiny.

What follows therefore is a specifically situated analysis of the market for, and user engagements with, digital distribution services in the UK. Here we focus on exploring broad trends in the specific conditions of the UK market for digital distribution services, before examining users of those services in terms of their viewing behaviors, experiences of viewing digital distribution services, and the tastes and values they place against what they watch. In particular, we will use empirical audience research to explore how the foundational ethos of public service broadcasting (PSB), which has underpinned UK media development since the early twentieth century, emerges throughout research participants' attitudes toward access to both television and film. As such, the specific characteristics of the UK film and television market are intertwined with audience attitudes as both industry and audience make sense of an ever-changing media landscape.

Digital Distribution in the UK: Market Context

Setting the scene for the remainder of this study, this section initially outlines broad trends over the decade 2002–11, which defined markets for film, television, and home entertainment consumption in the UK, before looking at how platforms and services for online viewing by digital distribution emerged in this context. By adding a new attraction competing for eyeballs in the economy of attention, digital distribution is inevitably locked into a relationship with established channels for the dissemination of film and television content: theatrical cinema exhibition, broadcast television, home video. Digital distribution services have emerged in the UK over a period in which the larger market context has seen the enduring stability of cinema attendances, the declining value of home video, and the expansion of the multichannel pay-TV economy (see Table 8.1).

In the first decade of the twenty-first century, the cinema-going audience remained relatively flat. Although gross theatrical box revenues grew from £755 million to £1,040 million, this did not result from any actual increase in cinema attendances: annual ticket sales were certainly subject to variation, but there was no discernible increase or decline in the theatrical audience as admissions fluctuated between 156 and 176 million per year. This stability appears significant in a context where unsubstantiated claims are made that theatrical exhibition is dying because film consumers are migrating to online outlets.[6] From this viewpoint, online viewing becomes the new threat to cinema's popularity, articulating a more modern version of the substitution effect, which Douglas Gomery identified with the post-World War II "blame television" hypothesis.[7] However, if the theatrical audience is relatively stable, then online consumption would appear to be expanding the viewing of film rather than replacing the cinema audience.

Technologies for online viewing may be relatively new, but their effect on the social dynamics of cultural consumption sit within longer-term trends toward the privatization and individualization of moving image viewing that stretch back to the first home cinema systems of the early twentieth century, and the subsequent popularization of television ownership and emergence of the home video market.[8] Since the earliest years of consumer videocassettes, media consumers in the UK have always been among the most voracious viewers of home entertainment. When DVD was introduced to the UK in the late 1990s, home entertainment entered a new boom phase before stalling in the midyears of the next decade as the value and volume of video retail and rental peaked; and when Blu-ray arrived in 2006, it failed to ignite any new interest in physical video. Based on the economic logic of the substitution effect, casual assertions are made that the physical video market declined because consumers moved toward accessing online the same forms of content previously bought or rented on video. Market data for revenues from UK online video-on-demand (VOD) services indicate, however, that VOD has not balanced the drop in sales and rentals of physical video: between 2006 to 2011, total consumer spending on physical rental and retail combined fell from £2,554 million to £1,762.8 million, a drop of £791.2 million; but by 2011 online VOD revenues had struggled to reach £51.8 million. By the end of the first decade of the new millennium, the market for physical video in the UK was certainly in decline, but any new market for online distribution was still in a nascent stage.

Of course, VOD revenues only represent the legal online market, and informal or illegal channels for online distribution form a vast shadow market. In this

TABLE 8.1 Key Market Data: UK Film, Television, Home Entertainment, and Broadband 2002–11

		2002	2003	2004	2005	2006	2007	2008	2009	2010	2011
Cinema											
Gross box office	£m	755	742	770	770	762	821	850	944	988	1,040
Admissions	m	175.9	167.3	171.3	164.7	156.6	162.4	164.2	173.5	169.2	171.6
DVD											
Consumer spending retail	£m	1,213.3	1,753.5	2,243.5	2,245.4	2,215.0	2,226.9	2,164.4	1,839.2	1,639.5	1,525.9
Units	m	89.9	145.0	196.5	211.2	227.0	248.1	252.9	234.6	210.1	191.8
Consumer spending rental	£m	165.1	262.9	358.4	376.9	339.5	293.8	276.1	267.5	248.5	236.9
Rental transactions	m	57.3	88.4	123.6	130.1	115.6	97.7	93.1	91.9	83.2	83.0
Blu-ray											
Consumer spending retail	£m					0.028	15.6	65.3	108.5	168.5	181.8
Units	m					0.001	0.8	3.7	8.4	13.0	15.3
Consumer spending rental	£m						0.97	7.49	17.37	29.43	37.54
Rental transactions	m						0.32	2.48	5.87	9.82	13.16
Television											
Multichannel households (analogue and digital terrestrial, satellite and cable)	%	44.7	48.0	56.7	64.9	71.8	80.3	87.2	89.6	92.1	93.1
Combined audience-share main PSB channels (BBC One, BBC Two, ITV, C4/S4C, and C5)	%	77.7	76.5	73.8	70.3	66.8	63.6	60.8	57.8	55.5	53.7
Digital TV adoption	%	38.5	43.2	53.0	61.9	69.7	86.3	87.1	91.4	92.5	96.0
Broadband											
Total broadband household	%	n/a	n/a	n/a	31	41	52	58	68	71	74
Mobile broadband households	%								12	15	17
VOD and NVOD											
Revenues TV-based VOD and NVOD	£m	62.6	67.6	72.7	73.5	67.2	74.5	95.7	100.9	107.3	113.9
Revenues online VOD	£m					0.1	0.5	6.2	22.2	39.1	51.8

Compiled from data in British Film Institute, *BFI Statistical Yearbook 2012* (London: British Film Institute, 2012), 9, 11, and 122; International Video Federation, *The European Video Yearbook 2012* (Brussels: International Video Federation, 2012), 104–5; Ofcom, *Communications Market Report 2011* (London: Ofcom, 2011), 97; Ofcom, *Communications Market Report 2012* (London: Ofcom, 2012), 119, 160, and 236.

context, a further substitution hypothesis has come into play around the "blame piracy" argument.[9] Yet this can only remain speculation, for the essential immeasurability of illegal distribution means no one can know with any confidence how much the informal economy is "stealing" viewers. Certainly the impact of piracy on the formal market cannot be dismissed, but neither can it be presumed or asserted as a one-cause explanation for the decline of physical video. Indeed, the huge boom in DVDs may have been among the foremost reasons why the market was destined to rapidly burn out.

In the UK television market, at the end of the 1980s analogue cable and satellite platforms were establishing both a multichannel environment and pay-TV economy, and from the late 1990s onward, the switch over to digital cable, satellite, and terrestrial services expanded multichannel provision. One effect of this change was the declining share of the audience captured by the five free-to-air networks (the license-fee-supported BBC One and BBC Two, and advertising-funded ITV, Channel 4, and Channel 5): as Table 8.1 shows, between 2002 and 2011, while the number of multichannel homes more than doubled, and digital television adoption massively increased, the combined audience share held by the five networks dropped from 77.7 percent to 53.7 percent. Consequently, by the end of that decade, the UK television landscape was broadly divided between the five networks, all operating according to public service principles, and the pay-TV economy facilitated by digital satellite provider British Sky Broadcasting (popularly known just as "Sky") and digital cable provider Virgin Media. With the main networks and their subsidiary channels already available for free over the digital terrestrial platform Freeview, the way was paved for television in the UK to go all digital, and October 2012 saw full analogue switch-off nationwide. In the midst of these changes, online distribution has extended the range of options by which established television services and new entrants aim to cultivate a market for flexible and mobile viewing.

Digital distribution in the UK has emerged as an arena characterized by a multiplicity of digital services for viewing film and television online. Variations between types of service are formed through differences in the categories of provider (broadcasters, producers or suppliers of content, telcos, or video rental services such as Netflix and LOVEFiLM), types of business model employed (PPV, SVOD, EST, or free), and the technologies of delivery (streaming and/or downloading). Among the multitude of service options, probably the most visible category is online add-ons to traditional broadcast television. In an extension of free-to-air broadcasting, all the major networks now offer free catch-up TV players openly available to anyone with Internet access, subject to geoblocking, according to territorial rights restrictions. Catch-up TV enables individual streaming and downloading of programs previously broadcast. Most notable here are the BBC iPlayer and Channel 4's 4oD, which provide free access to recently aired programs and some archived content. In the pay-TV market, Sky Go and the Virgin Media Player are online add-ons to subscription TV services, offering access to live or recently aired television but also on-demand films available as part of PPV or subscription film packages.

Second, there are hybrid digital terrestrial television (DTV) and broadband services. These combine access to the Freeview suite of channels through a conventional aerial with on-demand services delivered over broadband. BT Vision is the supplementary television platform for the broadband subscribers of telco BT, while YouView was formed by a consortium including the four TV networks plus BT and fellow telcos Arqiva and TalkTalk. In both cases, the Freeview digital channels are available by DTV, while the broadband component delivers all the catch-up services from the main networks. As BT partners with YouView, BT Vision is carried by both services, offering a range of on-demand packages specific to the service—e.g., Vision Box Office, Vision Kids—plus Sky Sports channels at an addition cost.

A third type of service comes from "rentmailers," i.e., companies who have built their business on delivering physical video and games by post to subscribers through mail order but who have now branched out into online digital distribution. In the United States, Netflix launched its rentmail service in 1999 and in 2007 branched out to begin streaming films online.[10] This pattern was reproduced in the UK, where leading rentmailer LOVEFiLM started its DVD mail order business in 2002 before launching LOVEFiLM Instant in 2010 as its digital distribution outlet. Integration of LOVEFiLM and the Internet retailer Amazon started in February 2008 when LOVEFiLM initially acquired Amazon's DVD rental business in Germany and the UK, and in return Amazon became the largest shareholder in LOVEFiLM. For consumers, the most direct evidence of this corporate marriage came from how browsing for film or television titles through Amazon's UK site produced links directing visitors to LOVEFiLM's own site. Subsequently, the two services were further integrated after Amazon used LOVEFiLM to power the video service offered on its Kindle Fire tablet computers, with the facility for users to sign into LOVEFiLM through their Amazon accounts.[11] LOVEFiLM faced aggressive competition when Netflix launched its UK service in January 2012, and it was another sign that physical video was becoming a thing of the past as the US company immediately decided to offer a streaming-only service.

Fourth are standalone online subscription services offering access to libraries of films and, in some cases, television programming as well. Whereas catch-up TV and rentmailer services make appeals to broadly conceived popular audiences, it is in this category where the greatest variety is to be found, as services are variously distinguished by the types of content offered but also the audience constituencies appealed to. For example, on-demand film and television service blinkbox (blinkbox.com) is majority owned (80 percent) by the UK's leading supermarket chain, Tesco, and bases its business on offering rentals of high-profile new releases. Also aimed at the popular audience, VOD service PictureBox, operated by media conglomerate NBCUniversal, appeals to the popular market by making films from the library of Hollywood studio Universal available for streaming through its proprietorial player or viewing through certain television providers. Film4oD (Film4OD.Film4.com), HMV On-Demand (HMVOnDemand.com), and EE Film (EE.co.uk/film) have taken established media or communication brands—respectively, the digital television channel Film4 of the broadcaster Channel 4, high street media retailer HMV, and mobile network operator EE—as the platforms to run on-demand film services. Film4oD, HMV On-Demand, and EE Film are all operated by FilmFlex, which is also the provider behind Virgin Media's Movies on Demand service. FilmFlex offers the same back-end functionality for each of these services but customizes the front-end design to make different appeals to their partners' respective customer bases.

Other standalone services, however, position themselves in the online market by offering alternatives to the popular. For example, as the company's original title, The Auteurs, suggests, MUBI (MUBI.com) is aimed at the art film audience, or what is now more commonly called the "specialized" market. Although originating in Palo Alto, California, MUBI now has offices in London, Paris, Istanbul, and Buenos Aires. UK consumers can access the service, which distances itself from the casual movie consumer to make self-conscious appeals to cinephilia. As the company's founder, Efe Cakarel, explains, MUBI is differentiated from other services

> in several ways: (1) curated content of independent, international and classic cinema. We select our titles one by one, we're about quality not quantity; we're not a video store; (2) we are a global platform—we are currently showing hundreds of films in every country in the world; and finally, (3) we unite this global audience and our curated library through a social network that helps film lovers around the world to find films they love and the people who love them, investing the social aspect back into film watching.[12]

To offer another example, UK consumers can also access the service of Hollywood-based firm MovieFlix (MovieFlix.com), which operates in a slightly different specialized niche, where for a monthly fee, subscribers gain access to an eclectic library of 4,000 archival feature and short films to download or stream. On MovieFlix, features and shorts from the silent era sit alongside 1970s martial arts movies, B-westerns of the 1930s and '40s, serial movies, and "health films" about the merits of tofu or nuts.

Finally are those channels for digital distribution that represent the informal economy. Again, there is considerable variety within this category alone. YouTube exemplifies the gray zone of online distribution, offering a platform for user-generated content while carrying advertising and corporately sponsored content. Operating outside the purview of the state, peer-to-peer file-sharing software (e.g., BitTorrent, Kazaa, and LimeWire) and cyberlockers (e.g., MediaFire.com, Megaupload, and RapidShare.com) transcend borders and integrate UK users into an expansive globalized connected viewing audience, which is simply impossible for the formal economy with the territorial rights management and the geoblocking technologies that characterize so much of it. By providing free access to content, much of the informal economy operates outside the field of pay transactions that defines the formal economy. This distinction is not so clear-cut, however: YouTube remains dependent on ad revenues, while cyberlockers have imposed charges for premium services (e.g., RapidPro) to give subscribers increased traffic capacity for transferring and downloading files. Both cases serve to illustrate how the informal sphere is now seeing, in Lobato's words, the "formalisation of the informal."[13]

New Players, Old Habits: Audience Behavior and Taste

Our research sought to explore how UK consumers are now interacting and engaging with these channels for digital distribution by conducting an online questionnaire (garnering 156 responses) and four focus groups (with a total of twenty participants) with young adult viewers (aged between 16 and 29). The questionnaire sample had a higher percentage of female (70 percent) than male (30 percent) respondents. Despite the dramatic changes discussed above, traditional attitudes and behaviors persist throughout the questionnaire and focus group participants. A significant percentage (88 percent) of the research group has access to film or television content via digitally distributed means. However, the vast majority of questionnaire responses described watching media at home (74 percent for film, 94 percent for television) via broadcast or DVD means and during television schedule peak hours (83 percent of the sample watched film or television between 6 p.m. and 11 p.m.). Less than 1 percent of the sample have taken advantage of the increased mobility of digital distribution platforms. Where connected viewing activities do occur, television content is more popular than film, with a total of 69.9 percent downloading at least one television episode per week, compared to 56.2 percent downloading at least one film per week. Similar sentiments were expressed in focus groups:

"I think it's harder to find films." (RES2 FG2)

"I don't watch that many films using online viewing, but I do have a lot of films on DVD, old school . . . online viewing is shorter." (RES1 FG4)

While the greater number of television episodes downloaded per week may be the result of numerous factors (including the comparative brevity, and subsequently shorter downloading times, of a single television episode compared to a film), this behavior reflects the dominance of catch-up TV services in the UK market.

Not only did research participants show a preference for television generally, but there is also significant preference for the major broadcasters' catch-up

FIGURE 8.1 User Ratings of Selected Digital Distribution Services in the UK

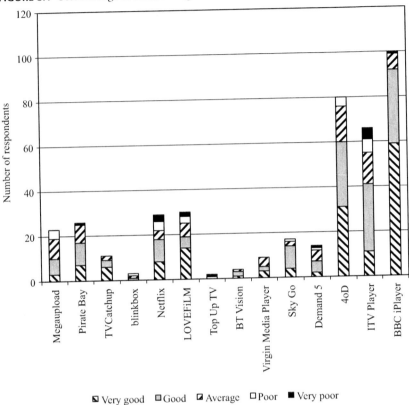

services (Figure 8.1). The first terrestrial broadcaster services to be established, BBC's iPlayer and Channel 4's 4oD, are clearly the most common platforms for digital distribution in the UK. They were equally the most highly rated services, with 54.6 percent rating iPlayer as "very good" and 30.4 percent giving Channel 4 the same rating, compared to the next-highest-performing service, LOVEFiLM (described as "very good" by 14.9 percent).

This reliance on established broadcasters, particularly those with strong public service remits, can be explained through a series of mutually reinforcing factors that relate to both the nature of technological change and the specific industry context of UK television. To a certain extent, favoring familiar market institutions can be understood through processes of cultural change. Although the digital distribution market is rapidly growing, the ability to access television or film content on anything other than the cinema screen or television set, or via Internet-based services, is still relatively new. As such, then, it is still in a state of emergence, a state that has consequences for audience taste and attitudes. Everett M. Rogers offers a foundational model for understanding how new technologies or concepts are adopted within communities. He positions innovations within closely related chronological development: "An adopter's experience with one innovation obviously influences that individual's perception of the next innovation to diffuse through the individual's system. In reality, the innovations diffusing at about the same time in a system are interdependent."[14] Such interdependence becomes even more significant when those innovations (even if not necessarily immediately succeeding one another) sit within the same sector of daily life; in this case, engagement with screen media. Elizabeth Evans has used Rogers's theories to explore the specific emergence of new technologies in relation to television viewing, arguing, "The unpredictability that emergent technologies create perhaps naturally leads to a reliance on something that is predictable."[15] Twinned with the broadcasters' development of branding strategies that facilitate "encouraging public loyalty" during intense industrial change, the established television broadcasters act as a signal of consistency and predictability in a moment of upheaval in the way that audiences can engage with media texts.[16] The fact that they remain the key focal point for connected viewing in the UK is partially an extension of their position as a key focal point in the UK's media industry more generally.

It is not simply the audience's familiarity with broadcasters such as the BBC and Channel 4, however, that results in their dominance of the UK digital distribution landscape. Both are heavily promoted on corresponding broadcast channels and are integrated in each institution's online spaces, increasing public awareness. The centrality of PSB to UK media policy also plays a significant role. The 2006 Charter Review of the BBC specifically gave the corporation responsibility over "helping to deliver to the public the benefit of emerging communications technologies and services," and online services were added to its preexisting radio and television services.[17] As a result, the BBC has invested significantly in the development of its iPlayer service, to the point where digital platforms are fully integrated into the television commissioning process.[18] Although not an explicit part of its remit until the 2010 Digital Economy Act, Channel 4 also clearly articulated its "experiments" in developing 4oD as part of its remit to be daring and innovative as early as 2006.[19] For both broadcasters, the development of online services has been a necessary part of their institutional strategies, with external policy factors playing a role absent in commercial broadcasters. This is not to say there is no development of online services by commercial broadcasters, as ITV Player, Demand 5, and Sky Go (which evolved from Sky Player, the UK's first online viewing service) indicate, merely that there is a more conscious policy *requiring* the BBC and Channel 4 to make such developments. Equally, we do not wish to suggest that such heavy investment automatically leads to popularity. However, whereas ITV Player and Demand 5 have seen few iterations of their online interfaces, both the iPlayer and 4oD have undergone multiple redesigns, with additional features being added in the case of the BBC and a wider range of content being made available by Channel 4. This greater investment was evident in the main criteria for awarding each service a rating of "very good," with both services primarily having been praised in questionnaire responses for the range and quality of their content and ease of their interface.[20]

Although clearly dominating the emergent digital distribution market in the UK, the extent to which public service broadcasters will continue this domination is a matter for future consideration as the market continues to grow and mature. As already described, commercial companies with little preexisting status in the UK market are starting to emerge as competitors to the major broadcasters, most significantly LOVEFiLM and Netflix. Neither service has yet reached the market position of iPlayer or 4OD, but questionnaire data indicate their potential to become key alternative choices. Although only a small number of respondents have used either service, those that have consistently rated them highly, often in preference to the traditional broadcasters. Of those who have used either LOVE-FiLM or Netflix, 48 percent ranked them as their favorite service, only slightly behind the BBC's iPlayer, ranked favorite service by 53 percent of those that have used it. However, 100 percent of participants who use LOVEFiLM or Netflix ranked them in the top three services they have used, compared to 93 percent for iPlayer and 85 percent for 4OD. The fact that every participant who has used these newer, purely commercial services considers them one of the best (even if not the best) services available demonstrates the potential for audience taste to change over the coming years. However, in turning to consider the values research participants placed on digital distribution services, the potential tension between commercial services that offer large-scale catalogues of content via a single interface and the universal access philosophy of public service media becomes apparent.

The Value of Digital Distribution: Access and Economics

Our survey participants placed emphasis on two key values that they find in UK digital distribution services. The first is in terms of accessibility. Although participants continue to prioritize traditional modes of viewing film and television content, online services provide a useful and strongly desired alternative when those traditional modes fail. The second relates more closely to issues around economic value and in particular an unwillingness to pay for downloaded or streamed content. As the following section will go on to explore, both relate to core principles of PSB or, as it is increasingly called, public service media (PSM). Much of the debate around PSM has focused on its role in developing citizenship and democracy, or the way in which public service resonates in individual programs.[21] However, the tastes and preferences demonstrated by this research group indicate that the founding ethos of PSM also serves an altogether more mundane and pragmatic purpose.

As Paddy Scannell and David Cardiff explore, the foundation of broadcasting in the UK rested on "the definition of broadcasting as a public utility to be developed as a national service in the public interest."[22] This has perpetuated throughout the twentieth century and into the twenty-first, with Graham Murdock arguing that the now more technologically expansive PSM can act as "a linked space defined by its shared refusal of commercial enclosure and its commitment to free and universal access, reciprocity, and collaborative activity."[23] While much work on PSM focuses on the latter two characteristics (see Moe, 2008; Iosifidis, 2010) or on how such ideals translate into content (see Bennett, 2006, 2008), the importance of "free and universal access" plays a key role in defining the development of digital distribution in the UK.[24] Indeed, PSB's ability to function is predicated on the necessity for all viewers to be able to access it, and throughout its history the BBC has been required to push the development of new reception technology.[25] It would be impossible for it to "promote a sense of social unity," something that was firmly in its founding principles, without all members of that society being able to watch or listen to it, for instance.[26] This has continued in the era of digital distribution, with the BBC's key policy regarding expanding iPlayer access across all digital platforms and devices becoming a key rhetoric in announcements about its ongoing expansion.[27] The core, eponymous assumption of PSM is that such content is a *service,* and should be made available to all, rather than a consumer good available to those who pay for it. In the case of online viewing, this then becomes twinned with attitudes that are equally core to the development of the Internet itself around open access and open source software. As Steven Weber has argued, "The conventional notion of property is, of course, the right to exclude you from using something that belongs to me. Property in open source is configured fundamentally around the right to distribute, not the right to exclude."[28] The resulting combination is a potent one that values free and easy access for all.

A belief in universal access to content manifests in both the behavior of questionnaire respondents and attitudes expressed by focus group participants. In terms of legitimate catch-up services, there is the chance to watch programs that have been missed or not known about until after they have aired, something that was raised as particularly valuable by a number of participants. The value of greater access is particularly apparent in the use of illegitimate sites that operate outside industrial copyright structures. Questionnaire respondents reported online viewing activity that was clearly driven by the desire to watch content they are unable to access otherwise, primarily that produced in the United States. Whereas only 18 percent use illegal sites to view films produced in the UK or European Union, 35 percent use them to access US-produced film. In the case of television, this division is even more pronounced with only 7.4 percent watching UK television illegally against 36.8 percent accessing US television illegally. Elsewhere, Evans has explored the central role that online services can play when broadcasters are deemed to have "failed," particularly in their treatment of imported drama.[29] This sentiment was echoed in the focus groups:

RES1:   I think most things I download would be TV shows, American
          TV shows . . . *Breaking Bad* is one of my favorite TV shows; it's

on such obscure channels at weird times, and you can never find them on, and the DVDs come out at weird times as well; you can't get them straightaway. (FG1)

RES2:   They're not always available; like, there's times that you go onto iTunes, and it's not there—

RES1:   Or one of you wants to watch *Game of Thrones* Season Two that's not yet out in the UK; even if you wanted to buy it, you couldn't buy it. (FG4)

The structure of global distribution results in delays before the release of US-produced content outside the United States. Online services are valued for providing greater access to this content, facilitating wider choice for audiences and extending PSB's principle of universal access.

However, merely having access to content does not fully account for research participants' attitudes toward digital distribution. The other branch of the "free and universal content" dictum was also presented through the research. In the questionnaire, a significant percentage of respondents said they would not be willing to pay for temporary access to digital content, though there is more willingness to pay small amounts to own such content, particularly if it is long form (i.e., feature films or television series) (Figures 8.2 and 8.3). There was additional evidence of a reticent attitude toward paying for digital content elsewhere in the questionnaire data: 46 percent of those who use subscription service LOVE-FiLM stated its cost is their least favorite feature (the highest percentage from the options provided), and 23 percent of Netflix users said the same (the second-highest percentage after "range of content"). Overall, cost of content was the third most important feature in ranking online services (47.6 percent), behind range of content (77.1 percent), and ease of use (53.3 percent) (Figure 8.4). Although there was some evidence of a willingness to pay small amounts to access online content, in the focus groups there was a much stronger reluctance toward additional payments for content:

RES2:   If I could just find it online, I wouldn't pay.
RES1:   I don't think anybody who downloads for free is really going to come across to a 'paying for it' philosophy. (FG1)

RES2:   You're not paying; you're not having to subscribe to things; that's certainly appealing.
RES1:   I always think I don't want to pay. (FG4)

INT: Why do you stream or download something?
RES 6:   Because it's free. (FG 2)

These issues of access to content and value for money perpetuate through research participants' attitudes toward digital distribution services.

FIGURE 8.2 Q. How Much Would You Be Willing to Pay to Rent Digital Versions of Content?

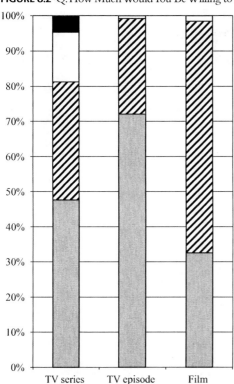

Of course, public service content in the UK is not "free" but is funded by the license fee paid by all television-viewing households. The tensions between public service and commercial priorities have long been a part of the BBC's activities in a situation that continues post-expansions into digital media.[30] However, the presence of the license fee in the UK has led to specific policies regarding further payments for public service content. The Communications Act 2003 and 2006 Charter Review explicitly require Channel 4 and the BBC to allow viewers access to their content for free, and although 4oD initially charged for some archive content, these charges were rapidly withdrawn.[31] However, at the same time, both institutions have a vested interest in exploiting their content for additional revenue. The BBC balances this tension by limiting online access to content for either seven days or the length of a season run; content is then licensed to BBC Worldwide and released via iTunes and DVD. Channel 4 equally makes some content available for a limited period, although some older pieces of content remain available beyond the catch-up cutoff. These "time limited" policies

FIGURE 8.3 Q. How Much Would You Be Willing to Pay to Own Digital Versions of Content?

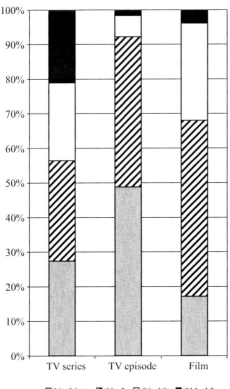

☐ Nothing ▨ £1–5 ☐ £6–10 ■ £11–15

FIGURE 8.4 Q. What Criteria Do You Use to Select Your Favorite Services?

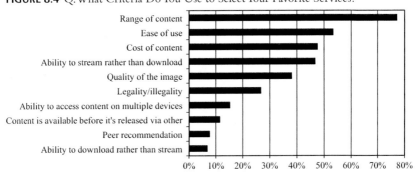

were the source of the most popular criticism of online viewing services, both in questionnaires and focus groups:

RES1:   It's annoying when things disappear, isn't it, especially, I think, the BBC. (FG4)

INT: Is there any way that the kind of services like BBC iPlayer or 4oD could be improved?
RES2:   Leave them on for a lot longer. (FG2)

RES2:   Not every show that's on telly is actually on the iPlayer, so there might be something that you really want to watch, and it's just not there.
RES3:   Like, they don't put *Family Guy* on it; even though they show it on BBC Three and stuff, they don't put it on iPlayer. (FG2)

Underlying these statements is a belief that television is a *service* rather than a commercial product; research participants believe that not only should content be made available to them, but they have a right to be able to watch it easily, on their own terms, and for little or no cost. One focus group participant specifically sees online services (primarily illegal ones) as a free alternative if one does not want to pay the cost of subscription services: "they could be on Sky or something, but if you don't have that then your only option really is to watch them online" (RES2 FG2). This belief perpetuates certain values being ascribed to that content that deny additional monetary payment. Connections between a reluctance to pay for online content and the license fee structure of PSB funding emerged directly from the focus groups:

RES8:   I think sometimes with, say, TV shows, I mean, I'm not old enough really to pay the TV people, I'm not the one paying for it, so it seems like it's coming for free, so then I think sometimes, like, when you have it illegally on the screen, it seems like the same thing, because that's for free, and the TV, on the TV, it's for free because, like, I'm not the one paying for it. So I think, for me, that's just kind of an association I make. (FG2)

RES1:   I pay the license fee, but I wouldn't specifically pay for streaming. (FG3)

In other discussions, such connections manifested less directly, in a general anticommercial sentiment regarding media content and a belief that if you can't pay, it is acceptable not to.

RES1:   It's free . . . we've been ripped off for so long with DVDs that it's about time we got our own back.

RES3:   I understand that sometimes the film industry will suffer, but I think they need to find a way round that, not me. It's not for me to sort of pay out, although it's money that I don't have. (FG1)

The discussions above indicate a clear ideological approach to film and television content that privileges the free access available via digital (particularly illegal) distribution avenues. Where the possibility for such content to have economic value (and so be "worthy" of payment on the part of the audience) was discussed, this became secondary to a greater insistence on free and universal access, the core principle of PSM.

Conclusion

In the UK, the film and television market has seen the rapid expansion of a wide variety of digital distribution platforms and services. Audiences are certainly beginning to embrace these outlets, although new technologies are being met with older, established patterns of viewing behavior. Despite opportunities for flexible time-shifted and mobile viewing, there still remains a ritualized sense of "prime time" in the online universe, as most consumption occurs at home in the evening hours. Tradition also weighs on notions of value. It may be specific to the UK context, but the principles of free and universal access foundational to PSB not only are influencing how online viewers are loyally drawn toward services from well-known PSB names like the BBC, but have also set in place ideological presumptions about the cultural and economic value of digital services. In the UK, for over ninety years the PSB model has deeply instilled belief among media consumers in their entitlement to obtain high-quality content for no (or at least no direct) cost. Even when considering film viewing, outside the usual parameters of the still-broadcasting-defined PSM, the ideology of "free and universal access" persists. As defining exemplars of, respectively, the formal and informal economies, the BBC and BitTorrent may appear poles apart, but arguably they share some common principles of service. Squeezed between these options, commercial digital distribution services must try to win the severely limited disposable income of consumers for whom a rich abundance of media content is readily available for free by not only informal but also formal channels. Although the share of the broadcast audience captured by the PSB networks may be declining in the UK, the same media institutions are cultivating new loyalties in the expanded terrain of PSM. Noting the forces at work in the UK context, as the landscape and market for digital distribution grow, it will not be enough to simply look at technology or content to draw conclusions about the state of the connected viewing universe. Returning to Turner's call for recognizing and respecting the specific conditions in which digital television is adopted, as the UK case suggests, empirical research demonstrates how specific residual values of cultural tradition can transcend and endure into the new media environment in ways that profoundly influence the manner in which those media will be viewed, used, and valued. Issues of access and value may play out differently in more explicitly commercial systems such as the United States, or even in other PSM-based European markets. It is necessary to further consider the unique combination of characteristics that define national and transnational media markets and how these characteristics may appear not just in industrial structures, but also in audiences.

Notes

1. Ramon Lobato, *Shadow Economies of Cinema: Mapping Informal Film Distribution* (London: British Film Institute, 2012), 39–40.
2. Lobato, *Shadow Economies of Cinema*, 95.
3. Graeme Turner, "Convergence and Divergence: The International Experience of Digital Television," in *Television as Digital Media*, eds. James Bennett and Niki Strange (Durham: Duke University Press, 2011), 48.
4. Turner, "Convergence and Divergence," 36.
5. Turner, "Convergence and Divergence," 35.
6. Renowned film critic Roger Ebert has offered one of the most direct articulations of this argument. In a 2011 blog post titled "I'll Tell You Why Movie Revenue is Dropping . . ." posted on his own website, Ebert speculated that one of the reasons why cinema-going audiences were declining was because of "[c]ompetition from other forms of delivery. Movies streaming over the Internet are no longer a sci-fi fantasy. TV screens are growing larger and cheaper. Consumers are finding devices that easily play Internet movies through TV sets. Netflix alone accounts for 30% of all Internet traffic in the evening. That represents millions of moviegoers. They're simply not in a theater."
7. Douglas Gomery, *Shared Pleasures: A History of Movie Presentation in the United States* (Madison: University of Wisconsin Press, 1992), 83.
8. See Paul McDonald, *Video and DVD Industries* (London: British Film Institute, 2007), 14–16; Anke Mebold and Charles Tepperman, "Resurrecting the Lost History of 28mm Film in North America," *Film History* 15, no. 2 (2003): 137–51; and Ben Singer, "Early Home Cinema and the Edison Home Projecting Kinetoscope," *Film History* 2, no. 1 (1988): 37–69.
9. Arguments that piracy negatively impacts legitimate revenues are widespread. To offer just one UK example, when the Film Policy Review Panel of the UK government's Department for Culture, Media & Sport published *A Future for British Film: It Begins With the Audience* . . . in 2012, the report argued that "[i]n the case of the film and television industries, studies have indicated that over 10 per cent of UK adults access infringing content online and that unlawful downloading costs these industries over £535m per year in the UK" (22). Among the most direct statements blaming piracy for an apparent "death of cinema" came in 2011 with the campaign video *The Last Cinema*, commissioned by the Federation Against Copyright Theft, the UK partner in the international antipiracy network sponsored by the Motion Picture Association. A short edit of the video ran in cinemas, with a longer version circulated through video sharing (see http://www.youtube.com/watch?v=7xuKllFofJ8). Opening on the exterior of a derelict theater, with "Cinema" displayed on the marquee, the camera moves through the mothballed interior. "RIP Last Cinema on earth" is written on a grimy wall, while in the auditorium, a few cinemagoers are found frozen in their seats covered in dust, with members of the audience gradually disappearing as the video progresses. Over this series of images cast in shades of dirty gray, doom-laden music adds to the apocalyptic tone, while a voice-over from actor John Hurt portends, "A moment of cinematic joy. An experience shared. All gone. Imagine. Love cinema? Hate piracy." For many UK citizens, the ominous resonances of Hurt's vocal abilities

were already well known, for he'd similarly voiced the infamous "Don't Die of Ignorance" public information commercial of 1987 warning against ignoring AIDS.

10. Netflix, "Company Timeline," https://signup.Netflix.com/MediaCenter/Timeline.
11. *BBC News,* "Lovefilm Ties Up With Amazon DVD," February 5, 2008, http://news .bbc.co.uk/1/hi/business/7228008.stm; *BBC News,* "Amazon Buys Remaining Stake in Lovefilm DVD Service," January 20, 2011, http://www.bbc.co.uk/news/technology-12239314; Lucy Spence, "Sign In to LOVEFiLM Using Amazon Account Details—for Kindle Fire and Kindle Fire HD Users," The Official LOVEFiLM Blog (blog), October 17, 2012, http://blog.lovefilm.com/uncategorized/sign-in-to -lovefilm-using-amazon-account-details-for-kindle-fire-and-kindle-fire-hd-users. html; Natasha Lomas, "Amazon's LOVEFiLM Powers Kindle Fire Video Service in the U.K., One Month Free Trial for Fire Buyers," TechCrunch, October 25, 2012, http://techcrunch.com/2012/10/25/amazons-lovefilm-powers-kindle-fire-video-service-in-the-u-k-one-month-free-trial-for-fire-buyers.
12. Paul Fileri and Ruby Cheung, "Spotlight on MUBI: Two Interviews with Efe Cakarel, Founder and CEO of MUBI," in *Digital Disruption: Cinema Movies On-line,* eds. Dina Iordanova and Stuart Cunningham (St Andrews: St Andrews Film Studies, 2012), 176.
13. Lobato, *Shadow Economies of Cinema,* 102.
14. Everett M. Rogers, *The Diffusion of Innovations,* 5th ed. (New York: Free Press, 2003), 15.
15. Elizabeth Evans, *Transmedia Television: Audiences, New Media, and Daily Life* (New York: Routledge, 2011), 14.
16. Catherine Johnson, "From Brand Congruence to the 'Virtuous Circle': Branding and the Commercialization of Public Service Broadcasting," *Media Culture and Society* 35, no. 3 (2013): 314–31.
17. Department for Culture, Media & Sport, *Broadcasting: Copy of the Royal Charter for the Continuance of the British Broadcasting Corporation* (London: The Stationery Office, 2006), 3.
18. A Freedom of Information request revealed that up to March 2011, the BBC had spent £10.5 million developing the iPlayer, and that the services costs £4 million per year to operate; Stephen Poppitt, "Cost of the BBC iPlayer Project," WhatDoTheyKnow, May 29, 2010, http://www.whatdotheyknow.com/request/cost_of_the_bbc_iplayer_project. See also Victoria Jaye, "Victoria Jaye: Commissioning for TV & iPlayer Content," BBC Commissioning, May 26, 2011, http://www.bbc.co.uk/commissioning/news/victoria-jaye-commissioning-for-tv-and-iplayer.shtml.
19. UK government, *Digital Economy Act 2010* (London: The Stationery Office, 2010), 29–30; Channel Four, *Review: Channel Four Television Corporation Report and Financial Statements 2006* (London: Channel Four Television Corporation, 2006), 26.
20. BBC—24.5 percent rated range of content, 25.5 percent rated ease of access, and 28.7 percent rated quality of content; Channel 4—53.8 percent rated range of content, 7.7 percent rated ease of access, and 15.4 percent rated quality of content. In both cases, these were the most popular responses for the broadcasters.
21. Graham Murdock, "Building the Digital Commons," in *Cultural Dilemmas in Public Service Broadcasting,* eds. Gregory Ferrell Lowe and Per Jauert (Gothenburg: Nordicom, 2005), 213–31; Hallvard Moe, "Dissemination and Dialogue in the Public Sphere: A Case for Public Service Media Online," *Media Culture & Society* 30, no. 3 (2008): 319–36; James Bennett, "The Public Service Value of Interactive Television," *New Review of Film and Television Studies* 4, no. 3 (2006): 263–85.
22. Paddy Scannell and David Cardiff, *A Social History of British Broadcasting: Volume One 1922–1939* (Oxford: Blackwell, 1991), 6.
23. Murdock, "Building the Digital Commons," 6.
24. See Moe, "Dissemination and Dialogue in the Public Sphere: A Case for Public Service Media Online"; Petros Iosifidis, ed., *Reinventing Public Service Communication: European Broadcasters and Beyond* (Basingstoke: Palgrave Macmillan, 2010); Bennett, "The Public Service Value of Interactive Television"; James Bennett, "Interfacing the

Nation: Remediating Public Service Broadcasting in the Digital Television Age," *Convergence: The International Journal of Research into New Media* 14, no. 3 (2008): 277–99.

25. Asa Briggs, *The History of Broadcasting in the United Kingdom – Volume Five: Competition, 1955–1974* (Oxford: Oxford University Press, 1995), 832–9 and 848–63; Andrew Crisell, *An Introductory History of British Broadcasting* (London: Routledge, 1997), 116.

26. Paddy Scannell, "Public Service Broadcasting: The History of a Concept," in *British Television: A Reader,* ed. Edward Buscombe (Oxford: Oxford University Press, 2009), 48.

27. BBC, "BBC Enters New Partnership to Bring BBC iPlayer to Sky," January 30, 2012, http://www.bbc.co.uk/mediacentre/latestnews/2012/iplayer-sky.html.

28. Steven Weber, *The Success of Open Source* (Cambridge, MA: Harvard University Press, 2004), 1.

29. Evans, *Transmedia Television: Audiences, New Media, and Daily Life,* 158–9.

30. Catherine Johnson, "Trading Auntie: The Exploitation and Protection of Intellectual Property Rights During the BBC's Monopoly Years," *New Review of Film and Television Studies* 7, no. 4 (2009): 441–58.

31. UK government, *Communications Act 2003* (London: The Stationery Office, 2003), 208; Department for Culture, Media & Sport, *Broadcasting: An Agreement Between Her Majesty's Secretary of State for Culture, Media and Sport and the British Broadcasting Corporation* (London: The Stationery Office, 2006), 7. This situation is reinforced by the consistent paralleling of developments within commercial UK television with free-to-air alternatives, most notably Freeview in response to multiplatform subscription services, and YouView in response to the integration of such subscription services with online catch-up services. Although PSB-originated content can be sold (via DVD or download), this only occurs after the initial period of free access, which can last up to a month.

References

BBC. "BBC Enters New Partnership to Bring BBC iPlayer to Sky." January 30, 2012. http://www.bbc.co.uk/mediacentre/latestnews/2012/iplayer-sky.html.

BBC News. "Amazon Buys Remaining Stake in Lovefilm DVD Service." January 20, 2011. http://www.bbc.co.uk/news/technology-12239314.

BBC News. "Lovefilm Ties Up With Amazon DVD." February 5, 2008. http://news.bbc .co.uk/1/hi/business/7228008.stm.

Bennett, James. "Interfacing the Nation: Remediating Public Service Broadcasting in the Digital Television Age." *Convergence: The International Journal of Research into New Media* 14, no. 3 (2008): 277–99.

Bennett, James. "The Public Service Value of Interactive Television." *New Review of Film and Television Studies* 4, no. 3 (2006): 263–85.

Briggs, Asa. *The History of Broadcasting in the United Kingdom – Volume Five: Competition, 1955–1974.* Oxford: Oxford University Press, 1995.

British Film Institute. *Statistical Yearbook 2012.* London: British Film Institute, 2012.

Channel Four. *Review: Channel Four Television Corporation Report and Financial Statements 2006.* London: Channel Four Television Corporation, 2006.

Crisell, Andrew. *An Introductory History of British Broadcasting.* London: Routledge, 1997.

Department for Culture, Media & Sport. *A Future for British Film: It Begins With the Audience . . .* London: The Stationery Office, 2012.

Department for Culture, Media & Sport. *Broadcasting: An Agreement Between Her Majesty's Secretary of State for Culture, Media and Sport and the British Broadcasting Corporation.* London: The Stationery Office, 2006.

Department for Culture, Media & Sport. *Broadcasting: Copy of the Royal Charter for the Continuance of the British Broadcasting Corporation*. London: The Stationery Office, 2006.

Ebert, Roger. "I'll Tell You Why Movie Revenue is Dropping . . ." Roger Ebert's Journal (blog). December 28, 2011. http://www.rogerebert.com/rogers-journal/ill-tell-you-why-movie-revenue-is-dropping.

Evans, Elizabeth. *Transmedia Television: Audiences, New Media, and Daily Life*. New York: Routledge, 2011.

Fileri, Paul, and Ruby Cheung. "Spotlight on MUBI: Two Interviews with Efe Cakarel, Founder and CEO of MUBI." In *Digital Disruption: Cinema Movies On-line*, edited by Dina Iordanova and Stuart Cunningham, 167–79. St Andrews: St Andrews Film Studies, 2012.

Gomery, Douglas. *Shared Pleasures: A History of Movie Presentation in the United States*. Madison: University of Wisconsin Press, 1992.

Iosifidis, Petros, ed. *Reinventing Public Service Communication: European Broadcasters and Beyond*. Basingstoke: Palgrave Macmillan, 2010.

International Video Federation. *The European Video Yearbook 2012*. Brussels: International Video Federation, 2012.

Jaye, Victoria. "Victoria Jaye: Commissioning for TV & iPlayer Content." BBC Commissioning, May 26, 2011. http://www.bbc.co.uk/commissioning/news/victoria-jaye-commissioning-for-tv-and-iplayer.shtml.

Johnson, Catherine. "From Brand Congruence to the 'Virtuous Circle': Branding and the Commercialization of Public Service Broadcasting." *Media Culture and Society* 35, no. 3 (2013): 314–31.

Johnson, Catherine. "Trading Auntie: The Exploitation and Protection of Intellectual Property Rights During the BBC's Monopoly Years." *New Review of Film and Television Studies* 7, no. 4 (2009): 441–58.

Lobato, Ramon. *Shadow Economies of Cinema: Mapping Informal Film Distribution*. London: British Film Institute, 2012.

Lomas, Natasha. "Amazon's LOVEFiLM Powers Kindle Fire Video Service in the U.K., One Month Free Trial for Fire Buyers." TechCrunch, October 25, 2012. http://techcrunch.com/2012/10/25/amazons-lovefilm-powers-kindle-fire-video-service-in-the-u-k-one-month-free-trial-for-fire-buyers.

McDonald, Paul. *Video and DVD Industries*. London: British Film Institute, 2007.

Mebold, Anke, and Charles Tepperman. "Resurrecting the Lost History of 28mm Film in North America." *Film History* 15, no. 2 (2003): 137–51.

Moe, Hallvard. "Dissemination and Dialogue in the Public Sphere: A Case for Public Service Media Online." *Media Culture & Society* 30, no. 3 (2008): 319–36.

Murdock, Graham. "Building the Digital Commons." In *Cultural Dilemmas in Public Service Broadcasting*, edited by Gregory Ferrell Lowe and Per Jauert, 213–31. Gothenburg: Nordicom, 2005.

Netflix. "Company Timeline." https://signup.Netflix.com/MediaCenter/Timeline.

Ofcom. *Communications Market Report 2012*. London: Ofcom, 2012.

Ofcom. *Communications Market Report 2011*. London: Ofcom, 2011.

Poppitt, Stephen. "Cost of the BBC iPlayer Project." WhatDoTheyKnow, May 29, 2010. http://www.whatdotheyknow.com/request/cost_of_the_bbc_iplayer_project.

Rogers, Everett M. *The Diffusion of Innovations*. 5th ed. New York: Free Press, 2003.

Scannell, Paddy. "Public Service Broadcasting: The History of a Concept." In *British Television: A Reader*, edited by Edward Buscombe, 45–62. Oxford: Oxford University Press, 2009.

Scannell, Paddy, and David Cardiff. *A Social History of British Broadcasting: Volume One 1922–1939*. Oxford: Blackwell, 1991.

Singer, Ben. "Early Home Cinema and the Edison Home Projecting Kinetoscope." *Film History* 2, no. 1 (1988): 37–69.

Spence, Lucy. "Sign In to LOVEFiLM Using Amazon Account Details—for Kindle Fire and Kindle Fire HD Users." The Official LOVEFiLM Blog (blog). October 17, 2012. http://blog.lovefilm.com/uncategorized/sign-in-to-lovefilm-using-amazon-account-details-for-kindle-fire-and-kindle-fire-hd-users.html.

Turner, Graeme. "Convergence and Divergence: The International Experience of Digital Television." In *Television as Digital Media,* edited by James Bennett and Niki Strange, 31–51. Durham: Duke University Press, 2011.

UK government. *Digital Economy Act 2010*. London: The Stationery Office, 2010.

UK government. *Communications Act 2003*. London: The Stationery Office, 2003.

Weber, Steven. *The Success of Open Source*. Cambridge, MA: Harvard University Press, 2004.

PART III
CONTENT AND ENGAGEMENT

9

CONNECTED VIEWING, CONNECTED CAPITAL

Fostering Gameplay Across Screens

Matthew Thomas Payne

The Promise of the Companion App

The summer can be a cruel time for avid gamers. Year after year, video game publishers schedule their big-budget titles for release just in time for the holiday season. Firms depend on increased seasonal spending to drive the sales of their big-budget franchise favorites, helping to secure returns on considerable investments. The upshot of this release strategy is that new blockbusters and anticipated sequels often do not hit store shelves until the fall at the earliest. Thus, gamers and game buyers have few major titles to look forward to during gaming's long summer months. There is, however, one brief and gleaming moment of over-hyped relief during this time: E3.

The Electronic Entertainment Expo, or E3, is an annual trade show that promises to both satiate and whet the appetites of voracious gamers with informational morsels and tidbits concerning upcoming software and hardware offerings. Part global marketing event, part corporate celebration of mainstream gaming culture, E3 features major presentations by industry leaders Microsoft, Sony, and Nintendo, as well as multiplatform game publishers including Ubisoft, Capcom, Konami, and Warner Bros., among others. And, as it does every year, the three-day Los Angeles event attracts the close scrutiny and fanfare of journalists and gamers alike, and it is broadcast and streamed live by a variety of cable channels and Internet sites.

In addition to showcasing the "latest and greatest" games and peripherals, the annual E3 show functions itself as a kind of game. It is a game of marketing discourse where firms compete to win best-in-show accolades from game critics, and build buzz for forthcoming franchises, sequels, and product lines. For example, the 2005 and 2006 shows were highlighted by the debut of the seventh generation of home consoles when Microsoft, Sony, and Nintendo teased their (then) "next gen" Xbox 360, PlayStation 3, and Wii platforms, respectively. Following Nintendo's lead with its wildly successful Wii, Sony and Microsoft revealed their own motion-sensitive devices at the 2009 show. Nintendo's dual-screen, 3D handheld device—the 3DS—garnered the lion's share of the positive press at the 2010 show. And multiscreen gameplay devices and multiscreen game support applications dominated the 2011 and 2012 E3s. For instance, at the 2011 show, Nintendo promoted the Wii's successor—its Wii U console—which has as its main selling point a controller with an embedded touch screen that allows for single- or multiscreen gameplay. Not to be outdone, at the following year's E3 Microsoft debuted its own multiscreen technology called SmartGlass. Nintendo and Microsoft were not alone in their push for multiscreen connectivity. Publishing giants Electronic Arts (EA) and Ubisoft were just a few of the other software companies that announced that their popular franchises would be launched with support services available via smartphones, tablets, and web browsers. Although it remains too early to predict how history will remember the seventh and forthcoming eighth console generations, there is mounting evidence that they will be known as those devices that connected viewing and gameplay practices across screens.

As recent E3 presentations make clear, publishers are increasingly turning to secondary screens to shore up their sales and expand their player communities. Game players, on the other hand, are looking to these additional screens to augment their gameplay, to supplement the information available on their primary screens, and to reconnect them with their online identities and fellow gamers when they are away from their home consoles and computers. Yet much of this community support infrastructure has been built seemingly on the collective faith of developers and marketers, representing a veritable "build it, and they will play" mentality. This chapter examines if the game industry's received wisdom is well founded, and if so, why these support efforts connect with players.

Like the other contributions to this anthology, this chapter argues that connected viewing means more than linking content across screens. Connected viewing is a technological achievement to be sure, but it is also a performative act. Sometimes second screens affect how consumers choose to reengage with their favorite media in new ways and in new places (as discussed by Ethan Tussey); sometimes second screens shape how users manage (Greg Steirer) and display (Chuck Tryon and Max Dawson) their digital collections; and sometimes socially networked second screens transform viewers into more active participants even as they are marked and tracked for audience measurement (Mark Andrejevic and Hye Jin Lee). In all these cases, the functioning of the multiscreen technology is indivisible from its contextual use; after all, it is the user that connects the screens. This chapter argues that when this fusion succeeds—when multiple screens are sutured and multimodal information is synthesized into a singular experience—connected viewing becomes more than the sum of its parts (or screens, as the case may be). This is perhaps no more evident than in the case of multiscreen video gaming.

Video game publishers for the home console market have, until recently, abided by a regrettable but necessary "release-and-forget" maxim. Without the means of extending their games' shelf lives—either by fixing broken code, or by adding new content—producers had to hope that the enthusiasm and profits from one title would bankroll the next. Now, through the online gaming services Xbox Live, PlayStation Network, and WiiWare, console publishers can update their titles as needed and offer downloadable content that extends the playability of their games. But publishers understand that gamers do not remain fixed only to their primary screens during play sessions. The ubiquity of mobile devices—in particular smartphones and tablets—in tandem with the increased availability of wireless Internet connectivity is not only enabling producers to extend their titles for longer periods on single screens, but it is also allowing them to use these technologies to extend the playability of games across screens. Enter the companion app.

Defining the companion app, or describing what it does exactly, is a deceptively difficult task. At its most basic level, companion apps assist gamers with their in-game activities. However, the definitional waters get murky after this initial level of abstraction. Owed in part to its novelty, the open and uneven nature of its development, the multiplicity of platforms where it might appear, and the sheer diversity of games that these apps support, there are few industry exemplars. There is no established design template. There is no checklist of essential services that these utilities ought to deliver to users. And there is, as yet, no set of best practices for the industry to follow. Until such a time comes, we can only look to the most popular games from the most popular genres for signs of what does and does not work.

To wit, one of the most popular genres in console and PC gaming for nearly two decades has been the first-person shooter. This was certainly the case in 2011 when *Modern Warfare 3* and *Battlefield 3* dominated the sales charts. In fact, *Battlefield 3* was EA's fastest-selling game in the company's storied history, and Activision's *Modern Warfare 3* was the fastest-selling product in entertainment history.[1] To date, *Modern Warfare 3* has sold over thirty million units, *Battlefield 3* has sold over fifteen million units, and each game has made over a billion dollars each.[2] These figures are all the more impressive when one considers how deeply the global recession has affected consumer spending on entertainment since 2008, suppressing even the so-called "recession proof" games industry.[3] But even before the economic downturn, producers in this more accurately labeled "recession-resistant" industry were devising strategies for amplifying gamers' play experiences by extending the reach of their titles beyond individual play sessions. It is not surprising that Activision and EA would turn to secondary screens to build brand loyalty, and it is not surprising that gamers would adopt these services and apps to gain a competitive edge.

This chapter examines Activision's Elite for *Call of Duty* and EA's Battlelog for *Battlefield* support services and companion apps to determine if these multiscreen and multiplatform utilities effectively aid those gamers seeking to better understand the gameplay activities unfolding on their primary screens. These companies' efforts were selected for analysis because of the broad appeal of their shooter franchises and because these firms were among the first-to-market with their support devices. Elite and Battlelog are accessible from web browsers, smartphones and tablets, and via the Xbox 360 and PlayStation 3 consoles. Using these utilities, players can customize their profiles, share their accomplishments via Twitter and Facebook, manage their player groups, participate in community events, and even mine their gameplay data to improve their tactics. Elite and Battlelog thus function as part social networking hub, part reference library, and part personalized report card. Gamers are free to consult these near-real-time resources from mobile apps or web browsers while they play on their primary screens, or they can check in when they are away from their consoles. Whether these two services are ultimately judged to be well designed or not, Elite and Battlelog will likely define shooter support applications to come because of their popularity.[4] Because users have an idea of their standing and achievement in a game (e.g., levels completed, their high scores, win-loss ratios, etc.), and are motivated to improve their in-game performance using the feedback that companion apps offer, truly connected viewing can do more than link a user's gameplay across devices—this connection can transform gameplay by giving users personalized feedback on their performance and strategies for future play sessions.

The Long Game of Gaming Capital

Although the support utility is a fairly novel innovation, it is not wholly without precedent. Many of the initial forays into generating increased interest around game franchises resemble practices seen in other sprawling, transmedia projects like those of *Harry Potter, Batman, The Matrix,* and *The Lord of the Rings.*[5] In these instances, producers refashioned their titles and IP into complementary media forms—be they novels, comic books, or action figures. But when done well, this process goes beyond mere adaptation; it presents diverse media users (including nongamers) with multiple points of entry for experiencing a transmedia or transmedial world.[6]

Despite the massive popular appeal and financial successes of the aforementioned properties, world building is not by itself a surefire commercial formula. For every success, there exist countless licensing failures. This is especially true in the games industry where producers often mistakenly presume that the allure of their coveted property—be it a superhero, a children's cartoon, or a famous athlete—will compensate for their game's technical and artistic shortcomings.[7]

Thus, in addition to a universe's stories unfurling across a spate of media, we are also witnessing increased opportunities for transmedia or connected play through second-screen platforms and services. Audience participation and play are, of course, at the proverbial heart of any discussion of media convergence, connected viewing, and fandom. And game franchises have been utilizing a range of transmedia storytelling and world-building strategies for decades, a practice resulting in what P. David Marshall calls the "new intertextual commodity."[8] Yet most companion apps are not just another means by which publishers migrate a game's backstory or lore to a second screen. Rather, these applications foster additional interactions with the game property. Transmedia play is less concerned with questions of content—i.e., whether a given property "makes sense" for a media format or platform (as is the case with transmedia storytelling)—than it is with *how* users engage simultaneously *and* asynchronously with properties across media devices. Given the game industry's expertise with crafting and selling interactivity, it is not surprising that its major firms have been leaders in cultivating connected play vis-à-vis their multiscreen apps.

The collective push by game producers to grow their connected viewing and play efforts begs two interconnected questions: First, why would any firm spend the time, resources, and money to develop and maintain a support service and its related mobile applications that will be made available to users for little to no money? And, conversely, what does the gamer have to gain by adopting such apps and services? The answer to the former is that content producers want to connect with gamers at multiple points along their purchase pathway. Adequate engagement and consumer outreach means year-round interactions, and not just a prelaunch marketing blitz. We might think of this strategy as being the marketing equivalent of Chris Anderson's "long tail" concept,[9] the key difference being that instead of a long distribution channel of eclectic items culminating in greater sales, the increased opportunities for interacting with a game property over time and over multiple devices result in a higher likelihood of consumers purchasing additional content, joining a game's player community, and developing a greater affinity for the franchise. That is, instead of a distributor benefiting over time from its "long tail" of products, the game publisher benefits from a "long game" development strategy where would-be gamers have multiple opportunities to engage in an expansive game universe. Industry research by Google confirms that mobile phones and secondary screens are key devices in gamers' purchasing decisions, and that multiscreen interactions will continue to increase.[10] Producers are scrambling to create welcoming environments around their titles because these spaces and apps grow their sales and brands. Said plainly: in the world of gaming, connected viewing begets connected purchasing.

The answer to the second question—what do players have to gain from introducing additional screens into their gameplay activities—lies in the performative nature of gameplay. Whereas expansion packs and additional content typically extend the playability of the game and its narrative, support apps hold the promise of bolstering users' gameplay performance and, with it, their personal sense of "gaming capital." This is why gamers, perhaps more so than other media users, have a vested, practical interest in effectively connecting their viewing across screens.

Services like Elite and Battlelog are popular among video gamers because they give users access to information that can directly improve their gameplay.

To borrow the old sports adage: gamers play to win. And when gamers can't win, they look for ways to improve their play so they might win the next time. They scrutinize detailed maps in game magazines. They share hints and codes with one another on Internet message boards. They strategize about team tactics before, during, and after multiplayer matches. They comb through FAQs and walk-throughs to discover the location of hidden "Easter eggs" and exploitable glitches. And they deconstruct YouTube videos to overcome difficult levels. In short: gamers want to be better than they are, and they seek out a host of resources to become better players and self-actualized avatars. Moreover, because enhancing one's knowledge of video games potentially bolsters one's gaming capital—or one's competency about a game's history, control interfaces, rules of play, etc.—it stands to reason that fostering this form of social knowledge within a play community may increase one's interest in the title and lead to additional interactions with the game company's properties over time and across screens. A quick word on gaming capital is in order before proceeding to the discussion of the research project.

Gaming capital is a fantastically useful, though at times frustratingly elusive, concept for thinking about what information gamers value and how it attains its value. First introduced by game scholar Mia Consalvo, the term is a reworking or recontextualizing of Pierre Bourdieu's "cultural capital" for the world of gaming—broadly understood as encompassing one's knowledge of games and how that knowledge is circulated and used.[11] Consalvo importantly recognizes that not only is gaming capital sought out by players and becomes instantiated in a diverse range of user practices and productions (including game mods, level walk-throughs and FAQs, and fan art), but that there are also no shortage of companies that seek to profit from selling the information that gamers value (e.g., game magazines, cheat devices, and official guidebooks). Gaming capital considered thusly moves us beyond Edward Castronova's idea of "avatar capital," which focuses primarily on the items and experiences accrued by the gamer's virtual persona that give the player more in-game mobility and gameplay options, and connects in-game practices with the paratexts surrounding games—including second-screen apps.[12]

The concept has been further developed. For example, building on Consalvo's work, Thomas Apperley and Christopher Walsh have subdivided gaming capital into Bourdieu's four original categories of capital—cultural, economic, symbolic, and social—for the purposes of thinking through how gaming functions as a new media literacy, and, as importantly, for operationalizing gaming capital for studies on the sociology of gameplay.[13] Olli Sotamaa assesses how game achievements, those items and awards unlocked during gameplay, operate as reward systems, and how these accolades do (and do not) serve as effective proxies for gaming capital.[14] Finally, political economist and game scholar Randy Nichols cautions us on neglecting those who have a hand in generating the apparatus of "gamer capital" but do not have economic access to it, most notably those responsible for assembling the hardware that allows gaming capital to happen at all. Moreover, the idea of gamer capital for Nichols forces "the question of how play, appropriation and reappropriation of game meaning, and the construction of meaning might be channeled, obstructed, or marketed by an industrial system."[15] In only a few years the scholarly attention to gaming capital has expanded from micro, in-game transactions to include global systems of capital and questions about how best to operationalize this demonstrably contextual concept. This chapter is another effort to examine gaming capital in action, and to understand how it motivates and mediates one's gaming experiences even as it, in turn, is mediated and monetized across multiple screens.

The second screen should not be thought of as being another content delivery device when it is working in conjunction with a primary screen. When gamers trace their gameplay from a primary to a secondary screen and back again with the goal of discovering more about a game world or seeking feedback on their play, it produces a potential wellspring of gaming capital for players and producers alike (although, to be sure, the nature of the capital produced may differ *considerably*). Gamers can learn more about play styles, tactics, strategies, characters, game mechanics, design choices, and analyze the personalized feedback of their previous in-game actions; in short, they learn more about what it takes to win, as well as the instrumental and noninstrumental information valued by a community of players. Likewise, publishers can learn more about their customers, including how they prefer to learn about their gameplay and that of others, as well as ways of extending their title's "long game" appeal. Because of this inherent dynamism, gaming capital should be conceived of as a virtual currency that can purchase credibility within a community, *and* as a system of exchange between gamers and content producers.

Thinking of gaming capital thusly forces deeper considerations of how game knowledge is engendered as users jump between multiple screens and interfaces, traversing the interactive texts and their supporting paratexts. This activity also begs additional questions that lie at the heart of this anthology on connected viewing technologies and user practices. In particular, when the technological means for extending a game experience bridges multiple screens and motivates users to further explore a fictional world or virtual identity, will these moments of connected viewing and play result in users achieving a better competency with the game? The remainder of this chapter answers this question—the one that implicitly justifies the companion app's raison d'être—namely, do Elite and Battlelog prove their efficacy to gamers looking to improve their gameplay vis-à-vis multiscreen utilities? The answer to this question is not limited to determining whether or not EA and Activision designed effective support tools. Rather, the answer to this question has broader implications for a range of connected viewing practices independent from gaming because the underlying process is about cultivating meaningful connections for users across screens, a process that transforms data into knowledge, or in the case of video games, gameplay into capital.

Analyzing *Call of Duty*'s Elite & *Battlefield*'s Battlelog

To determine whether Elite and Battlelog amplify players' levels of gaming capital, I enlisted the assistance of fifteen research participants selected from the undergraduate and graduate sections of my spring 2012 Video Game Studies class at the University of Alabama. The participants included eleven undergraduates and four graduate students, all of whom were in their early to mid-twenties. Two participants were women, and two were students of color. The remaining research participants were white men. The participants had a broad range of gaming experiences—from being novice gamers to being lifelong fans.

Playing games is, as media scholars are fond of emphasizing, a necessary step for critically assessing their computational design and cultural meaningfulness.[16] Accordingly, over the course of six weeks, the participants collectively played approximately 550 hours of *Modern Warfare 3* and *Battlefield 3* while utilizing their support utilities on phone and tablet apps (e.g., Android, iPhones, iPad), and web browsers on Mac and PC laptops, and the lab's desktop PC. The participants kept daily journals of their online play and took notes on their research partners' gameplay actions during these play sessions. Additionally, the students responded to weekly take-home reflection prompts, and completed questionnaires regarding their use of the support applications. The reports and gameplay journals were collated, synthesized, coded, and used to generate more precisely worded writing prompts and questionnaires. These responses were, in turn, collated and coded again. This iterative process resulted in the narrowing down of the project's emergent concepts and themes until the participants' core experience of using these services came into focus—a qualitative methodology and process known as grounded theory. As I discuss shortly, this project finds that these second-screen services amplified the participants' engagement by imparting insider knowledge and winning strategies for subsequent play sessions.

First-Screen Wars, Second-Screen Boot Camps

Given the nature of the games they support, it is useful to think of Elite and Battlelog as virtual boot camps whereby players can become more efficient and skilled joystick soldiers. Players must put a wealth of information into action to excel in these titles' intensely competitive, multiplayer game spaces. Perfecting the art of the online kill does not come easy. Gamers must be fluent with titles' weapons, vehicles, maps, control schemes, gameplay modes, etc.; they must recognize their own strengths and weaknesses in a variety of dynamic play situations; and they must communicate effectively with teammates. Elite and Battlelog address all these demands in some capacity (although they do so to varying degrees of emphasis and user satisfaction[17]).

If Elite and Battlelog are their games' online boot camps, then we can further subcategorize the services' educational features along these lines: as informational example, participants lamented the construction of one of *Modern Warfare 3*'s maps after they reviewed how a round had unfolded. They determined that there were too few options for movement that resulted in frustrating bottlenecks. Second-screen apps highlight a host of design choices—both good and bad.

The Companion App as Mobile Barracks

As the research group's heat map conferences illustrate, gaming capital is communal. It is a form of social currency that displays its value when it is exchanged. Gamers often improve their gameplay when they play together. Sometimes this means playing with one another in the game, and sometimes it means observing others playing. This was true for gamers in video arcades of the 1970s and 1980s. Before popular game magazines and before the modern-day version of the Internet, novice gamers would routinely improve their gameplay by watching over the shoulders of experienced players. Games—digital and analog, video based and tabletop—have always been social events. EA and Activision amplify the sociability of their games with their multiscreen support services by giving users a socially networked view of gaming expertise in a post-video arcade era—one that implicitly sanctions what proper gaming capital looks like by giving players numerous ways of comparing their performance to other gamers.

Elite and Battlelog are virtual barracks that embrace their games' competitive and cooperative elements. On the competitive side, the services' leaderboards chart the games' global point leaders, the players' own rankings, and the rankings of their friends. These services regularly promote competitions that pit single players and teams (or clans) against one another. These tournaments are not limited to showcasing only gameplay skills, however. There are also media-based competitions that challenge players to compile or capture the best montage or images of destruction. Together, these social networking features and events promote a competitive gaming hierarchy in their communities with empirical stats and a host of head-to-head bouts.

EA and Activision likewise promote in-game cooperation through their connected viewing companion utilities. It is possible (and encouraged) in Elite and Battlelog to create player clans with customizable names and insignias. Gamers can also study and copy other players' load-outs—the combinations of weapons, accessories, and perks—to experiment with new choices. Elite also has a feature called Elite TV, which provides gamers with original content ranging from interviews with studio personnel to advertisements for upcoming content and televised contests between professional e-Sports squads. Together, these second-screen group-building features and videos promote an inclusive gaming community for the primary gameplay screen.

Whether gamers are looking to Elite and/or Battlelog to give them a better sense of how they rank in an official gaming hierarchy, whether they use these apps to grow their social ties with fellow players—or, more likely still, a little of both—the research participants overwhelmingly wanted to keep their gaming achievements and activities partitioned from their preexisting social networks. This may be bad news to firms looking to leverage the popularity of extant social networking sites to spread their marketing efforts through electronic word-of-mouth. The participants felt that Activision and EA insisted too strongly on linking their services to social networking sites like Facebook and Twitter. To be clear, the participants liked having the option of sharing gameplay information through these services. But due to gaming's social stigma, especially that of violent military shooters, participants did not want their gameplay activities advertised to their nongame networks. This suggests that gaming capital does not automatically translate well to other social circles, and when it is expressed in a new forum, it is unlikely that it will retain the values and meanings that it held for its original community of players. It therefore makes sense that companion app producers give users plenty of options for customizing how their gaming accolades are shared with fellow gamers and nongamers alike. This also means that the same gaming capital that can tether screens together when their union benefits the user can also be disruptive when the gaming capital that is lauded in one social circle is ridiculed in another.

Beyond their ability to act as veritable field manuals, after-action reports, or mobile barracks, perhaps the greatest strength of these companion services is their ability to shape the participants' in-game activities and discussions. The Internet is a fantastically unruly and unpredictable place—a fact that holds true for online game spaces. But over the course of using these apps, it became evident from observational reports and the journal entries that participants were relying on Elite and Battlelog both as the primary instruments for evaluating their gameplay *and* as the platforms for devising their collective strategies. Thus, support apps can aid publishers in shaping the kinds of conversations and gameplay activities that are sanctioned and rewarded by a gaming community. Second-screen devices like Elite and Battlelog are potentially powerful tools for publishers because they allow firms to frame, structure, and privilege certain gameplay acts and information over others, which gamers come to value. It would seem that companion apps are virtual mints of gaming capital. It also stands to reason that the stronger the ties between screens and the more popular a support app becomes, the greater its ability to prime its gamers' interests, activities, and purchasing decisions.

Still, support services and companion apps are no techno-panaceas for publishers looking to grow their consumer bases and coffers. It is not surprising that the participants who most appreciated the deep informational resources of Elite and Battlelog had played *Modern Warfare 3* and *Battlefield 3* previously. The group's novice gamers' first impressions of the companion services and apps were less favorable, however. These data-tracking utilities may prove to be of limited value when it comes to courting new players, especially novice gamers, because they do not yet possess the values shared by a community of play. The sophisticated visualization of gameplay data that wowed experienced players, alienated casual gamers. This does not mean that support apps are useless for expanding a gaming community; rather, it is likely instead that the data-rich environment alongside the games' steep learning curves does little to welcome newcomers.

Support apps are attractive for publishers because they offer opportunities for new "long game" revenue streams. Yet there remains the potential for consumer backlash if a firm is perceived as mishandling the monetization of premium content and services. This underscores that gaming knowledge, skill, and know-how are not the same for players as they are for the firms looking to capitalize on gaming capital. Game publishers should tread carefully here. This study's participants were suspicious of the push to monetize future gaming experiences if it meant creating tiered groups of gamers—those who pay for premium content and services, and those who do not. This was especially the case for powerhouse publishers like Activision and EA because of the participants' shared feeling that these companies are doing well financially and need not charge them for all manner of additional content. Instead, the participants recommended that gamers should be given trial access to premium content. Users want to know what they will be missing if they choose to go without. The game's support app—which may or may not link directly to premium content—should remain free, however. As if heeding the advice of the project's participants, Activision announced before the launch of 2012's *Call of Duty: Black Ops 2* that a full version of Elite would be available to all *Call of Duty* players free of charge.[19]

The participants identified areas where Elite and Battlelog could be improved, and recommended that these companion apps should consider adding the following features:

- Access to video replays, and ability to share clips via Facebook or Twitter
- Ability to buy additional content through the second-screen application
- Access to level/map generators and more user-generated content
- Ability to comment on levels, maps, guns, load-outs, etc.
- Real-time communication with community managers through the app
- Ability to report cheating, "trolling," or "griefing" through the app
- Player-to-player alerts notifying friends of future play times

A common theme of these recommendations is their insistence on opening the support systems and companion apps up to more user-generated content. Not only would such a move tacitly and effectively expand the operating definition of what constitutes gaming capital for these game communities by giving users more power in determining the discursive contours of their online support spaces, but it would also introduce unwelcome content management issues for Activision and EA. Elite and Battlelog are not wikis or open-source platforms, after all; rather, they are highly regulated and controlled corporate game spaces. Indeed, the wars waging in the virtual trenches of *Call of Duty* and *Battlefield* are only the most obvious battles taking place in and around these games. The battle over gaming capital is the battle over cultural legitimacy, and this ongoing struggle has far greater repercussions for gamers and media firms than any of the games' virtual firefights.[20] This push and pull is about what counts as meaningful information, who can access it, how it can be used, and who can capitalize on it and to what end.

Connected Screens, Connected Capital

Elite and Battlelog are many things in one. Perhaps more importantly, they serve two masters to different ends. First, these companion apps hold a number of attractions for motivated gamers. These support services are community organizers that promote upcoming events and content. They are customization tools that give users control over their avatars and online identities. They are social hubs that bring players together to compare stats and strategies. And they are visualization tools that give players exacting statistical feedback on their play, and on the gameplay of others. These multiscreen interactions stand ready to amplify the status of gamers within their play communities and increase their knowledge of the things that matter to that community. Support services and their companion applications bolster the gaming capital of players by giving them a better "grip" on the gameplay experience and mastery over the game property.

These companion applications also serve the needs of their second major constituency: their producers. Provided publishers can convince gamers of their practical benefit, support services can become an effective springboard for producers seeking to promote additional fare, be it minor digital add-ons or major franchise sequels, extending the "long game" of their IP and brand. Elite, Battlelog, and similar support platforms are spaces crafted to extract a more traditional form of financial capital from information-hungry gamers. This is their key attraction for publishers.

Despite the research project's focus on games, support utilities need not be limited to the world of gaming. Indeed, content creators of all stripes—whether they work in film, television, comics, or another expressive mass medium—can give their users the opportunity to experience a felt sense of connection to their favorite fictional worlds vis-à-vis multiple screens. Consumers who are motivated enough to seek out support aids do so because they want to be more than knowledgeable consumers. Simply put: they want to master the property irrespective of medium. Support apps succeed when they function as a framework for earning personal achievement over or through the IP.

And herein lies the utility of gaming capital as a practical idea for technology design and as an analytical concept for research. With respect to design, producers should evolve their second-screen apps into better instruments with which consumers can master IP. This means increasing the functional connectivity between primary and secondary screens. Currently, most support apps are little more than informational resources that too often simply re-present information that is already available through the game. However, producers could tether primary and secondary screens together in real time to deliver unique, multiscreen experiences. This is the direction that Nintendo and Microsoft are forging with their Wii U and SmartGlass technologies. If these innovations are an accurate forecast of things to come, future connected screens will not just be data displays—they will be remote controls.

Second, as a research idea, gaming capital reminds us that there is more to the elusive concept than its financial capitalization. There is, of course, no shortage of instrumental value to producing, procuring, and circulating actionable game information (some of which will invariably be monetized by firms). Yet that is not the whole of it either. Because gaming capital functions as a contextual currency, the system reveals information that is of explicit and implicit value to a gaming community. That is, gaming capital reveals a complex sociology of play that cannot be captured by sales numbers alone, and that offers a potentially alternative discourse and value system to the publisher's "official" version of what matters as depicted in its guidebooks, press releases, and across its multiscreen support apps.

Notes

1. In recent years, there has been no video game genre more popular among avid gamers, and more commercially lucrative for producers, than the "military shooter." Take Activision's *Call of Duty* franchise, for example. The publisher's last three installments—*Modern Warfare 3* (2011), *Call of Duty: Black Ops* (2010), and *Modern Warfare 2* (2009)—hold first-day sales records, with each annual release outperforming the previous year's offering ($400, $360, and $310 million, respectively). Or, to put the franchise's cultural and commercial dominance in different terms, having moved over fourteen million units domestically, *Black Ops* is estimated to be in one of every eight US households. Dana Jongewaard, "Call of Duty: Black Ops in 1 of 8 U.S. Households," *IGN*, March 14, 2011, http://uk.wii.ign.com/articles/115/1155422p1.html.
2. Antone Gonsalves, "'Call Of Duty: Black Ops' Shatters Sales Record," *Information Week*, November 11, 2010, http://www.informationweek.com/news/security/app -security/228200776.
3. Jay Yarow and Kamelia Angelova, "Chart of the Day: Video Game Industry Not So Recession Proof After All," *Business Insider*, November 13, 2009, http://www.businessinsider .com/chart-of-the-day-total-video-games-sales-2009-11.
4. Mike Luttrell, "Battlefield Premium Hits 800,000 Subscribers," *TG Daily*, July 2, 2012, http://www.tgdaily.com/games-and-entertainment-brief/64431-battlefield -premium-hits-800000-subscribers; and Fred Dutton, "Call of Duty Elite Has 10 Million Users, 2 Million Pay," Eurogamer.net, May 9, 2012, http://www.eurogamer.net/articles/ 2012-05-09-call-of-duty-elite-has-10-million-users-2-million-pay.
5. Henry Jenkins, *Convergence Culture: Where Old and New Media Collide* (New York: New York University Press, 2006); and Kristen Thompson, *The Frodo Franchise: The Lord of the Rings and Modern Hollywood* (Berkeley: University of California Press, 2007).
6. Lisbeth Klastrup and Susana Tosca, "Transmedial Worlds - Rethinking Cyberworld Design," in *Proceedings: 2004 International Conference on Cyberworlds*, Los Alamitos, CA. (Institute of Electrical and Electronics Engineers, 2004), 409–16.

7. Robert Alan Brookey, *Hollywood Gamers: Digital Convergence in the Film and Video Game Industries* (Bloomington: Indiana University Press, 2010).
8. P. David Marshall, "The New Intertextual Commodity," in *The New Media Book*, ed. Dan Harries (London: British Film Institute, 2002), 69–82.
9. Chris Anderson, *The Long Tail: Why the Future of Business is Selling Less of More* (New York: Hyperion, 2006).
10. James Getomer, Michael Okimoto, and Jennifer Cleaver, "Understanding the Modern Gamer: What Google Search Data Says about Gamer Behavior," Google Whitepaper, http://www.thinkwithgoogle.com/insights/library/studies/understanding-the-modern-gamer/.
11. Mia Consalvo, *Cheating: Gaining Advantage in Videogames* (Cambridge, MA: MIT Press, 2007).
12. Edward Castronova, *Synthetic Worlds: The Business and Culture of Online Games* (Chicago: University of Chicago Press, 2005).
13. Christopher Walsh and Thomas Apperley, "Gaming Capital: Rethinking Literacy," in *Changing Climates: Education for sustainable futures: Proceedings of the AARE 2008 International Education Research Conference.* http://oro.open.ac.uk/20850/.
14. Olli Sotamaa, "Achievement Unlocked: Rethinking Gaming Capital" (paper presented at the Future and Reality of Gaming Conference, Vienna, Austria, 2009).
15. Randy Nichols, "Bourdieu's Forms of Capital and Video Game Production," in *The Game Culture Reader*, eds. Jason C. Thompson and Mark Ouellette (Newcastle upon Tyne: Cambridge Scholars Publishing, forthcoming).
16. Judd Ethan Ruggill and Ken S. McAllister, *Gaming Matters: Art, Science, Magic, and the Computer Game Medium* (Tuscaloosa: University of Alabama Press, 2011); and Frans Mäyrä, *An Introduction to Game Studies* (Thousands Oaks, CA: SAGE, 2008).
17. At the time of the study, Elite offered more functionality than did Battlelog. The participants overwhelmingly preferred this deeper service and—as a consequence— enjoyed playing *Modern Warfare* more than *Battlefield*.
18. Sotamaa, "Achievement Unlocked," 2009.
19. Dean Takahashi, "Call of Duty Elite Goes Free as Activision Charges Only for DLC for Call of Duty: Black Ops II," *Venture Beat*, October 15, 2012, http://venturebeat.com/2012/10/15/call-of-duty-elite-goes-free-as-activision-charges-only-for-dlc-for-call-of-duty-black-ops-ii/.
20. Consalvo, *Cheating*, 2007.

References

Anderson, Chris. *The Long Tail: Why the Future of Business is Selling Less of More.* New York: Hyperion, 2006.
Brookey, Robert Alan. *Hollywood Gamers: Digital Convergence in the Film and Video Game Industries.* Bloomington: Indiana University Press, 2010.
Castronova, Edward. *Synthetic Worlds: The Business and Culture of Online Games.* Chicago: University of Chicago Press, 2005.
Consalvo, Mia. *Cheating: Gaining Advantage in Videogames.* Cambridge, MA: MIT Press, 2007.
Dutton, Fred. "Call of Duty Elite Has 10 Million Users, 2 Million Pay." Eurogamer.net, May 9, 2012. http://www.eurogamer.net/articles/2012-05-09-call-of-duty-elite-has-10-million-users-2-million-pay.
Getomer, James, Michael Okimoto, and Jennifer Cleaver. "Understanding the Modern Gamer: What Google Search Data Says about Gamer Behavior." Google Whitepaper. http://www.thinkwithgoogle.com/insights/library/studies/understanding-the-moderngamer/.

Gonsalves, Antone. "'Call Of Duty: Black Ops' Shatters Sales Record." *Information Week,* November 11, 2010. http://www.informationweek.com/news/security/app-security/228200776.

Jenkins, Henry. *Convergence Culture: Where Old and New Media Collide.* New York: New York University Press, 2006.

Jongewaard, Dana. "Call of Duty: Black Ops in 1 of 8 U.S. Households." *IGN,* March 14, 2011. http://uk.wii.ign.com/articles/115/1155422p1.html.

Klastrup, Lisbeth, and Susana Tosca. "Transmedial Worlds—Rethinking Cyberworld Design." In *Proceedings: 2004 International Conference on Cyberworlds,* 409–16. Los Alamitos, CA. Institute of Electrical and Electronics Engineers, 2004.

Luttrell, Mike. "Battlefield Premium Hits 800,000 Subscribers." *TG Daily,* July 2, 2012. http://www.tgdaily.com/games-and-entertainmentbrief/64431-battlefield-premium-hits-800000-subscribers.

Marshall, P. David. "The New Intertextual Commodity." In *The New Media Book,* edited by Dan Harries, 69–82. London: British Film Institute, 2002.

Mäyrä, Frans. *An Introduction to Game Studies.* Thousand Oaks, CA: SAGE, 2008.

Nichols, Randy. "Bourdieu's Forms of Capital and Video Game Production." In *The Game Culture Reader,* edited by Jason C. Thompson and Mark Ouellette. Newcastle upon Tyne: Cambridge Scholars Publishing, forthcoming.

Ruggill, Judd Ethan, and Ken S. McAllister. *Gaming Matters: Art, Science, Magic, and the Computer Game Medium.* Tuscaloosa: University of Alabama Press, 2011.

Sotamaa, Olli. "Achievement Unlocked: Rethinking Gaming Capital." Paper presented at the Future and Reality of Gaming Conference, Vienna, Austria, 2009.

Takahashi, Dean. "Call of Duty Elite Goes Free as Activision Charges Only for DLC for Call of Duty: Black Ops II." *Venture Beat,* October 15, 2012. http://venturebeat.com/2012/10/15/call-of-duty-elite-goes-free-as-activision-chargesonly-for-dlc-for-call-of-duty-black-ops-ii/.

Thompson, Kristen. *The Frodo Franchise: The Lord of the Rings and Modern Hollywood.* Berkeley: University of California Press, 2007.

Walsh, Christopher, and Thomas Apperley. "Gaming Capital: Rethinking Literacy." In *Changing Climates: Education for sustainable futures: Proceedings of the AARE 2008 International Education Research Conference.* http://oro.open.ac.uk/20850/.

Yarow, Jay, and Kamelia Angelova. "Chart of the Day: Video Game Industry Not So Recession Proof After All." *Business Insider,* November 13, 2009. http://www.businessinsider.com/chart-of-the-day-total-video-games-sales-2009-11.

10

CONNECTED VIEWING ON THE SECOND SCREEN

The Limitations of the Living Room

Ethan Tussey

During the early seasons of *The Office* on NBC, episodes concluded with an invitation to the viewer to visit the official website for the show. This invitation is an example of what John T. Caldwell has called "second shift media aesthetics," a strategy used by television networks to "channel" audiences from one conglomerate-owned platform (broadcast network) to another (the official website).[1] By the final two seasons, fans of *The Office* were being channeled to an additional digital platform, NBC Live, a "second screen" experience designed to "enhance" the viewing of NBC shows. Actor Rainn Wilson, known for playing Dwight Schrute on the program, served as pitchman for a second-screen application that promised to bring social network conversation and insider information to the viewers during first-run broadcasts.[2] The NBC Live app represented the television network's increased expectations of fans of the show by applying the "second shift viewing" strategies associated with the official website to "simultaneous multiscreen viewing" on a mobile device.

One year later, NBC discontinued the NBC Live app and replaced it with a more established app, Zeebox, developed by a British company.[3] The broadcast network's decision to employ multiple apps in such a short time reveals the television executives' interest in creating second-screen content to complement first-run broadcasts. Neil Smit, president and CEO of Comcast Cable and executive vice president of NBC's parent company, Comcast Corporation, explains the strategy when describing how these apps "offer a unique nationwide TV companion experience that will make viewing live TV more engaging, compelling and fun."[4] Smit's description of this connected viewing app as a "TV companion" for "live TV" is a telling label for a potentially disruptive digital technology. NBC Live and Zeebox are second-screen apps designed to make mobile devices support traditional living room viewing practices. Such viewing practices then further serve traditional business models, as apps like Zeebox give networks the ability to target viewers with ads on the second screen to supplement those airing on television.[5]

On the surface, Comcast's promise to engage audiences through digital technology would seem to support claims made by Henry Jenkins and Axel Bruns that online platforms provide audiences with opportunities to participate in and cocreate consumer culture.[6] Jenkins and Bruns believe that the emergence of digital technologies can be mutually beneficial for producers and consumers because it allows producers to learn more about their consumers while also giving consumers the ability to demand and create content that is more useful to their lives. Jenkins describes the digital era as a potential win-win scenario where fans are given more access to and ownership over the media properties they cherish while companies earn devoted audiences and creative collaborators. Adapting the work of Pierre Levy, Jenkins predicts that the Internet will lead to increased collective consumption in which people will contribute their individual expertise to examine and debate popular culture.[7] He believes that the collective action built around popular culture will translate to more serious purposes like political action.[8]

Early in his book *Convergence Culture,* Jenkins describes mobile technology as a "Swiss army knife" that could be pivotal to shaping the future of media consumption because its devices would allow consumers to use participatory culture in their everyday lives.[9] In some ways, Jenkins's prediction has come true, as over half of all cell phone owners use their mobile devices to engage with media properties by sharing their thoughts and opinions with friends.[10] These devices enable collective discussion, a form of audience engagement that television and cultural studies scholars have argued is especially important to a public understanding of social issues.[11] Beyond collective discussion, smartphones, tablets, and laptop computers provide a means of production through their ability to capture audio/video and easily distribute it via Internet connections.[12] These production and distribution capabilities can lead to user-generated content that adds a variety of perspectives to the cultural zeitgeist and shapes understanding of media texts.[13]

Not only do mobile technologies offer a means of production and distribution, but they also allow consumers to access and use popular culture to navigate social and political relationships in public places. For example, a person may use his or her mobile phone to show a YouTube clip to a friend during a shared commute, or he or she might share highlights of the previous evening's football game with a coworker at the watercooler. In both examples, the selection of the content and the place where it is shared have a political calculus and social meaning attached. According to television scholar Anna McCarthy, media technology has long shaped the political and institutional expectations of public spaces through different components of visual culture, including airport television networks (e.g., CNN's Airport Network), waiting room televisions, and point-of-purchase advertisements in shopping centers.[14] Before the widespread adoption of mobile media devices, these authoritative public screens shaped the meaning and use of media culture outside the home by offering societal norms and codes of conduct influenced by the political agendas of those managing the public space.[15] As digital technology has evolved, mobile devices offer a media toolkit for those looking to bring their own visual cultures and political agendas to everyday locations. Michel de Certeau has argued that people have often used media technology in public spaces as a tactic for reclaiming their agency in power relationships with employers, coworkers, and society at large.[16] Barbara Flueckiger explains that people use mobile devices as a tactic to navigate their environment; usage is governed by an "associative mechanism" by which a person encounters something in his or her world and uses his or her phone in response. For example, a person may see someone on a train, notice he or she has a shirt of a favorite musician, and then use his or her phone to play that musician's latest song to indicate a kindred spirit.[17] Mobile devices are an important tool for self-expression and navigating public spaces as they allow consumers to tap into their fandom and express it outside the home.[18] By offering a means of accessing, producing, and distributing culture, mobile devices have the potential for realizing the political action and media engagement that digital proponents have predicted. Yet connected viewing apps created by the major media companies largely limit the audience's ability to use culture to navigate public spaces. Instead, these apps focus the audience on the private space of the living room.

The limitations of these connected viewing apps were examined in a course I created on connected viewing at the University of California, Santa Barbara in 2011. Evidence from seminar discussions and student journals that chronicled students' experiences using connected viewing apps indicated that most applications replicate linear viewing experiences on new devices. The functionality offered on connected viewing apps does not encourage long-term engagement and creativity, the kind one might find in transmedia storytelling or a wiki-based collaboration, the kinds of participatory cultural opportunities that mobile technologies have the potential to facilitate.[19] In my class, we discussed participatory culture and the types of thoughtful meaning-making that have been markers of active audiences, but we found that connected viewing apps do not facilitate this kind of creative engagement. Instead, these apps offer "synchronicity" and "access" as ideal forms of interactive engagement. We felt that because connected viewing apps limit engagement, they are simply the latest example of a "digital enclosure," where emergent audience practices are identified and repackaged in ways that affirm the traditions of the entertainment industry instead of transforming them.[20] This chapter identifies the functionality and the interactive capabilities that define media-conglomerate-owned connected viewing apps and shows that this technology represents *boardroom fantasies*—to borrow a term from Caldwell—in which new technologies are harnessed to serve established practices and ignore the ways this technology might work beyond a living room viewing context.[21]

During the class, students were asked to use connected viewing apps in a variety of different contexts. For the first month of research, the students received a connected viewing allowance (determined by the costs of required technology) to help lower the costs of access. Each week, the class was assigned a particular time to use a certain category of connected viewing apps. The students made journal entries about their experiences and then discussed them as a group in class. I also instructed students to use the Facebook and Twitter functionality on these apps to create posts on their social network feeds while they used these technologies as a way to confirm they were using the apps during the assigned times. During the second month of research, the students were assigned weekly connected viewing usage, but the choice of technology and expenses were left to them. By removing the connected viewing allowance, I hoped to discover if their initial experiences were enough to entice them to purchase the technologies on their own. As a group, we developed a definition of different categories of connected viewing apps to describe the variety of functionality offered. These categories can be described as "companion viewing apps," "franchise apps," "social networking apps," and "'TV Everywhere' apps"; and they offer the following capabilities:

Companion Viewing Apps

Companion viewing apps include pocket BLU, Disney Second Screen, Yahoo's IntoNow, MTV's WatchWith, TBS's Big Bang Theory app, and Zeebox. These apps allow the viewer to sync his or her mobile device with the primary screen and receive information that corresponds with the action on the primary screen. The experience is similar to the VH1 show *Pop Up Video* or the TV series *Mystery Science Theater 3000* as it blends information and entertainment on the second screen, offering two ways of engaging with content, either through the program itself or through the commentary about the program.

Social Networking Apps

Social networking apps attempt to replicate the peer-to-peer conversation on social network sites such as Facebook and Twitter. Apps such as HBO Connect, Showtime Social, USA's Chatter, and Bravo's Tweet Tracker replicate and integrate social networking features but focus the conversation around particular media properties. These apps provide a concentrated social network conversation similar to those of chat rooms and bulletin boards dedicated to particular media franchises or television networks.

Franchise Apps

Franchise apps condense the features of an official website of a television show or film. These apps allow audiences to watch preselected clips, gain access to "catch-up" episodes, play games, and engage in fan contests. Examples of companion apps include the Warner Bros. app editions of *The Dark Knight, Inception,* and the Harry Potter series; USA's Psych Vision app for *Psych;* TNT show apps for

Leverage, Rizzoli and Isles, and *Falling Skies;* Comedy Central's Tosh.0 app; and E!'s The Soup app.

"TV Everywhere" Apps

"TV Everywhere" apps provide audiences with access to full-length content via digital distribution methods like electronic sell-through (iTunes purchases), transactional video-on-demand (Amazon video rentals), subscription video-on-demand (Netflix), or ad-supported content (Crackle). These apps qualify as connected viewing because they provide access to the Internet, use recommendation algorithms based on social network data, and offer an interactive interface for engaging with content. This category of apps boasts the most variety of options as television networks and media conglomerates have embraced "TV Everywhere" apps to distribute content digitally.[22] Each of these apps enables the user to watch television or films on his or her digital devices. Examples of these apps include Hulu Plus, CNN App, PBS's app, NBC App, TNT App, USA's app, TBS's app, Flixster's app, Crackle's app, the ABC Player app, the Showtime Anytime app, the WatchESPN app, and HBO GO's app.

Taming the Mobile Screen

Through these four categories of connected viewing, apps offer users different ways of engaging with media content, all designed to support traditional television watching as opposed to offering a way for consumers to use culture in public spaces. Companion viewing and social networking apps make this distinction most evident by offering content that syncs with the living room screen. Both companion apps and social networking apps operate through "synchronicity," which, according to John R. Carlson and Joey F. George, creates a "sense that all participants are concurrently engaged in the communication event."[23] While emphasizing synchronicity replicates the sense of community and the "public forum" of live television, it also conveniently complements the advertising business model of television. The television business works by selling audiences to advertisers. Yet this business model has been disrupted by time-shifting technologies, DVRs, and on-demand services, which enable consumers to view content on their own schedules and reduce the importance of watching television when it initially airs. Fewer viewers results in lower advertising rates.[24] The promotion of "synchronous" second-screen functionality reestablishes the need to watch content when it is first broadcast. The prevalence of synchronous functionality in connected viewing apps defines digital engagement in terms of live television viewing and helps deliver valuable live audiences to advertisers.

By privileging synchronous functionality, these apps position connected viewing as an act of intense fan labor that requires two screens instead of as a relaxing pastime that offers ways to discover new content and conversations. Synchronous functionality is constantly asking viewers to prove that they are engaged with the television show they are supposed to be watching. In addition to the constant requirement to multitask, my students were frustrated by the clumsy way connected viewing apps integrated their social network profiles into the viewing experience. One student complained that when she tried to use the USA Chatter site to discuss the show *Psych,* the aggregation tool the site used to find relevant social network conversation repeatedly featured comments about psychology that were irrelevant to the discussion of the show. Most students preferred their preexisting social networks like Facebook and Twitter to specialized connected viewing apps because their friends were already on these sites, they did not have to constantly attend to activities, and they had control over their conversations (for example, they could be snarky about the content they were watching and not fear that it would be censored by the filters on the connected viewing app). In an effort to make the interactivity and conversation on connected viewing apps more relevant than that on Facebook and Twitter, these apps construct rigid filters that limit conversation, intimidate viewers, and aggregate irrelevant information.

Filtering social network conversations might be desirable to audiences that want to talk to like-minded fans during a live episode, but the students I worked with were much more likely to use connected viewing apps on reruns or while surfing channels. In fact, my students felt second-screen apps distracted them from their initial viewing of a favorite television show, or spoiled the narrative by revealing plot points before they occurred on the television screen (a particular problem given the time delay between East Coast and West Coast airings of television shows). One student summed up the class attitude toward synchronous engagement by explaining that she enjoyed using television as a starting point for her online exploration but found it annoying that the connected viewing app wanted to automatically alert her friends about her viewing habits for "fear that it may define" her.[25] Connected viewing apps are undergoing changes to address some of these shortcomings, but my students were left with a bad impression and were much happier to have the flexibility that Facebook, Twitter, and text messaging offered them.[26]

Some of the frustrations my students felt with the synchronous functionality of these connected viewing apps are related to media companies' efforts to ensure advertising synergy between primary screens and secondary screens. For example, the makers of the companion app Zeebox signed a deal with Comcast-NBCUniversal and HBO to provide specialized second-screen content for the connected viewing app.[27] The Zeebox app attempts to keep the viewer from changing the channel by offering curated social network conversation and links to official web pages, merchandise, downloads, and online polls. The app is able to deliver the appropriate second-screen content because the second-screen device is linked to the cable box through a networked Wi-Fi connection. While audience members' attention may not be on the primary screen when they are engaged with all these secondary features, they are still engaged with a digital extension of that media property. Syncing the Internet to the cable box is a fitting techno-logical requirement for the app given the way Zeebox asks audiences to use their second screens as a supplementary service for the established television industry. The partnership between the technology company and the media conglomerates means that a person could potentially be accessing the Internet through his or her Comcast Internet service provider, while watching NBC (owned by Comcast) on his or her Comcast cable service and using the Zeebox app with special synchro-nized content provided by Comcast.

By emphasizing synchronicity, these connected viewing apps are difficult to use without the living room television. Synchronous content is designed to foster community, but these apps exclude those who are not in front of a television screen. My students did use these apps when they were outside the home, during breaks from class or work, to review social network conversation from the night before and relive online discussion of their favorite shows. But even this activity was frustrating as these apps privileged the conversations of the show's creators, actors, and promotional arms over user-generated content. For example, the Zee-box app featured an NBC News Twitter feed to accompany the 2012 presidential election coverage. There is no function on the Zeebox app that allows the user to create a specialized Twitter feed. Instead, the app offers predetermined Twitter hashtags (a practice that Twitter recommends to its television partners) in an effort to shape online conversation and organize viewer "buzz" to support traditional measurements of success, such as ratings.[28] If all viewers use the same hashtag to discuss a program, this can raise the profile of the show by making the hashtag a "trending topic" on the social network, alerting people who are not watching to tune in to a particular channel and join the conversation. To join in this conversa-tion, the viewer needs to get inside, find a television, and use his or her mobile device to interact with it. Thus media conglomerates' efforts to link first screens and second screens by predetermining the terms of interactivity (through pro-moted hashtags) limit the mobility of these connected viewing devices.

Watching DVDs on Your Mobile Device

Not all second-screen apps are designed to support linear programming. Fran-chise apps and "TV Everywhere" apps define connected viewing in terms of "access" instead of in terms of "synchronous" multiscreen engagement. Media scholar Chuck Tryon has examined the marketing of these connected viewing apps and uses the term *platform mobility* to describe the type of access these apps provide. Platform mobility refers to the ability to watch content on one device and continue watching content in another location on a different device.[29] This functionality brings the cultural activities of home entertainment from the living room to any location, allowing fans to escape their surroundings by rewatching their favorite content on mobile devices. Key to platform mobility is its emphasis on the individual viewing experience, the ability to use media content to escape public surroundings. According to television scholar Lynn Spigel, the ability to use technology to create a privacy bubble has historically been a key selling point of portable media.[30] Connected viewing apps provide this personalized viewing experience in two ways: by offering the extra features and behind-the-scenes videos typically found on DVDs, and by providing on-demand access to full-length movies and television shows for "lean back" viewing in any location. This push to make "any room your TV room" shifts the connected viewing context from public to private, making "connected viewing" the way one uses media to escape public interactions rather than the way we use media to facilitate discussion. "TV Everywhere" apps were by far the most popular connected viewing apps used by the students in my class because they were easier to work into public places than those that needed to be synchronized to a primary screen. Though these apps were popular, students did not use them in the traditional living-room, "lean back" fashion. For example, some students used connected viewing apps on their commute by starting an episode of a favorite show on Netflix and listening to the soundtrack while they walked to class. Sound was also important for students who used connected viewing apps as background noise for their homework or studying. Others used these apps to share favorite scenes with friends during breaks between their classes.

Nevertheless, these apps made this nontraditional type of engagement difficult by clogging screens, hindering multitasking, and slowing the processing speed of the mobile devices. Unfortunately, media conglomerates have been so fixated on getting their content on mobile screens that they do not seem to consider whether audiences want to watch movies on their mobile devices in the same ways that they watch them in their living rooms. The most vocal supporter for these types of apps is Time Warner CEO Jeff Bewkes, and he has strongly advocated for the widespread adoption of digital policies that provide customers with digital access as an "added value" incentive for purchasing a DVD or cable subscription.[31] The Dark Knight app created by Warner Bros. Digital Distribution is a good example of such efforts to translate strategies from established markets to the connected viewing context. For the same price as a DVD, a person can purchase the "app edition" of the popular Batman film, which includes a digital download of the movie, behind-the-scenes extras, social network integration, interactive video trivia, soundboard, ringtones, art gallery, and audio commentary.

Though my students enjoyed the initial viewing of these franchise apps, they also reported that they would have little interest in using them once the class was over because the extra content loses its allure after its initial access. The problem stems from the fact that the companies that create these apps are attempting to use their experience creating home entertainment products, like DVDs with superior visual and sound qualities, without acknowledging the difference in desires of the living room audience and those of the mobile audience. The desire of media conglomerates to create a digital product that supplements diminishing DVD revenues, without destroying the DVD business, has encouraged digital distribution divisions to replicate familiar consumer experiences instead of providing viewers with content more appropriate for the mobile context. Specifically, students wanted functionality that would give them more ability to use content in a public context that would go beyond simply watching clips or full-length episodes.

Conclusion: Access and Synchronicity vs. Control

During the course of the semester, my class learned that media conglomerates are disciplining disruptive mobile technology by designing connected viewing apps that support traditional ways of watching media content. Our analysis of connected viewing apps occurred early in their evolution, and in the short time since we conducted this research, digital divisions have developed new functionality and created a variety of new mobile viewing options. Despite these developments, the emphasis on interactivity through "synchronicity" and "access" has remained the standard strategy.

The limitations on the connected viewing experience are concerning given the growing prevalence of apps as the preferred way of engaging with the Internet on mobile devices.[32] Apps offer convenient access to web pages and direct navigation to particular online activities. In exchange for these conveniences, apps limit the ways audiences can engage online content. In the case of connected viewing apps, audiences are largely limited to synchronizing their second screens to action on a primary screen or using their second screens to access and watch previously aired television shows or movies. These options are examples of *closed interactivity*, a term Lev Manovich uses to describe digital design that attempts to "externalize the mind's operations" by asking users to "identify with someone else's mental structure."[33] If a user wants to use an app to engage with a media franchise while commuting, the functionality of the app forces the user to think like the app designer who thinks in terms of the living room screen. Whereas Manovich is concerned with the subjectivity that is built into interface design, Jonathan Zittrain has critiqued the economic interests behind the proliferation of apps and online services by claiming that they are transforming the Internet from its open-platform roots toward a more closed system controlled by a few media companies.[34] Using a similar argument, Chris Anderson and Michael Wolff explain that apps make the Internet more business friendly by replacing browser-based navigation, which allows users to find content through search algorithms that treat all websites (more or less) equally, with a system that privileges established brands.[35] In short, apps make the Internet we know easier to use, but they also make the Internet we have yet to discover less likely to appear. This could lead to a future where mobile connected viewing looks no different than living room viewing.

The development of connected viewing apps is the latest effort of media conglomerates to colonize digital platforms to support existing business models. In the past, IP holders have created digital products that emphasize certain interactivity while limiting audiences' ability to use content in a variety of creative endeavors. For example, Alisa Perren has argued that media conglomerates have established digital distribution windows that complement existing physical distribution windows, and thus restrict the potentially limitless availability offered by digital storage and streaming access.[36] These digital contracts replicate television syndication and licensing deals, treating digital platforms as another outlet and revenue stream for watching television instead of as a distinct audience engagement opportunity. Thus the distinction between digital and physical distribution business models is largely superficial. Beyond the replication of business strategies, digital content is distinguished aesthetically through promotional materials; as Max Dawson has observed, it is defined by an "aesthetic of efficiency," short-form clips and webisodes "unbundled" from long-form content, in an effort to promote more lucrative live broadcast television.[37] Like the research done by these two scholars, analysis of connected viewing apps reveals an effort to replicate existing industry practices, which consequently limit the ways digital technology could distinguish itself as a more creative outlet for participatory culture.

The limited functionality of these apps is particularly concerning as media companies begin to treat second-screen activity as market research. Consider, for example, the Nielsen audience research company's plans to create a Twitter TV rating that measures the "reach of TV conversation on Twitter."[38] It is troubling to think that Nielsen's audience measurement shortcomings may soon be translated to digital measurement.[39] The creative exchange between television viewers, outside media conglomerate mediation, is part of what makes social network conversation such a promising example of audience engagement.[40] Much of the value of this experience could be damaged as the definition of connected viewing is tied to the living room screen.

Mark Andrejevic has warned against the interactivity that media corporations offer, as he believes it is a façade of democratic participation designed to reinforce commercial values and conduct market research.[41] This is a consequence of the media conglomerates' efforts to support established business models and build on the experiences learned while programming for other entertainment mediums. In addition, the producers of connected viewing apps would face myriad legal, copyright, and residual issues should they begin creating apps that give the user greater control over content. The few examples of connected viewing apps that offer viewers the ability to control content are built with a variety of safeguards to protect against legal challenges. For example, the IntoNow app by Yahoo offers an image-capturing function called CapIt that allows viewers to take screenshots of the programs they are watching, comment on those screenshots, and send them to their social networks. Similarly, Universal's U-Control offers an interface for selecting favorite scenes from DVDs and saving them to an online file for later viewing. These tools produce content similar to the user-generated Internet memes found on sites like Tumblr, as they enable viewers to add personal expressions and commentary to on-screen content. Yet the functionality of

CapIt and U-Control is only available for a few titles and limits the distribution of the user-generated content to approved platforms. Nevertheless, the technology's expanded functionality deserves notice as it represents an effort to use media content beyond simply watching it.

In a discussion with Warner Bros. executives about the possibilities for customized control in connected viewing apps, one of the members of the marketing staff asked if a media-centric version of Pinterest, an online bookmarking social network, would offer the control my students desired. This is an intriguing proposition as Pinterest allows users to aggregate images, web pages, and links to their favorite content, and offers a way for users to access these collections on their mobile devices, display them to friends, and use them in a variety of contexts. If clips, audio, screen captures, and conversations about media could be collected by users and stored on a social networking platform, this would go a long way to changing the way media conglomerates approach interactivity on connected viewing apps. It would allow a personalized media toolkit for sharing, manipulating, and using media to navigate the public sphere. Enabling this control over content would require a shift in IP protection that more directly reflects Henry Jenkins and Lawrence Lessig's call for IP holders to adopt practices that offer audiences a participatory role in the production and distribution of media content.[42] At the moment, the focus on access and synchronicity in connected viewing functionality supplements established business models and limits the public use and mobile engagement of media content. Until consumers begin demanding, and paying for, the right to control content on their mobile devices, media corporations will continue to promote interactivity that supports established business models and limits the more creative and social uses of creative audiences.

Notes

1. John T. Caldwell, "Second-Shift Media Aesthetics: Programming, Interactivity, and User Flows," in *New Media: Theories and Practices of Digitextuality*, eds. Anna Everett and John T. Caldwell (New York: Routledge, 2003), 132.
2. The link for the NBC Live video now sends users to the Zeebox app. See http://www.nbc.com/nbc-live/.
3. Mike Snider, "Zeebox Looks to Amp Up the Second-Screen TV Experience," *USA Today*, September 27, 2012, http://usatoday30.usatoday.com/tech/story/2012/09/27/hbo-nbc-universal-and-comcast-add-zeebox-tv-app/57846184/1.
4. Zeebox, "Zeebox Makes U.S. Debut with Game-Changing TV Companion Experience; Launches for iPhone, iPad, iPod Touch, Android and the Web," press release, September 27, 2012, http://zeebox.com/press/27-sep-2012-zeebox-us-debut.
5. Zeebox cofounder Anthony Rose explains that the app allows networks to serve advertiser messages on multiple screens and customize those ads for specific audiences. Mike Snider, "Zeebox Looks to Amp Up the Second-Screen TV Experience," *USA Today*, September 27, 2012, http://usatoday30.usatoday.com/tech/story/2012/09/27/hbo-nbc-universal-and-comcast-add-zeebox-tv-app/57846184/1.
6. Henry Jenkins refers to this concept as "participatory culture," while Axel Bruns developed the term *produsage* to describe the blurring of lines between consumption and production. Henry Jenkins, *Convergence Culture: Where Old Media and New Media Col-*

lide (New York: New York University Press, 2006); and Axel Bruns, *Blogs, Wikipedia, Second Life, and Beyond: From Production to Produsage* (New York: Peter Lang, 2008).

7. Jenkins, *Convergence Culture,* 5.
8. Jenkins, *Convergence Culture,* 4.
9. Jenkins, *Convergence Culture,* 5.
10. Pew Research Center, "The Rise of the 'Connected Viewer,'" July 12, 2012, http://www.pewresearch.org/2012/07/12/the-rise-of-the-connected-viewer/.
11. Horace Newcomb and Paul M. Hirsch, in their seminal essay, "Television as a Cultural Forum," use the work of Jurgen Habermas to argue that television provides a common place for people to come together to discuss social issues. Similarly, John Ellis has argued that television culture represents a process of "working through" social problems through the familiar narrative tropes and conventions of storytelling. See Horace Newcomb and Paul M. Hirsch, "Television as a Cultural Forum," *Quarterly Review of Film Studies* (Summer 1983): 45–56; and John Ellis, *Seeing Things: Television in the Age of Uncertainty* (New York: St. Martin's Press, 2002).
12. Gerard Goggin provides a detailed overview of the ways mobile technology has facilitated creative consumption in his book *Global Mobile Media* (New York: Routledge, 2011), 47.
13. For examples of how user-generated content, such as fan fiction and fan-made videos, challenges traditional readings of media franchises and leads to political discussions, please read Henry Jenkins, *Textual Poachers: Television Fans and Participatory Culture* (London: Routledge, 1992); Constance Penley, *NASA/TREK: Popular Science and Sex in America* (London: Verso, 1997); Matthew Hills, *Fan Cultures* (London: Routledge, 2002).
14. Anna McCarthy, *Ambient Television: Visual Culture and Public Space* (Durham: Duke University Press, 2001), 2.
15. McCarthy, *Ambient Television,* 7.
16. I am referring to the way de Certeau's concept of *la perruque* has been used to describe active engagement with consumer culture. *La perruque* originally referred to the practice of factory workers using tools of their employer for their own designs. Michel de Certeau, *The Practice of Everyday Life* (Berkeley: University of California Press, 1984), 25.
17. Barbara Flueckiger, "The iPhone Apps: A Digital Culture of Interactivity," in *Moving Data: The iPhone and the Future of Media,* eds. Pelle Snickars and Patrick Vonderau, 171–83 (New York: Columbia University Press, 2012).
18. Consider these articles as examples of the various ways that people are engaging online video and media content on their second screens outside the home. Nielsen Newswire, "Wasting Time Online, Especially at Work," July 9, 2008, http://www.nielsen.com/us/en/newswire/2008/wasting-time-online-especially-at-work.html; and Gautham Nagesh, "Pew: Minorities More Likely to Use Mobile Web," *The Hill,* July 7, 2010, http://thehill.com/blogs/hillicon-valley/technology/107547-pew-minorities-more-likely-to-use-mobile-web.
19. Jonathan Sterne has made the point that interactivity is only meaningful when an audience has time to reflect on its engagement. In Sterne's estimation, clicking the "Like" button or retweeting is too immediate to be meaningful participation. Read more Jonathan Sterne, "What if Interactivity Is the New Passivity?," FlowTV.org, April 9, 2012, http://flowtv.org/2012/04/the-new-passivity/.
20. Mark Andrejevic introduced the concept of "digital enclosure" as a description for corporate-controlled websites that monitor fan activity and attempt to monetize certain audience activities. Suzanne Scott has explained how this practice has evolved to model preferred fan behavior for a larger audience. For more on this concept, see Mark Andrejevic, *iSpy: Surveillance and Power in the Interactive Era* (Lawrence, KS: University Press of Kansas, 2007); and Suzanne Scott, "Repackaging Fan Culture: The Regifting Economy of Ancillary Content Models," *Transformative Works and Cultures* 3 (2009), http://journal.transformativeworks.org/index.php/twc/article/view/150.

21. Caldwell, "Second-Shift Media Aesthetics," 139.
22. I am making a distinction between the app version and website version of these digital platforms and services.
23. John R. Carlson and Joey F. George, "Media Appropriateness in the Conduct and Discovery of Deceptive Communication: The Relative Influence of Richness and Synchronicity," *Group Decision and Negotiation* 13, no. 2 (2003): 191.
24. Steve McClellan described time-shifting technologies' implications for advertising as early as 2008. Steve Mcclellan, "TV Ads are Less Effective, Survey Says," Adweek .com, February 20, 2008, http://www.adweek.com/news/television/tv-ads-are-less -effective-survey-says-94977.
25. Student Diary No. 1, Connected Viewing Diary, March 4, 2012.
26. The third version of Yahoo's IntoNow app is an example of the ways that second-screen apps are evolving. While the app still privileges simultaneous engagement, it also offers the ability to grab screen captures of the content the user is watching, which allows conversation to continue on Facebook and Twitter long after a show's initial airing has ended. According to the designer of the app, Adam Cahan, these new features are "born out of the [audience] behaviors we're seeing." The development of functionality that enables audiences to use culture as opposed to simply viewing culture is a positive sign. Daniel Frankel, "Yahoo Unveils Version 3.0 of Its IntoNow Social TV App," paidContent.org, July 30, 2012, http://paidcontent.org/2012/07/30/yahoo-unveils -version-3-0-of-its-intonow-social-tv-app/.
27. Chris Tribbey, "Second-Screen App Gets Comcast, NBC Universal Backing," *Home Media Magazine,* September 27, 2012, http://www.homemediamagazine.com/ universal/second-screen-app-gets-comcast-nbc-universal-backing-28435.
28. For evidence of how Twitter influences television ratings, see "Twitter on TV: A Producer's Guide" on the Twitter website (https://dev.twitter.com/media/twitter-tv), and read the Media Industries Project's interview with Betsy Scolnik, a social media consultant for a variety of media organizations, including Wolf Films and *National Geographic*. Betsy Scolnik, Media Industries Project interviews, November 10, 2011, http://www.carseywolf.ucsb.edu/mip/article/betsy-scolnik.
29. Chuck Tryon, "'Make Any Room Your TV room': Digital Delivery and Media Mobility," *Screen* 53, no. 3 (Autumn 2012): 288.
30. Lynn Spigel, "Portable TV: Studies in Domestic Space Travel," in *Welcome to the Dreamhouse: Popular Media and Postwar Suburbs,* 31–59 (Durham: Duke University Press, 2001).
31. Matthew Lasar, "Is Comcast and Time Warner's 'TV Everywhere' TV for Everyone?," *Ars Technica,* June 24, 2009, http://arstechnica.com/tech-policy/2009/06/is-comcast -and-timewarners-tv-everywhere-tv-for-everyone/.
32. Charles Newark-French, "Mobile Apps Put the Web in Their Rear-view Mirror," Flurry Blog (blog), June 20, 2011, http://blog.flurry.com/bid/63907/Mobile-Apps -Put-the-Web-in-Their-Rear-view-Mirror.
33. Lev Manovich, *The Language of New Media* (Cambridge, MA: MIT Press, 2001), 61.
34. Jonathan Zittrain, *The Future of the Internet—and How to Stop It* (New Haven, CT: Yale University Press, 2008), 104–7.
35. Chris Anderson and Michal Wolff, "The Web Is Dead. Long Live the Internet," *Wired,* August 17, 2010, http://www.wired.com/magazine/2010/08/ff_webrip/all/1.
36. Alisa Perren, "Business as Unusual: Conglomerate-Sized Challenges for Film and Television in the Digital Arena," *Journal of Popular Film and Television* 38, no. 2 (2010): 72–8.
37. Max Dawson, "Television's Aesthetic of Efficiency: Convergence Television and the Digital Short," in *Television as Digital Media,* eds. James Bennett and Niki Strange, 204–29 (Durham: Duke University Press, 2010).
38. Nielsen Press Room, "Nielsen and Twitter Establish Social TV Rating," press release, December 17, 2012, http://www.nielsen.com/us/en/insights/press-room/2012/ nielsen-and-twitter-establish-social-tv-rating.html.
39. For a detailed explanation of the inequalities of the television ratings system, see Eileen Meehan, "Why We Don't Count: The Commodity Audience," in *Logics of Television:*

Essays in Cultural Criticism, ed. Patricia Mellencamp, 117–34 (Bloomington: Indiana University Press, 1990).

40. For an example of this creative consumption, consider the act of "hate watching" as it has been discussed by two panels of Flow participants at the Flow Conference 2012, http://flowtv.org/conference/schedule/.

41. Mark Andrejevic, *iSpy: Surveillance and Power in the Interactive Era* (Lawrence, KS: University Press of Kansas, 2007).

42. Lawrence Lessig, "Lucasfilm's Phantom Menace," *Washington Post,* July 12, 2007, http://www.washingtonpost.com/wp-dyn/content/article/2007/07/11/AR2007071101996.html.

References

Anderson, Chris, and Michal Wolff. "The Web Is Dead. Long Live the Internet." *Wired,* August 17, 2010. http://www.wired.com/magazine/2010/08/ff_webrip/all/1.

Andrejevic, Mark. *iSpy: Surveillance and Power in the Interactive Era.* Lawrence, KS: University Press of Kansas, 2007.

Bruns, Axel. *Blogs, Wikipedia, Second Life, and Beyond: From Production to Produsage.* New York: Peter Lang, 2008.

Caldwell, John T. "Second-Shift Media Aesthetics: Programming, Interactivity, and User Flows." In *New Media: Theories and Practices of Digitextuality,* edited by Anna Everett and John T. Caldwell, 127–44. New York: Routledge, 2003.

Carlson, John R., and Joey F. George. "Media Appropriateness in the Conduct and Discovery of Deceptive Communication: The Relative Influence of Richness and Synchronicity." *Group Decision and Negotiation* 13, no. 2 (2003): 191–210

Dawson, Max. "Television's Aesthetic of Efficiency: Convergence Television and the Digital Short." In *Television as Digital Media,* edited by James Bennett and Niki Strange, 204–29. Durham: Duke University Press, 2010.

deCerteau, Michel. *The Practice of Everyday Life.* Berkeley: University of California Press, 1984.

Ellis, John. *Seeing Things: Television in the Age of Uncertainty.* New York: St. Martin's Press, 2002.

Flueckiger, Barbara. "The iPhone Apps: A Digital Culture of Interactivity." In *Moving Data: The iPhone and the Future of Media,* edited by Pelle Snickars and Patrick Vonderau, 171–83. New York: Columbia University Press, 2012.

Frankel, Daniel. "Yahoo Unveils Version 3.0 of Its IntoNow Social TV App." paidContent.org, July 30, 2012. http://paidcontent.org/2012/07/30/yahoo-unveils-version-3-0-of-its-intonow-social-tv-app/.

Goggin, Gerard. *Global Mobile Media.* New York: Routledge, 2011.

Hills, Matthew. *Fan Cultures.* London: Routledge, 2002.

Jenkins, Henry. *Convergence Culture: Where Old Media and New Media Collide.* New York: New York University Press, 2006.

Jenkins, Henry. *Textual Poachers: Television Fans and Participatory Culture.* London: Routledge, 1992.

Lasar, Matthew. "Is Comcast and Time Warner's 'TV Everywhere' TV for Everyone?" *Ars Technica,* June 24, 2009. http://arstechnica.com/tech-policy/2009/06/is-comcast-and-timewarners-tv-everywhere-tv-for-everyone/.

Lessig, Lawrence. "Lucasfilm's Phantom Menace." *Washington Post,* July 12, 2007. http://www.washingtonpost.com/wp-dyn/content/article/2007/07/11/AR2007071101996.html.

Manovich, Lev. *The Language of New Media.* Cambridge, MA: MIT Press, 2001.

McCarthy, Anna. *Ambient Television: Visual Culture and Public Space*. Durham: Duke University Press, 2001.

Mcclellan, Steve. "TV Ads are Less Effective, Survey Says." Adweek.com, February 20, 2008. http://www.adweek.com/news/television/tv-ads-are-less-effective-survey-says-94977.

Meehan, Eileen. "Why We Don't Count: The Commodity Audience." In *Logics of Television: Essays in Cultural Criticism,* edited by Patricia Mellencamp, 117–34. Bloomington: Indiana University Press, 1990.

Nagesh, Gautham. "Pew: Minorities More Likely to Use Mobile Web." The Hill, July 7, 2010. http://thehill.com/blogs/hillicon-valley/technology/107547-pew-minorities-more-likely-to-use-mobile-web.

Newark-French, Charles. "Mobile Apps Put the Web in Their Rear-view Mirror." Flurry Blog (blog), June 20, 2011. http://blog.flurry.com/bid/63907/Mobile-Apps-Put-the-Web-in-Their-Rear-view-Mirror.

Newcomb, Horace, and Paul M. Hirsch. "Television as a Cultural Forum." *Quarterly Review of Film Studies* (Summer 1983): 45–56.

Nielsen Newswire. "Wasting Time Online, Especially at Work." July 9, 2008. http://www.nielsen.com/us/en/newswire/2008/wasting-time-online-especially-at-work.html.

Nielsen Press Room. "Nielsen and Twitter Establish Social TV Rating." Press release, December 17, 2012. http://www.nielsen.com/us/en/insights/press-room/2012/nielsen-and-twitter-establish-social-tv-rating.html.

Penley, Constance. *NASA/TREK: Popular Science and Sex in America.* London: Verso, 1997.

Perren, Alisa. "Business as Unusual: Conglomerate-Sized Challenges for Film and Television in the Digital Arena." *Journal of Popular Film and Television* 38, no. 2 (2010): 72–8.

Pew Research Center. "The Rise of the 'Connected Viewer.'" July 12, 2012. http://www.pewresearch.org/2012/07/12/the-rise-of-the-connected-viewer/.

Scolnik, Betsy. Media Industries Project interviews. November 10, 2011. http://www.carseywolf.ucsb.edu/mip/article/betsy-scolnik.

Scott, Suzanne. "Repackaging Fan Culture: The Regifting Economy of Ancillary Content Models." *Transformative Works and Cultures* 3 (2009). http://journal.transformativeworks.org/index.php/twc/article/view/150.

Snider, Mike. "Zeebox Looks to Amp Up the Second-Screen TV Experience." *USA Today,* September 27, 2012. http://usatoday30.usatoday.com/tech/story/2012/09/27/hbo-nbc-universal-and-comcast-add-zeebox-tv-app/57846184/1.

Spigel, Lynn. "Portable TV: Studies in Domestic Space Travel." In *Welcome to the Dreamhouse: Popular Media and Postwar Suburbs,* 31–59. Durham: Duke University Press, 2001.

Sterne, Jonathan. "What if Interactivity Is the New Passivity?" FlowTV.org, April 9, 2012. http://flowtv.org/2012/04/the-new-passivity/.

Tribbey, Chris. "Second-Screen App Gets Comcast, NBC Universal Backing." *Home Media Magazine,* September 27, 2012. http://www.homemediamagazine.com/universal/second-screen-app-gets-comcast-nbc-universal-backing-28435.

Tryon, Chuck. "'Make Any Room Your TV Room': Digital Delivery and Media Mobility." *Screen* 53, no. 3 (Autumn 2012): 287–300.

Zeebox. "Zeebox Makes U.S. Debut with Game-Changing TV Companion Experience; Launches for iPhone, iPad, iPod Touch, Android and the Web." Press release, September 27, 2012. http://zeebox.com/press/27-sep-2012-zeebox-us-debut.

Zittrain, Jonathan. *The Future of the Internet—and How to Stop It.* New Haven, CT: Yale University Press, 2008.

11

STREAMING U

College Students and Connected Viewing

Chuck Tryon and Max Dawson

Since the 1990s, demographers, marketers, politicians, pundits, educators, and journalists have proposed a number of names for the generation of Americans born between 1980 and 2000. Some, including "The Millennials," "Generation Y," and "Generation Next," locate this generation in time, positioning it as the latest in a succession of generations that includes Generation X, the baby boomers, and the Silent Generation. Others, including "Digital Natives," "The Net Generation," "Generation N," or the "Digital Generation," define it in terms of the technologies its members use. Such analyses frequently explain the peculiar identities, values, and lifestyles of this generation's members as consequences of their lifelong engagements with digital media, and the Internet in particular.[1] Don Tapscott, the founder of the consulting firm nGenera Insight and the author of a number of books on youth and technology, calls this generation "N-Geners," and suggests that its members have internalized the interactive, participatory culture of the Internet.[2] Similar contentions are found in books, newspaper and magazine articles, and research white papers on this generation. For example, a 2005 study by Forrester Research proposes that American youth "have an innate ability to use technology, are comfortable multitasking while using a diverse range of digital media, and literally demand interactivity as they construct knowledge."[3]

The idea that those Americans born between 1980 and 2000 constitute a "Digital Generation" has attracted a significant amount of attention in the press and strong support from within the business community. However, scholars in a variety of fields, including Henry Jenkins, David Buckingham, and Siva Vaidhyanathan, have criticized this hypothesis on the grounds that it is predicated on technological determinism and essentialism.[4] As these authors have argued, the Digital Generation hypothesis overstates the influence that digital technologies have exerted over the identities, values, and lifestyles of members of this age cohort—so much so, in fact, that it cannot account for the influences of other political, sociological, economic, and cultural factors, such as the war on terrorism or the prolonged series of economic crises experienced by global financial markets since 2000.[5] Furthermore, it is predicated on a baseless assumption: that members of this generation share similar experiences with and attitudes toward digital technologies. Observes Siva Vaidhyanathan, "Talk of a 'digital generation' or people who are 'born digital' willfully ignores the vast range of skills, knowledge, and experience of many segments of society. It ignores the needs and perspectives of those young people who are not socially or financially privileged."[6] Not all millennials were "born digital." In fact, many members of this generation still find themselves with limited access to some digital and mobile technologies. The Digital Generation hypothesis obscures the unavoidable fact that gender, class status, region, ethnic backgrounds, linguistic competency, and educational background all exert strong influences on how young people interact with digital media.[7] A more precise approach, we argue, would take into consideration the various locations where students consume media and the resources available to them when they watch movies and television series. This approach does not strictly follow the logic of a "digital divide," in which some students have access to digital tools while others lack them. Instead, we found that students across our campuses consume media differently depending on where they happen to be watching, a conclusion that might lead us to pay more attention to *site specificity* when seeking to define the practices of connected viewing. Thus, instead of relying on facile binaries between digital natives and digital immigrants or between two sides of a digital divide, we argue that students participate in viewing cultures that develop as a result of a wide range of social and technological factors.

These critiques of the Digital Generation hypothesis challenge prevailing constructions of this age cohort by complicating essentialist assumptions about how American youth interact with new digital media. Our research was motivated by a desire to subject assumptions about how millennials interact with the "old" media of television and cinema to scrutiny. Some proponents of the Digital Generation hypothesis have argued that young people's lifelong engagements with digital technologies have decisively shaped their attitudes toward and use of film and television. These observers identify members of this generation as early adopters of new video platforms, but also as early rejectors of existing video platforms and practices, such as cutting the cord on cable television subscriptions. For example, Tapscott argues that N-Geners harbor distaste for the "passivity" of broadcast media. Not only do young people dislike television, Tapscott contends, but they also have difficulty relating to Americans who were reared on (and by) television. "Because the Net is the antithesis of TV," Tapscott writes, "the N-Generation is in many ways the antithesis of the TV generation."[8] Media industry analysts have observed that young people have already rejected "the old-fashioned way" of watching television—that is, watching programs "live" during their scheduled timeslots while "lounging on a couch, remote control in hand, surfing through the channels."[9] Similarly, some film critics have suggested that the "Digital Generation" has rejected traditional ways of experiencing cinema. Neal Gabler argues that young moviegoers with short attention spans interact with film primarily through the framework provided by social media. As a result, their tastes in film tend to be biased in favor of the new, blockbuster releases that are the subjects of discussions among their peers on Facebook and Twitter.[10]

Our study interrogated these essentialist assumptions about the film- and television-viewing habits of young people by examining video consumption on the campuses of two American universities: Northwestern University (NU), a highly selective private university in the Midwest with 8,443 students; and at Fayetteville State University (FSU), a historically black university in the South with an enrollment of 6,285. Research was conducted over three stages spanning a period of five months. The first stage involved focus groups of eight to twelve students at each university. These sessions produced insights into how students watch films and television shows. Stage two consisted of an online multiple choice survey with questions covering topics including television set ownership rates, cable and satellite penetration, and Netflix use. In all, 134 FSU students and 125 NU students replied to the survey. The third and final stage involved one-on-one follow-up interviews with twelve to fourteen students at each university. During these interviews, we asked students questions about how they find, watch, and share content. We also invited them to demonstrate these processes to us. Interviews were conducted in facilities equipped with a variety of networked devices, including an Apple iPad, a Roku "smart TV" device, a PlayStation 3 video game console, and a laptop computer. Participants also had access to video-on-demand services (including Netflix, Hulu Plus, and HBO Go), the cloud-based digital video locker system UltraViolet, and electronic sell-through stores (including Amazon and Apple iTunes). These media performances allowed us to observe how young people access video content, albeit in the artificial environment of the laboratory.

The results yielded by this two-site study contradict essentialist assumptions about the media habits of members of the so-called "Digital Generation," highlighting the diverse practices that college students engage in as they watch films and television programs. Students' preferred methods for finding, watching, and sharing video content, not to mention their motivations for renting or purchasing content, vary widely between the two campuses. Perhaps the most dramatic differences pertain to how students access content. For example, FSU students are far more likely to own television sets than NU students and far less likely to engage in appointment television viewing. By contrast, while many NU students emphasized the importance of staying current with buzz-worthy new television programs, very few watch these programs "live"—that is, when they air. The study also revealed the existence of significant variations *within* each of the student populations we surveyed. On each of the two campuses, students' viewing habits appear to change based on the resources available to them in the residences they inhabit. Habits thus change dramatically as students move, for instance, from freshman dormitories to on-campus apartments or from one off-campus rental to another. These changing behaviors illustrate that generational explanations alone cannot account for contemporary viewing practices. As Barbara Klinger argues in her research on the movie-viewing habits of college students, "reception is deeply affected by a host of variables, including the gender, race, and class of viewers, the sphere—national or local—in which viewing takes place, and the social structures that surround the interactions between people and media texts."[11] More specifically, we found that students' viewing habits are strongly shaped by the material and social conditions that exist within the dormitories, apartments, and shared houses that they occupy. *What* students watch and *how* students watch are very much factors of *where* students watch.

The findings of our study of connected viewing on these two campuses resonate with concepts advanced by prior scholarship on the site specificity of screen media technologies, forms, and consumption practices. Exemplary of this scholarship is Anna McCarthy's work on the placement of television sets in nondomestic environments, which highlights the heterogeneity of television's identities and uses outside the home.[12] The concept of "site specificity," McCarthy writes, "is useful even when, or especially when, it is taken out of its art context and applied to the discourses and practices of television's installation in everyday places, because it captures some of the flexibility and adaptability of the medium and its microlevel uses."[13] McCarthy's recognition of the flexibility and adaptability of television complements an extensive body of literature on the site specificity of domestic television. For example, Lynn Spigel's work on television's initial diffusion in the United States underscores the degree to which postwar television structured and was structured by the physical and social spaces of the homes (and even the rooms) into which it was installed during the 1940s and 1950s.[14] The ethnographic studies conducted by British cultural studies scholars such as David Morley, Charlotte Brunsdon, Shaun Moores, and Ann Gray similarly suggest that our experiences with screen media are shaped by family and household relations, which are themselves organized by the spaces of domesticity.[15]

The concept of television's site specificity offers a means of complicating the essentializing claims of the Digital Generation hypothesis. Instead of asserting that young people consume screen media in a uniform fashion determined primarily or even solely by their identity as "digital natives," this concept alerts us to the myriad ways in which hyperlocal social and spatial contexts influence viewers' encounters with screen media. As McCarthy argues, television may mean different things and fulfill different functions depending on whether we encounter it in our homes, in the waiting room of a hospital, or the food court of a shopping mall. Drawing on McCarthy's thesis, we propose that the "television" a college student watches at her parents' home during her summer vacation may differ quite dramatically from the "television" she watches on her laptop in her dorm room or on the large flat-screen set in the lounge in the student center. The same may be said of college students' consumption of films or any other screen texts. If the media consumption habits of American college students display distinct patterns or commonalities, we suggest that it is because they consume media in similar environments and under similar circumstances, and not because of their membership in a "Digital Generation."

The concept of the site specificity of screen media adds nuance to scholars' and industry professionals' understandings of connected viewing. The promoters and proponents of connected viewing technologies have actively encouraged consumers to regard their products as a means of liberating themselves from the spatial and temporal confinement enforced by media such as broadcasting and cinema. For instance, Apple, the digital video recorder manufacturer TiVo, and major US wireless carriers including Verizon and AT&T have embraced both a rhetoric and an aesthetic of mobility to differentiate connected viewing technologies from existing screen media.[16] Certainly, connected viewing technologies problematize conventional understandings of the relationships between screen media and place, the majority of which are informed by the specific material conditions and institutional politics of television's broadcast era and the "golden" age of cinema spectatorship. However, our study of the media habits of college-aged students suggests that the connectivity engendered by new technologies does not supersede the site specificity of screen media. Quite the contrary, connected viewing may in fact help give rise to unique viewing cultures localized around specific campuses, dorms, or student apartment complexes. For this reason, our essay places emphasis on the mundane connected viewing practices of our students, using details and anecdotes to challenge and complicate assertions about a homogeneous "Digital Generation" and the placelessness of connected viewing.

America's fourteen million full-time college students make up only a small portion of the eighty million Americans who were born between 1980 and 2000. From a demographic standpoint, they are not representative of this generation as a whole, and the students included in our study offer only a limited sample of the overall college population. Furthermore, their status as college students affords many of them high levels of access to technologies and the technological know-how of their teachers and classmates. With this in mind, we have avoided making sweeping generalizations based on our findings. While the members of our sample all belong to the so-called "Digital Generation," their engagements with film and television are every bit as diverse as they are.

Local Practices, Local Tastes

Our research yielded a number of distinctions between the habits and attitudes of the student populations who comprised our two samples. Device ownership varies dramatically between student groups at NU and FSU. While only 36.9 percent of NU respondents own television sets, all respondents own laptop or desktop computers. By comparison, 87.9 percent of the FSU students surveyed own television sets, and 79.5 percent computers. This distinction might initially invite us to conclude that NU students are more likely to be early adopters of new media technologies. However, in actuality, more FSU students surveyed reported using mobile technologies such as digital video recorders, tablet computers, mobile phones, and video game consoles to watch films or television programs than their counterparts at NU, while students at NU more frequently use laptop or desktop computers, or engage in collective viewing practices around a shared screen. Device ownership might also be shaped by the fact that FSU students are far more likely to commute to campus, while NU students can pool resources in their shared dorm rooms and suites. Therefore, while a number of factors influence device ownership and usage, one important consideration is where students live. The different types of residences on a particular campus may be homes to distinctive *viewing cultures*—small, informal groups with their own device biases and customary modes of consumption. For example, basic cable television services are available to students who live in FSU dormitories, with the costs included in dorm fees, while students living in on-campus apartments have access to satellite television, also subsidized by student fees. Dorm and apartment residents may also take advantage of FSU's broadband network to stream or download content over the Internet. However, not all FSU students live on campus, or even in the campus's immediate vicinity. A significant portion of the FSU student body commutes to campus from homes that they share with parents, spouses, or children, where many of them may rely on family cable television, Internet, and cell phone services.

Depending on where they live, FSU students may have access to quite different programming services, channel lineups, and viewing devices. For instance, students living off campus are much more likely to use mobile devices to watch movies and television shows than their dorm-dwelling counterparts. In fact, the viewing of video content on mobile devices among FSU commuter students, as compared to those living in dorms, may be a response to the specific conditions that exist in the mixed households that these students occupy. Students who live with their parents, for example, may opt to watch on mobile devices when the alternative is watching programs selected by their parents on their families' communal living room sets, while young parents may yield the household's main television set to their children. No one single factor alone dictates the platforms on which college students watch video content. Rather, these decisions are made on a case-by-case basis, and are influenced by a number of factors, including the environment in which the viewing will take place.

FSU students in our research pool enjoy far greater access to television sets and cable or satellite television subscriptions than NU students in the study. As a result, the majority of FSU students surveyed watch television on television sets. Compared to our NU sample, they are less likely to use subscription video-on-demand (SVOD) services, such as Netflix and Hulu Plus, or websites to catch up on recent programs. However, the FSU students are far more likely to watch television "live"—that is, when programs initially air. Of the FSU respondents, 69.5 percent watch television "live," compared to only 30.3 percent of the NU students, who are far more likely to engage in appointment viewing. This distinction is even more pronounced for students living in FSU's dorms, where 84.4 percent of students reported that they typically watch television as it is being broadcast. More than 75 percent of the NU sample reported that the majority of their viewing takes place *after* programs initially air on television. Again, the conditions existing within student residences appear to be a major factor driving this tendency. Cable and satellite television services are not available in NU dormitories. Instead, students have the option of using an Internet protocol television service known as NUTV. The NU students who participated in focus groups and one-on-one interviews were extremely vocal about their dissatisfaction with NUTV, suggesting that its poor picture quality and confusing interface drive them online in search of alternative sources of television programming. Thus, many students turn to SVOD services such as Netflix, which 44.6 percent of NU students reported using as their go-to source for television and film content. Students also compensate for the inadequacies of NUTV by pooling resources. For example, one dormitory keeps a master list of all the television and film DVDs owned by its residents for the purpose of facilitating the sharing of content. Within that dormitory, the inhabitants of a suite of four double rooms opt to spend a portion of a discretionary fund set aside for social activities on a shared Netflix account. In this dormitory and others on the NU campus, the rooms of students who own their own television sets often become hubs for communal social activities. A student who owns a set might host a student who has access to an HBO GO account for a group screening of one of the premium cable network's original dramas. As this summary suggests, an unsatisfactory video delivery system like NUTV may have the unintended side effect of fostering account sharing and communal viewing among college students. Another unintended side effect of the poor quality of the television service available to NU students is that many dorm dwellers patronize peer-to-peer file-sharing networks and streaming video websites that make content available without the consent of copyright holders. While our survey did not include a question about peer-to-peer sharing and streaming, 22.3 percent of the NU students polled used a write-in option to indicate that they have used websites such as Megavideo.com and LetMeWatchThis.com to access content in violation of copyright. Cost—or, more precisely, students' desires to avoid paying for content—certainly motivates students to seek out content from these and other peer-to-peer sites. However, in this particular case, the absence of viable legal alternatives may also be a factor. By denying dormitory dwellers access to cable or satellite television services in their rooms, the NU administration has inadvertently fostered an on-campus viewing culture that is biased toward SVOD services, peer-to-peer networks, and streaming. These complaints illustrate that piracy, despite efforts to attribute it to a "pricing problem," cannot be blamed on the cost of media alone.[17]

Film and Television as "Social Media"

At NU and FSU, we observed the existence of viewing cultures oriented around both individual and collective forms of media consumption. Students at NU often emphasized the social nature of their media use. FSU students, by contrast, are more likely to watch alone or to use media as a form of cocooning. One factor that may influence FSU students' solitary viewing habits is that 71 percent of FSU undergraduates are commuter students and live off campus (by comparison, only 41 percent of NU undergraduate students live off campus, and the vast majority of these students live within walking distance of the NU campus).[18] Commuter students at FSU, and in particular those who live with their parents, spoke to us about using media to carve out private times and spaces within their families' homes. One student described watching Hulu on her laptop as a way of finding a modicum of privacy, stating, "It's, like, my own space. . . . I don't get along with my family, and we don't have [shared] favorites." While this respondent's parents prefer sports and "old cop stories," she tends to favor content that she finds "scary" or "fun." Similarly, another student discussed his habit of spending several hours a day alone watching Netflix. This student estimated that he often spends two to three hours a day watching Netflix in the campus student center and another two hours at home, using this practice as an "escape" from his daily life. However, even students who live in the dorms at FSU often described solitary viewing experiences, with several students explicitly emphasizing tastes in movies and television shows that they believe go against campus taste cultures in order to distinguish themselves from their classmates.

By comparison, NU students regularly watch together. Multiple interview subjects reported that they attend weekly get-togethers for their favorite programs—for example, *Parks and Recreation* (NBC), *Game of Thrones* (HBO), and *Breaking Bad* (AMC). These gatherings typically occur on the same days on which these series air, a few hours after their initial airings. Thus, for instance, one NU student, a resident of an off-campus apartment, hosts roommates and friends for weekly screenings of the most recent episode of *Game of Thrones* on Sunday nights. Because many of this gathering's regular attendees are unavailable to watch the show when it airs at 8 p.m. Central Standard Time, the group uses a shared HBO GO account to watch later in the evening. The NU students placed great emphasis on the importance of keeping up with current shows, even if it means getting the latest episodes from peer-to-peer websites. As one student explained, "I don't want to go hang out with my friends the next day having not seen the latest episode because I was otherwise preoccupied." In this sense, NU students use peer-to-peer services to follow their favorite shows, but also to secure their positions within social groups defined in large part by their members' shared cultural competencies. In fact, interviews with NU students suggested that these social imperatives—and not the allure of free content—are what drive many of them to patronize peer-to-peer services. Thus, even when technological resources may be similar, students at our universities tend to follow social norms that might be shaped by unique aspects of their campus cultures.

"I Don't Want to Pay a Whole Bunch of Money for Something I Don't Use Too Much"

During interviews and focus groups, students at both universities stressed that cost is a determining factor in the decisions they make about what and how they watch. That said, we contend that many of our respondents grossly underestimate their monthly entertainment expenditures. As noted above, many students at both universities openly acknowledged their use of peer-to-peer streaming and download sites to access content for free. Another source of "free" (albeit advertiser-supported) content is YouTube: a number of FSU students indicated that they use the site to watch movies and television shows that have been broken up into short segments and uploaded by other viewers, an option that many FSU students prefer to peer-to-peer downloads because of software on campus that blocks access to sites that contain unauthorized content, such as The Pirate Bay. Students also get "free" content from one another. In addition to the long-standing practice of sharing DVDs from their personal collections, some share their account log-in information for subscription services such as Netflix, HBO GO, and Hulu Plus. This practice is far more common at NU, perhaps on account of the fact that NU dormitory dwellers lack access to cable or satellite services in their rooms.

However, these practices don't stop when students leave the communal space of the dorm. In fact, we found that students who live off campus share video subscriptions with friends and family members. A majority of the NU students interviewed use SVOD accounts registered to their parents. A 20-year-old male NU student acknowledged that both his HBO GO and Netflix accounts are actually registered in his older brother's name:

> I don't know how many devices they let you run it on, but my brother in Indianapolis is using the same HBO account and unless we're watching it at the same time, which so far has never even happened, we're both golden.

Another NU student bluntly acknowledged, "I think I've given my [Netflix] account to, like, five other people." Similarly, an FSU student bragged about sharing his monthly subscription, suggesting that he was going to "use the hell out of it" by sharing the password with trusted friends and family members. To some extent, account sharing is an extension of the campus tradition of students lending their DVDs, CDs, or VHS tapes to friends. Like these older practices, account sharing serves as part of the bonding experience that takes place on college campuses as students develop new friendships and adjust to new circumstances, including changing entertainment budgets. It is a way of sharing resources and, to some extent, sharing expressions of personal taste. If five years ago an NU student would have lent a friend a DVD of her favorite HBO series, today that student might give her friend her parents' HBO GO password.

The practice of account sharing is only one of a number of factors that allow college students to ignore the real financial costs of their media consumption habits. As noted above, the cost of video and Internet services is typically included in students' dormitory fees. Many of the FSU students interviewed do not see themselves as paying for cable television or Internet access. Instead, they regard these services as essentially free. Similarly, NU students who use their parents' Netflix or HBO GO accounts described these SVOD subscription services as sources of "free" content. The majority of students on both campuses estimated their monthly entertainment budgets to be $25 or less (see Table 11.1). If the hidden costs of cable, Internet, and SVOD services were factored into these budgets, they would undoubtedly surpass $25.

Interviews and focus groups on the two campuses revealed that many college students regard content as "free" when they do not pay for it, even if someone else they know does. One 19-year-old female NU student concisely articulated this attitude:

> I'd say, I think, that my budget is probably $0. I use my cousin's Netflix, so I don't pay for it. And I watch streaming or HBO GO, things like that are free—a friend's HBO GO so . . . I don't pay for it.

Students are insulated from having to come to terms with the real costs of the content they consume by the unique conditions of campus life, where bandwidth is copious (and subsidized by dormitory fees), parents pay cell phone bills, DVDs change hands freely, and information about the newest peer-to-peer sites is widely available. SVOD services such as Netflix and HBO GO may also bear some responsibility for distorting college students' conceptions of the value of content. Many college students have some knowledge about the business side of the entertainment industry. They can, for example, rattle off the budgets or box

TABLE 11.1 Estimated Monthly Entertainment Budgets

Estimated monthly entertainment budget	Fayetteville State University	Northwestern University
$0–25	66.9%	69.7%
$25–50	23.1%	22.1%
$50–75	4.6%	4.1%
$75–100	3.1%	2.5%
More than $100	2.3%	1.6%

offices tallies of the newest blockbusters. Few, however, understand the arcane economic arrangements that allow for film and television programs to be delivered
to their laptops or game consoles. The entertainment industries face considerable
challenges in educating members of this population on these matters. Failing
to educate this generation will reinforce the misconception that television and
movie content is or should be free, an attitude that students may take with them
after graduation, as they move into the workplace and start lives of their own.

Platform Surfing vs. Active Viewing

Iterations of the Digital Generation hypothesis frequently stress that the media
consumption styles practiced by members of this age cohort bear little resem-
blance to those of older Americans. However, in focus groups and interviews,
many of the students in our samples described behaviors that are at least superfi-
cially consistent with established consumption styles. For example, a number of
our respondents use Netflix in a manner reminiscent of channel surfing on television. That is, rather than watching a specific program or film, they "surf" Netflix's
content categories until something catches their interest. These Netflix "surfers"
watch the beginning of a movie or program before committing to watching it in
its entirety. One FSU student repeated on several occasions during his interview
that if a video does not capture his interest within the first five minutes he moves
on to something else. By comparison, students at NU reported using Netflix as
a kind of electronic companion or video wallpaper, much in the way that television is used. As a 21-year-old female NU student explained, she and her two
roommates in an off-campus apartment often "have on Netflix almost just as
background noise. Like you would just a TV show." Along with her roommates
(and many of her NU classmates), these young women frequently use Netflix as a
form of "ambient television," despite the fact that they also subscribe to a basic
cable package.[19] In both cases, however, students adapt practices typically aligned
with older forms of TV consumption—channel surfing and background noise—
to their use of SVOD services.

While many students are not thrilled with Netflix's library of titles, most
identified it as the most convenient source for films and television programs.
Among members of this age group, convenience often trumps other factors,
including cost and personal preferences. Students "watch Netflix" like older
generations of Americans "watch television," using it to sample content that
they would not watch otherwise, simply because it is easily available. By contrast, the members of our samples are unlikely to use platforms or providers that
they perceive to be inconvenient. An unresponsive user interface or a cumbersome log-in process is all it takes to drive students away. Students report that
they want to do the right thing by content creators, whether that means paying
for access or watching ads. But when "the right thing" is something they regard
as unnecessarily inconvenient, they find paths of less resistance. For example, a

number of NU students expressed frustration about how inconvenient it is to catch up on *How I Met Your Mother* at CBS.com. Some now watch the show on peer-to-peer sources, while others have given up on watching it altogether. Similarly, many students reject the current cloud movie storage system with the most industry support, UltraViolet, which not only requires users to create logins for each studio but also demands that students enter an authentication code for each title they purchase.

Physical Media in the Age of Streaming Video

The practices of owning content are also shaped—in complex ways—by issues of geographic location. Respondents on both campuses acknowledged that their media-purchasing habits have changed in recent years, following a trend that is well documented in the entertainment industry. Many NU students indicated that they frequently purchased films and, to a lesser extent, television programming on DVD while in high school. Few have maintained these habits since matriculating in college. More than 30 percent of NU students interviewed reported that they no longer purchase DVDs or Blu-rays. Among those NU respondents who still purchase DVDs, many do so for the purpose of adding titles to personal collections. However, during follow-up interviews, a number of NU students admitted to owning DVDs that they have never actually watched. In some instances, students purchase DVDs of films or series they have already seen, just to add them to their personal libraries. In other cases, students reported that they purchase titles primarily so that they can share them with friends or display them to others. One 20-year-old female student at NU explained that many of the DVDs she purchases "sit on my shelf, and they're wrapped. I still haven't opened them to watch, but I'm just happy that I own them." Thus, collecting and displaying DVDs at NU, at least in some cases, serves as a means of expressing personal tastes and of sharing those tastes with others.

The distinctions between campus viewing cultures were also reflected in how students use DVDs. Of NU respondents, 35.2 percent stated that they purchase DVDs for the purpose of sharing them with others, compared to only 28.1 percent of FSU respondents. FSU students often purchase DVDs of films and television series that they have not seen, with nearly half of the FSU respondents living on campus reporting that they have engaged in this practice. Of FSU students, 74 percent have purchased at least one DVD in the last year. Follow-up interviews and online survey comments suggested that many of those purchases were of DVDs for their children. FSU respondents who are parents stated that they use DVDs as electronic babysitters, with one respondent stating that she buys "DVDs that my children [will want] to watch over and over." In this sense, FSU students fit neatly within the industry strategy of producing movies and television shows that can be used as inexpensive and inoffensive entertainment for children. This reliance on DVDs as electronic babysitters may also explain the popularity of Redbox for FSU's student population, as compared to NU's. While

Redbox has been dismissed by some scholars as cinematic fast food—convenient, but unhealthy, given that it offers access to only the most popular films—students at FSU frequently professed how much they "loved" the kiosk service.[20] The value of Redbox may be related to FSU's larger number of commuter students who can stop at a kiosk while driving home from school, a practice that fits neatly with Redbox's strategy of targeting car owners living in suburban locations and parents with young families, demographic categories that exclude most NU students. This appreciation for Redbox was borne out in our survey results, which showed that approximately 33 percent of FSU respondents use it at least once a month (by contrast, 62.3 percent of NU respondents have never used Redbox). Thus, even when it comes to the use of DVDs, the unique living circumstances and cultures of the two campuses powerfully shape the tools and technologies that students choose to use to consume media.

Conclusion

Our comparative study of the undergraduate student media consumption habits at FSU and NU challenges many of the underlying assumptions on which the Digital Generation hypothesis is based. Members of this generation are often identified as technologically adventurous creators and consumers of content who defiantly reject the "old" ways of consuming content. In fact, where the Digital Generation hypothesis sees homogeneity, we find diversity: a diversity of habits, of tastes, and of attitudes. College students' engagements with media technologies and content are as diverse as they are. Furthermore, it appears that students' habits, tastes, and attitudes are highly susceptible to environmental influences. The students' living environments appear to have a far stronger influence on how they consume film and television than does their membership within the so-called "Digital Generation."

At the same time, there is some overlap between our student groups, especially when it comes to the values and beliefs that inform media consumption. For example, students at both schools have had their attitudes about the value of media content altered by fast, cheap, and easy digital distribution methods. Students at both schools also share the view that paying full retail price for DVDs or digital downloads is not realistic. However, these commonalities may attest more to the economic circumstances facing college students than to the existence of a shared value system. In this regard, we argue that connected viewing entails two related phenomena. First, students have access to a wide range of movies and television shows through subscription and transactional video-on-demand services. They can connect to programs through digital tools. Second, these students also connect with one another, both online and off, in their dorms and apartments, often sharing movies, television shows, and even passwords, even while they also share their tastes with one another.

This research makes visible a small selection of the heterogeneous media consumption practices that exist on America's college campuses. Our contention is that these practices are products of the special circumstances that exist in these spaces, and not manifestations of a generation's homogeneous tastes and attitudes. The nature of this relationship will only reveal itself through further study of the viewing cultures that exist on these and other American college campuses, as well as those of other campuses worldwide. These studies should engage carefully with the unique viewing protocols associated with individual campuses, attending not only to the specific demographics of individual student populations but also to the tools available to them. Media studies scholars have created an extensive body of literature on the relationships that exist between the spaces, practices, and ideologies of domesticity and Americans' engagements with screen media.[21] A much smaller, and yet no less significant, corpus of scholarship examines the consumption of media in nondomestic spaces, including bars, doctors' offices, workplaces, and public transportation.[22] With a few notable exceptions, however, media studies scholars have not explored media consumption on college campuses.[23]

College campuses are unique social spaces. They are equal parts public and private, domestic and nondomestic. They are concentrated hives of social interaction and experimentation, and they are saturated with bandwidth and technology, making them ideal settings for observing how media users might adapt to changes in viewing practices. In these socially and technologically connected environments young people pool content, resources, and know-how—and in the process devise their own idiosyncratic ways of finding, accessing, and engaging with film, television, and other media. Whether or not aspects of these viewing cultures will carry over to students' lives after college is impossible to predict. In fact, many students expressed a desire to purchase big-screen television sets and to rebuild their DVD and Blu-ray collections after graduating from college. That said, the prospect that the media habits young people cultivate while in college might not survive beyond graduation is no reason to exclude these colleges from our analyses of contemporary media culture. By examining how young people find, access, share, and view video content in dorm rooms, off-campus apartments, and commuter students' homes, we stand to trade truisms about the habits of the so-called "Digital Generation" for insights into the many factors that shape their diverse attitudes toward and engagements with a variety of media forms.

Notes

1. Marc Prensky, "Digital Natives, Digital Immigrants," http://www.marcprensky.com/writing/prensky%20-%20digital%20natives,%20digital%20immigrants%20-%20part1.pdf; Ian Jukes, Ted McCain, and Lee Crockett, *Understanding the Digital Generation: Teaching and Learning in the New Digital Landscape* (New York: Corwin, 2010); Don Tapscott, *Growing Up Digital: The Rise of the Net Generation* (New York: McGraw-Hill, 1998).
2. Tapscott, *Growing Up Digital*, 26.
3. Forrester Research, "Get Ready: The Millennials Are Coming!," quoted in Mark Bauerlein, *The Dumbest Generation: How the Digital Age Stupefies Young Americans and Jeopardizes Our Future* (New York: Penguin, 2008), 73.

4. Henry Jenkins, "Reconsidering Digital Immigrants," *Confessions of an Aca-Fan* (blog), December 5, 2007, http://henryjenkins.org/2007/12/reconsidering_digital_immigran.html; David Buckingham, "Is There a Digital Generation?," in *Digital Generations: Children, Young People, and New Media,* eds. David Buckingham and Rebekah Willet, 1–13 (Mahwah, NJ: Lawrence Erlbaum Associates, 2006); Siva Vaidhyanathan, "The Generation Myth," *The Chronicle of Higher Education* 55, no. 4 (2008): 7.

5. This is in contrast to past discussions of generational differences, which in many instances suggested that generations were defined by traumatic events such as wars or natural disasters. See Buckingham, "Is There a Digital Generation?," 4.

6. Vaidhyanathan, "The Generation Myth," 7.

7. Nielsen Newswire, "America's New Mobile Majority: A Look at Smartphone Owners in the U.S.," May 7, 2012, http://blog.nielsen.com/nielsenwire/online_mobile/who-owns-smartphones-in-the-us/.

8. Tapscott, *Growing Up Digital,* 26.

9. Dawn C. Chmielewski and Meg James, "TV Networks Try to Connect with Young, Tech-Savvy Multitaskers," *Los Angeles Times,* June 16, 2012, http://articles.latimes.com/2012/jun/16/business/la-fi-digital-kids-20120617.

10. Neal Gabler, "Perspective: Millennials Seem to Have Little Use for Old Movies," *Los Angeles Times,* July 14, 2012, http://www.latimes.com/entertainment/news/movies/la-ca-film-novelty-20120715,0,4176050.story.

11. Barbara Klinger, *Beyond the Multiplex: Cinema, New Technologies, and the Home* (Berkeley: University of California Press, 2006), 139.

12. Anna McCarthy, *Ambient Television: Visual Culture and Public Space* (Durham: Duke University Press, 2001).

13. Anna McCarthy, "The Rhythms of the Reception Area: Crisis, Capitalism, and Waiting Room TV," in *Television after TV: Essays on a Medium in Transition,* eds. Lynn Spigel and Jan Olsson (Durham and London: Duke University Press, 2004), 186.

14. Lynn Spigel, *Make Room for TV: Television and the Family Ideal in Postwar America* (Chicago: University of Chicago Press, 1992).

15. David Morley and Charlotte Brunsdon, *The Nationwide Television Studies* (London: Routledge, 1999); Shaun Moores, *Interpreting Audiences: The Ethnography of Media Consumption* (London: SAGE, 1993); Ann Gray, *Video Playtime: The Gendering of a Leisure Technology* (London: Routledge, 1992).

16. See, for example, Max Dawson, "Little Players, Big Shows: Format, Narration, and Style on Television's New Smaller Screens," *Convergence* 13, no. 3 (August 2007): 231–50; Chuck Tryon, "Pushing the (Red) Envelope: Portable Video, Platform Mobility, and Pay-Per-View Culture," in *Moving Data: The iPhone and the Future of Media,* eds. Patrick Vonderau and Pelle Snickars (New York: Columbia University Press, 2012), 124–39; Steven Groening, "From 'A Box in the Theater of the World' to 'The World as Your Living Room': Cellular Phones, Television, and Mobile Privatization," *New Media & Society* 12, no. 8 (2010): 1331–47.

17. Joe Karaganis, ed., *Media Piracy in Emerging Economies* (New York: Social Science Research Council, 2011).

18. In fact, virtually all of NU's first-year students live on campus, providing them with ample opportunity to share in connected viewing practices with their classmates.

19. McCarthy, *Ambient Television.*

20. Wheeler Winston Dixon, "Red Boxes and Cloud Movies," FlowTV.org, July 21, 2011, http://flowtv.org/2011/07/red-boxes-and-cloud-movies/.

21. See, for example, Spigel, *Make Room for TV;* Morley and Brunsdon, *The Nationwide Television Studies;* Moores, *Interpreting Audiences;* Gray, *Video Playtime.*

22. See, for example, McCarthy, *Ambient Television;* Ethan Tussey, "Foam Finger Cubicle: Selling ESPN360 as Workspace Media," FlowTV.org, October 17, 2009, http://flowtv

.org/2009/10/foam-finger-cubicle-selling-espn360-as-workspace-mediaethan-tussey-ucsb/; Groening, "From 'A Box in the Theater of the World.'"
23. For example, see Klinger, *Beyond the Multiplex*, as well as Sharon Strover's contribution to this volume.

References

Bauerlein, Mark. *The Dumbest Generation: How the Digital Age Stupefies Young Americans and Jeopardizes Our Future*. New York: Penguin, 2008.

Buckingham, David. "Is There a Digital Generation?" In *Digital Generations: Children, Young People, and New Media*, edited by David Buckingham and Rebekah Willet, 1–13. Mahwah, NJ: Lawrence Erlbaum Associates, 2006.

Chmielewski, Dawn C., and Meg James. "TV Networks Try to Connect with Young, Tech-Savvy Multitaskers." *Los Angeles Times*, June 16, 2012. http://articles.latimes.com/2012/jun/16/business/la-fi-digital-kids-20120617.

Dawson, Max. "Little Players, Big Shows: Format, Narration, and Style on Television's New Smaller Screens." *Convergence* 13, no. 3 (August 2007): 231–50.

Dixon, Wheeler Winston. "Red Boxes and Cloud Movies." FlowTV.org, July 21, 2011. http://flowtv.org/2011/07/red-boxes-and-cloud-movies/.

Gabler, Neal. "Perspective: Millennials Seem to Have Little Use for Old Movies." *Los Angeles Times*, July 14, 2012. http://www.latimes.com/entertainment/news/movies/la-ca-film-novelty-20120715,0,4176050.story.

Gray, Ann. *Video Playtime: The Gendering of a Leisure Technology*. London: Routledge, 1992.

Groening, Steven. "From 'A Box in the Theater of the World' to 'The World as Your Living Room': Cellular Phones, Television, and Mobile Privatization." *New Media & Society* 12, no. 8 (2010): 1331–47.

Jenkins, Henry. "Reconsidering Digital Immigrants." *Confessions of an Aca-Fan* (blog), December 5, 2007. http://henryjenkins.org/2007/12/reconsidering_digital_immigran.html.

Jukes, Ian, Ted McCain, and Lee Crockett. *Understanding the Digital Generation: Teaching and Learning in the New Digital Landscape*. New York: Corwin, 2010.

Karaganis, Joe, ed. *Media Piracy in Emerging Economies*. New York: Social Science Research Council, 2011.

Klinger, Barbara. *Beyond the Multiplex: Cinema, New Technologies, and the Home*. Berkeley: University of California Press, 2006.

McCarthy, Anna. "The Rhythms of the Reception Area: Crisis, Capitalism, and Waiting Room TV." In *Television after TV: Essays on a Medium in Transition*, edited by Lynn Spigel and Jan Olsson. Durham and London: Duke University Press, 2004.

McCarthy, Anna. *Ambient Television: Visual Culture and Public Space*. Durham: Duke University Press, 2001.

Moores, Shaun. *Interpreting Audiences: The Ethnography of Media Consumption*. London: SAGE, 1993.

Morley, David, and Charlotte Brunsdon. *The Nationwide Television Studies*. London: Routledge, 1999.

Nielsen Newswire. "America's New Mobile Majority: A Look at Smartphone Owners in the U.S." May 7, 2012. http://blog.nielsen.com/nielsenwire/online_mobile/who-owns-smartphones-in-the-us/.

Prensky, Marc. "Digital Natives, Digital Immigrants." http://www.marcprensky.com/writing/prensky%20-%20digital%20natives,%20digital%20immigrants%20-%20part1.pdf.

Spigel, Lynn. *Make Room for TV: Television and the Family Ideal in Postwar America*. Chicago: University of Chicago Press, 1992.

Tapscott, Don. *Growing Up Digital: The Rise of the Net Generation*. New York: McGraw-Hill, 1998.

Tryon, Chuck. "Pushing the (Red) Envelope: Portable Video, Platform Mobility, and Pay-Per-View Culture." In *Moving Data: The iPhone and the Future of Media*, edited by Patrick Vonderau and PelleSnickars, 124–39. New York: Columbia University Press, 2012.

Tussey, Ethan. "Foam Finger Cubicle: Selling ESPN360 as Workspace Media." FlowTV.org, October 17, 2009. http://flowtv.org/2009/10/foam-finger-cubicle-selling-espn360-as-workspace-mediaethan-tussey-ucsb/.

Vaidhyanathan, Siva. "The Generation Myth." *The Chronicle of Higher Education* 55, no. 4 (2008): 7.

12

THE CONTOURS OF ON-DEMAND VIEWING

Sharon Strover and William Moner

Introduction

The media marketplace has witnessed an increase in the amount and types of viewing devices available to consumers. From the traditional television set to pocket-size mobile devices to laptop computers, people now have a surfeit of choices available for entertainment purposes. Many of these devices perform multiple functions, are portable, and afford tremendous personalization opportunities. Technology, distribution, reception, and content developments all influence the new connected viewing/using habits; Internet-enabled digital devices in particular engender alternative temporal and spatial engagement opportunities.

In the broadcast-centric environment of the 1990s, television shows were delivered to audiences through fairly standardized mechanisms. The decade featured over-the-air broadcast to television set receivers, cable television delivery to set-top cable boxes and, commonly, a recording device to enable time-shifting. While audiences could enjoy a limited selection of programs, viewers remained subject to a flow of programming options rather than exercising much autonomous choice over their selections. Only the remote control threatened to break the flow, with its opportunities to zap, zip, and graze.[1] The VCR and the DVD player (and later the TiVo service) expanded opportunities to experience television programs, films, and videos in the home. These devices created another window for home viewing, and distributors quickly adjusted and exercised selective control of the supply of film and video to shape audience expectations across their distribution horizons. While some sharing of media occurred among friends, individual demand for content largely remained subject to the limited selection available commercially or through physical video rental stores.

This situation worked well for media industries that leveraged windowing to achieve maximum revenue opportunities from successive audiences, and it allowed audiences to exercise consumption behavior at different price points. Media industries knew where to reach an audience and how to structure purchasing behaviors. People's engagement profiles were technologically and spatially limited. VCRs enabled limited forms of interactivity (program preselection, time-shifting), but industries maintained their entrenched distribution models that enabled the "flow" model of programming and control to persist.[2] While many scholars were excited by these forms of "interactivity," they clearly pale in comparison to the choices and operations available today.[3]

As broadband Internet and wireless services emerged as entertainment distribution technologies in the late 1990s and into the twenty-first century, online video and media distribution services also developed to both create and meet the demand for content. An assortment of viewing apparatuses and user points of control have grown in an iterative fashion, and both new types of content and new platforms have been alternately contested and adopted by incumbent industries. By 2010, audiences could download or stream television programs through a variety of authorized and unauthorized services, and viewing no longer required a television set.[4] A "film" can now be viewed on a TV screen, a laptop, a mobile device, a tablet, or a gaming console, given Internet access to a service provider, and no longer requires physical media such as DVDs. To patch together entertainment opportunities in this splintering environment, a savvy viewer/user might possess the combination of a multifunction receiving device, broadband Internet service, and additional personal media devices for communicating about programming content. Researchers have only begun to grapple with these dynamics of connected viewing engagement.

A generational shift in viewing media finds its vanguard in young people, especially those in colleges where high-speed Internet networks are common and the environments for sharing and creating are rich. Students engage with various devices to view television and film content, partake in online conversations about media, and even participate in remaking or remixing content to shape their own experience, defining the new connected viewing environment. Students will view in waves as some things "go viral" on YouTube, and routinely access video and music programs via online services such as YouTube, Netflix, or Hulu, engage media through BitTorrent networks that provide access to both authorized and unauthorized content, and search for entertainment via Google or Bing web search engines. A typical student's connected media environment now includes entertainment offerings inclusive of YouTube videos, a Facebook news feed, shared photographs, personal videos, content libraries available on Netflix and Amazon, Twitter feeds, instant messaging, online chat, BitTorrent networks, and many others. In contrast to the users of programming available in the conventional "flow" configuration, the student audience has come of age in a connected environment rife with content available on demand and shared through a multitude of distribution platforms.

Our study investigated the behaviors associated with media engagement among university student populations in divergent locations: a large research-based university in the United States, a US community college setting with broader age and income ranges, and two four-year universities in Portugal. Our intent was first to describe some of the new "viewing" behaviors among these groups of users/participants, and second, to understand the influence of mobility and temporality as well as services available (cost, platforms) on patterns of engagement. The broader goal of this study was to unpack how connected viewing operates at this moment in time, and to enlarge discussions around the ideas of platform and choice. The background of media industries and their ability to structure choices was highlighted by the opportunity to compare two different environments—those of the United States and Portugal—where viewing/using opportunities vary.

Literature Review

The concept of television has shifted in the past decade to include any screen or device that delivers television programming. "Television," therefore, has been increasingly reframed as a platform for content delivery rather than a simplistic one-way medium, belying its technological mode of delivery. Just as Lynn Spigel and Jan Olsson differentiate "TV" from "television,"[5] characterizing the latter as the expanding terrain of multiple viewing and interacting experiences, we note that in the first decade of this century the words we can use to distinguish platform from content, form from delivery method, or uses from distribution method, have multiplied into a combinatory plenitude. This mesh of imprecise descriptors around platforms, settings, content, and user behaviors complicates any attempt to understand engagement. While some might understand television delivery at the signal level (e.g., cable, DSL, or over-the-air antenna-based signal processing), viewers increasingly understand viewing of programming to be dependent on a mix of intermediaries such as smartphones, laptops, or services like Hulu. The idea of "reception" fails to capture people's interactions with media content.

The television industry has reframed its discourse, favoring the term *content* in place of the more arcane concept of *programming*. By making the move to *content,* television producers and industries recognize the multimodal delivery systems available to audiences and respond by fragmenting their offerings across multiple devices and multiple modes of viewing. However, the literature on audiences or users has not entirely caught up to the alterations in how we engage media. The audience literature pays scant attention to peer production models of distribution and use that excite many scholars, users, and advocates of participatory media such as Yochai Benkler,[6] or to the types of viewing environments constructed by YouTube.[7] Understanding how viewers find and engage content in a nearly "ubiquitous computing" environment (i.e., where high-speed broadband connections are available) is fettered by the industrial models that presuppose conventional advertising exposure as their point of departure and the more static conceptions of viewers often found in the television literature. Contemporary viewing/using patterns that acknowledge multiple devices and platforms, including Facebook, complicate conventional definitions of audience activity, going well beyond Stuart Hall's articulation of reception or uses and gratifications theories of motivation.[8]

Scholars such as Henry Jenkins[9] or P. David Marshall[10] have referred to the new generation of viewers as being more *committed* viewers of network-created (but not broadcast-distributed) series television, of forming social relationships and initiating fan behavior around certain content through Internet-based fan sites or YouTube or other similar apparatuses.[11] However, there is so much heterogeneity in viewing/engaging processes that this claim must be tempered. First, what once was studied as a single-site, home-based activity has now become an activity that can occur in multiple areas of the home via cable and wireless, in the workplace via broadband, at school via laptop or tablet, or on the bus or at other places via mobile devices and networks such as Wi-Fi and 3- and 4G. Second, the shift becomes more pronounced when considering the convergent and multipurpose uses of gaming devices, set-top boxes, broadband-connected tablets, and smartphones, streaming servers, and home entertainment servers.

Further, the connected viewing *environment* also may affect the selection of content. As Beverly Bondad-Brown et al. point out, "sharing information about online content, helping filter and evaluate the vast amount of Web site content, exchanging opinions of it, and providing others with online links to content, represent considerably more ways that one may become exposed to, and engage with, online user-shared video content than for traditional TV."[12] Are users of new video technologies the committed viewers of content that Jenkins discusses? Alternatively, is their use of these media more spontaneous and "uncommitted" (in the fan sense)? How does the intensely social domain of using and working with online media alter older notions of engaging?

Some characterize the new engagement experience as a "highly personal medium of individualized, privatized consumption";[13] however, there are differences across devices and screens, and much content on YouTube, for example, defies the conventional notion of *privatized* content, instead underscoring viral qualities and social media. Using portable devices does not imply that people are simply migrating the same content they would engage on a computer screen or another home-based large-format screen. Rather, portable devices interact with individuals' attention spans, spatial locations, privacy, bandwidth or connection speeds available, and sense of aesthetics (i.e., some content is less acceptable on a small screen). New ways of thinking about mobility with respect to content must acknowledge the role of place as well as types of content. Jason Farman's notion of portable media users as *bricoleurs,* creating highly uneven media experiences depending on time, place, and purpose, is pertinent here.[14]

Furthermore, the use of so-called "companion" devices to the television screen also demands attention.[15] Beyond the idea of a simultaneous second screen, some scholars have suggested reformulating the idea of entertainment to encompass the social nature of media, whether by suggesting a rebranding of interactive TV systems as "social TV"[16] or recognizing that audiences have extended their entertainment considerations beyond the traditional logics of the existing system.[17] To fully understand the notion of social TV, studies in this environment cannot ignore the role of social media, particularly Facebook. Statistics from the service comScore, for example, show that even by 2011 Facebook had become more important for online linking than conventional portals.[18] This social media site currently occupies a central role as a communication and entertainment platform for its users. For example, young adults are heavy users of Facebook,[19] and many post their own content or link to or repost content through it. As of 2011, 71 percent of online adults in the United States watched videos on sharing sites such as YouTube or Vimeo.[20] How do Facebook and other social networking sites affect viewing patterns and behaviors, and if significantly, what might this mean for the structure of entertainment or taste cultures in the near future?

As streaming services have emerged, new pressure points for businesses and for users have materialized among industries that barely would have been thought of as "media industries" ten years ago. In the case of Netflix's streaming video service, broadband service providers now fear the loss of their ability to control content by controlling bandwidth.[21] Amazon, for years heavily identified with books and then a wide array of retail products, is now squarely in the digital content domain with its Kindle, related e-publishing products, and streaming services via Amazon Prime. Apple, originally a computer company, is central to the content delivery system with the iTunes Store. Competing technology from BitTorrent, a legal technology optimized for sharing large files (such as video), pushes against the boundaries of legal downloading and streaming even as iTunes authorizes and commercializes these same processes. Authorized distribution through a service such as iTunes or Netflix depresses unauthorized file sharing. However, such services often limit sharing of content, or impose certain limitations on bandwidth or speed or cost or time of access, all factors that can influence how people engage content.

Barry Brown and Louise Barkhuus[22] identify a number of shifts in the viewing habits of the DVR and "peer-to-peer" television viewers. While television in the broadcast era was largely ephemeral, their informants described archiving behavior with DVRs and peer-to-peer downloading. For example, users of BSkyB's Sky+ DVR service record several episodes of a series on their devices and then watch multiple episodes in order in one sitting. (Some of the viewers archive the episodes to DVD, but the poor reliability of DVD recording devices makes them poor systems for archiving.) Archiving is also common among the Internet viewers of TV programming. Such viewers use a peer-to-peer service like BitTorrent to download programming and then keep it on high-capacity hard drives as a personal collection. As Brown and Barkhus discuss with regard to British file-sharers, some used BitTorrent to view series unavailable in the UK, while others preferred to use illicit Internet content to watch at their convenience.

While some peer-to-peer viewers use BitTorrent as a supplement to viewing as shows continue to air, nearly all the DVR users exclusively watch time-shifted television. This is in contrast to the interviewed VCR users, who only time-shift on occasion. Such results raise questions about how streaming alters notions of engagement. How might data caps imposed by Internet service providers and account-sharing practices[23] influence engagement patterns? What are users' attitudes toward the legality and illegality of certain practices?

In summary, alterations in media industry approaches to cross-platform content and entirely new opportunities for people to themselves generate content have joined with highly tailorable and mobile platforms to upset the norms of television viewing characteristic of the 1990s. How Internet-based content sources, alongside various user-owned technologies (e.g., mobile devices) that operate in mobile spaces, shape people's connected viewing habits was the core question here. Our concerns focused on 1) how viewers/users engage with mediated visual entertainment, particularly with respect to the role of user-generated content and the time and place affordances associated with mobile devices; 2) how Facebook or other social media function in selecting or creating content; and 3) how authorized or unauthorized services for obtaining content come into the new user calculus.

Research Questions and Methods

The increasing use of broadband- and wireless-based technologies, Internet-enabled devices, multifunction devices, and portable media platforms suggests new dimensions to the idea of audience or user activity. Our study begins to grapple with shifts to connected viewing by examining several related aspects of contemporary device usage and media content delivery. This study's goals were primarily descriptive rather than causal, and it relied on both quantitative and qualitative data in order to understand how people engage new media forms and platforms. We focused on three major questions:

1. How do viewers/users engage with new, especially second-screen, "television" or visual entertainment? Mobile technologies may facilitate engaging or producing content in new ways and places, adding a dimension to user engagement that previous models do not capture. How do time and space affect engagement?
2. How do Facebook or other social media figure in the viewing experience, especially in selecting, creating, and circulating content? If users are spending a great deal of time on Facebook and with other social media, do social networks channel viewing choices?
3. What is the role of authorized and unauthorized services in downloading or streaming content? The value proposition and threat of illegality may influence how and what people view in different circumstances. How do users conceptualize value?

We administered surveys to three different college student populations and also conducted eight focus groups of approximately ten students each with students from one four-year university from the spring of 2011 through the summer of 2012. Our nonrandom survey samples included US-based community college students (N = 433), students attending a four-year public university (N = 490), and elite university students at two similar sites in Portugal (N = 500). The college student population was targeted in order to explore the population most likely to incorporate new media technologies into their daily lives. The international setting contrasts with the United States because Netflix, Hulu, and iTunes did not offer video services to Portugal at the time of our data gathering, but peer-to-peer downloading services, many with unauthorized access to popular media fare, are common.[24] The four-year universities in the United States and Portugal are similar in terms of catering to full-time students and offering broadband and wireless Internet access on campus. The universities also tend to be less diverse in terms of income, age, and ethnicity than in our community college setting in the United States. The community college sample contributes broader income and social class ranges to our analysis. Our focus groups probed more deeply into how devices, time, and location configure viewing and the pleasures of engagement.

Survey data were gathered through a questionnaire administered in person during undergraduate college classes. The cross-sectional, purposive sample members had the opportunity to decline to complete the survey, although most students chose to provide responses.

The questionnaire items examined the following dimensions of the research questions:

1. Engagement: The devices commonly used, how much time people spend with them, where they use them, and which sources of content they routinely engage measure engagement. Understanding where and when mobile devices are used is important, and the role of specific places and social settings in user behavior provides insights into temporal and spatial aspects of engagement.

2. Social media functions and content manipulation: Questions measured Facebook and other social media services in terms of frequency of use, how such services function for discovering new entertainment, the utility of their recommendation services, and how frequently these applications are used to communicate *about* programs being viewed, especially how often people produce content via Facebook.

3. Authorized/unauthorized sources of content: Questionnaire items assessed whether people use file-sharing services such as BitTorrent or an authorized service such as iTunes, and whether people keep or delete media content. We also inquired about the choice process for entertainment fare, specifically whether people prefer an on-demand selection process or an unbroken flow of programming typified by broadcast television or cable television scheduling.

The survey contained both open- and closed-ended questions, and the open-ended responses were content coded. The closed-ended survey questions asked about personal viewing habits across delivery systems, device usage, recommendation systems, and characteristics of viewership. The same ideas were accessed in the focus groups with probes on social settings and the time dimensions of media use, engagement with apps and other software, and attitudes toward peer-to-peer media file sharing.

In terms of characterizing the technology and platforms in Portugal and the United States, we note that Portugal ranks lower than the United States in terms of general household broadband penetration,[25] but the universities in our sample are located in heavily populated cities in Portugal where broadband and mobile wireless services are readily available (which is not always the case in the country's interior). Cable TV services in Portugal are marketing DVRs and on-demand services, but no streaming or downloading video services were available through their networks or those of the DSL provider Portugal Telecom at the time of our study. The US university and community college are located in a city characterized by plentiful Wi-Fi access locations throughout the city and home-based access from three cable and broadband providers. Both US campuses feature a broadband network available for free to any registered student through Wi-Fi or Ethernet. Mobile phone Internet access is readily available, albeit for the standard data service fee.

Results

Engagement

It is clear from our results that different platforms are amenable to different engagement styles. The critical issues regarding what screen is used have to do with time available, content desired and viewer investment, and whether one is in an environment conducive to group viewing as opposed to personal viewing.

The *laptop screen* is the screen of choice because of its ability to easily link to streaming content, its ability to play DVDs, and its portability to different viewing environments. However, the community college students use a laptop less frequently (54 percent cited it as a frequently or very frequently used device for viewing) than do four-year college students (75 percent US, 68 percent Portuguese). It is viewed as a personal device, and one amenable to both multitasking and selecting content that is pleasing just to oneself. The *smartphone screen,* on the other hand, supports viewing bursts and short content, its size allowing it to be personal even if it is used in a public space. It serves to fill in otherwise unoccupied (or lightly occupied) time periods. In a theme that takes shape across several data points, however, we found that our community college sample uses a mobile phone to view content more frequently than is the case at the US four-year university: 25 percent reported this frequently or very frequently, compared to about

TABLE 12.1 "Regularly Used" Program Services by Sample (%)

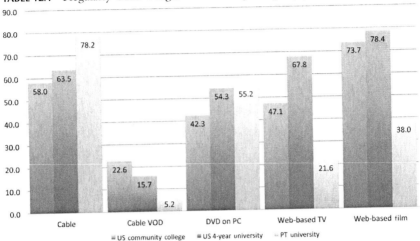

11 percent having said the same from the four-year US students and 12 percent from the Portuguese students.

All three of our sub-samples exhibit high rates of subscription to cable television services, but rather low rates of using cable video-on-demand (VOD). The utilization of web-based services such as Hulu or NBC.com for television programs dramatically exceeds cable VOD for the US populations, as does using web-based services such as Netflix and YouTube for film/TV (Table 12.1). Correspondingly lower figures in web-based services for Portuguese students reflect the lack of such services' availability. Respondents repeatedly noted that Hulu and Netflix are valued because they are legal, present no concerns about viruses or malware, and are convenient and easy to use. Above all, web-based services are flexible in terms of what they provide and when. As one focus group participant put it, "Well, I guess on, like, Hulu, you don't have to watch . . . on a scheduled time, so I just, like, grab a time. Like, I'll just go on and look for it. Whenever I have free time." Several people mentioned the problem of data caps, and many consider this an issue in their choice of how to obtain programming.

Our populations do watch DVDs on their PCs, often obtaining them from Redbox (in the United States) or from friends; using DVDs seems to reflect interest in a higher-quality image, in particularly valued content, or in content amenable to group viewing (such as a blockbuster movie) on a large screen. When people *download* content, a significant majority prefer to keep the file on a hard drive for a long time as opposed to deleting it soon after viewing, suggesting that viewers tend to collect media for repeated access.

Higher cost, confusing interfaces, too many ads, and inconsistent audio-visual quality create disincentives for using certain services (Table 12.2). Focus group

TABLE 12.2 Annoyance Ratings (1=no effect; 4=much less likely to use)

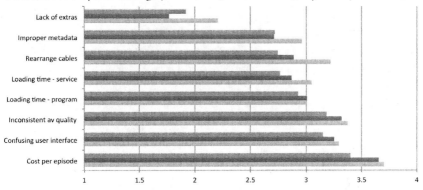

respondents noted that a certain number of ads are tolerable, but that too much clutter and pop-ups are strong negatives.

In terms of where entertainment content viewing/using occurs, there are some contrasts: the Portuguese and community college students spend more time in their living rooms than is the case for the four-year US university students; we know that more Portuguese students do live with their families, and that more community college students also have families and are older, perhaps explaining this finding. However, the embeddedness of portable devices is evident in that over 50 percent of all three samples do view content in their bedrooms, often using laptops or phones. Again, the prominence of mobile devices for the community college sample stands out in that those students reported viewing on mobile phones far more than students from the other two samples did (18 percent versus 5 percent for the other US sample and 2 percent for the Portuguese sample).

A cross-tabulation of mobile phone use with use of Facebook, YouTube, and e-mail—the primary sources of entertainment for the sample—produces mixed results. First, the use of Facebook is so dominant that the device platform does not appear to matter: people are on Facebook a lot, wherever they happen to be and whatever technology is in their hands (there is no statistically significant difference across these platforms). YouTube is a somewhat different story. The people creating and sharing content via this video platform rely more heavily on mobile phones; their frequent use of the mobile is associated with YouTube content; many focus group participants commented on the utility of the phone for "spending time" with YouTube videos. People who reported a heavy dependence on the mobile phone for viewing also frequently use collaborative software (e.g., Google Docs, now Google Drive) to share content. Mobile devices seem to be associated with increased activity in content creation and sharing, and active participation in connected media environments.

Facebook and Social Media

Facebook is central to all sampled students, who use it not only to keep up with friends and family but also to recommend viewing content, to take a look at what others have recommended, and to make recommendations or to create their own content. Among US students, 95 percent of the four-year and 77 percent of the community college students use Facebook to share or discover content, and a slightly lower 71 percent of the Portuguese students reported the same. Its use is banal: "Interviewer: What's your next step after you capture a video? Subject: I usually just picture mail or Facebook." Importantly, many people access Facebook through their phones and end up browsing content linked through Facebook on their devices. Even people who rarely post still browse Facebook or Twitter and follow up on people's recommendations for content; as one participant said,

> Usually videos I watch will be via Twitter, like someone I follow will be like, 'Hey, check out this video, it's really cool,' so if I don't have my laptop I'll use my phone. That's pretty much the only time [I use the phone for viewing].

Our focus group commentary illustrates that many people sign up as Facebook fans for celebrities, movies, or other programs on Facebook, and that those sites in turn become recommendation sources to their friends. Along with Facebook, respondents frequently use YouTube and Netflix (in the United States) to find items to watch (Table 12.3), with YouTube having been cited as the most useful in terms of referrals to content. In response to the question "What services do you use to share *your* creative work?," students primarily cited Facebook, YouTube, and e-mail, in that order. Clearly, Facebook embeds a variety of communicative purposes, and its messaging is now used as a substitute for e-mail. These results are parallel across all three samples and contribute to connected viewing practices.

Among US students, using Facebook for *responding to others' content* dwarfs all other services: 95.9 percent of the US sample reported using Facebook to share or comment on content *created by others,* and nearly two-thirds do so several times a day. In other words, secondary circulation of shared content and commentary is extremely common. YouTube has lighter use, but it is still prominent. Such results underscore that sharing content is common, and that this element of connected viewing—sharing and commenting on other people's content—is practically a daily activity. When we asked focus group members how they find content, word-of-mouth and Facebook were dominant. However, the use of various dedicated apps or extensions for specific content also appeared:

> One thing that I used for TV on phones—my brother bought it—was either five dollars or eight. You get every March Madness game on the go, on your phone. And so we were hanging out over spring break, and we would share his phone and watch it, but that was really nice.

TABLE 12.3 Average Frequency of Use for Discovering Content (0=low; 4=high)

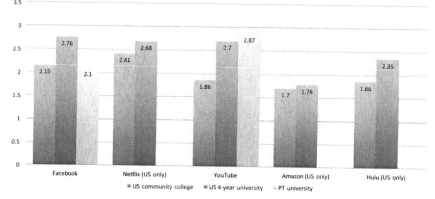

Another respondent explained,

> If you go on Firefox, you can download DownloadHelper, and you can download YouTube videos, fragments of different shows, movies that are in several parts. I'll go ahead and download all of that so [I can watch] when I don't have [an] Internet connection.

Authorized/Unauthorized Content

Recording programs and especially accessing them from online sources are the norm, and a busy lifestyle raises expectations and motivations for immediate gratification regarding video content. Interestingly, in our focus groups people often expressed frustration with not being able to get just-aired TV content right away, and this becomes a motivation to turn to unauthorized sources for content. The large percentage of people who prefer an on-demand style of watching media as opposed to a flow style ("regular" TV) underscores this drive (Table 12.5). As one respondent said,

> It seems that like our generation is very . . . in the now. We don't want to wait, you know, we're really impatient. You know, so there's something really cool that just comes out, we're like, yeah, we have to see it. If we have to wait a week? We cannot wait one week. If it's two days? We still don't want to wait two days.

We interpret the lower numbers for the Portuguese sample in the "on-demand" category as indicative of more limited opportunities for streaming content. Focus groups also confirmed a certain amount of account sharing among family members and friends in order to access on-demand content through Slingbox or HBO GO, a practice they believe is entirely legitimate.

TABLE 12.4 Average Frequency of Helpfulness for Content Discovery (1=rarely; 4=frequently)

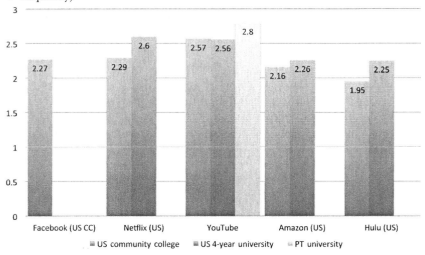

TABLE 12.5 Preferences for Flow or On-demand (%)

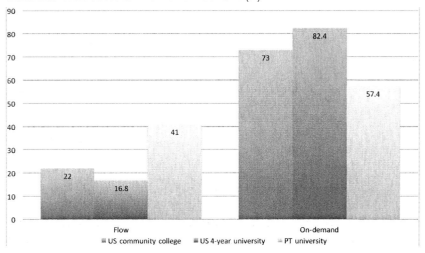

The US populations overwhelmingly prefer an on-demand configuration to an uninterrupted flow of content typical of an older broadcast model. The Portuguese population does not vary as significantly between those who prefer a flow (41 percent) versus those who prefer on-demand content (57 percent). These observations lend credence to the idea that access to on-demand, authorized streaming content—and the devices that facilitate an on-demand lifestyle—shapes the way in which audiences engage with media.

TABLE 12.6 Viewer Preference for Authorized or File-Sharing Sources (%)

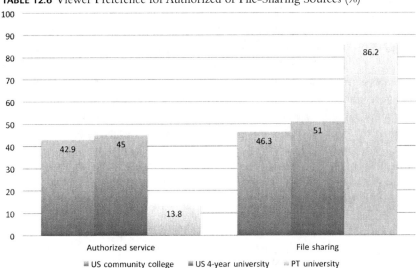

In response to the question "Given a choice between file sharing and using an authorized source, which would you choose?," a stark contrast is evident between Portugal and the United States (Table 12.6), probably because Portugal lacks many authorized streaming services. The slight preference for file sharing over authorized services within the United States represented by surveys results is probably a reflection of cost, ease of use, and file-sharing services' ability to provide the content people want (according to our focus groups). Students are familiar with a plethora of sources for unauthorized programming, but they said they actually would prefer an affordable, user-friendly, authorized alternative.

While US respondents expressed concern over poor image quality, viruses, and possible litigation when using unauthorized services, they remain undeterred. According to one respondent, problems include "viruses (*agreement*), spam, incorrect content—like, it will have one description, and you're expecting *Little House on the Prairie*, but you get porno (*laughter*)." Several people explained that deficiencies in the official distribution system encourage their use of such services: from their perspective, the market successfully creates desire to watch, but then unfairly inhibits viewing. While many people conceded the justice in compensating people for the effort required to make a good film, this does not always offset their turn to unauthorized sources in order to get it when they want it.

Our motivation for asking this question stemmed from the differences in the US and Portuguese media systems. The US media system offers access to several authorized downloading and streaming services, and authorized services like

Netflix and Hulu were ranked highly by US respondents for accessing media: four-year college students indicated they stream daily (34 percent), weekly (36 percent), or monthly (12 percent), and although the levels are lower with community college students (62 percent reported streaming monthly or more often), such services are clearly popular. However, it is clear that most focus group members are well aware of how to access unauthorized content, and they will do so if they cannot easily access it through authorized means.

In contrast, the Portuguese media system does not feature access to Netflix or Hulu, nor do Portuguese students have access to a popular authorized streaming service. Instead, Portuguese respondents turn to cable TV at a rate of 45.5 percent, followed by 28.4 percent who choose streaming media for their primary source of entertainment; the latter is most likely a selection of rerun broadcast television programs offered through their provider. Given the lack of popular authorized sources in Portugal as opposed to the plentiful access in the United States, one might presume that unauthorized services are among those used in the file sharing so popular in Portugal among college students. Only 13.6 percent of Portuguese respondents reported preferring to access content from an authorized service, much lower than the response from US respondents.

Discussion

Our results suggest that users/viewers are evolving to expect opportunities to create and use content in various forms and in various places. There is striking similarity across the three different samples we surveyed to explore these issues. While students may not typify the adult audience due to the typical student's lack of financial resources and limited time to spend with media, they are early adopters of technology and set the agenda for how other generations engage with entertainment programming of various sorts. Portable devices such as laptops and phones are commonplace utilities for connected viewing, and there is ample evidence among our sample that much time is spent in a "lean forward" fashion, rather than a "lean back" fashion: leaning forward to create and interact, rather than leaning back to just consume. Using a laptop computer is nearly as common as using a television for entertainment, and one-tenth of our sample uses various devices for entertainment in public places rather than in the home, a trend most pronounced among the US students.

Mobile devices allow people to use content in new ways and at new times, prompting new ways of characterizing engagement that depend on where one is, how much time one has, and with whom one wants to watch. Along the dimensions of location, time, and group dynamics, a more reasonable typology of connected viewing activity may emerge in the terms illustrated below (Table 12.7) rather than in terms of rigid programming preferences or genres. With mobile devices, opportunities to nibble on quick bursts of content or to participate in a viral moment greatly expand ideas about how people find and

TABLE 12.7 A Typology of Engagement

Time	Content	Where	Who	Source
Now	Sporting events, reality TV finales, award shows (Oscars, Emmys), other event-based content	TV/large monitor, scores and information— mobile	Shared group experience (in-person or connected)	Live broadcast or stream; often 2nd screen for additional info
Soon after release	Contemporary serial TV	Laptop, TV/ large monitor	Groups, friends	Hulu, Netflix, other online
Buzz and interest dictate timing	Contemporary TV, film	Laptop, DVD	Alone, friends	Redbox, Netflix, other online
Anytime	Older content	Laptop	Alone, passing time	Netflix, DVD, Hulu
As circulates through social media; downtime	Clips (e.g., YouTube); Facebook links	Mobile or connected device	Alone; social connections through fan clubs, etc.	YouTube, Facebook

consume media. Certain types of content adapt to new dimensions of time and place afforded by mobile technologies.

Social networking services are a part of the mix for creating, sharing, and locating entertaining content. We found that e-mail, YouTube, and Facebook are the most popular services for sharing content and commenting on others' content, and arguably the types of interactions one has with each are unique. The level of discussion around content—three-quarters of the sample reported communicating about content they see—underscores the extent to which this interactivity is commonplace, a part of a daily wave of communication that is voluminous and meaningful. The social networks fostered by each of these applications are vital to the contemporary circulation of content among young users.

Facebook epitomizes the "on-demand" culture that our results on file sharing and downloading explore. The ability to quickly upload or download, the opportunity to sample a range of content, and the chance to share one's own work simply and immediately are what the contemporary culture desires. This is a paradigm shift away from the notion of programmed content channels that structure viewing. As Jeremy Butler puts it, "The future of media convergence . . . depends upon media companies' ability to compete with the real-time screen's user agency, navigable space, temporal simultaneity, and virtual sense of shared space."[26]

While the mobile phone occupies fledgling status in terms of its utility for content creation and distribution, the disparity among our samples may illustrate that mobile is going to occupy an increasingly important role in content connections.

The mobile smartphone, along with the laptop, offers portable opportunities for the connected viewing and creative engagement that enmesh users. Many people use their smartphones to connect on Facebook, a service that is a contemporary fulcrum of content engagement. Mobile-phone-based access to the Internet is surprisingly high among the community college sample, and this may reflect a pattern observed in other data, namely that lower-income and minority populations are using phones rather than computers for Internet access.[27] While we cannot say exactly why mobile phone use for content access is higher among community college populations, other studies have found that phone-based Internet access often has to do with not owning a computer or not being able to afford both a cell phone as well as a home broadband connection.[28]

Finally, unauthorized content is a typical component of the digital diet. Its use is in part a by-product of a highly effective marketing system that creates demand. File sharing of both authorized and unauthorized content is so habitual in so many domains that exalt the social (Facebook and its linking) that carving out a particular use of shared files as illegal goes against the grain of a raft of other routine and popular activities within digital life.

This study suggests that mobile devices such as laptop computers and smartphones coincide with more ubiquitous broadband and Wi-Fi networks to thoroughly embed opportunities for engaging digital content in more places and at more times than ever before. The rapid growth of social network sites and their use by young adults in particular has created a new domain for content circulation, alongside content platforms such as YouTube that have exponentially expanded content types and availability. How we theorize "viewers" and viewing activity across connected viewing domains requires new metrics and conceptualizations of engagement that must be cognizant of a transformed socio-technical calculus of platforms, devices, mobility, content, time, and social circumstances.

Notes

1. Robert V. Bellamy Jr. and James R. Walker, *Television and the Remote Control: Grazing on a Vast Wasteland* (New York: Guilford Press, 1996).
2. Raymond Williams, *Television: Technology and Cultural Form* (New York: Schocken Books, 1974).
3. Mark R. Levy, *The VCR Age: Home Video and Mass Communication* (Newbury Park, CA: SAGE, 1989).
4. For example, as of January 2012, Netflix reported twice as many streaming subscribers as DVD subscribers. See http://gigaom.com/2012/01/25/netflix-streaming-vs-dvds/.
5. Lynn Spigel and Jan Olsson, eds., *Television after TV: Essays on a Medium in Transition* (Durham, NC and London, UK: Duke University Press, 2004).
6. Yochai Benkler, *The Wealth of Networks: How Social Production Transforms Markets and Freedoms* (New Haven, CT: Yale University Press, 2006).
7. Jean Burgess and Joshua Green, eds., *YouTube: Online Video and Participatory Culture* (Cambridge, MA: Polity Press, 2009).
8. Elizabeth M. Perse, "Audience Selectivity and Involvement in the Newer Media Environment," *Communication Research* 17, no. 5 (1990): 675–97; Mark R. Levy and Sven

Windahl, "The Concept of Audience Activity," in *Media Gratifications Research: Current Perspectives*, eds. Karl Erik Rosengren, Lawrence A. Wenner, and Philip Palmgreen (Beverly Hills, CA: SAGE, 1985), 109–22.

9. Henry Jenkins, *Convergence Culture: Where Old and New Media Collide* (New York: New York University Press, 2006).

10. P. David Marshall, "Screens: Television's Dispersed 'Broadcast,'" in *Television Studies After TV: Understanding Television in the Post-Broadcast Era*, eds. Graeme Turner and Jinna Tay (London and New York: Routledge, 2009), 41–50.

11. Marshall, "Screens," 41.

12. Beverly A. Bondad-Brown, Ronald E. Rice, and Katy E. Pearce, "Influences on TV Viewing and Online User-shared Video Use: Demographics, Generations, Contextual Age, Media Use, Motivations, and Audience Activity," *Journal of Broadcasting & Electronic Media* 56, no. 4 (2012): 471–93.

13. Marshall, "Screens," 41.

14. Jason Farman, *Mobile Interface Theory: Embodied Space and Locative Media* (New York: Routledge, 2012).

15. Santosh Basapur et al., "Field Trial of a Dual Device User Experience for iTV," in *Proceedings of the 9th International Interactive Conference on Interactive Television* (New York: ACM, 2011), 127–36; Pablo Cesar, Dick C.A. Bulterman, and Jack Jansen, "Leveraging User Impact: An Architecture for Secondary Screens Usage in Interactive Television," *Multimedia Systems* 15, no. 3 (2009): 127–42.

16. Konstantinos Chorianopoulos and George Lekakos, "Introduction to Social TV: Enhancing the Shared Experience with Interactive TV," *International Journal of Human-Computer Interaction* 24, no. 2 (2008): 113–20.

17. Tara McPherson, "Reload: Liveness, Mobility, and the Web," in *New Media, Old Media: A History and Theory Reader*, eds. Wendy Hui Kyong Chun and Thomas Keenan (New York: Routledge, 2005), 240–52.

18. comScore, "It's a Social World: Top 10 Need-to-Knows About Social Networking and Where It's Headed," December 21, 2011, http://www.comscore.com/Insights/Presentations_and_Whitepapers/2011/it_is_a_social_world_top_10_need-to-knows_about_social_networking.

19. Joanna Brenner, "Pew Internet: Social Networking," Pew Research Center's Internet & American Life Project, February 14, 2013, http://www.pewinternet.org/Commentary/2012/March/Pew-Internet-Social-Networking-full-detail.aspx.

20. Kathleen Moore, "71% of Online Adults Now Use Video-Sharing Sites," Pew Research Center's Internet & American Life Project, July 26, 2011, http://www.pewinternet.org/Reports/2011/Video-sharing-sites/Report.aspx.

21. Jon Brodkin, "Time Warner, Net Neutrality Foes Cry Foul Over Netflix Super HD Demands," *Ars Technica*, January 17, 2013, http://arstechnica.com/business/2013/01/timewarner-net-neutrality-foes-cry-foul-netflix-requirements-for-super-hd/.

22. Barry Brown and Louise Barkhuus, "The Television Will be Revolutionized: Effects of PVRs and Filesharing on Television Watching," in *Proceedings of the SIGCHI Conference on Human Factors in Computing Systems* (ACM, 2006), 663–6.

23. Jenna Wortham, "No TV? No Subscription? No Problem," *New York Times*, April 6, 2013, http://www.nytimes.com/2013/04/07/business/streaming-sites-and-the-rise-of-shared-accounts.html?pagewanted=all&_r=0.

24. iTunes initiated movie rentals in Portugal in late 2011.

25. Organisation for Economic Co-operation and Development, "Broadband Penetration Per 100 Inhabitants," May 6, 2013, http://www.oecd.org/statistics/.

26. Jeremy G. Butler, *Television Style* (New York: Routledge, 2010), 167.

27. According to Pew's 2012 study of cell Internet, "half of African-American cell Internet users do most of their online browsing on their phone, double the proportion for whites (24%). Two in five Latino cell Internet users (42%) also fall into the 'cell-mostly'

category. Additionally, those with an annual household income of less than $50,000 per year and those who have not graduated college are more likely than those with higher levels of income and education to use their phones for most of their online browsing." Aaron Smith, "Cell Internet Use 2012," Pew Research Center's Internet & American Life Project, June 26, 2012, http://www.pewinternet.org/Reports/2012/Cell-Internet-Use-2012/Key-Findings.aspx.
28. Ibid.

References

Basapur, Santosh, Gunnar Harboe, Hiren Mandalia, Ashley Novak, Van Vuong, and Crysta Metcalf. "Field Trial of a Dual Device User Experience for iTV." In *Proceedings of the 9th International Interactive Conference on Interactive Television*, 127–36. New York: ACM, 2011.

Bellamy Jr., Robert V., and James R. Walker. *Television and the Remote Control: Grazing on a Vast Wasteland*. New York: Guilford Press, 1996.

Benkler, Yochai. *The Wealth of Networks: How Social Production Transforms Markets and Freedoms*. New Haven, CT: Yale University Press, 2006.

Bondad-Brown, Beverly A., Ronald E. Rice, and Katy E. Pearce. "Influences on TV Viewing and Online User-shared Video Use: Demographics, Generations, Contextual Age, Media Use, Motivations, and Audience Activity." *Journal of Broadcasting & Electronic Media* 56, no. 4 (2012): 471–93.

Brenner, Joanna. "Pew Internet: Social Networking." Pew Research Center's Internet & American Life Project, February 14, 2013. http://www.pewinternet.org/Commentary/2012/March/Pew-Internet-Social-Networking-full-detail.aspx.

Brodkin, Jon. "Time Warner, Net Neutrality Foes Cry Foul Over Netflix Super HD Demands." *Ars Technica*, January 17, 2013. http://arstechnica.com/business/2013/01/timewarner-net-neutrality-foes-cry-foul-netflix-requirements-for-super-hd/.

Brown, Barry, and Louise Barkhuus. "The Television Will be Revolutionized: Effects of PVRs and Filesharing on Television Watching." In *Proceedings of the SIGCHI Conference on Human Factors in Computing Systems*, 663–6. ACM, 2006.

Burgess, Jean, and Joshua Green, eds. *YouTube: Online Video and Participatory Culture*. Cambridge, MA: Polity Press, 2009.

Butler, Jeremy G. *Television Style*. New York: Routledge, 2010.

Cesar, Pablo, Dick C.A. Bulterman, and Jack Jansen. "Leveraging User Impact: An Architecture for Secondary Screens Usage in Interactive Television." *Multimedia Systems* 15, no. 3 (2009): 127–42.

Chorianopoulos, Konstantinos, and George Lekakos. "Introduction to Social TV: Enhancing the Shared Experience with Interactive TV." *International Journal of Human-Computer Interaction* 24, no. 2 (2008): 113–20.

comScore. "It's a Social World: Top 10 Need-to-Knows About Social Networking and Where It's Headed." December 21, 2011. http://www.comscore.com/Insights/Presentations_and_Whitepapers/2011/it_is_a_social_world_top_10_need-to-knows_about_social_networking.

Farman, Jason. *Mobile Interface Theory: Embodied Space and Locative Media*. New York: Routledge, 2012.

Hall, Stuart. "Encoding/Decoding." In *Culture, Media, Language: Working Papers in Cultural Studies 1972–79*, edited by Stuart Hall, Dorothy Hobson, Andrew Lowe, and Paul Willis, 107–16. London: Unwin Hyman, 1979.

Jenkins, Henry. *Convergence Culture: Where Old and New Media Collide.* New York: New York University Press, 2006.

Levy, Mark R. *The VCR Age: Home Video and Mass Communication.* Newbury Park, CA: SAGE, 1989.

Levy, Mark R., and Sven Windahl. "The Concept of Audience Activity." In *Media Gratifications Research: Current Perspectives,* edited by Karl Erik Rosengren, Lawrence A. Wenner, and Philip Palmgreen, 109–22. Beverly Hills, CA: SAGE, 1985.

Marshall, P. David. "Screens: Television's Dispersed 'Broadcast.'" In *Television Studies After TV: Understanding Television in the Post-Broadcast Era,* edited by Graeme Turner and Jinna Tay, 41–50. London and New York: Routledge, 2009.

McPherson, Tara. "Reload: Liveness, Mobility, and the Web." In *New Media, Old Media: A History and Theory Reader,* edited by Wendy Hui Kyong Chun and Thomas Keenan, 240–52. New York: Routledge, 2005.

Moore, Kathleen. "71% of Online Adults Now Use Video-Sharing Sites." Pew Research Center's Internet & American Life Project, July 26, 2011. http://www.pewinternet .org/Reports/2011/Video-sharing-sites/Report.aspx.

Organisation for Economic Co-operation and Development. "Broadband Penetration Per 100 Inhabitants." May 6, 2013. http://www.oecd.org/statistics/.

Perse, Elizabeth M. "Audience Selectivity and Involvement in the Newer Media Environment." *Communication Research* 17, no. 5 (1990): 675–97.

Smith, Aaron. "Cell Internet Use 2012." Pew Research Center's Internet & American Life Project, June 26, 2012. http://www.pewinternet.org/Reports/2012/Cell-Internet-Use-2012/Key-Findings.aspx.

Spigel, Lynn, and Jan Olsson, eds. *Television after TV: Essays on a Medium in Transition.* Durham, NC and London, UK: Duke University Press, 2004.

Williams, Raymond. *Television: Technology and Cultural Form.* New York: Schocken Books, 1974.

Wortham, Jenna. "No TV? No Subscription? No Problem." *New York Times,* April 6, 2013. http://www.nytimes.com/2013/04/07/business/streaming-sites-and-the-rise-of -shared-accounts.html?pagewanted=all&_r=0.

CONTRIBUTORS

Mark Andrejevic is Deputy Director of the Centre for Critical and Cultural Studies at the University of Queensland. He is the author of *Reality TV: The Work of Being Watched, iSpy: Surveillance and Power in the Interactive Era,* and *Infoglut,* as well as numerous articles and book chapters on reality TV, digital media, and surveillance. His current research explores ways in which interactive media technologies double as forms of productive monitoring and surveillance. He runs the Personal Information Project at the University of Queensland, where he studies Australians' attitudes toward the collection and use of their personal information.

Joshua Braun is Assistant Professor in the Department of Film, Video, and Interactive Media at Quinnipiac University, and a former graduate fellow of the National Academy of Sciences. He received his PhD in Communication in 2011 from Cornell University, where his dissertation work earned him the Anson E. Rowe Award for outstanding research. His work examines sociological questions surrounding the online distribution of television and news. Joshua is currently a member of a National Science Foundation working group on cultural production in the digital age, and his papers have appeared in a number of journals, including *Communication Theory, Journalism Practice,* and *Communication, Culture & Critique.* He is presently at work on a book for Yale University Press about the development of MSNBC's online distribution infrastructure. Joshua is also a former science journalist whose work has appeared in *Seed Magazine* and on WNYC's *Radiolab.*

Max Dawson consults on the television industry and social media for Frank N. Magid Associates in Los Angeles. Prior to joining Magid, he held academic appointments at Northwestern University and Indiana University. His research on television and new media has appeared in journals such as *Convergence, Technology and Culture,* the *Journal of Popular Film and Television,* and *Popular Communication,* in addition to numerous edited collections. More about his scholarship and consulting work can be found at maxdawson.tv or on Twitter at @fymaxwell.

Elizabeth Evans is Lecturer on Film and Television Studies at the University of Nottingham, UK. Her research focuses on the relationship between narrative experiences and technology, with a particular focus on audiences for television, games, pervasive drama, and transmedia texts. She is the author of *Transmedia Television: Audiences, New Media, and Daily Life,* which examines the impact of new media technologies on television-viewing habits. Her research has also been published in *Media, Culture & Society, Participations,* and a number of edited collections.

Jennifer Holt is Associate Professor of Film and Media Studies at the University of California, Santa Barbara. She is the author of *Empires of Entertainment* and co-editor of *Media Industries: History, Theory, and Method.* Her work has appeared in journals and anthologies including *Cinema Journal, Jump Cut, Moving Data,* and *Media Ownership: Research and Regulation.* She is also a Director of the Carsey-Wolf Center's Media Industries Project at UCSB.

Aynne Kokas, PhD, is currently the Baker Institute fellow in Chinese media and a sustainability postdoctoral fellow at the Chao Center for Asian Studies at Rice University. Starting in August 2014, she will be Assistant Professor of Media Studies and Media Policy at the University of Virginia. Kokas's current research focuses on the circulation of US environmental media and pollution data on Chinese social networks. She is also revising a manuscript examining Sino-US media joint ventures, titled *Shot in Shanghai: Blockbusters, Social Networks and the Story of Sino-U.S. Media Convergence.* Kokas has been a Fulbright scholar and a Social Science Research Council fellow in Shanghai, and a Chinese Ministry of Education fellow in Beijing, where she spent a year studying media production in the Chinese studio system at the Beijing Film Academy. Fluent in Chinese and Spanish, Kokas also speaks German and Korean. She holds a BA from the University of Michigan and a PhD from the University of California, Los Angeles.

Hye Jin Lee received her PhD in Mass Communications from the University of Iowa. Her research focuses on critical cultural and media studies, television studies, feminist media studies, video games and digital play, and new media and communication technologies. She is currently the editor of *Books Aren't Dead*—a monthly podcast interview series with feminist authors of recent books on media, science, and technology—for Fembot (FembotCollective.org), a scholarly community of faculty, graduate students, media producers, artists, and librarians who are dedicated to promoting research on gender, new media, and technology.

Paul McDonald is Professor of Cinema and Media Industries in the Department of Culture, Film and Media at the University of Nottingham, UK. His research concentrates on the home entertainment business and on the commerce of conglomerate Hollywood. He is the author of *Video and DVD Industries* and *Hollywood Stardom*, and co-editor of *The Contemporary Hollywood Film Industry*. For the British Film Institute he jointly edits the International Screen Industries book series. Currently he is co-editing the forthcoming collection *Hollywood and the Law*.

William Moner is Instructor of Communications at Elon University and a PhD candidate in Media Studies at the University of Texas at Austin in the Department of Radio-Television-Film. He holds an MS in Multimedia Technology from Duquesne University. His research investigates the material and historical aspects of interactive media, particularly the preservation of websites and other communication artifacts that originate and are distributed online.

Elissa Nelson was the project lead of the Connected Viewing Initiative at the University of California, Santa Barbara during its inaugural year. Currently, she teaches Film and Media Studies at Purchase College, State University of New York, and does independent media research consulting in New York City. She received her PhD from the Department of Radio-Television-Film at the University of Texas at Austin and her MA from the Cinema Studies Department at New York University. Her research focuses on the convergence of the media industries, including the growth of digital distribution, the relationship between Hollywood and the Internet, and the increasingly connected structures of the television and music industries; genre studies, specifically teen films of the 1980s; and youth in film and marketing.

Matthew Thomas Payne is Assistant Professor in the Department of Telecommunication and Film at the University of Alabama. He earned his PhD in Media Studies from the University of Texas at Austin and holds an MFA in Film Production from Boston University. Matthew is a co-editor of *Flow TV: Television in the Age of Media Convergence* and *Joystick Soldiers: The Politics of Play in Military Video Games*. Matthew is currently working on a book project that examines the production, marketing, and reception of popular military-themed "shooter" video games following the September 11 terrorist attacks. More information about Matt's work is available at mattpayne.com.

Kevin Sanson is the Research Director of the Carsey-Wolf Center's Media Industries Project at the University of California, Santa Barbara, where he oversees the development of MIP research initiatives and resources. His current book project focuses on the spatial dynamics of media production and examines issues of location, labor, and creative identity in emergent media hubs. He most recently completed a critical study of the role film, television, and digital media production plays in the economic and cultural strategies of Glasgow, Scotland, focusing especially on the experience of media workers. He is co-editor of *Distribution Revolution: Conversations about the Digital Future of Film and Television*. He also serves as part of the founding editorial collective of *Media Industries*, the first peer-reviewed, open-access journal for media industries research.

Gregory Steirer is Assistant Professor of English and Film Studies at Dickinson College. His research focuses on the impact of technological and economic changes on the production and consumption processes surrounding old and new media forms. His current book-length project, *Narrative Inc.*, examines big-brand media franchises and the changes they have wrought to traditional processes of narrative creation and consumption. His work has appeared in the journals *Postmodern Culture,* the *International Journal of Comic Art,* and *Women and Performance.* He also keeps a blog, *Cultural Production,* on which he publishes work on convergence culture, marketing, and popular media.

Sharon Strover is the Philip G. Warner Regents Professor in Communication at the University of Texas at Austin, where she teaches communications, telecommunications, and technology-related courses and directs the Telecommunications and Information Policy Institute. Some of her recent research projects examine the digital divide, immersive media, new media markets and participatory culture, rural broadband deployment, and telecommunications regulation. She has worked with several international, national, and regional government agencies on telecommunications policy matters, including the US Department of Agriculture's Rural Utilities Service, the US Federal Communication Commission, the government of Portugal, the Center for Rural Strategies, the European Union, the Appalachian Regional Commission, the Rural Policy Research Institute, the Ford Foundation, the European Union, and the Public Utility Commission of Texas, among others. She has published articles and chapters on technology and telecommunications subjects in numerous journals, and has been the editor or co-editor of three books. Dr. Strover received her undergraduate degree from the University of Wisconsin-Madison and her graduate degrees from Stanford University.

Chuck Tryon is Associate Professor in the Department of English at Fayetteville State University. His research focuses on the transformations of movie and television consumption in the era of digital distribution. He is the author of *Reinventing Cinema: Movies in the Age of Media Convergence* and *On-Demand Culture: Digital Delivery and the Future of Movies,* both from Rutgers University Press. He has also published essays in the *Journal of Film and Video, Jump Cut, Popular Communication,* and *Screen,* as well as the anthologies *Moving Data: The iPhone and the Future of Media* and *Science Fiction Film, Television, and Adaptation: Across the Screens.*

Ethan Tussey is Assistant Professor of Communication at Georgia State University. His work examines the relationship between the entertainment industry and the digitally empowered public. He has written articles on digital creative labor, online sports viewing, and workplace media usage as a contributor to *Saturday Night Live and American TV, Digital Media Sport: Technology, Power and Culture in the Network Society,* and *Spreadable Media: Creating Value and Meaning in a Networked Culture.* He is the coordinating editor of *In Media Res* and a member of the Atlanta Media Project.

Patrick Vonderau is Associate Professor and Senior Lecturer at the Department of Media Studies at Stockholm University. His most recent book publications include *Moving Data: The iPhone and the Future of Media, The YouTube Reader* (both with Pelle Snickars), *Films that Work: Industrial Film and the Productivity of Media* (with Vinzenz Hediger), and the forthcoming *Behind the Screen: European Contributions to Production Studies* (with Petr Szczepanik). Patrick is an editorial board member of *Media Industries* (MediaIndustriesJournal.WordPress.com); a co-editor of Germany's leading media studies journal, *Montage;* and a cofounder and previous Steering Committee member of the European Network for Cinema and Media Studies (NECS.org).

INDEX

The annotation of an italicized "f" or "t" indicates a reference to a figure or a table on the specified page.

resource; as performance feedback; and as social hub. Although this framework is a loose one, it emerged from the coding of the participant feedback, and it helps clarify students' game experiences with their connected screens. The following subsections highlight the opportunities and challenges facing support utilities like Elite and Battlelog that foster connected viewing experiences that aim to increase players' levels of gaming capital.

The Companion App as Field Manual

At the risk of generalizing a fantastically diverse group: video gamers are a pragmatic bunch. This tends to be the case because so much of their gameplay is goal oriented. It is perhaps not surprising that the experienced gamers in the research group enjoyed tracking their game stats and digging into the supplemental information about the weapons, vehicles, and maps. They appreciated having the freedom to consult another screen that would not interrupt the game flow and could be accessed while waiting for the next firefight to begin. These participants boasted of their performances during and between rounds to their fellow players, and would often announce the stats that Elite and Battlelog highlighted on their profile pages like K/D ratios (one's number of kills versus one's number of deaths) and various accolades for combat achievements (the same kinds of awards that Sotamaa discusses with respect to displays of gamer capital[18]).

The group's experienced gamers were also most impressed with those features that explicitly addressed their desire to improve themselves as gamers. One such example is Elite's (aptly titled) "Improve" feature, which provides users with overhead schematics of *Modern Warfare 3*'s multiplayer maps, showing the location

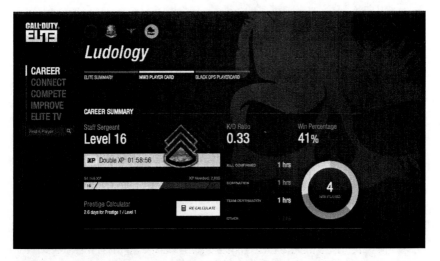

FIGURE 9.1 *Call of Duty's* Elite App

FIGURE 9.2 *Battlefield*'s Battlelog App

FIGURE 9.3 Participants Play Together and Take Notes on Their Gameplay

FIGURE 9.4 A Participant Tracks his Performance Stats using Second-Screen Applications

of key items. Participants would often access Improve before the beginning of a round so they could strategize before the firefight commenced. During longer down periods, these gamers would also review Improve's video guides. These five-minute walk-through videos feature a voice-over narrator who discusses the maps' major landmarks and regions, and who makes recommendations on how one might best opponents. During extended gameplay sessions, it was not uncommon to see participants huddled around one of their teammates' screens to debate the video's suggestions.

Elite and Battlelog function as mobile, easy-to-access repositories of producer- and user-generated data. But they are more than simple FAQs or tools for aggregating tips. Rather, companion apps are interactive gateways for personally enculturating users on a title's history and cueing them to those pieces of information that its play community values.

The Companion App as After-Action Report

The principal appeal of Elite and Battlelog is that they track a wealth of personal gameplay data and alert players to forthcoming achievements. This is a technological affordance that offline and noninteractive media simply do not possess. That is, no matter how detailed and well designed an official guidebook may be, it can never collect information on one's gameplay and make recommendations based on that data. The two services' career pages foreground the player's big-picture numbers that serve as communicative shorthand when discussing one's soldiering, including K/D ratio, win percentage, and military rank. Beneath this top layer there exist far more granular data, including the player's score per minute (think: points odometer); proficiency with weapons and vehicles including accuracy, kill count, and even headshots; gameplay awards collected (e.g., for repeatedly securing a site, destroying vehicles, etc.); and—in the case of *Battlefield 3*—a library of dog tags from stabbed opponents. And because these ID tags include the victims' personal gamer tags, they serve as rather grisly display trophies of one's battlefield dominance.

These services and apps also tease players with achievements to come. It is common practice for designers to entice players into spending long hours with their games by tempting them with unlockable items. The *Call of Duty* and *Battlefield* franchises embrace this design convention, as do most shooters. After a certain number of kills, victories, experience points, etc., the player is granted access to coveted items like new guns, different skins for avatars and weapons, and devices that can change one's gameplay. The research participants reflected positively on tracking their progress on their second screens. This activity also imbued the repetitive firefights with new goals, structuring users' gameplay in rounds that lacked explicit objectives beyond the common "kill or be killed" imperative. Indeed, a few of these items were so tempting for participants that they occasionally played in counterintuitive ways to access these goods. These reward systems not only motivate players to track their accomplishments via the support apps, but also serve as empirical proof of players' gaming capital—evidence that can be conspicuously displayed in physical and virtual venues.

But the research team's favorite screen utility, by far, was Elite's "heat map" feature. This visualization tool maps a recent round of combat over a level schematic in dramatic pools of green, yellow, and red, representing the locations and frequencies of player kills and deaths. Part of the utility's appeal is its visual design. The maps allow players to transcend their games' limited first-person perspectives by presenting them with a bird's-eye view of a battle's action in its totality.

The heat maps also proved to be a social magnet because of their practical application for team play. Indeed, it was not uncommon for participants to gather around the lab's PC desktop and review together the previous round's action, and devise strategies for the next. The secondary screen became a physical rallying point for the participants to discuss winning tactics and to flex their gaming knowledge. And because the maps aggregate the round's action, they are an easy means by which gamers can assess their performance, as well as monitor and surveil the gameplay of others.

Despite their popularity among the research participants, the heat maps also revealed a potential liability of support utilities. The close feedback that the heat maps provide drew gamers' attention to the producers' design choices. For